"Drawing from some unlikely sources—Friedrich Nietzsche, SIA, and Avenger films, to name a few—as well as from his direct experience working with young adults, Rut Etheridge invites the reader to consider a way out of the pain of dehumanization—by not putting humans first. *God Breathed* diagnoses the depth of modern Western culture's problems and, by doing so, shows us how to reconnect with an active, life-giving God through serious wrestling with the Bible—yes, even its hardest parts! This book exudes a deep commitment to the flourishing of *every* young person, no matter where they are in their lives when they pick up this book."
ELIZABETH W. CORRIE, director, Youth Theological Initiative, Emory University

"Etheridge creatively diagnoses the condition of our age and opens the way for us to see that if we truly want to find ourselves we need to read and encounter God's book. Truly scholarly and truly accessible, *God·Breathed* is the kind of book that brings strong conviction wrapped in genuine love for God and others."
VINCENT BACOTE, director, Center for Applied Christian Ethics, Wheaton College; contributor, *Keep Your Head Up: America's New Black Christian Leaders, Social Consciousness, and the Cosby Conversation*

"It is difficult to find good books targeted for a young adult reading audience. They are usually dumbed-down, trying too hard to connect, or cheesy. And yet this is often the time of life when people have serious and meaningful questions about the Christian faith. Rut offers us a "Schaeffer-esque" blend of philosophy, theology, and apologetics that connects with the questions about God that Christians and unbelievers alike wrestle with in our current cultural context. He takes his audience seriously and points them to something (Someone) altogether delightful. I will be giving this one away!"
AIMEE BYRD, author, *No Little Women* and *Why Can't We Be Friends?*

"Whereas many critiques of culture complain and scold, Etheridge decides instead to explain and counsel—and does so supremely well. He speaks to people both inside and outside the church, as well as those feeling caught in between. His message about Christianity and contemporary culture is clear. Each chapter feels like it was written with both passion and compassion."

RUSSELL HAITCH, professor of theology and human science, Bethany Theological Seminary

"...this *tour de force* of biblical ethics, philosophy, and theology presents a timely challenge for readers at any stage to understand who they are in relation to God, God's word, and God's world...I highly recommend it!"

WHITNEY GAMBLE, associate professor of biblical and theological studies, Providence Christian College

"Among other things, three stand out about this book: it is theologically and philosophically shrewd, pastorally wise, and engagingly written (with a dizzying array of real world connections to life in late modernity). Clearly, Rut has his finger on the pulse of the current generation of young adults. But anyone looking for sturdy, tried, and true belief in a rapidly shifting age will do well to take up and read."

MARK ROBINSON, pastoral mentor, Western Pennsylvania Adult and Teen Challenge

"Rut Etheridge's God Breathed is a culturally relevant theological *tour de force* which speaks directly into the hearts and minds of its readers. This book is heavy in every sense of the word, but if you are willing to mine its depths I can promise you that you will emerge from its pages edified, enriched, and empowered because the One to whom Rut is drawing his readers is the One who speaks the words that are truly spirit and life."

ANTHONY T. SELVAGGIO, author, *A Proverbs Driven Life* and *7 Toxic Ideas That Are Polluting Your Mind*

"I was very heartened to see someone write a book as brave and honest as this one. Scholarly, engaging, and remarkably accessible, this book takes history seriously and refuses to simplify complex issues. Drawing from early Church fathers through Descartes, Kant, and Nietzsche to purveyors of pop culture and advocates of atheism, Rut addresses contemporary cultural issues from a perspective many would prefer not to consider—but that cannot be ignored."

JANIE HARDEN FRITZ, professor of communication and rhetorical studies, Duquesne University

GOD BREATHED

GOD BREATHED

Connecting through Scripture to God, Others,
the Natural World, and Yourself

Rut Etheridge III

Crown & Covenant
PUBLICATIONS

©2019 Rut Etheridge III,
Crown & Covenant Publications
7408 Penn Avenue
Pittsburgh, PA 15208
crownandcovenant.com

ISBN: 978-1-943017-28-7
e-book: 978-1-943017-29-4
Library of Congress Control Number: 2019940695

Printed in the United States of America

To all of you whom I've ever had the honor to call my student, especially those who are now with the true teacher. I love you all.

Contents

Foreword

Rut loves music. Every chapter of this book he has written starts with song lyrics. A few years ago he invited me to play Flyleaf songs for his students. But it was also important to him that I talk about the stories behind the songs, especially our biggest song, "All Around Me," written about the salvation encounter I had with God on the day I planned to commit suicide as a sixteen-year-old atheist.

A beautiful thing about Rut is that he listens closer to lyrics than most people. I think it's because he loves God. Lovers of God tend to look closer into God's artwork than others. As a musician, I've found irony in being given a stage: The audience you want to connect with on a personal level generally dehumanizes you because you're on stage. But not Rut. He has the heart-wrenching reverence to call every one of us God's image-bearers, assigning us all the same eternal value and worth, the same level of attention, stage or no stage.

The first time I took the stage was not for music. I was four years old. My five-year-old brother and twenty-year-old mother were part of a play in downtown Ft. Worth, Texas, at a theater called The Caravan of Dreams. Making my way through the backstage area felt like treasure hunting through the ruins of a hundred deconstructed stories in piles all over the place. It was full of costumes, wigs, props, and set pieces.

I have a faint memory of falling asleep in an antique, worn-in leather chair amid the rubble during late-night rehearsals. Just before drifting off to sleep, I would lean in close to the intricately engraved brass buttons, delighted to find each one unique. The details were so seemingly infinite that surely the artist had no intention of anyone else actually seeing any further than the shiny, golden gleam against the rich, brown leather. Including these microscopic details must have been just an expression of who the artist was.

When you encounter artistry like this, you can feel the artist's sheer delight in creating through the richly minded details designed by the artist and left everywhere he or she has been. Focusing in on this kind of artwork is not done to see what the artist left for you to see. Take Emily Dickenson: her work wasn't for others but a product of her being who she was. No, you look not to see what the artist left for you but to see a glimpse of the glory of who the artist truly is. When examining this kind of heart-overflow art, it's difficult to look away. The rabbit trail of life-beyond-necessity, that is beauty in all the artist does, is too fascinating. There is enough beauty on the surface to make you fall in love, but when you're intrigued you explore deeper and there comes a sweeping away of the heart, a gasp, a disorienting wonder. My lip trembles as I lean into these wonder-filled antique buttons in my mind. This close to this image-bearer's art I can smell the metal and almost taste it as I marvel at the way the artist's lingering thoughts engraved in the buttons are their own universe of revelation. That's how the God of creation does everything.

You can find revelation of who God is and what God is like in every direction you look, in every soundwave, in every second of time that passes, in every blade of light that reveals swirling dust particles in the air. From the atomic level to the galaxies, he is the artist behind it all, and he is endlessly awesome in all his artwork as Creator. As we ponder his works, understanding unfolds to resonate with the eternity he has written on the heart of humanity. We can get lost in endless awe of just one facet of who he is and what he is like.

Whenever I find truth in any place I immediately know that it is guaranteed to be a biblical principle on display. As a smart aleck atheist who met God on the day I planned to commit suicide, I was not one to take people's word for what they said about God. I wanted to know for myself. What I found in the Bible when I read it for myself was staggering. In the Bible I found Truth. The most profound, living, mind-blowing truth after truth after truth. I have always been a lover of truth. To find that the Bible was a book of truth was crazy enough, but then to find that it was alive and word-for-word breathed from the mouth of God, words which God intended for me to read and understand and learn so I could actually know Him—are you serious?! This is still absolutely astounding to me.

The sad truth is that many people who want to know the real God have written off the notion that the Bible could actually be God's word to them personally. Many don't consider the Bible a legitimate way to come close to God. The truth is, though, this very reality is the most phenomenal thing about the Bible.

Imagine that the Scriptures are what they say they are in 2 Timothy 3:16 with the Greek word *theopneustos*: God-breathed, given by his Holy Spirit. Hebrews 4:12 declares that God's word is *living* and *active*. Wait, what? This book is alive? And active? Meaning it could talk to me?

It makes me think of the scene from *The Never Ending Story* where Bastian starts to read about himself in the book he has stolen from a book store. As he reads the words he is justifiably freaked out; he screams and throws the book across the room. He was having what my writer friend Timothy Willard calls a "numinous experience," a very personal encounter with a reality we've all had a sense of since we were children: that there is more to life than the physical world we see. The Bible brings very personal, numinous moments, but they make you want to lean in and look closer. The Bible will bring you awe, make your heart burn, make you cry, and make you laugh with tears of joy, because Scripture speaks to exactly what you are thinking, wrestling with, and questioning. The Bible is indeed alive.

It's sad to think the most important thing humanity has in written form is so misquoted, misunderstood, neglected, and maligned. I was excited to read Rut's book because most people I hear talking about the Bible don't have love in their voice, and Rut's book addresses so many of the issues that most people have with reading the Bible. I am so thankful Rut was brave enough to write it.

I think Rut's courage comes from his love. He loves like the God he worships. Fearlessly. It only took an afternoon having a meal with Rut's wife and children while he played video games with my three-year-old son to know that he loves like our heavenly Father. It wasn't just the way his kids were so kind and thoughtful, his wife so empowered and brilliant, or the great peace, playfulness, and joy that filled the atmosphere of his home—it was how he treated my three-year-old's questions and storytelling. He listened to him like a three-year-old image-bearer of God was speaking and deserved his full attention and thoughtful response. When I read the book you are about to read, I could see Rut's playfulness and reverence for others' perspectives on every page. But I could see his love and reverence for them is deeply rooted in his love for the God in whose image we all were made.

This book actually changed my life. The last chapter healed deep things in my heart in relationship to music. I have never heard anyone talk in such a completely pure and holy way about music. This helped me see what music is actually meant for, and I was humbled to a mess of tears that I still cry when I think of it. This book is a very important one. I pray you will receive it in love and find your heart open to reading the Bible with new eyes, like I did. It will bring your heart to life.

—*Lacey Sturm*
Pittsburgh, Pennsylvania, 2018

Acknowledgments

"Grateful" barely scratches the surface of my deep respect and appreciation for those whose contributions were so crucial to this project.

Evelyn, my heart's deepest smile and my best friend. You are the spark and steadfastness, the fire and fortitude of our family. Your light shines in our children and warms every life you touch and serve with such relentless selflessness. You leave me, a man of far too many words, speechless. I love you. Thank you for 20+!

Isaiah, Callie, Calvin, Josiah, and Sylvia: You are and have my heart. Your mom and I are so proud of each of you. Each of you is, and all of you are, an endless joy to us. May you grow every day in the grace, knowledge, wisdom, freedom, courage, and love of our Savior, who gave us to you and you to us. Love you forever, no matter what.

Lacey and Josh Sturm, for believing in and making this

project a priority in your family's life and work. Lacey, I knew your writing before I knew your music and they both rock, hard! Your work is simultaneously gentle and fierce, always straight from the heart and aimed at freedom. You understand profoundly the passions and pains of this generation of young adults. Thank you, daughter of God, for introducing so many to our heavenly Father's heart.

Natalie Auell, for having the courage of unconventional thought in a context that tends to discourage it. Your request was like a shout calling down an avalanche of blessings on this project and my work and ministry as a whole. Thank you! And may the Lord continue to bless your musical artistry.

Rachel Tyson, visual artist of deep intuition and empathy. You understood my vision for this book before I finished the first sentence describing it to you. Your perfect expression of its soul made a priceless birthday gift for my oldest daughter; every time I see that painting in her room I remember why I wrote this book and the effect I hope it has on its readers.

Dale and Holly Miller, for opening your beautiful home for visits during three consecutive summers. Thank you for providing space and time for my soul to stretch, breathe, and exercise as this book took shape. And the nearby mountains weren't bad for that, either! Thank you for your sincere and superlative hospitality.

Shelley Davenport Davis, for freelancing an editorial overview of this project at its most monstrous, when I'd lost the leash for the beast. As a fellow writer, you helped me regain focus and perspective; your philosophical and editorial insights taught this temperamental tome some humility and self-control.

Janna Bassette, for personal encouragement and support of this project from so very early on. That you were excited for it and liked the early chapters gave me great confidence in continuing. And thanks for forgiving me when I slammed your favorite "superhero." You know I'm right on that point!

Zack Bowman, rockstar philosopher and philosophical rockstar. It's been my privilege to know you since you were a boy. It's an honor to call you friend. Thank you for your help in research, your beautifully disturbed outlook on life, your courageous and sensitive spirit. God bless you from Providence to Interboro Avenue and wherever his heart leads yours.

Lindsey McCracken and Grace Acosta, for help in research and so much of the tedious and time-consuming work necessary to get this thing done. Thank you for heartfelt feedback, insights, and encouragements. Thank you for persevering!

Matt, Dan, and Joel. Colleagues and Cobra Kai brethren. True and faithful friends. Thanks for honesty and safe, unguarded conversations. Matt, thank you for early review work. Your ministry among young adults is true and beautiful and a model for this book. Your insights and critiques were empowering.

Rick Gamble, Barry York, and Sensei Robert Haynes: thank you for mentorship, friendship, and guidance through many years. Particular conversations with each of you were pivot points in my life and are reflected in this work more than you know. Thank you for understanding me, for wisdom from cross-shaped lives faithfully lived.

Crown & Covenant Publications staff. What were you thinking?! Little did you know what a high-maintenance author you were signing when you took a chance on me. Thank you especially for scheduling flexibility when I was, for years, tending to serious family health issues. Thanks for being there the whole way professionally and personally.

U2, Twenty One Pilots, The Killers, Florence and the Machine, Sia, Bleachers, Steel Train, Bruce Springsteen, Sheryl Crow, Radiohead, Linkin Park (RIP, Chester Bennington), Brandi Carlile, Counting Crows, Alicia Keys, Elton John, Skylar Grey, Jessie Ware, Halsey, Ingrid Michelson, Disturbed, Breaking Benjamin, Fionna Apple—your stellar musical artistry is a clear window into the tremors, traumas, and triumphs of humanness, especially in our day and age. I wanted to interact with your work so much more, but it's really hard and expensive to get permission to quote you! Alas, I could have made you famous...

Coffee houses throughout Western Pennsylvania, North Carolina, Tennessee, Indiana, and California. Special thanks to local gems Café Kolache, Generoasta, National Grind, and Beaver Falls Coffee and Tea Company. From your in-house vibe to your wondrous caffeinated creations—You are the best work offices! And to coffee itself; thank you. No explanation needed.

The opinions expressed in this book do not necessarily reflect those of the particular people so important to it, nor its publisher or my employer—but they would, if those people knew what was good for them. Amen.

1

The Bible Could Mean
So Much More to You

"Well, my sense of humanity has gone down the drain
Behind every beautiful thing there's been some kind of pain…
I've been down on the bottom of a world full of lies
I ain't looking for nothing in anyone's eyes…
Don't even hear a murmur of a prayer
It's not dark yet, but it's getting there…"
—Bob Dylan, "Not Dark Yet"[1]

"Where we're from, there's no sun; our hometown's in the dark.
Where we're from, we're no one; our hometown's in the dark."
—Twenty One Pilots, "Hometown"[2]

You've been robbed. Not by purchasing this book, I hope!
You've been robbed on a much deeper level, and the theft took
place long before you were born.

This theft is directly related to the deepest pains in people's
lives, including yours. It's not so much physical pain, though it
definitely rises to that level. It's the unease you feel when silence
falls around you and the whispers start within you. It's the uncertainty way down deep where you struggle to understand what
makes you, you. It's that painful, frustrating friction between your
desire to belong and your desperation to be left alone, between
your desire to be truly known and your paralyzing fear of the very
same thing. Sound familiar?

The theft didn't cause these tensions; they're as old as humankind—well, almost. We'll get to that later. The theft removed
our hope of finding any resolution to these troubles. The thieves

managed to convince us that that these struggles of the soul are all in our heads. They said we're better off not seeking answers to the questions these pains produce because there are no knowable answers to be found, and we believed them. We still do.

As a culture, we no longer believe that we can know truth— *big* truth, meaning-of-life kind of truth, the kind of truth that might address and even appease our deepest anxieties, the kind of truth the Bible claims to be.

Instead, we've come to believe that we cannot know reality as it actually is, that there is no absolute truth. Or, if absolute truth does exist, we cannot know it with any real confidence—practically the same thing. But do you notice something a bit off about these beliefs?

These claims self-destruct as soon as they're made. *The reality is that we cannot know reality as it is.* We're absolutely sure that there is no absolute truth. Or, the more modest version: *We're very confident that any absolute truth out there cannot be known with any real confidence.* Each of these statements violates the principle it's meant to express before the sentence stops. Shouldn't we be suspicious of ideas that can't even be stated without imploding?[3]

Pointing out these inconsistencies is nothing new.[4] The stunning thing is that we don't care about them. Somehow, as children grow up in this culture, they come to accept such self-destructing statements as, well, absolute truth. The suicidal inconsistency of these ideas doesn't seem to bother us at all. This is how we know a crime has been committed.

We never accept inconsistencies when it comes to the things we care about. If someone gives us 10 dollars but tells us he's given us 100, we don't shrug and say: "Well, who's to say what's true anyway?" We call shenanigans on it and demand proper payment. But when someone slips us the idea that we cannot know truth and calls it truth, and we sincerely believe it, that's evidence that something is missing within us—something that would stop that philosophical transaction and at the very least say, "Wait. What?!" When we don't even pause at that kind of proposition, it's evidence that something's been stolen from us.

This robbery has reached into all of our hearts. Even if you affirm that the Bible is knowable absolute truth, don't you find that there's something missing in your desire to know it?

Be honest: Are you ever bored with the Bible? Or at least, does reading it ever feel like a chore? How often do you pick it up, and how quickly do you put it down? It's one thing to avoid the Bible because we have a hard time understanding it. That's natural, and that's where this book seeks to help. But if we're Christians, something major must be missing from our hearts if we are at all disinterested in the word of our Lord.

If we really, truly believed that the Bible is the word of God, and that through it, we can actually get to know God, then how could we ever regard the Bible with anything less than the utmost awe and eagerness to explore? But that awe and eagerness are missing from the hearts of so many Christians today, and that's a crime.

How did the thieves get away with it? In chapter 3, we'll explore the crime story in more detail, but suffice it to say for now, the thieves had a lot of help…from Christians.

"I Can Do It Myself, Dad!"

Sometimes Christians make the best criminals, or the best unwitting accomplices to a crime. About five centuries ago, in what may have been the Christian church's "Doh!" moment of the millennium,[5] a Christian mathematician in France tried to prove God's existence beyond the shadow of a doubt. That effort is questionable to begin with, but he made matters so much worse by trying to prove the existence of the God of the Bible without seeking any help from the Bible. He thought that the Bible would be just fine with that.

Renee Descartes (1596–1650) understood the Bible to say that human reason, by itself, could teach us everything we needed to know about God.[6] Kind of makes you wonder why we would need the Bible then, right? Hold that thought.

Descartes thought that, by the process of proper reasoning, he could discover the most basic, fundamental, knowable, indubitable truth. Once he found that rock-solid knowledge, that truth buried deep beyond the reach of any reasonable doubt, he could use the process of proper reasoning to build upon it other truths that we could also know with absolute certainty, including the knowledge of God's existence. Like a toddler who wants to impress his dad by trying to ride a bike on his own, Descartes was as sincerely desirous of honoring God by his unaided effort to prove God's existence as he was confident that he could pull it off. And oh, was he confident. And oh, did he crash.

Descartes was sure that, as a result of his writings, and with a little editorial advice from a world-famous theology faculty (along with their money and endorsement), "there will be no one left in the world who will dare to call into doubt...the existence of God."[7] The effort was a spectacular fail. Likely suspecting as much, that faculty never endorsed it.

Descartes went wrong at the very beginning. He decided that the most basic truth of which he could be absolutely sure was that he was thinking. "I think, therefore I am." In other words, I know I exist because I recognize that I'm thinking. Descartes thought that was the bedrock for building human knowledge. But wouldn't belief in the God who created him be even more basic than that? After all, how did "I" get here to begin with? And how did "I" get the capacity to recognize that "I" is thinking? And without any help from outside "I," how can "I" be sure that "I" is thinking correctly? And why does anyone like philosophy?!

By trying to ground true knowledge in the thinking self and by placing supreme confidence in human reason rather than God's revelation of himself in Scripture, Descartes inadvertently treated the Bible like the bench player I was on my high school basketball team: I was necessary to fill the roster, but utterly unnecessary to win the games. I barely counted as eye candy.

Descartes made supreme confidence in human reason intellectually fashionable. His work resulted in the rise of Rationalism, which exalts human reason as the infallible guide to absolute truth and the arbiter of what counts as absolutely true. Reason, not God's revealing himself and his will in Scripture, would rule the new world to come. Major advances in science, coupled with the church's apparent disdain for them, seemed to confirm that hypothesis.

The nail in the coffin of Christian confidence in Scripture may have come when people began to distrust the Bible even as God's guide to a good moral life. Europeans in the rising eighteenth century were weary from so many wars; in many of them, all sides claimed scriptural support for their slaughter of other people. Maybe the Bible was no good at all, at least as a direct word from God.

The separation from Scripture that Descartes accidentally spurred wasn't supposed to last. He merely meant to prove, especially to non-Christians, the reasonableness of the faith that Scripture details. But like so many separations meant to strengthen a relationship, it ended in divorce.

More and more leading Christian thinkers rejected Scripture as a means of attaining absolute truth. But Rationalism wouldn't last as an alternative. The man whose work undermined Rationalism was still a big fan of human reason unaided by divine revelation. But reason had to know its limits. Reason could never reach beyond the thinking self like Descartes thought it could, much less grab hold of God. And that was just fine with this philosopher. This man convinced people to abandon any hope of hearing directly from God, to which more and more people responded: "Sweet!"

The separation was seismic, and it set the stage for thieves to swoop in later and snatch from people's hearts any rising hope of a personal encounter with a personal God. Such encounters were declared absolutely impossible. This declaration of independence from God shook up the Western world; we feel the aftershocks in those suicidally inconsistent, soul-crushing ideas embraced as absolute truth today.

In what has to be the biggest irony in the history of Western philosophy and theology, the man who insisted upon this separation between us and God was named Immanuel, which means: "God with us."

Caution: Low Ceiling

Immanuel Kant (1724–1804) taught that God is too great to be understood by us mere mortals. We can't know for certain any particular details of who God is and what he does in this world, other than that he's really powerful and really good. All of the particulars having to do with God, and therefore our knowledge of him, the origin of the universe, the end of history—all that stuff is up in God's territory, and God has a "No Trespassing" sign firmly posted in the heavens. Following Kant's lead, Christian leaders increasingly taught that all of our knowing happens beneath what we'll call throughout this book *the ceiling of self*.

Beneath the ceiling of self, we can never get beyond ourselves in our knowledge of reality. All we have is perception. The further we go with this idea, truth becomes simply something each culture creates so it can get by for a season, nothing more. We build truth like ants build their homes, in community and not for long. But wouldn't the idea that truth is a societal construct be itself a mere construct of society? And therefore incapable of accurately describing reality and always subject to change?

Despite the gaping cracks in its consistency, the ceiling is taught these days as self-evident truth. It's set like philosophical concrete in our collective conscience, having hardened over our heads the past several centuries. It's so thick these days that many people in our culture, especially young people, have no idea that the ceiling is man-made. They feel they have no right, and really no need, to question its structural integrity. The ceiling provides the perfect cover for the cosmic theft we've been considering, and it keeps conditions perfect for that crime to be recommitted every generation.

Sound a bit vague? Here are some popular statements that steal our confidence that truth can be known. Notice how these statements, like their parent statements we considered above, self-destruct.

"Don't judge people." Because the ceiling prevents us from knowing what's ultimately right or wrong,[8] we have no right to say that what someone else believes or does is actually wrong. But if you forbid me from judging, you're saying that what I'm doing is wrong—and that's judging me. And what's even more offensive to this self-destructing standard, you're also telling me what to do. You're not the boss of me. BOOM!

"Perception is reality." Under the ceiling, perception is the only reality we have access to.[9] But doesn't that mean that this idea is also just someone's perception, that it can't possibly reflect reality? BOOM!

One more. This one falls apart in a funny way, but if we believe it as truth, it literally kills: "Beauty is in the eye of the beholder."

Imagine telling someone you're really attracted to: "You are absolutely gorgeous." And in the next breath: "*BUT*, beauty really is in the eye of the beholder." You deserve to be slapped for that. What you're saying is: "It's not how you look; it's my looking that makes you beautiful. If you look good, well, you're welcome."

We could put it poetically:
> Thou art beautiful, true.
> But thy beauty belongs not to you.
> Doubtless, this certain truth you'll see:
> Thy beauty lies not in thyself, but in me.
> Now kiss me, baby!

You might say, "But physical beauty *is* just a matter of perspective, of preference. It's not a right or wrong thing." Are you sure about that?

What if a girl starves herself to satisfy her standard of beauty, or some cruel community's standard? Is she right about what's beautiful? Can you say that the community is wrong?[10]

We certainly have our preferences, but is beauty *only* a matter of personal preference and majority opinion? Beneath the ceiling of self, yes.

Beneath the ceiling of self, no one and no-thing is truly, ultimately, beautiful. No scarlet sunset over a glittering ocean can command any praise higher than community consensus. If there is beauty outside of us, we'll never really know that we've encountered it. We can never be confident that our souls have touched and tasted true beauty.

Beneath the ceiling of self, not even the Son of God will be truly lovely to us. The Bible tells us that Jesus had no special physical attractiveness (Isaiah 53:2). But as we'll see throughout this book, what Jesus said and did is beautiful beyond description (Psalm 45). In his words and deeds shone the light of heaven, in whose nourishing beams all of life's beauties bloom. This is the light that the ceiling of self keeps out.[11] And when it's dark, the thieves come out to play.

Stolen Election

The thieves are people who benefit from being unquestioned in their efforts to enforce particular ideas. They can be found anywhere, and they're usually everywhere—in education, politics, industry, and oh yes, the church. You can spot a thief by his refusal to ground his ideas in any principle greater than his own preferences, unless he defines the terms of that greater principle.

The thieves insist that the ceiling is real because in the

darkness it creates, they seize godlike power in society. So much of that power comes from defining the terms by which society operates.

The quietest but most important battles in public policy happen on the field of language, long before the public ever sees a proposed policy. If I define the terms, I control the public conversation and can steer popular opinion in my direction, no matter how unjust my policy proposal is. If I get to define "justice," then I can label anyone who disagrees with me an opponent of justice and slander them into silence.

Let's say I'm in the United States Congress (rigged election for sure) and I'm pushing legislation that, in the interest of "justice," would shut down all roller coasters in the country. The reason: That slow climb up the tracks makes me hate life and everyone around me, especially the people laughing at me as I tremble. Plus, I don't trust the teenage punks who run the ride to have checked my harness correctly—(no offense to any of you punks who have this job). It's unjust for me and every other American man who cries easily to have to endure that kind of emotional abuse at an amusement park. Therefore, away with coasters! You say, "Just don't ride the coasters." But that's not good enough for me. No business should be allowed to do something that causes nervous investors to liquidate their assets. It's unjust to even create this potential. You don't like my policy? What, you don't like *justice*?!

However, if "justice" has an established, inviolable definition already—if it goes beyond the personal preference of the powerful—then I cannot hijack the term to serve my jacked up policy. Coasters will remain open; jobs will be saved. Rejoice, thrill-seekers and punks everywhere!

This is why it's so crucial to the thieves that society believes in the ceiling. Beneath the ceiling, thieves are kings. Sadly, we're all too willing to comply, because in the dark beneath the ceiling, in the absence of God's intrusive voice, we who do the thieves' bidding are promised lots of power, too.

Down here, we are the builders of "truth" and the makers of meaning. Down here, we define life's terms. We define ourselves and our rights, which is to define life for everyone else. To define yourself is to deify yourself. Down here, beneath the ceiling of self, we *are* God.[12]

The Wonder(less) Years

We're not God. The ceiling is so transparently a fake that a child can see right through it. And that's not to say that children are unintelligent. It's to say that we desperately need their wisdom, their brightness in the dark beneath the ceiling. Kids have the courage to question the ceiling, and that's why the thieves start to work on them as early as they possibly can.

The demands of life below the ceiling of self wage war against our deepest instincts. We humans are naturally and boundlessly curious. Our earliest thoughts are ones of wonder, of seeking. We look up to a sun-bathed sky and our imaginations open like spring. We study what's under rocks, poking and prodding the earth to discover the countless creatures swarming within it. It's just like the title to a *Calvin and Hobbes* anthology: *There's Treasure Everywhere!* And when we're young, we wonder what, or who, put all that gold there to be discovered. We are hardwired with worshipful instincts.

Children ask big, searching questions, the intelligence of which adults so often miss. Kids ask because they believe that there are answers (and that adults are holding out on them). Just try to get a little kid to stop asking "Why?" Better yet, *don't!*

The question of "why" can wrap its arms around the universe. It defies simplistic, surfacey responses and forces shifty adults to do some digging for real answers. "Why?" threatens to punch right through the ceiling of self, and that's why the thieves feel so threatened by it.

For fans of the ceiling, it's bad enough that kids believe truth can be known. What's even worse is that kids believe it will thrill them. Children love to ask "Why?" and they love to say "Wow!" The searching, sparkling eyes of a child suggest that the ceiling is a lie.

A child's excited laugh as she learns reminds us that something is buried alive within us, deep beneath the philosophical silt of lesser, self-focused ideas and affections, the soul-suffocating dust that the ceiling of self dumps upon our deepest instincts. A child's joy in knowing is like a tornado siren to the thieves: their anthill of "truth" is about to be blown apart. So the thieves try to reduce that storm of wonder to a gentle, harmless, impotent breeze.[13]

The best way to reduce and control wonder is to bat it back to the wonderer, adding some flattery to make it stick. Children are often encouraged to find within themselves the answers to their heart's biggest questions. This guarantees that whatever answers they find will be small, self-referential, and only applicable to them.[14]

It is a theft to convince children to be satisfied with answers philosophically smaller than their questions.[15] The trick in pulling off the heist is to make small sound big, to make confinement sound like freedom. Thieves tell kids: "You can believe whatever your heart tells you about God. Faith is special; it's just between you and God. So celebrate Christmas at home. At school, we celebrate 'Sparkly Season'!"[16] We expect kids to be impressed with our bland substitutes for the spiritual substance they crave. It's heartbreaking when it works.

Telling kids that life has no knowable, ultimate meaning sounds harsh. So we say it softly, using condescending language that says more about our intelligence than theirs. "You can be whatever you want to be." That statement is a viper, smooth and deadly. It numbs children's minds with the promise of godlike power to define themselves, leaving their souls defenseless against reality and crushing their desire to reach beyond themselves for truth. Trying to mold an unbending reality into their image will exhaust them, and lead them to call upon promise-making, politically powerful thieves for help. Eventually, they're reduced to simpering, morally lifeless, unquestioning slaves to whatever societally constructed truth the empowered thieves approve.

Here's another snakelike statement: "Always follow your heart; be true to yourself!" So what happens when a bully follows his heart by beating the life out of another student? We need responses to bullying that run as deep as the pain it ignites in victims (and the pain that bullies may be venting by their violence).

Lacey Sturm, musician and author, writes: "I don't believe bullying is the main thing that makes us want to die. I believe that it can be a trigger for people like my young self who already feel unsure about their purpose and identity—people prone to sadness, people restless with a world that seems to offer so many shallow answers to the deep questions that make their hearts heavy."[17] Sometimes following our hearts is exactly what hurts us, and others. Our hearts are much better at asking questions than providing answers.

When a child's questions are never allowed to touch truth greater than what she can build herself, or what's been built for her by thieves– when she never learns that those questions are appetizers for a great feast awaiting her, served beyond the thieves' reach, her hunger for truth begins to die. Her curiosity starts to crumble. When the *whys* keep crashing against the ceiling of self, the *wows* begin to fade.

From "Whatever!" :) to "Whatever" :(

As it's advertised, life beneath the ceiling of self sounds exhilarating. Who doesn't want to be God? But honestly, should you be trusted with almighty power? Should I? We want it, but would life really be good if we had it? What would life be like for others if you were God? Yikes, right? Me, too.

Children are naturally curious, but they're also naturally selfish. "Childlike" is a compliment; "childish" is an insult. To get their own way, kids are willing to kill. When a toddler tries to strangle another child who's playing with a toy he wants, we see the cruelty we're capable of at such a young age. Imagine if that toddler were stronger, and if no adult swooped in to stop the strangling. Now imagine that same toddler grown up, his god-complex never challenged, and in charge of biological weapons, or the Center for Disease Control.

This is not to say that we're all terrorists in the making, but it is to say that something terrible lurks within every one of us— the desire to dictate life for ourselves and therefore everyone else, to be exactly who the thieves say we are. But if we're honest, we know the world needs a much better god than we can be. We've got issues. These issues can't be solved beneath the ceiling of self. If we're incapable of getting beyond ourselves, how can we possibly improve ourselves? Too bad for the world.

In the '90s comedy show *Seinfeld*, the main character, Jerry, begins to date a woman who seems a lot like him—intelligent, observant, funny, narcissistic, and criminally indifferent toward most other people. At first, it's awesome. No arguments because no disagreements! But then he realizes with growing horror that she is exactly like him. As he watches her in public, he gets to see himself on display in society. He can't take it. He dumps her, explaining later to his friends: "I can't be with someone like me. I *hate* myself!"

It's bad enough to see yourself replicated in a girlfriend. What about in a god? And that's the horribly depressing truth about the ceiling of self: it's actually a cosmic mirror. Down here, if we're humble enough to look above us for God, all we can see is ourselves staring back.

A look in a mirror can be excruciating. We see the flaws immediately and we know some are irreparable. It's just who we are. We try to change, to find and express in a physical way our truest self, or maybe to hide it. But no matter how much we exercise, starve ourselves, or mangle our bodies, the mirror always shows the same soul staring back at us. Somehow we can still see our deepest insecurities, our most hated imperfections. Then we're not in the mood for self-worship. We'd rather go the other direction.

In our self-loathing, we start to wonder if others have the same problems. Do you ever get jealous of people who seem so comfortable in their own skin? While they float carefree through an enchanted existence, you feel ground-bound in a cursed life.

There's no good reason to think the floaters have it figured out. Each of us is a self, and as hard as the self tries, the self, by itself, can't become what the self so deeply desires to be: better.

We naturally want what's higher than the ceiling of self. But if someone above punches through the ceiling to lend a helping hand, he might start bossing us around. And thieves have taught us that it's better to die than to give up our godhood. After all, if we challenge our own claim to deity, we might think about challenging theirs.

Some people love the mirror effect, at least at first. Feeling independent and in control, they dance beneath the ceiling of self. But then a friend dies. Suddenly they're forced to face the ultimates in life, truths that don't respect their godhood. They realize that they've been deceived. Though teachers and superstar athletes have told them otherwise, they know they can't be whatever they want to be. They're not gods.

Those hard moments of self-realization are pivotal. They provide a turning point at which we could question the ceiling of self. Life's ultimates, especially death, clearly have access to us; could it be that we might have access to real answers about them? On what credible, consistent basis can we dogmatically say, "No way!"

This is why the biblical book of Ecclesiastes tells us that it's better to go to the house of mourning than to the house of feasting (chapter 7, verse 2). Better to go to the funeral than to the frat party. At the funeral, you're forced to think, deeply. But at the frat party, the revelers give you too little time and hand out too many intoxicants for you to manage some serious, sustained, sober thought.

At the funeral, our hearts begin to ask big, kid-like questions again. "Why?" "What will happen when I die? Is it possible to know?" "Is there something beyond death I should live for while I'm alive?" But the thieves have taught us to suppress those questions and to snuff out any hope they kindle. "Grow up. Those questions are for the weak and superstitious." Or more softly: "Maybe there are answers. If so, your heart will lead you to them." Yeah, that's helpful.

Those same ceiling-piercing questions surface the morning after the big party, and the major moral mistake made while there. What if the blush of shame is a spark of color signaling a better, brighter way of life within our reach? The question rises in our hearts: "Why am I living like this?" But it bounces off the ceiling of self and comes back a scream: "BECAUSE YOU'RE A GOD! You can do whatever you want! Don't be ashamed. You just need the right drink to help you deal with the hard parts of being divine. It's those questions that are killing you. There are meds to make them quiet, you know."

When the question of *why* never surfaces, it seeps out of us in a different, darker form. "Why" turns into "Why *not?*" Might as well go back to the bottle(s) and party as much as possible before the next funeral, or to forget the latest mistake. Might as well swing from that chandelier hanging down from the ceiling of self. "One, two, three drink. One, two, three drink. Throw em back, till I lose count. I'm gonna swing from the chandelier....I'm gonna live like tomorrow doesn't exist." This song is not a celebration of independence; it's a scream for help: "Help me, I'm holding on for dear life, won't look down, won't open my eyes. Keep my glass full until morning light, 'cause I'm just holding on for tonight."[18]

When our souls can't fly higher than the ceiling, we start to look for more interesting levels of low. "Matt," who shared his personal story on Dr. Jean Twenge's research website, said that the only reason he didn't attempt suicide as a thirteen-year-old was the thought of tomorrow. Hold on; it's not as hopeful as it sounds. Matt writes, "Even though that day and the preceding days basically sucked, tomorrow may suck in a novel way."[19]

Nate Reuss, formerly of the band Fun., sings triumphantly about a blazing night of substance abuse, begun in a bar where his friends "are in the bathroom, getting higher than the Empire State....Tonight, we are young. So let's set the world on fire, we can burn brighter than the sun." Sounds inspiring. But here's what he means by burning bright: "I just thought maybe we could find new ways to fall apart. But our friends are back, so let's raise a cup, 'cause I found someone to carry me home."[20] At least he has friends.

Community: None of Us Is as Dumb as All of Us[21]

In the alleged absence of God and his speaking to us, we turn to each other. We're much more attuned these days to our need for community. Less individualism is good, but being part of a community cannot solve the problem of the ultimately helpless, lonely self. A community is an assembly of selves. There is strength in numbers, but that's what makes community potentially scary, too.

Without any ultimates to guide the community, there's limitless potential for the abuse of its members.[22] What the group loves one day it might hate (and punish) the next. "Group think" is not usually considered a good thing, so it's probably not a good way to guide a community.

Whether it's a single or communal voice, the scream for personal significance rebounds hard off the ceiling of self. We put our deepest selves out there, up there, to touch something or someone of real meaning, only to be disappointed...again. The fast trip back to the ground ends in a hard crash. There are only so many crashes a heart can take before it codes.

Sometimes, to keep from flatlining, we pull back from the community. To protect what little life our hearts have left, we adopt apathy as self-defense. But it's often an irritable indifference, like a coat of cheap primer on a red wall. Beneath the surface, we're nervous, anxious, angry, and ready to explode.

Counselor Amy Solman notes that half of college students admit that they have been stressed to the point that they couldn't function in the past year, and there are more than 1,000 reported suicidal deaths on college campuses in the U.S. every year. The American College Heath Association found that 44.6% of all students surveyed among American colleges felt hopeless; 56.6% felt very lonely; 49.9% felt overwhelming anxiety; and 29.5% felt so depressed that it was difficult to function.[23] As Twenge puts it, "Being young has not always carried such a high risk of being anxious, depressed, suicidal, or medicated."[24]

All You Need Is Love

In this angst-ridden, affirmation-seeking atmosphere, it's increasingly difficult for people to think of love as anything beyond self-service. In romantic relationships beneath the ceiling of self, we reserve the right to make sexual intimacy mean anything we want it to—an act of affection or just a distraction—so we're often far freer in giving it out. Thus, the hookup culture, especially alive on college campuses.

In the hookup culture, sex is sometimes said to be meaningless. Huh? If one of life's most intimate and intense human interactions can be called meaningless, maybe it's not being done right.

Exclusivity is a vital part of intimacy, but exclusivity demands restraint. And why should gods restrain themselves? So we trade intimacy for animal instinct, and the ability to gain and give trust dies in the exchange. We'll sleep with everyone, but we have a hard time trusting anyone, and we wonder why no one else trusts us.

Some who once hoped for better than this lifestyle become so desperate for real affection that they'll take its cheap substitute from a selfish jerk. We know we're being used, but we don't want to be alone. We use the users. We give up the years of our greatest strength and give away all kinds of intimate "firsts" to people for whom we care so little and who care so little about us. We know it will scar us and we'll likely regret it eventually, but who's to say whether we'll ever make it to "eventually"? Or, we convince ourselves that we really do love the other person, or that the other person really does love us. But then our partner fails us, or we fail our partner. Despite our desperate efforts, we can't make that initial infatuation last, and we eventually wonder who we're kidding with the effort.

This is the "new normal" of young adult life in our culture. This is "freedom" beneath the ceiling of self. This is as good as life gets when we're God.

Isn't it about time we call shenanigans on the ceiling of self?

Maybe you want to call shenanigans on what you've read so far. I understand if you don't trust my take on things. But it's not just my take. I'm not inventing new things; I'm urging forgotten things, stolen things. In bygone days and in contemporary cultures away from the wealthy, "enlightened" West—and among many minority communities within it[25]—the gold of God's word has enriched souls and societies. It is the basis for so many of the freedoms, and so much of life's fullness, that we in the West are forsaking for slavery to thieves and shallow-living beneath the ceiling of self.

Just imagine for a moment: What if our innate perception that there really is more to life than can be seen, and that we can know it—what if that perception actually matches reality? What if we have access to absolute truth, and it's absolutely true that God loved the world so much that, despite our efforts to make him back off, he became one of us to forgive and free us so that we could really start living? And what if God gave us a book (?!) to tell us all about it?

The thieves say, "No way. Absolutely no way is that stuff possible." Or in their politer moments, "Maybe, but you can't be sure, so please be quiet about it." But we have to admit: There could be a God, and if so, God could do all this. And if God *could*, don't we have to seriously deal with the possibility that he did?

What if you could have a soul-satisfying encounter with the living God, a satisfaction that keeps you hungry for more? And what if, in meeting this God, you meet your truest self—you as you are with the ceiling of self exploded, your deepest instincts unburied and your soul set free to soar?

Even as a Christian—maybe especially as a Christian—that might be really hard to imagine. But just because something is really hard to imagine doesn't mean it's not real. The Bible says all of the above is very possible and is itself a vital means of making it happen. This book aims to show how.

Maybe you say, "I've read the Bible and my soul didn't exactly soar." Well, it's hard to know you're having an experience when you've been taught that such an experience is impossible. And as we'll see in the next chapter, many believers have never really, truly encountered the one in whom they claim to believe. To one degree or another, the ceiling of self has kept all of us in the dark.

That's why we've spent so much time here discrediting the literally in-credible idea that nothing of the above is available to us.

That idea is criminal, and you've been a victim long enough.

2

The Bible Takes God Seriously:
Do Christians?

"God created man in his own image. And man, being a gentleman, returned the favor."
—Mark Twain

"They look for a paycheck,
 As if you needed workers…"
—Lacey Sturm, "Heart Work"[1]

I mean it, guys," Chad says during testimony time on the final night of the church youth group's ski retreat. Snow falls silently outside the towering lodge windows as his peers huddle in front of him. The warm glow of the fireplace lights their faces as they gaze with squinty-eyed sincerity upon the young man who's just rededicated his life to the Lord. Chad's face is constipated, frozen between pain and pleading as he struggles to express what's deep within. "I'm tired of just pretending to love God. I want all of us, right here, right now, tonight—to *literally* be on fire for Jesus!"

Smiles spread across the room and heads nod encouragingly. A few grammar geeks snicker, exchanging knowing, self-congratulatory looks. What Chad means, of course, is that he wants everyone in the room to really love Jesus and to live like it. What he *said*, though, is a pretext to terrorism.

Imagine if one of the geeks panicked and screamed, "I knew

it! Chad's gone berserk! We're all gonna die!!" That reaction fits Chad's words perfectly, especially if Chad's life shows a pattern of emotional instability. (We'll come back to that later.) But Chad didn't really mean what he said. He was completely sincere, but his words did not match his intended meaning—good thing for the youth group! But here's the tricky part: *Chad doesn't believe his own statement, but he believes that he does believe it.*

For Chad, it was a semantic slipup. If a grammar geek corrected him, he'd probably laugh—or call the geek a legalist.[2] But among Christians living in the wealthy West beneath the ceiling of self, the problem of believing that we believe our statements about Jesus, when in reality we actually don't, goes way beyond grammar games; it's a crisis of faith we might not realize we're having. But like the freaked-out grammar geek, others are noticing, and they're unnerved.

We Believe We Believe

If you're not a Christian, or if you're seriously questioning whether you want to remain one, do you ever listen to Christians articulating their faith and feel like responding, "Hold on. Do you really *believe* that? Do you really think the Bible is right on that point? Do you realize what that would *mean?*" Maybe you're a Christian and you've been asking yourself the same questions. It's unnerving, isn't it? But sometimes a freak-out is the first step toward sanity.

The Bible's claims are heavy. Here are a few biblical basics about Jesus: Jesus Christ is God (!), is both God and human, having been born of a virgin (!!), and after being publicly executed by crucifixion, rose body and soul from the dead (!!!).[3] Feeling the gravity of these claims means we're taking Scripture seriously. It ought to unnerve us when Christians don't feel that weight, and especially when those who don't sincerely believe that they do.

The magician and avowed atheist Penn Jillette says he doesn't mind when Christians tell him that, unless he believes in Jesus, he'll go to hell. He figures if Christians really believe he's on his way there and don't warn him, they must really hate him.[4] Pretty compelling logic. By that standard, how many Christians who claim to believe that there is a real place called hell are guilty of this kind of hate crime?

Sometimes people who reject Christianity take statements of Christian faith more seriously than the on-fire believers who speak them. They recognize what the Christians don't: a drastic disconnect between actual belief and sincerely stated belief.

Whether you're a Christian or not, you can feel the difference between merely affirming a Christian belief and actually believing it to be true—even if you just pretend to believe! Say this statement out loud: "God raised Jesus Christ from the dead, and he's alive right now." No big deal, right? (Unless you just said that in public and people are staring.) Now say it again, with conviction. If necessary, just pretend you really believe it: *God raised Jesus Christ from the dead. And he's alive—right now.* Even pretending that it's true gets your heart going a bit, doesn't it? What should it do to our souls then, if we really do believe it? The simple answer is—a lot!

Odd That We Are Not That Awed

In the New Testament letter that goes by his name, a prominent church leader named James[5] blasts faith that is all talk. His thesis is that genuine belief in the true God authenticates itself through the believer's heartfelt actions in keeping with God's law (James 1:19–25). Our actions reveal our true affections; our behavior reveals our true beliefs.[6] According to James, if we hear God's word, affirm it, but then fail to do what it says, we're fooling ourselves if we think we actually believe it.

Like Chad, James is fed up with fake faith. He writes to Christians, "You believe that God is one? You do well." Feel the simmering sarcasm, the warm flattery setting us up for a burn? James commends his readers' faith for its doctrinal accuracy. There is indeed only one God, and God is self-existent and self-sufficient. So true! So far, so good. Then comes the fire. "Even the demons believe, and they shudder!" Ouch!

James knows that demons are vile creatures who hate God, but unlike self-deceived Christians, they take God seriously. They have the decency to shudder in fear as they contemplate him. Jesus got the same reaction from demons. All Jesus had to do was approach someone suffering demonic possession and the hellish spirits would howl in hatred and terror (Luke 8:26 and following). They knew who he was. How can it be, then, that people who claim to know and love and worship this very same Lord can sometimes barely stifle a yawn when he's talked about, and can hardly stay awake when they close their eyes to pray to him?

The easy answer is that Jesus isn't around anymore like he was 2,000 years ago. But even back then, not everyone who encountered Jesus understood who he really was. As we'll see later, those who really got it eventually responded to Jesus with either a demonic hatred and desire for his death or all-out worship and a willingness to die for him. And you don't have to see God in the flesh to know him personally.

The Bible is written to and for people who've never seen Jesus, telling us that we can be so close to him that he becomes our very life (John 20:31, Colossians 3). The Apostle[7] Peter wrote to Christians who had never seen Jesus but who truly believed in him; they were filled with "joy inexpressible and full of glory" (1 Peter 1). But as we look around us at Christians in our culture, and within us if we are Christians, don't we find, by and large, a relatively "meh" attitude toward the Almighty?

Isn't it common for Christians to talk about Jesus with far less interest than we show for our favorite team, music, or food? If the objects of our truest affections all met in one event—if we could eat our favorite food at the big game with our favorite band playing the postgame concert—wouldn't that be heaven? But then we're brought down to earth by remembering that we have to get up early the next morning for church, just to worship some resurrected God-man. *Borrringgg.* "Oh look, fly ball!...Wait, what?! HOME RUN! Game over! Bring out the band! Pass the grub! I am *so* sleeping in tomorrow!"

Don't get me wrong. I love sports, Boston-based sports especially. These are God's blessings. Remember the 2004 ALCS, Yankees fans? Heh heh. And I love music and food, too. Alternative Rock! Chowda! These are ways to experience God's goodness, and we should praise him for them. But why is it when we're called to turn our attention away from the gifts to pay more attention to the giver, we so easily lose focus and interest?

The statement that James cites, "God is one," comes from the great prophet Moses in the Old Testament book Deuteronomy (6:4)[8] and is followed immediately by a command to respond to God in the only manner worthy of him, a command that Jesus calls the first and greatest commandment (Matthew 22:37): "You shall love the Lord your God with all your heart, with all your soul, and with all your strength." When it comes to loving God, it's all-in. So isn't something off if worshipers of the Lord of heaven and earth can't wait to leave the worship service on Sunday to sing and dance before the gods of the gridiron? Who, or what, is truly our first love?

You might say: "I'm not bored with God; I'm bored with church." Fair enough. But what if there was just the tiniest chance that, in the midst of some truly blameworthy boringness at church enacted in Jesus's name, we might, if only for a few fleeting moments in worship, actually interact personally with the true and living God? Shouldn't the mere possibility make us willing to camp out the night before like we would for a concert or film we can't wait to see?[9] Shouldn't we be willing to miss the big game or scrap the lunch plans if they conflict with the public worship of the God we love? If not, then don't we Bible-affirming believers have to admit that, as it can be in a troubled marriage, we've become bored with our first love?

But think of that for a second: bored with *God*. How can that be? There's a sense in which it can't be.

Up in Flames

The idea of God is incendiary. In the Bible's book of Proverbs, the author asks, "Can a man carry fire next to his chest and his clothes not get burned?" (6:27). Even a few seconds of serious thought that a being worthy of the title "GOD" *might* exist should spark something inside of us. So shouldn't the belief that God does exist be a blaze in the depths of our being?[10]

For the biblical prophets, the fact that God exists and has spoken was sometimes too much to bear. But torturously, it was too compelling not to share.[11] Jeremiah is called "The Weeping Prophet." He foresaw and lived to see awful judgment upon his people, and his perennially hard-hearted countrymen hated and brutalized him for decrying the wickedness that incurred it. Jeremiah wanted out of his miserable ministry. But the only thing harder than speaking for God was not doing so. "If I say, 'I will not mention him, or speak any more in his name,' there is in my heart as it were a burning fire shut up in my bones, and I am weary with holding it in, and I cannot" (Jeremiah 20:9).

There is something utterly compelling about the idea of God, and something irrepressible about the sincere belief that God exists. If we're Christians, shouldn't our souls dance if we truly believe that God has spoken and we have access to his words, or break down and cry depending upon what God has to say? And that's exactly how we can spot the sometimes unseen disconnect between true faith and faith that's all (sincere) talk. Our true regard for God is revealed in our regard for his word.[12]

There's a sad but clear logic to it: If you don't care much about God, you won't care much about what he says.[13] On the other hand, if you're enthralled with God, you'll hang on every word he says as if your life depends on it—because if God is real, it does. Jesus says: "Man shall not live by bread alone, but by every word that proceeds from the mouth of God" (Luke 4:4). And that's what makes the big picture of allegedly Bible-believing Christianity in America so bleak.

It's common in contemporary Christian America to resent a ten-minute drive to church and to spend sermon time silently willing the preacher not to exceed the unwritten but deadly serious twenty-minute time limit. True, some pastors are boring. So are some writers, and people like me who are both are the worst! But if the presentation is at least a credible effort from a credible source—someone who believes that the Bible is God's word, has prayerfully and studiously prepared to preach as such, and who sincerely cares for the people listening and speaks to their hearts— couldn't we muster some patience? After all, the Bible is the word of God. Why does God's word not get more love from people who claim to love God? Jesus says that God's word is vital for life; many Christians seem to disagree.

Sociologist Dr. Jonathan Hill notes that only 8% of young people in the United States who self-identify as Christians actually read their Bible with any regularity.[14] Of course, stats can vary depending on how you define terms and ask questions. So let's make it personal: if you're a Christian, how much practical difference would it make to your daily routine if you no longer had access to the Bible?

Maybe there's a happy, or at least hopeful, irony at play in all this. Perhaps many Christians in this culture, despite constant access to God's word, have never truly approached the Bible *as*

God's word. That's unnerving, because it means that people who claim to love Jesus may not know Jesus as the Bible proclaims him. But that also means there's hope. It means that our "meh" attitude might not be directed so much toward Jesus and his word as toward our personal perceptions of them as perpetuated by the church. This is exactly why God gave us books in the Bible like James, to cut through the calluses of our self-deceit, to show us what's healthy or rotten in our souls beneath them, and to reveal what we truly believe—or don't. Self-deceit comes easy beneath the ceiling of self.

The Bible has always been subjected to the criticism that its claims aren't true. But beneath the ceiling of self, we're convinced we can't know truth anyway. Down here, we don't bother ourselves with whether the Bible is inaccurate. Down here, we believe that the Bible is impossible. God can't speak, much less write us a book. And if he could, we couldn't understand his words anyway. Even as Christians, our sometimes unrecognized belief in the ceiling of self keeps us from truly understanding what the Bible is, and therefore from truly believing what the Bible says.

"Happy" Days

No matter how sincerely we believe something and how passionately we may defend our belief, if something deep within us knows that what we believe is all just a matter of opinion anyway, it's easier and easier to treat that belief casually—even belief in God. Beneath the ceiling of self, our certainty that we cannot know absolute truth automatically segregates faith from "real life." It makes matters of faith matters of mere opinion, and it sets the stage for a life full of separations.

Beneath the ceiling of self, belief can't touch actual truth. So if you're feelin' the faith one day, God must be there. If not so much the next day, then maybe he's not. Down here, something is only really true if I believe it, because my believing makes it true. So God's existence and goodness ebb and flow with my sense of them; they rise and fall based on the relative intensity of my sincere feelings about them. Beneath the ceiling of self, God and the Bible can be as important, or unimportant, as individual believers feel they are at the moment. We can sincerely claim that the Bible is "true" while ignoring its commands in our daily thoughts and decisions.

We feel obligated to obey Scripture only to the extent that we feel it connects to "our truth," "our reality." So we can sincerely claim faith in the true and living God and feel precious few pangs of conscience when we live like there's no God at all.

It's been observed that Christian college students will put their faith in a "lockbox" for four years (five, if they're "super seniors"!) so they can participate in the pervasive party scene, even to illegal extents. How can Christians think that Jesus is okay with being ignored until they get their bachelor's degree? Love them or hate them, Jesus gives all kinds of commands about preserving our souls and bodies in purity,[15] and he allows no time-outs in the process. Self-control is one of the primary signals that a person's life is truly led by the Lord (Galatians 5:22 and following), and yet so many Christian high schoolers who claim Jesus as their Lord and the Bible as his word can't wait to totally lose control at college. But putting faith in a lockbox isn't just a young-adult thing.

Christians of all ages, and in every place and period of time, learn to lock their faith away so their favorite sins can come out to play. James calls this double-mindedness and self-deceit (chapter 1), and he joins the other biblical authors in calling all Christians to seek God's forgiveness for it (chapter 4). But beneath the ceiling of self, Christians don't need to distinguish between serving Jesus and serving the desires that Jesus calls sinful (see Matthew 5–7). Jesus asks, "Why do you call me 'Lord, Lord' and not do what I tell you?" (Luke 6:46). Down here, Christians have essentially learned to reply, "Thanks, Jesus. I'm sure the people you were talking to back then really needed to hear that challenge. But for me, if something makes me feel good, and if I feel good about it, that's all the proof I need that God is good with it, too."

Beneath the ceiling of self, to discover oneself is to discover the greatest truth that can be known, and to express one's true self is the most meaningful, beautiful thing that can be done. Down here, self-expression and self-satisfaction are truth. "Clap along if you feel like a room without a roof….Clap along if you feel that happiness is the truth….Clap along if you know what happiness is to you..."[16]

That song by Pharrell Williams might be the most addicting piece of audio recorded this century, and its lyrics are alive with the painful irony of our times. How many children have sobbed themselves to sleep at night because Mom or Dad, or both, have decided that happiness isn't with each other anymore? And how many have been guilted into getting over it for the sake of the new family being formed against their will? Their hearts cry, "I don't want to meet your friends, and I don't want to start over again. I just want my life to be the same, just like it used to be. Some days I hate everything…everyone and everything. Please don't tell me everything is wonderful now!"[17]

But if Mom and Dad feel bound by God's words about marriage and family to keep their vows and to live up to their responsibilities as parents, if happiness isn't "me first, finding my truth," then that crying child can clap for joy instead. There's hope for her, for the family she might form in the future, and even hope for real happiness for her struggling parents. Within a family, the hurt we feel and inflict is especially intense and painful, so none of this suggests that reconciliation and healing are even in the same galaxy as easy. But Jesus said, long before Christian clichés were a thing: "With God, all things are possible" (Matthew 19:26).

Jesus teaches that, for us, our relationships, and the world itself to be made whole, we've got to set our sights higher than our hell-bent pursuit of personal happiness. As we'll explore throughout this book, this does not mean that our hearts are left out of the Bible's picture of human wholeness and world peace—it's just that we're not the centerpiece. That's a hard lesson to learn beneath the ceiling of self.

You would think the public worship of God would be the perfect setting for us to get out of our own heads for a bit, to be reminded that life is way bigger than we are and about way more than our personal happiness—and that this might, maybe ironically, make us happy! You would think the worship service would provide us with demolition materials for the ceiling of self. But it turns out that the ceiling of self is set up in our churches, too.

"Your Own Personal Jesus"[18]

The ceiling of self is especially deceptive when it's set up in church, where it's more like a skylight. Through a skylight, you can see stormy or sunny weather clearly, but you're not actually experiencing it. And if you look closely enough as you gaze into the heavens, you'll sometimes see your own reflection.

Christianity beneath the ceiling of self involves the sights and sounds and language of biblical Christianity, but the ceiling prevents us from actually experiencing it. As the builders of truth and the makers of meaning, we feel the freedom to redefine biblical terms, even the term "Jesus." We're so accustomed to conditions down here that fashioning life to fit our image is instinctive; we don't often realize we're doing it. When we think we're gazing in faith upon God's son, we might, if we look more closely with a biblically informed scrutiny, see a savior whose politics, prejudices, personal life preferences and even physical appearance make us think we're looking in a mirror.[19]

Have you ever seen the Jesus with shock-blond hair and electric blue eyes? I mean, as much as I'd like to look like my Savior, there's no way the real Jesus looks like me. He was a Hebrew man and recognizable as such.[20] And truth be told, my hair is not blond; it's a beautiful shade of gone. My eyes are blue, though—profoundly so. Kind of like frozen lightning. But that's beside the point. There's no way in heaven or earth that Jesus looked like me, or so many other images of him based in our often ethnocentric imaging of the Lord.

You can imagine a young boy thrilled at seeing the blond, blue-eyed "Jesus" in a picture Bible. "Daddy, I didn't know *Thor* was in the Bible!"

Dad's pumped; his boy is interested in the Lord! "No, son, that's Jesus!"

The boy's face droops, but suddenly his eyes widen: "Wait—Jesus is *Thor*??"

"Uhh…no, son…but, um, there's a lot of ways Jesus is *like* Thor! Let's think about that…" And so begins a dad's loving, desperate quest to make God incarnate exciting by comparing him to the true object of his boy's affection, the Norse god of thunder. At least it wasn't the Hulk! Or Hawkeye. That'd be the best argument ever for atheism.

When our portrayals of Jesus look so much like us, our culture, our politics, our superheroes (see chapter 8 on this), what does that say except that Jesus is the biggest and best expression of our personality-driven and culturally conditioned life preferences?[21] Perhaps the Bible's silence regarding Jesus's physical features is not meant to incite our imaginations on the topic, but to rein them in and focus them on what he said and did. Should there really be so many images of Jesus among people who all claim the same faith? Is the biblical image of Jesus really meant to be a Rorschach?

Maybe this is a significant but unheralded reason why so many have left the church, and why some will never give church a chance.[22] The Jesus worshiped among some Christians is nothing but a projection of the people gathered in his name. And no offense, but they're not exactly worthy of worship. And this might also help to explain why churches in America are so segregated. We want a Jesus of people, by people, and for people like us.

Following the lead of our false god, sometimes we want worshipers who don't look and act like us to keep their distance, and we let them know it. In some churches, if you show up with tattoos or unnatural hair coloring, or a different skin color or socio-economic status, you're guaranteed to be the subject of lots of suspicious staring, even as the pastor calls the church to set their eyes on Thor, I mean, Jesus. The real Jesus is not like that.

Throughout the Bible, the Lord calls his worshipers out for practicing favoritism and for the terrible way they treated foreigners and strangers among them—another theme struck in James's lightning bolt of a letter (James 2).[23] But beneath the ceiling of self, even when we try to mend the social divides among us, we're prone to reinforce them.

The Bible constantly calls for love-based reconciliation in the name of Jesus. But the idea in Scripture is to find common ground by worshiping the same Savior, not to invent as many versions of the Savior and ways to worship him as there are people needing to be reconciled.[24]

The most obvious segregations among churchgoers are based on race, but there's segregation even within racially monolithic churches, too—age segregation. Rather than uniting people of differing ages and backgrounds, worship is instead arranged according to the separation-inducing preferences of each. It's well intentioned, but is it really well with the church when different demographics of people are ushered off to different parts of the building to praise God according to their personal stylistic preferences (which they could do to their hearts' content at home or elsewhere)? Wouldn't it be beautiful, and a better picture of the bond all believers share through Christ, to be together as a full, integrated body of believers? What does it say about the allegedly unifying power of Jesus when his people, *in the same congregation*, don't know one another? When they never worship alongside people very different from them, or even alongside their own kids?

It's significant that parts of the New Testament written to particular churches would have been read to whole congregations. Ephesians is one such letter. It was written by the apostle Paul, whom we'll get to know later, and it was meant to be circulated among many congregations. In chapter 6, Paul addresses children directly.[25] This means that the kids were in the worship service to hear his words, which means that it was the expectation among early Christians for kids to be with adults in worship and to listen intently—for at least five chapters! And Ephesians is no "children's sermon."

Ephesians is considered by some to be the most significant document ever written.[26] This high praise is based largely on the letter's socially staggering commentary on its subject matter. Paul means to unite very different kinds of people to worship Christ and to break down ancient, entrenched barriers of hostility between them. How sad that when this letter is preached in churches today, it's so often to deeply segregated congregations who miss the tragic irony and forfeit the blessing of applying God's unifying truth right there among themselves.

While keeping our helpful age-specific ministries intact, wouldn't it be wonderful if, for the main worship service, we gathered everyone who could be there, were intentionally inclusive instead of intentionally divided, so we can be side by side as very different people possessing and expressing one uniting faith in the Savior of the whole world?[27]

Yes, having everyone in the same room creates logistical problems, especially in big churches. Yes, young kids can have a hard time sitting still in the worship service, and nurseries for the youngest are a godsend. But, as one dear friend in the ministry says when the kids pipe up as he's preaching, "If we can hear them, it means we have them." It will require patience on the part of adults, and some loving help for struggling parents, but this is where believers can shine in the selfless, uniting love meant to mark followers of Christ (John 13:35). And if the crowd can't fit the room, then maybe instead of amassing big numbers spending big dollars at one worship site, we can start more churches and do more philanthropic work in more neighborhoods, not least so that pastors can, in these smaller settings, really get to know the people in the worshiping community and beyond.[28] God already feels so impersonal to so many. If we're just a face in the crowd to the ministers who teach God's word, why should we think God feels differently?

Wouldn't it be worth the struggles, and wouldn't it be a shocking, stereotype-defying sight for Christianity's critics to see such love, such diversity within unity among people who claim to believe in the one true and living God?

I Gotta Be Me

But don't we all have different, personality-specific ways of relating to God, and shouldn't that be reflected in the way we praise God? The Lord certainly relates to us personally, and it's wonderful—essential, in fact—to have time alone with God. But it seems we want alone time with the Lord even in the worship gathering.

Sometimes we try in our minds to block out all the others around us, as if to say it's just us and Jesus there in that place, in that moment. The Bible, however, calls us to be fully aware of and rejoicing in one another's presence, partly so that we can teach and encourage one another as we're praising God together.

Paul writes in chapter 3 of Colossians: "Let the word of Christ dwell in you richly, teaching and admonishing one another in all wisdom, singing psalms and hymns and spiritual songs, with thankfulness in your hearts to God." Our singing to God in the church is not meant to be a solo! We're to interact and instruct one another as we praise God. God even gives us words with that dynamic built in.

For example, we say "Hallelujah!" when something really great happens, like "Yes! Finally!" That's cool, but "hallelujah" is actually a Hebrew word by which we address other people; it's a command that means "Hey you, praise the Lord!" It's hard to have a hallelujah time together when we're trying our best not to pay attention to all the "yous" around us.

With all eyes facing ahead, or totally closed, anonymity is easy in the church, and that means so is isolation, and loneliness. The well-intentioned effort to make God feel personal to us—it's just you and Jesus—might make the nervous person who's unaccustomed to worshiping God feel the opposite. The Lord means for us to feel his presence in the acknowledging, loving company of the worshiping community that claims his name.

Sometimes we want anonymity in the church, because anonymity provides autonomy (literally, self-law). When we do look around in church, if we don't like what or who we see, we can just go worship somewhere else. Or, despite the Bible's call for Christians to keep assembling in public worship (Psalm 122, Hebrews 10:25), we'll just stay home or take a walk in the woods to worship. Beneath the ceiling of self, how we worship God is our call, not God's.

Sadly, segregation of all kinds is a normal part of worship among Christians in this culture; it's the inevitable result of efforts to create unity that respects individuality but that is fatally, sometimes unknowingly, founded upon a core commitment to individual*ism*. This is a Western thing, not a biblical thing (as we'll see especially in chapter 6). The Bible calls us to reach beyond ourselves in order to know God, to open ourselves up in and to the presence of others seeking to do the same.

When we Christians present to would-be worshipers a god no greater than ourselves, than our politics, than our personality-driven preferences and culturally driven conveniences, the spiritual inquirer turns skeptic and says, "Sorry. You've actually got nothing here for me. I don't have to wake up earlier on Sunday, much less give away my money, to worship myself."

This Is No Time for Tears!

We should think about one final form of segregation that occurs in churches beneath the ceiling of self: the walls we put up in front of people already feeling on the outs with God because of deep personal pain in their lives or the rising religious doubt that often comes with it. Sometimes we build those walls by the songs we raise in praise of God.

Our worship songs paint the truest picture of our real beliefs about God. As one Bible teacher puts it, "Show me a church's songs, and I will show you their theology."[29] A church's songs tell us what the people gathered believe about God, and what they believe God wants to hear from us. If worship songs spend little or no time in lament and even anger, little or no time expressing fear and doubt and not simply for the sake of a quick correction and counterpoint, then isn't it only right for a heart trembling in these ways to conclude that God himself just doesn't want to hear such things from us?

What kind of Savior would Jesus be if he didn't step into the shadows where you sometimes find your soul? But how can you meet him there when you've been taught, at least implicitly because it seldom happens at church, that you can't talk to God (much less sing to him) with bleak or angry words?

The answer is not to make the Christian faith an angst fest, as if a sulk is braver than a smile and relentless discouragement is more honest than unceasing happiness. It's good and godly in life to splash in the puddles and dance in the watery sunlight after the rain. There's a time to sprint on hot sand under a cloudless sky toward the welcoming menace of the mighty ocean—oh, how I wish that time was now!—and to sing our thanks to God for it all. As we'll see in the final chapter, the Bible's own songs spend lots of time in the sun, but they also spend a good amount of time—most of their time, in fact—in the darkness. Despite that obvious cue from God's own word, so much teaching material and especially praise material bearing the label "Christian" refuses to let life's very real darkness sink in.[30]

Church historian Carl Trueman wrote a blog piece entitled "What Can Miserable Christians Sing?"[31] He put this question to several evangelical crowds in his native U.K., and each time the crowd burst into laughter as if the idea of a faithful Christian feeling miserable was absurd. Bono from U2—the greatest Irish quartet *ever*—laments the lack of realism in popular Christian music. "Write some songs about your bad marriage…"[32] he says. He sees the disconnect between real life in the world and popular expressions of Christianity in the wealthy West.

Even when worship songs acknowledge the shadows, we tend to move quickly to sunshine, implicitly telling the hurting heart: "Turn that frown upside down! Things are just fine because Jesus is alive!" It's true that Jesus is alive; it's not true that things are just fine.

While Christian young adults and those who minister to them are doing better at admitting and addressing their fears and doubts among one another, church can still feel like the place where you go to feel bad for feeling sad, where you're thought a reprobate for feeling rage, and where faith is pretending really hard that you're happy.

The true Jesus never tells people to pretend that life is anything other than it is. We'll explore the Bible's sometimes unnerving but always straightforward realism—found especially in its own songs—as we go throughout this book.

For now, we've got to ask of any piece or collection of praise music, ancient or modern, traditional or contemporary: How theologically deep and biblically broad is our material? Can our repertoire reach deep and honestly into hearts haunted by life's hurts, and does it actually conduct such hearts to the Savior who can truly shepherd their souls? Here's a sobering test to apply to our worship music: To what extent could our words directed to God apply equally well to another god, or any god, or no god, or a friend, or a lover, or even a pet? Is there anything distinctive about our songs that would let a first-time hearer know that we're praising the God of the Bible? As sincerely as we may sing vaguely worded praise, without God's word practically and powerfully present in our songs, we have to wonder who we're really worshiping. We should wonder the same about sermons.

Preach It!

God's written word was meant to be preached. Paul writes, "Faith comes through hearing, and hearing through the word of Christ" (Romans 10:17). In sounding a call for missionary preaching to people who've not yet heard about Jesus, Paul asks, "How are they to believe in him of whom they have not heard?" (verse 14). Paul wrote this letter in Greek, the common language throughout the Roman Empire in Paul's day, and there's a cool thing happening in the way he phrases this question. It could be, and probably should be, translated: "How can they believe him whom they have not heard?" In other words, to hear the word of Christ preached faithfully, on the Bible's own terms, is to hear Christ himself speaking. Paul considered the preaching of Scripture to be the voice of Jesus in the world. So whose voice is missing from Christian worship services when Scripture is all but ignored in the sermons?

Whether you're a regular churchgoer (or once were), an occasional visitor, or an outside observer, see if the following feels familiar: The sermon gets so little time in the worship service, or at least the Bible gets very little time within the sermon. Messages can be filled with heartwarming stories and jokes, but their connection to Scripture is sometimes circumstantial at best. Hearers walk away knowing the speaker much better than they did upon entering the service, but not necessarily knowing Jesus any better. We might call these "selfie sermons"; the Bible is in the background but the preacher looms large front and center.

The flipside of selfie sermons can be heard in some churches where lengthy preaching is the norm. In these settings, the focus on self is insidious. Though the sermon may be central to the worship service, it's heavily loaded with theological terms known only to the theologically astute churchgoer. The preachers make little effort to engage the hearts of those for whom those terms are a foreign language. And when people have no idea what the preacher is talking about, he blames it on God: "Well, I can't open their hearts to understand. Only God can do that."[33] These churches are less popular than those that promote individualism in the sincere effort to respect individuality, and that's probably a profound blessing.[34]

God makes it clear in Scripture that his worshipers should never be satisfied with what they might consider proper form and doctrinally pure words in worship. In the first chapter of the prophecy of Isaiah, God builds an indictment against his faithless people. What's his grievance? Lousy lyrics in their praise songs? Sermons not sufficiently loaded with seventeen-letter theological terms[35] nor sufficiently critical of other denominations? Nope. God grieves that when his people worship him, their hearts just aren't in it.

God says he's weary of the mindless, heartless, nonchalant performance of religious rites he himself had prescribed. The people were in effect saying that God should be good with their apathetic worship because they were doing it by the book. But remember what Moses and Jesus taught: we're to be "all in" as we love God. Fiery, impassioned ignorance and its mirror opposite, the emotionally indifferent performance of rote religious routine, are opposite sides of self-worship.

Beneath the ceiling of self, cut off in obvious and subtle ways from God's word, which James describes as a mirror to our souls, Christians cannot see what's really going on in their thoughts and feelings and words about God.

It Feels So Right; It Can't Be Wrong!

If things are this spiritually bleak in the typical Christian experience of the West, how do we explain the palpable sense of drawing near to God while we hear sermons and sing songs that, upon further scrutiny, actually speak so little about God? Behold once again the subtlety of the ceiling.

Have you ever thought about yourself in a sad situation, and gotten teary-eyed in the process? But then you realize you're not getting emotional because you're contemplating a sad situation; the emotions come from contemplating yourself getting emotional in that sad situation. At first you think it's the other people and the circumstances you're imagining that are moving you, but then you realize that it's really all about you. You're moved to tears by the thought of your being moved to tears.

In the same way, maybe when I feel especially moved while worshiping God through empty words preached, sung, and prayed, maybe what I'm actually enthralled with is not so much God as the idea of my being enthralled with God. Maybe I'm worshiping my worship,[36] or worshiping myself worshiping. I mean, it is rather cool when you think about it. *Me*, being enthralled with God... wow, I'm awesome...I mean, he's awesome!

I remember a particularly moving time of worshipful singing in a chapel service when I was in college, but I don't at all remember what I was singing. And it's not just because it's been longer than I like to admit since I've been in college. Even then, I realized most of the way through the song that I had no idea what I was singing; it was just a sweet tune. I could have been singing the recipe for oatmeal cookies and felt just as close to God. And while contemplating and eating cookies can have profound spiritual effects upon us, shouldn't there be something distinct, special, about worshiping God? Something that distinguishes it from a rock concert, cool as those can be, and that doesn't make Cookie Monster a patron saint?

At a good concert, there's a palpable sense of transcendence and spirituality. But what would happen if the band suddenly got specific and told its audience to find the source of that transcendence in the God of the Bible? Deep and powerful and true stuff can happen at the concert, gifts from God the original and consummate artist. But we tend to love gift more than giver. For

Christians, worship is the backstage pass. After the blaring sights and sounds, it's the intimate conversation with the one who created wonders like the music that thrills our souls, the one whom James calls the giver of every good and perfect gift (James 1:17).

In worship, there should be a directness about praising God with biblical content that would likely drive fans away in droves from the concert.[37] But aren't there Christian rock and hip-hop concerts blasting songs with thoroughly biblical lyrics? Definitely. But do we depend so much upon that atmosphere to feel close to the Lord that, unless it's replicated in church, we're just not feeling the faith? If so, could it be that we secretly get our spiritual highs from the adrenaline rush of the concert atmosphere, a high we'd likely feel regardless of the religious orientation of the band and the venue? Could it be that our deeper affection is for the style rather than the substance? We should ask the same of Christian concert-goers who prefer classical music and choir-singing and therefore want the same in church.

This is not to say that musical style is neutral. Some styles just can't communicate a song's substance. Imagine Beethoven's "Ode to Joy" performed on kazoo, or Metallica's "Enter Sandman" the same. But how much would the substance of our faith suffer if we couldn't praise God through our personally preferred styles of song? To what extent have we equated Jesus with the culturally driven way we think about and praise him?[38] These are unnerving but essential questions to explore. But there's a remarkably positive upside to the downer of discovering that our faith is more dependent than it should be upon our favorite styles of music and message.

If, when we're really feeling the faith, truth might actually be far away, then when we're feeling nothing, truth might actually be close by. Feelings are vitally important to faith; it's just that, beneath the ceiling, we've learned to equate them with truth. Thank God, the way we feel about life is not always the way life really is. Same with our feelings about God. Much more on this in our final two chapters.

The less Christian faith and worship are rooted in Scripture,[39] the more room there is for the seeds of self-worship, so tiny and subtle at first, to gain ground. And self-worship is no delicate flower thinly rooted in a tiny pot. It's a bulbous gourd with freakish growing power that runs all other life out of the garden. Once self-worship gets rooted in Christian worship gatherings, it grows under the guise of worshiping God. Scripture and the Savior it proclaims get crowded out of the place. It's hard to meet the biblical Jesus in church when we make so little use of the Bible in worship.

God's written word must be the centerpiece of any understanding and expression of Christianity. Only Scripture can sober us when we're unknowingly drunk on self—either bright-and-happy drunk or depressed-and-mean drunk. God's word reveals his heart to us; it also reveals our hearts to us.

The Bible brings God close, busting right through the ceiling of self. When it's read and taught, preached and prayed, studied and sung on its own terms, the Bible speaks to us with a voice not our own, but from a heart that knows us better and loves us far more than we know and love ourselves. Taking the Bible on its own terms takes effort: a sincere, all-in commitment. But beneath the ceiling of self, we've learned that spiritual stuff should come easy, cost little, and leave us in total control of the terms.

(Mis)Education

Down here, spiritual stuff isn't a matter of what's true; it's a matter of what's true to you.[40] A Bible passage can mean pretty much anything you want it to, regardless of what it meant to the original readers and hearers. So why sweat serious scriptural study?

Biblical illiteracy is pathological among Christians in America. Some Christians reared in this culture learned Scripture from kind-hearted church leaders eager to serve, but not necessarily equipped by deep study or good communication skills to teach. Unprepared and unnerved as they encounter challenges to their faith from people thriving in life without it, some double down hard on the fundamental biblical truths they've been taught, militantly ignoring any and all "worldly" thoughts that might upset them. Others live nervously, and often secretly, with doubt like a ticking time bomb in their souls, fearing the imminent explosion of a biblical faith whose grasp on real life feels increasingly shaky. (Much more in chapter 4 about when that bomb goes off.)

Others learned Scripture from teachers who seemed very well studied but who came off as personally cold and distant, never bothering to kindly explain Scripture's unfamiliar words and ideas. If the Bible teaching they get is dry and disengaged from their real-life contexts, people can logically conclude the same of the God Scripture proclaims.

Both scenarios above assume efforts by church leaders to teach. That doesn't always happen. One of my college students wrote me a note on his exam, lamenting that his many classes in preparation for church membership never really interacted with the Bible at all.

Church culture is like broader culture in so many ways, including its chronic underestimation of the young people within it. Sometimes older Christians don't believe that young people are interested in or capable of deep biblical learning.

One student sat in my office, deeply distressed because his mentors in youth ministry said he might not have what it takes to be a good youth pastor. Why? Because he didn't sincerely love the Lord or know how to communicate God's word to young people? Nope. He loves his Savior and Scripture, and he gets along really well with the young people to whom he wants to minister. But his favorite Bible classes were the upper level theology classes. That made him a misfit among his mentors. This pained him to the point where he asked if it was really okay for him to like these classes so much, given that he wants to minister Christ to young people. *Yes!* Jesus thinks so, anyway.

When Jesus cited Deuteronomy 6:5 for a crowd culturally conditioned to divide head from heart in its approach to knowing, he substituted "mind" for "strength." Jesus meant the same thing Moses did—loving God is all in—but he wanted to be sure we knew that "all in" included mind. Sadly, in Christian education undergraduate level and below, Bible class is sometimes the joke in an otherwise serious academic curriculum.[41] James would not consider this schooling Christian at all.

James tells the majority of Christians that they should not seek to be teachers within the church, because God will hold them to a higher degree of accountability than Christians who serve in other ways (James 3). And whether they held church office or not, all of God's people were expected to deeply study his word, as a matter of love, and in their various life contexts to teach young people to do the same (Deuteronomy 6:7). But the desire for deep, intellectually stimulating and satisfying biblical education dies easily beneath the ceiling of self.

Down here, there's a lot of well-meaning, honest intention and fully felt emotion going on among Christians, for sure. But perhaps it's just enough of the faith to render us immune to the real thing. James is all about exposing fake faith for the sake of encouraging the real thing, so he gives us two more tests to help us distinguish between faith that takes God seriously and the subtle self-worship with which we confuse it.

You've Lost That Loving Feeling

James calls believers to practice two things we often lack in this psychotically fast-paced culture: patience and perseverance.[42] Even when we have a decent grasp of the Bible's basic teachings, James tells us that real, living faith puts that teaching into practice, and does so through life's trials and tribulations over a stretch of time. "But the one who looks into the perfect law, the law of liberty, and perseveres, being no hearer who forgets but a doer who acts, he will be blessed in his doing" (James 1:25).

In the same way that we can inadvertently worship our worship, we can also put faith in our faith. We trust in our sincerity; the assurance that we are in "God's will" comes from remembering the time we recently rededicated ourselves—again—to love God "like never before." That kind of faith can't sustain us long-term. It grasps nothing beyond us, so it's not worth holding on to.

If our faith is in our faith, our impatience in waiting for God to "show up" might make us question whether he was ever there to begin with. We're desperately depressed until the next retreat, revival meeting, or theology conference reminds us of God's constant presence. But then there's the inevitable letdown between times of faith stimulation; and these deflations can be devastating. *Just ask Chad.*

As we first met him, Chad was "on fire," "all in," "sold out," "totally pumped"—thankfully, none of it literally. But remember, we caught Chad at a good moment, right at the close of a winter retreat. He was fresh in his renewed faith like a new coat of powder, fallen from a generous night sky, glistening like a field of diamonds in the day's rising light. But if Chad fits the stereotype, what happens to that powder-fresh faith the next day, and especially the day after that?[43] It gets plowed and pressed, and, depending upon the wildlife surrounding it, pooped on. As temperatures rise, the sweet surface on which skis fly turns to slush and muck, neither hot nor cold. Apathy regains control and old faithless habits come back with a vengeance, dominating life and discouraging faith, until the next retreat comes to the rescue. Until then, the daily slog of life reduces Chad's spiritual fire to a dying ember. C'mon, Chad!

It's easy to criticize Chad, but to some extent, we Christians are all Chad. Across the denominational spectrum in the wealthy West, why does our faith's vitality depend so deeply on the missions trip or the ski retreat? On the concert or the theological conference where celebrity pastors and theologians speak and sign autographs, or the new shipment of old theology books? Is this sometimes flaring, often fading faith the kind of belief that the Bible says "overcomes the world" (1 John 5:4)?

Christians in our culture need to ask a hard question that insightfully critical non-Christians beg us to ask ourselves: do we really even know our own God?

Living faith might truly be there, longing to stretch and stride forward, but it often bangs its head and falls concussed beneath the ceiling of self. For our faith to stand and step forward with integrity, we need to fight the seductive power of self-made reality and self-focused spirituality. We need to stop practicing a virtual faith beneath the ceiling (or skylight) of self. We need to step outside and feel the elemental force of the faith we claim.

The Bible takes us there in its first seven words.

This Might Hurt...

The Bible's opening sentence hurls a javelin at any bubbles of self-worship we may float within beneath the ceiling of self. It's ten words in English, seven in the Old Testament's original language, Hebrew: "In the beginning, God created the heavens and the earth." There's nothing fancy or provocative about the wording itself. It's a straightforward statement, but it reveals a Being whose staggering power is actually painful to think about.

Think of it: If God was there in the beginning, then He is beyond time. He came "before" time. But hang on. "Before" only has meaning with reference to time. Yet God is, somehow, prior. He is first, but without a beginning. There was a "time" in which

God was all there was. But "then," out of no-"thing," God created every-"thing." Ouch!

At least one benefit of pain is that it humbles us.[44] Pain slows us down and reminds us that we are dependents, creations. There is not one single need we have that we can meet completely or even partially by our own will and power. Even our breathing most often takes place without our conscious consent—thank God! All of life is this way. There is not one single part of life or our lives over which we have true, total control.

If we took time to consider how essentially dependent we are as creatures, we might freak out. But once again, a freak-out might be the first step toward sanity. It could help us admit that we are not the gods we claim to be beneath the ceiling of self.

The Bible's first words tell us how we got here, how anything got here, how "here" got here! They answer that ultimate, childlike, too often unasked question of why—and provide quite the "wow" in doing so. Scripture's opening words put us in the only posture of heart from which we can rightly understand and respond to the rest: humility.

Human pride makes no sense in the presence of the being we meet personally in the pages of Scripture. But the painful humbling that God's word induces is not a harmful hurt. As we'll explore more fully later, God designed us to relate to him very personally, and in love. And contrary to what some skeptics say (see chapter 4), the humility to which Scripture calls us is not mindless.

Remember, Jesus makes sure we know that an all-in love for God requires the full powers of our mind. By taking aim at our foolish pride, Scripture clears the way for a vibrant, growing life of the mind, lived toward God and others in love.

Scripture opens by putting first things first in every category—logically, chronologically, philosophically, and morally. According to the Bible, the first and most fundamental and knowable fact in all of reality is that *God is*. Every bit of truth begins there, and therefore so does every bit of true knowledge. Sorry, Mr. Descartes! "Unless we first think rightly about God we shall be in basic error about everything else."[45]

The Bible has inspired some of history's greatest intellects; it has also infuriated some of them. The reason one intelligent person is utterly in awe of Scripture and another thinks Scripture is utterly awful has to do with ethics, not IQ. It's a matter of what we think should be true, what we assume without exhaustive proof is true, and whether we're willing to accept truth that contradicts our desires.

The humility that accepts the Bible's first ten words as true simply admits that we are not in ultimate control—of anything. So if we are to know anything, do anything, say anything, *be* anything, we are dependent upon God. Everything besides God, which means every "thing" there is, ever was, or ever will be, owes its existence to God, finds its true worth and meaning in relationship to God, and is only truly knowable and explainable in reference to God —and that includes us. This is what Descartes missed, and why his well-intentioned efforts at honoring God eventually took his fans so far away from the Lord. If we refuse to acknowledge the first and most fundamental fact in reality—God IS—we will literally fight like hell against the second, which is like it: we are not he.

Sure, we might admit that we're not almighty, but we do think, especially in America, that we have fundamental, sovereign authority over at least one thing: our own lives. God disagrees. And that's what people really don't like about the Bible (see chapter 8). That's why we in the church keep God at a distance in our alleged efforts to create the most authentic Christian experience we can. As we'll see next chapter, it's why the ceiling of self was built to begin with.

The Bible teaches that we can know God. Not exhaustively, but truly. Belief in the ceiling of self assumes that, if God is there, God either cannot, or has never wanted to, speak to us in a way we can understand. And it calls that assumption humility. But according to the Bible, it's not a high view of God that requires a rejection of Scripture as his word; it's a high view of ourselves that requires that.

God says through the Old Testament prophet Isaiah, "Heaven is my throne, and the earth is my footstool; what is the house that you would build for me, and what is the place of my rest? All these things my hand has made…But this is the one to whom I will look: he who is humble and contrite in spirit and trembles at my word" (Isaiah 66:1–2).

That was Jeremiah's attitude, as well as that of Isaiah and the other prophets.[46] Their sincere, all-in, pained but persevering service to the Lord changed the world. And that's because their faith had no ceiling. There are believers like them in the world today.

It's to Die For

My pastor ministered for a time in Eritrea. He describes how hard it was to come back to American culture after his work in Africa was done. The Eritrean Christians would enter the church auditorium with a joyful solemnity, a reverent eagerness. Whole families and singles entered the worship room, happily and willingly, as if they really believed they were about to encounter the living God. These African Christians were convinced that, in addition to the privilege of talking to God in prayer, they would actually hear God's voice through the preaching of the Bible, even if the divine voice sounded through a middle-aged American Caucasian from Jersey. And if my pastor preached sermons long enough to give TED-talk loyalists an aneurysm, the people wanted more, not less.

When he was in Kenya, the people expected a pastor to preach for three hours straight, to take a break, and then to go for another three hours in the evening. But when my pastor got back to the States after his years in Africa, the typical vibe in the room before he preached was: "Give me something good, and make it quick." When we're merely critics of sermons, consumers and customers of church rather than worshipers who are eager, conscientious hearers of God's word, we can't possibly, truly and deeply, believe that the Bible really is the word of God.

When asked in an interview what Irish people have that defines them as Irish, Bono replied: "It's what they haven't, that defines them." So, too, with Christians who don't believe in the ceiling of self. If the relatively casual Christianity in America were typical of Christianity around the world and throughout history, we could chalk Chad's problems up to typical Christian life—but if that were the case, we may never have heard about Jesus to begin with.

The Christian faith tends to spread most powerfully when it's persecuted. There's a morbid logic to it: if Christianity is violently opposed, it means it's making an impact. Sure, God sometimes grants peace and prosperity to Christian communities. But by and large, what Christians have experienced in America is far from what the Bible tells us to expect of a life lived for Christ, far from what's played out painfully in world history and in our day beyond the wealthy West.

In cultures where the ceiling of self is set up, Christian knowledge of Scripture tends to go down. But where Christianity's vital signs are strongest in the world, the Christians truly believe that the Bible is nothing less than the word of the living God. Their lives more than pass the tests James gives for faith's proof of life.

Christians in other countries risk being hunted down and killed simply to hear one more sermon, to attend one more prayer meeting, to sing and pray perhaps for the last time in this life alongside fellow believers. They could avoid all that trouble by practicing a purely private faith, which is by definition a societally irrelevant faith, the only kind that increasingly testy governments in the West will tolerate. But James says that's dead faith. And there are those who'd rather die than try to live it out. They'll give up their jobs, their homes, even their lives for the sake of God's word, to be around it and to broadcast it as best they possibly can as long as God gives them life in this world.

Christians in countries that exalt another god face the same threat of death. If they'd only convert, or at least keep quiet and submit in practical terms to the rules of the nation's religion, they could live in relative peace. But these Christians know that true peace means more than an absence of conflict. If believing the Bible brings conflict, so be it. After all, the Bible is the word of *God*, not just a book full of people's opinions about God.

Christians in Communist countries dodge government agents who seem to be on every corner, following new and random routes to their secret worship assemblies. And yet, they know that their meetings aren't really secret, or at least that they won't stay that way for long. The government knows, and when it decides to act, any of those Christians in the assembly may turn up "disappeared." Yet still they get together, as often as they can. Why?

Religious fanaticism? That's too easy an answer. While lots of people do lots of crazy things in the name of religion (or lack thereof), the difference, as cliché as it sounds, comes down to Jesus. Not Jesus the idol we fashion according to our definitions. But Jesus as he is, as the Bible presents him to us. And it comes down to these persecuted Christians embracing Jesus's own view of the

Bible. Christianity in the wealthy West needs to recover not only Scripture's view of Jesus, but Jesus's view of Scripture.

Contrary to everything essential about life beneath the ceiling of self, Jesus insisted that, in Scripture, God had spoken—clearly, definitively, and with authority. The most vital churches in the world are the ones who believe him, and who prove it in their faithful, often behind-the-scenes, and often painful perseverance.

The Bible tells these hunted Christians to keep assembling in Jesus's name to worship him, and God in turn promises to be with them in a special way when they do. And he really, really is (2 Corinthians 6:17–18, Hebrews 10:25). At the heart of these not-so-secret, but oh-so-spiritually-alive assemblies is the written word of God. The same Bible with which so many of us are bored. As Jesus once told a Samaritan woman, in a conversation we'll examine later, these humble, sincere, Scripture-believing Christians are the kinds of worshipers God seeks (John 4).

Such worshipers are definitely found in the West, too, but it seems impossible to say that their attitude is status quo here. Often, when this spiritual vitality surfaces and starts to grow, the ceiling of self drops a new load of dust on it, the narcissism and consumerism that cover and try to kill it.

As persecuted Christians know, sometimes it takes a violent storm to blow away the self-centered dust and debris that collect on our souls, to water the roots of faith buried beneath the polluted surface, to allow life and growth. Maybe that's why the political storm clouds seem to be gathering over popular Christianity in the West. It's time for God's church here to grow up.

O Come, O Come, Immanuel

Westerners do not trust in Kant's ceiling because we're wiser than non-Westerners. And it's not even that persecuted Christians in other lands have never heard of Kant's ceiling, or thought deeply about it. I've spoken to representatives of newly rising churches in the Far East. They've studied the ceiling and they watch in sadness as we suffer the soul-crushing consequences for still believing in it, the consequences we considered last chapter and will examine again in chapter 4 especially. They've lived under the reign of thieves. They watch and they warn that the ceiling is the perfect setup for the ascendancy of governments like those that try to kill them for worshiping a god other than the state, and that make life in general miserable for the vast majority of people in their countries. The state is a cruel god, but a "true" god beneath the ceiling of self.

Christians who've suffered the tyranny of that god find it stunning that we in the West who have such constant access to the Bible live as if the Immanuel of sacred Scripture is subject to the Immanuel of modern philosophy. Their hearts break as we serve the gods that breed beneath Kant's ceiling.

The churches that follow that Immanuel and treat the Bible as less than it claims to be are dying. They're hemorrhaging members. To be unimpressed with the word of God is to practice an unimpressive Christianity. Philip Jenkins writes: "The churches that are doing best in the world as a whole are the ones that stand farthest from Western liberal orthodoxies, and we should learn from their success."[47]

Living without the ceiling allows marked-for-death Christians to see clearly what's most important in life. They know that the ceiling is silly, and that the societies that choose to live beneath it are suicidal. Meanwhile, their faith, built upon the conviction that the Bible is the word of God, is blooming like spring across the globe.

One member of a viciously persecuted church put it this way in an outstanding paper he wrote for a class I taught: "To conserve the worldview of the Bible and to keep the Word of God as the starting point for interpreting everything is the most important aspect of Christendom today." This Christian is not self-deceived. He understands and believes his own words. His life shows it.

That same student went back to his homeland, to preach the Bible to his countrymen, to tell them about the Jesus it proclaims. Government officials arrested him, beat him bloody, and sent him home with the order to knock it off, and to warn other Christians he knew to do the same. After his wife bandaged him up, he asked her to prepare a huge dinner. He was going out and into the neighborhood to personally invite people to their home for a wonderful meal, and to hear all about their Savior.

Back to those good and necessary questions from people who reject the faith and that Christians contemplating the same are asking themselves: Do you really *believe* that? Do you really think the

Bible is right on that point? Do you realize what that would *mean*? These suffering, victorious Christians who possess such vital, self-less, Scripture-filled faith have an answer. Happily and humbly, they say: "Yes. Hallelujah! Yes, we do."

For centuries now in the West, we've been listening to the wrong Immanuel.

3

The Bible Is the Word of…*God*

"…On that same day the madman entered divers churches and there sang a requiem. Led out and quietened, he is said to have retorted each time: 'what are these churches now if they are not the tombs and sepulchers of God?'"
—Friedrich Nietzsche, *The Gay Science*[1]

"Grand speeches pour out with the rain
On streets where no one's listening…"
—Lacey Sturm, "Life Screams"[2]

The soul of the nation is at stake, and the young emperor is afraid to act. The old-school samurai master Katsumoto begs the boy to feel the strength of who he is—the emperor of Japan is divine! But this emperor feels powerless against Japan's lesser leaders, politicians lobbying hard to Westernize the empire. Katsumoto used to be the boy's teacher; it's agony to see his former pupil paralyzed with fear. Yet his student is also his master, and he must speak cautiously, reverently. "Forgive me for saying what a teacher must—You are a living god! They will do what you want!" The disheartened boy replies: "I am a god, *if* I do what they want."

Later, Japan's leaders assemble in the emperor's presence to discuss a looming treaty with the United States. Omura, the leading pro-West politician, whose work Katsumoto's samurai had been undermining, is there to lead the meeting. And then enters

Katsumoto as the personal guest of the emperor. And he's brought his sword.

Omura notices, but he fears no physical attack. Self-control is the essence of the samurai way. He does, however, fear Katsumoto's empowering presence, symbolized in his sword. The samurai personifies the empire's ancient warrior spirit, venerable and fierce, and a samurai's sword is his soul. Katsumoto is a clear and present danger to Omura's plans, but the cunning politician is prepared: he has already declared the assembly a no-sword zone.

In the most respectful of terms, Omura informs Katsumoto that, so sorry, he must relinquish his weapon. Katsumoto refuses. "This sword serves the Emperor; only he may command such a thing." Suddenly, the conflict over the sword brings the larger dilemma into sharp focus, and forces a choice. Will the young god embrace the new, mechanistic ways of an increasingly industrialized world or hold to the old, honored traditions of a simple, courageous, spiritual life?

Katsumoto bows before the emperor, arms and hands extended, offering his sword, his soul, to his master. The emperor hesitates. Omura notices, and grins like a jackal spotting a lost, injured gazelle. The predatory politician pounces. He shouts, "The emperor's voice is too pure to be heard in this assembly!"

A tear falls from Katsumoto's eye. He knows all is lost. Who in the assembly of emperor-worshipers could protest such a statement? On Omura's terms, to call for the emperor's speech is to drag him down to the level of mere mortals. The one who wants the god in the room to keep quiet suddenly seems to be his most reverent servant, and the one who truly reveres him suddenly seems to be a powerless, old-fashioned fool.

Flattery silences the god in the room, creating an artificial distance between him and his worshipers, a distance that the faithful feel bound to maintain out of loyalty to him. Katsumoto submits quietly and is escorted from the assembly. The warrior knows that he'll be expected to commit ritual suicide to salvage what's left of his dignity. Samurai cannot live with the shame of defeat, and it's clear to Katsumoto that his lord no longer requires his service. Well played, Mr. Omura.

If you're familiar with popular Hollywood films with culture clash at their heart, it's no spoiler to tell you that the troubled

Eastern island empire is eventually saved by a white Westerner, the film's main character. Our hero even gets the wife of the samurai he kills earlier in the film to fall for him. But it is Tom Cruise we're talking about. What widow, despite her grief, could resist the way Cruise rocks a kimono? But back to matters at hand: the way a false worshiper fakes true believers into accepting the silence of their god.

Omura's praise did not glorify the emperor; it bound and gagged him. Its conniving brilliance was its unassailable implication that the divine emperor wanted to keep quiet. To suggest otherwise would be blasphemy. Of course, one word from the emperor could have called Omura's bluff and destroyed his plans for the empire. But as yet, the young god had not grown a divine spine. For the time being, Omura's subtle subversion made him seem like the emperor's most loyal servant.

This scene from *The Last Samurai* illustrates well the opportunistic flattery with which modern-era Christianity, following the lead of Immanuel Kant, praised the God of the Bible.

The Sound of Silence

Unlike the young emperor, the God of the Bible is not afraid to speak his mind. But Kant's ceiling of self undercut the longstanding belief among Christians that God had already spoken up by way of the Bible. That conviction was already falling on hard times, and people were increasingly open to the idea that a silent God was actually more worthy of worship than one who spoke, especially one who could tell you all you needed to know about himself in a book. Kant thought he was doing God and Christianity a huge favor by building the ceiling of self and separating God from the Bible.

The Bible's God had not been polling well in Western Europe for quite a while by the time Kant came on the scene.[3] People were on fire—literally—in the name of Jesus, killing and being killed for particular formations of biblical doctrine or the proclamation of rich Christians' property rights. By Kant's day, influential Christians were wide open to worshiping a god who would preside over the universe without being too pushy, who would encourage societal advances in science and art. They wanted a Christianity not bound by a book.

On top of all that, trendy biblical scholarship suggested that Bible-based faith wasn't much different from ancient pagan mythology, and that we couldn't even be sure when and by whom the biblical books were written. There seemed to be little that was unique in the Bible's content and much that was questionable in the Bible's composition.[4]

Maybe modern mankind didn't need the Bible, or at least the parts about angels and resurrections, heaven and hell—all the stuff that encouraged an unscientific, superstitious outlook on life. It's not the Bible's fault, thought Kant. What can you expect from an ancient book written by superstitious—er, philosophically immature—people whose theological thinking wasn't fortunate enough to be forged in an age of reason like his? The Bible did its best, and it was good for the days in which it was written. But now, among more enlightened people, it was giving God a bad reputation. Kant's ceiling would give God the space and time he needed to clean up his image.

Kant taught that the best access to anything "absolute" in life would come by way of reason and science, not religion and Scripture.[5] So he attempted to liberate God from the laughable idea that humans could gain detailed access to his thoughts—*pfft*, as *IF!*— and from the book that claimed to be that access.

When it came to knowledge, Kant ascribed all power and authority to the knower. The knower rules in the realm of knowledge, no longer having to bow before the thing to be known in order to learn, even if that "thing" is God. Some have called this shift in philosophy "Copernican."[6] While Descartes thought we could know things as they are, Kant thought that we could only know things as they appear to us. We cannot know reality and God as they are. For some, this was permission to say "good riddance" to the good book, and hello to a God worth worshiping.

Kant's declaration that God is too high and lofty to speak directly to us[7] made him seem like the most pious guy in the room of Western Christianity. He propped himself up as God's ultimate PR agent and handler. He would let us know how and when God could be accessed. Kant the philosopher gave people theological justification to believe, whether disingenuously or sincerely, that it was impossible to get a direct word from God, no matter what the Bible said. God's voice was too pure to be heard in the world.

But if God is silent, whose voice will fill the void? Why, the one who respects him too much to listen to him, of course! By hailing the emperor as too high and lofty to be heard by his subjects, Omura ensured that his own voice would rule the assembly and therefore the empire itself. Kant lacked Omura's malice, but the effects upon Western Christianity were the same as the politician's power grab in Japan. Just like Omura's, Kant's alleged act of worship forced loyal believers to bow before a new god in the name of honoring the true god.[8] By building the ceiling of self, Immanuel Kant unwittingly put the finishing touches on a temple for the god of modern-era Christianity.

God: The Good European and the Perfect American[9]

Because we have no real access to his thoughts and words, this god is not at all insistent that you think of him according to particular theological categories and classifications. His goal in being worshiped is simple: to help you be a better person. For Kant, moral improvement was the only real purpose of religion. Who cares if your perception of God is radically different from someone else's? If you're both decent people, why stress over doctrinal details?

To help you be the best you that you can be, Kant's god will keep a respectful distance and keep his opinions to himself. Or, if you'd like him to feel close, he can do that, too. This god is totally user friendly. The dominant philosophy of the day determines the primary form he'll take, though he's quite happy to adjust to individual preferences as well. Many American Christians worship this god without realizing it. In some ways, it's in our nation's DNA to do so.

Historically, Kant's ceiling served the silent, distant, and aloof god of the Deists, who enjoyed the presence of America's third president among their ranks. Deists revered God for his aversion to performing miracles and his total respect for the autonomous desires of individual people and nations.

Deism had "hopped the pond" from Europe to America and taught people to worship a stately, righteous, eminently reasonable divine presence who dwelled above the ceiling, but whose presence we could feel beneath it in society's basic building blocks like liberty and justice.

Thomas Jefferson wrote: "I tremble for my country when I reflect that God is just." But Jefferson also took a razor to the Bible—no kidding, he actually cut it up!—removing from it all of that awful stuff about bloody ceremonial sacrifices for the forgiveness of people's sins, and that literally incredible stuff about people rising from the dead. "God" would not be so uncouth as to actually involve himself with humanity, let alone to do what the Bible says God did in Jesus—actually become human. Ewww! Why would God do that? A righteous architect of the universe with a dignified disinterest in matters beneath him? Why, yes! Quite so. A relational god incarnate nailed to a cross to save the world? Hell, no! No such being could be worshiped by scientifically enlightened people.

Immanuel Kant didn't like Deism,[10] but his own view of God didn't do much better than Deism's distant, nondescript God. Whatever their particular ideas about God, the leading Enlightenment intellectuals in Europe and America were basically united in their religious devotion to autonomous (self-ruling) human reason—human thinking unaided and unrestricted by divine revelation, by the word of God.

According to Enlightenment thinking, autonomous reason will tell us everything we need to know about God and therefore about how to be a good person. We can learn all worthwhile religious truth by looking inward, looking by reason to reason. Autonomous reason, even in matters concerning God, is our ultimate authority and guide. To reason, I mean, to God, be the glory!

But what if our reasoning is ever wrong? After all, a logical argument can be valid, but not sound. It can be completely consistent on its own terms, but have nothing to do with truth and reality. If being a good human being required being a Red Sox fan, and you're a good human being, then Sox nation is glad to have you! But much as it pains me to admit, the first premise is not true. You can be a good human being and like...and like...the Yankees. There, I said it.

So if logically consistent reasoning isn't enough to connect us to truth in everyday life, how could it be enough to connect us to truth about God? Or, how could it ever go the other way and rule God out? Couldn't God break through the barrier of our limitations in knowing? And wouldn't we need him to, in the event that our reasoning was leading us to valid but unsound conclusions about him? NO! says Kant. If God broke through the ceiling to correct our unaided thinking about him, that would be cheating.[11] Reason, as he understood it, told us all we needed to know about God and therefore all that God wanted to say to us.

Kant taught that properly functioning human reason (as he defines proper function) is God's voice within us. If God wants to add anything to it, he needs to run what he wants to say by that truest and purest of standards. "Inward divine revelation is God's revelation to us through our own reason. It must precede all other revelation and serve as a judge of external revelation. It has to be the touchstone by which I know whether an external revelation is really from *God*; and it must give me proper concepts of him."[12]

For Kant, human reason is the gatekeeper for God's revelation. If reason rules an idea it out, then that idea is not from God. God can say nothing to us if what he says doesn't make sense to properly functioning reason.

Contrary to Kant's requirements, the Bible plainly declares certain mysterious things to be true, and sometimes doesn't explain to us how they can be. But for Kant, if we can't reach what we can know by way of autonomous human reason, it's either falsehood or it's truth we don't need to know. So miracles, for instance, are out. Even if supernatural acts of God did happen, how could you know, except by way of reason, that they were really from God?

But lest we think this gives autonomous human reason too much power, Kant writes this about reason: "If it is honest and free of prejudice, it still has to discover many deficiencies and weaknesses even in the most complete system of theology possible for it. And certainly it must not boast about its knowledge of God. If a higher revelation has disclosed some clearer insight into its relation to God, reason should accept this revelation with thanksgiving and use it rather than rejecting it."[13] A higher revelation like the Bible, maybe? Nope. Haven't you been listening? Reason tells us that God can't speak directly to us unless reason approves it.

Never mind the rather ridiculous idea that our reason could ever be totally free of bias and prejudice. "Quite impossibly, the Enlightenment had a prejudice against prejudice."[14] How could reason ever recognize a higher revelation than itself, much less bow to it? Would autonomous reason really give up its throne? And if it did so, presumably it would have to do so on the basis of...well, autonomous reason. So reason, by reason's means and only in a matter consistent with its dictates, would recognize in some revelation a higher, clearer view of God and humbly bow and adjust accordingly?

There's a German word for this kind of thinking: Bullgeschichte.[15]

Be Reasonable!

Can God really be restrained and silenced by our arbitrary rules about autonomous reason? And can human reason alone, unaided by God's revealing himself, really handle all that's necessary to know about God? This is God we're talking about! But according to Kant, God needs to keep a respectful distance from us, to give us an immense amount of autonomy.

Kant thought we needed independence from God's coercive power and even any incentives God might offer as encouragements to live a good life. Otherwise, how could he ever hold us accountable for our own actions? Nope. We've got to do it on our own. "Man *himself* must make or have made himself into whatever, in a moral sense, whether good or evil, he is or is to become." Kant taught that, by following what he called the categorical imperative, to never do anything that you would not want to see everyone else doing, people could make themselves worthy of God's assistance (which will still come by way of autonomous reason).

But will human beings really be on their best behavior relying solely on God's having endowed them with a fine sense of reason? Have you met any humans? Ah, but who needs realism when you've got reason!

Modern-era God-fearers wanted a divine justice without a divine Jesus; they wanted to be good people without the good book. But Jefferson and other Deists didn't reject everything about the Bible. They thought that certain portions were helpful toward good ethics, and that a national morality partly based in the Bible could create and sustain the new nation's ethical substructure. A few excerpts from God's laws on morality—summarized in the Ten Commandments (Exodus 20, Deuteronomy 5)—could build a good framework for society.[16] But all the miraculous stuff and the idea that the Bible is God's direct word to us—we could pitch it all into the Dumpster at our nation's construction site. The problem, though, is that the moral principles that Jesus advocated are impossible to maintain without grounding them in the truths about God that Kant said were impossible to know.

Jesus's famous command "Love your neighbor as yourself" draws its strength and staying power from the one that comes immediately before it, the command to be all in in our love for God (Matthew 22:37–40). In order to really know how to love and serve your fellow human being, you've got to know and love the God who designed humanity. And as we'll see throughout this book, God tells us much about himself that Kant would find quite unreasonable.

Jesus gives these two commands to summarize, in order from top to bottom, the two "tables," sections, of the Ten Commandments. Kant's ceiling served as a horizontal guillotine, decapitating the Decalogue. Severed from their head, the commands about loving our neighbor might, like a recently axed chicken, retain some life in them, but not for long. Take only the ninth commandment, for example: "Do not bear false witness against your neighbor." In other words, no slander. But beneath the ceiling of self, who's to say what's true, and therefore what's false? And as Jesus was once asked by someone seeking to justify his prejudices, "Who is my neighbor?" (Luke 10:29).

If God's moral law is so accessible in the recesses of our reason, and if we are so capable of making ourselves worthy of God's assistance in keeping it, why do so many, many people do the opposite?[17] Kant freely admitted that his own era and those before him were full of examples that call into serious question whether people would, or even could, live out the categorical imperative.[18] But one of the major blind spots in the Enlightenment was its refusal to really learn from history, or at least to be properly humbled by it.[19] History is so *then*; this is now! We're better and brighter than all those who came before us, and so many others around the world wallowing in ignorance now. The Enlightenment was all about "an unbounded faith in progress, a belief in perfectibility and the imminent elimination of pain and suffering."[20]

Benjamin Franklin wrote: "The rapid progress the sciences now make, occasions my regrets sometimes that I was born so soon. It is impossible to imagine the heights to which may be carried in a hundred years, the power of man over matter....All diseases may by sure means be prevented or cured, not excepting even that of old age, and our lives lengthened at pleasure even beyond the ante-diluvian[21] standard."[22]

Despite its deliriously high hopes for humanity, though, by casting God to society's periphery (or rearview mirror), the Enlightenment set us up for slavery in the name of freedom. Isaac Kramnick writes: "The secular perfectionism of the Enlightenment is a dangerous anticipation of the social messianism...writ large in modern totalitarian movements."[23] And without a word from God as to the value of all human life, certain people are inevitably regarded as less entitled to an Enlightened society's pleasures and protections.

The Enlightenment claimed to champion the individual's rights over and against the systematic repressiveness of institutions like the church and the state, especially when the two joined forces. But the Enlightenment defined an individual as a male property owner. Sorry, ladies. Oh, and it really helped if you were a white male property owner, and being wealthy and well-educated was great, too. "There were class, gender, and racial restrictions in 'the race of life.' An occasional uneducated poor man might make it into the competition, but strict barriers kept virtually all women and people of color from the starting line."[24] But other than that, the Enlightenment was all about the little guy!

The spirit of the Enlightenment seemed to say, *Oh, if only the rest of the world was so wise, wealthy, and white as the West! What a day of rejoicing that would be! But alas, we must be patient with those who are not as bright, not as white, as we. Less enlightened people may at first be pitied and tolerated, but eventually the powerful and privileged must reeducate society's less enlightened members, or if they refuse to learn, just eliminate them. Sad, yes, but it's for the greater good. It's all about compassion, really. And we don't need the Bible to teach us how to be compassionate.*[25]

White Wash

Recent studies show that those in our culture who identify as "nons"—no religious affiliation of any kind—are likely to be old, wealthy, and white.[26] This is what makes the boom of Christianity among non-white people around the world, which we thought about last chapter, such a stunning, stinging example of poetic justice. They're finding that God's word is the key to unlock the fetters of the totalitarian governments to which they've been chained since before their birth, while those in the West who boast of their freedom from God increasingly volunteer themselves for political and social slavery. Just like with Omura, when a nation's god is silent, her politicians will gladly take that god's place.

But you couldn't tell any of the above to Jefferson, Kant, and others. For Enlightenment thinkers, if we could dream it (by reason), we could do it! *We could achieve peace. We could build a league of nations, presided over by the most reasonable people and build the kingdom of God on earth. Science is the only Savior we need in this life. But because God got all this going, and will deign to help us when we prove ourselves morally worthy of it, he gets all the credit. Far be it from us to claim glory! It's God who's made us the most reasonable, unbiased people there's ever been. Thanks be to God, we're bold, unafraid, unbound by the Bible, ready to save humanity and to rule a brave new world beneath the banner of autonomous human reason. It's the age of Enlightenment, baby! The future's so bright, we've got to wear shades!* But the sky's-the-limit optimism of the Enlightenment was galactically naïve.

The Enlightenment mingled legitimately high hopes with deadly hubris. Kramnick describes the perspective of a key figure in the "Counter Enlightenment": "The Enlightenment, for de Maistre, was guilty of the satanic sin of pride, seeking to give to man the power and insights of God." Regarding the French Revolution, "'These apostles of tolerance, humanity, intelligence, virtue, and reason,' he thundered, 'had left France littered with corpses and tombs.'"[27] According to still other critics of the Enlightenment, the movement's attempt to keep God and the world separated "bore its final fruit in Auschwitz."[28] History shows us that human autonomy leads to human atrocity.

Sure, we've made great strides in science. But with every disease we've cured, it seems we've also invented new and even more horrible ways to afflict our fellow human beings. We cured polio, but we created the dirty bomb. Humanity is, and almost always has been, a mess. And some of humanity's most "enlightened" people have been its cruelest.[29]

Contrary to Kant's views, it's much more reasonable to think that there is something deeply, maliciously ill in the heart of humanity, something fundamental to the human condition and incurable by merely human means. The Bible has been telling us this for millennia: the autonomy that Kant and the Enlightenment prized above all things has never been our salvation; it's been our sickness.[30]

Left completely to our own devices, individuals and societies don't do good things as we govern ourselves, at least for very long. Thank God we don't have power proportional to our desire for godhood! We're not good gods, but deep down, "Everybody wants to rule the world." Ten minutes in a room full of toddlers, or adults, demonstrates human depravity on all kinds of levels. (And just imagine if you could see into people's thought life, to see what's going on beneath the surface of their smiles...and imagine if others could see through ours as well...eesh!)

In the end, Kant's view of human nature, and therefore of human potential, was just plain unreasonable. But he thought his view was better than the Bible's. He soundly criticized the Bible's understanding of human nature and how it became corrupted.[31] Kant believed God had nothing particular to say about that, or anything else, really. The words that could have made this profound thinker wise to the true nature of humanity, that could have tempered the Enlightenment before its violent self-worship binge and the horrible hangover it's given humanity, these words Kant ruled out of reason's bounds and therefore ultimately untrue or unimportant for humanity to know. For humans to prosper, they had to be autonomous. And for that to happen, God had to keep his mouth shut.

Unfortunately for Kant's theory, human nature is not so noble as to be restrained by an inner, speechless sense of God's moral gravitas.[32] We didn't always do what was right when God did speak, so why would we start when he went silent?

Kant died at the opening of the nineteenth century, so he never saw the global atrocities that would open and define the twentieth. Two world wars within the first half of the new century! And ever since, we're only a few bad decisions and bad tempers away from a three-peat. So much for the silent, stately edition of Kant's god; so much for the age of reason.

What if God Was One of Us?[33]

Two centuries after Kant, we've kicked back hard against the idea that reason rules all. A postmodern society believes that there's more to knowing, and to what can be known, than our reason can reach.[34] Christians have realized that knowing God is about a lot more than reason and systems of theology, and that there are mysterious aspects of life that are very real, but not very explainable— even by science. It's acceptable now to be spiritual. Being religious is frowned upon, because religion comes from outside and suggests an external authority, whereas spirituality wells up from within. Spirituality touches only as much of the transcendent as the spiritual person wants, and allows God to speak only to the extent that the worshiper wants to listen.

By and large, Christians have rejected Rationalism's uptight version of a knowable God as well as Kant's uptight version of an unknowable one. Many who call themselves evangelical Christians have loosened up, worshiping instead the ultra-chill God of suburbia (who somehow fancies himself so relevant to the inner city). Unlike the distant god of the Deists, this god is above all things relational.

This god doesn't mind at all when his worshipers give him the Heisman in order to watch the big game. In fact, as far as this god is concerned, watching the big game can be worship. After all, if Jesus is Lord of everything, then anything we do is worship!

Christians would be wise to learn the lesson taught to us by the first installment of *The Incredibles*, the story of people with special capabilities being shoved to the shadows of a society that mandated mediocrity in the name of fairness. The heroes recognize: if everything is special, then nothing is special. Similarly, if everything is sacred in the same way, then nothing is really sacred. A god who says "Whatev" when it comes to worshiping him may sound really sweet, but it's the sick kind of sweet. And not the sweet kind of sick, either. It's icky sickly sweet, sweet to the point of making you sick.

What else are we to think of a god who morphs into whatever form his creatures want? The rush for the worshiper is great at first. God is everything you want! But then you realize, he's *everything* you want. Eventually, you should probably ask him, "Can't you come up with an original thought? Maybe give me some kind of pushback so I can develop some spiritual muscle? Grow a divine spine, will ya?!"

To be fair, Kant would cringe at the self-indulgence that goes on today in the name of Christianity. But in the wise words of every young child in conflict with another: "He *started* it!" Of course, the situation is always more complex than that. But whatever led to the scuffle, and however many children were involved, at least one kid did something definitive that gets at the core of the conflict and leaves lasting marks on others, maybe even scars. Kant was just that kind of kid.[35] By insisting that God cannot really be known, Kant introduced us to a god who isn't worth knowing.

By insisting that we cannot know anything as it actually is and that we must never even try to, by insisting that all we have in knowledge is our perceptions, that our minds form reality more than they receive and learn it, and by insisting that when it comes to knowing God, the details of his personality don't really matter, what else but self-indulgent religion could Kant reasonably expect?

Under the ceiling of self, one's favorite way of knowing becomes the exclusive or at least the primary way by which God can be known. This is how the worshiper (unwittingly) becomes the worshiped.

For Kant, God could be known through autonomous human reason. For others, feeling is the primary way of knowing God, even to the point of irrationality: we're most faithful when we're willing to take unreasonable leaps of faith. Whether we call it knowledge or not, our favorite way of connecting to God becomes the cage we create for him.

Beneath the ceiling of self, Jesus can be the prude or the party dude, and even his own word can't tell you otherwise. Because of his laid-back nature, the party dude version is much more comfortable being identified with the Bible. But by no means is he strapped down to what Scripture says about him; he's quite happy to let believers decide for themselves what the Bible means. And in this way especially, we still feel Kant's influence today in matters far beyond religion.

Kant's work centuries ago paved the way for contemporary popular thought on language and meaning (see chapter 5), giving the reader firm interpretational authority over what she reads—we can never know what the author meant by those words, anyway—and in general giving the knower firm interpretational authority over what is known, and even authority to decide what can be known. It's the ultimate philosophical promotion for people who want God's job.

As we look back on life since Kant built the ceiling in order to honor God, we have to ask: What kind of real God would be okay with all of this? What being worthy of the title "God" would bow so easily to the whims of his worshipers and keep his mouth shut until they allowed him to speak? If God is so reduced, why bother believing in a god at all?

For some clear thinking on what it means to take God seriously, let's turn to a Christianity-despising, Bible-berating atheist who eventually went certifiably nuts.

Meet Friedrich Nietzsche.

Wrecking Ball[36]

Friedrich Nietzsche (October 1844–August 1900) had the courage of his convictions.[37] He said that people in his day were already living like practical atheists, as if God had not spoken in the Bible. So why bother claiming to be Christians? What good is faith in a distant, silent god?

Nietzsche thought that a real god would not act the way Christian society was demanding. Nietzsche saw himself as a prophet bringing truth too heavy for God's self-deceived worshipers to bear, but too compelling for him not to share. The Christian West needed to man-up and face a hard reality: If God is silent, it's not because he's distant. It's because he's dead.

According to Nietzsche, the biblical concept of God did not die of natural causes. He was murdered by the Western world that once worshiped him. Walter Kaufmann summarizes Nietzsche: "Faith in God is dead as a matter of cultural fact, and any 'meaning' of life in the sense of a supernatural purpose is gone. Now it is up to man to give his life meaning by raising himself above the animals and the all-too-human....Our so-called human nature is precisely what we should do well to overcome."[38]

Nietzsche heralds God's death in many of his works, perhaps most bitingly and even beautifully through the words and antics of a character whose clear thinking made a cerebrally numbed society think he was mental. Nietzsche describes a crowd mocking a man who claims to be searching for God. "Is he lost?" someone calls, clearly impressed with himself.

> The madman jumped into their midst and pierced them with his eyes. "Whither is God?" he cried. "I

will tell you. *We have killed him*—you and I. All of us are his murderers. But how did we do this? How could we drink up the sea? Who gave us the sponge to wipe away the entire horizon? What were we doing when we unchained this earth from its sun? Whither is it moving now? Whither are we moving? Away from all suns? Are we not plunging continually? Backward, sideward, forward, in all directions? Is there still any up and down? Are we not straying as through an infinite nothing? Do we not feel the breath of empty space? Has it not become colder? Is not night continually closing in on us? Do we not need to light lanterns in the morning? Do we hear nothing as yet of the noise of the gravediggers who are burying God? Do we smell nothing as yet of the divine decomposition? Gods, too, decompose. God is dead. God remains dead. And we have killed him."[39]

The pompous herd of people simply stares and blinks in response. Ohhhhkaaaaay...

In his day, Nietzsche tried to get Christians (and everyone else) to recognize that they didn't need God, especially the Christian God, to get by in life. They'd already been living like that, in practical denial of the Bible's God, but were for no good reason still clinging to the stupid belief that there is a god and to some of the moronic moral strictures that came with the Christian god's book. They were too dense to realize that they no longer needed to carry around the dead weight of their decomposing deity. They were free to be what man could be, and should be: autonomous, a god who rules himself in the midst of a swirling universe of repetitive chaos.

Nietzsche would say that real autonomy, unlike Kant's view of it, was not driven by a sense of moral duty. If we're truly autonomous, "morality" as we've long thought of it—as a duty owed to God, to others, to ancestors, whoever—is meaningless. If we're truly a law unto ourselves, then let's get to it! No more hypocritically saying that God's existence is necessary for us to be good people but then turning a deaf ear to anything he wants to tell us about himself. In other words, no more of Kant's crap.

Nietzsche appreciated Kant's view that we can only know things as we perceive them, but he called Kant a "crafty Christian" for his attempt to divide life into the real world—what Kant called the "noumenal" world, God's territory—and the world we see, our territory, the "phenomenal" world of our perceptions,[40] realms divided by the ceiling of self. Nietzsche didn't believe in the ceiling because he didn't believe in anything above it.

Nietzsche also criticized Kant's attempt (and that of many others whom Kant's work seemed to justify) to retain Christian morals while dumping basic Christian doctrine. He called out the hypocrisy of societal leaders in England who stressed the need for Christian morality all the more urgently given the people's rejection of the Christian God.

> If you abandon the Christian faith, at the same time you are pulling the *right* to Christian morality out from under your feet. This morality is *very* far from self-evident: this point needs highlighting time and again, English fat-heads notwithstanding. Christianity is a system, a synoptic and *complete* view of things. If you break off one of its principal concepts, the belief in God, then you shatter the whole thing: you have nothing necessary left between your fingers.[41]

As we've seen from his summary of the Ten Commandments, Jesus agrees.

We in the West would be wise to listen to Nietzsche's dark sayings as we increasingly reject Judeo-Christian principles while stubbornly insisting we can maintain the moral fruit they can only bear when rooted in God's word. In some ways, Nietzsche is Christianity's blasphemous best friend. Oh, how he would have hated that statement! But at least when it comes to taking God seriously, to reacting viscerally to the claims of God's word, he provides the mirror image of a true believer.

Christians should be as fervent in their faith as Nietzsche was vehement in his unbelief. (He even gave one of his books the rather subtle title *The AntiChrist*.) In this way, he saw life far more clearly than Christians who, beneath the ceiling of self, blur the lines between themselves and God.

Nietzsche's work was a storm of acid rain falling on the

ceiling, burning through it to reveal an empty sky above, no signs of a divine Savior. It was silly to imagine a separation, a distance, between us and God because God was never there to begin with.

To Nietzsche, the idea of God, especially as the Bible portrayed him, was the real fictitious ceiling; theism was the real barrier between humanity and the achievement of our true potential as the most interesting animals on earth. But because Nietzsche's outlook on life was based upon the same principle that built Kant's ceiling—its insistence upon the reality, necessity, and rightness of human autonomy—it suffers from the same debilitating blindness.

Both Kant and Nietzsche believed that man was actually capable of achieving better things, of being better beings, and of doing so all by himself. While Kant lamented humanity's lack of good moral living, he was optimistic that the wordless backbeat of God's moral law, set to reason, could keep us in tune with life's best rhythms so all people could make beautiful music together. Nietzsche despaired more deeply at the underdeveloped state of Western humanity and of his German countrymen in particular. (He even felt the foreboding philosophical signs of the rise of Germany's barbaric Reich. He despised what the German people were becoming.)[42] He felt that we were still so far away from being authentically human, of being really good at being godless.

Nietzsche held out hope, or at least longed deeply in his soul for someone to rise from the bland ranks of the "all too human" masses as a shining example of what man could be. Nietzsche was looking for his own kind of messiah, someone he called "the Overman."

The overman would conquer human nature's depressing, repressive tendencies and pointless moralizing and shine, radiant with the dark light of an anti-messiah, as a fully authentic human. But by what standard could the "authentic man" measure his achievement of authentic humanity, except against all the sad sacks before him who failed to arrive as he had at this pointless, self-defined summit of human glory? A climb that could only be achieved, it would seem, by the decimation of all who'd compete for the title and the subjugation of any who'd challenge his reign. After all, what kind of overman would he be if he allowed anyone, or any moral law, to rule over him? Christian author and apologist[43] C. S. Lewis writes: "All pictures yet offered us of the superman are so unattractive that one might well vow celibacy at once to avoid the risk of begetting him."[44]

Nietzsche's philosophical work, and even his own version of messianic hope, is all demolition. It's supremely and even ingeniously effective in tearing down, but it leaves nothing to build with.[45] It's also hypocritical. To claim so vehemently that so many others are wrong, one has to be very confident in one's own view of what's right. "Ironically enough, Nietzsche speaks as if he knows what the truth is (not Christianity). Absolute suspicion, like absolute skepticism, is impossible in practice. What we have in Nietzsche and his ilk is finally an apologist for *another* faith."[46] Ultimately, faith in the supremacy of self. And that's not good for anyone else.

If there is no God, then no one—not Kant, not Nietzsche, not you, not I—has a real right to complain when people destroy other people's lives. They're just doing what they think is right, achieving their own authenticity. Why should they care what Nietzsche or anyone else thinks of their truth, their reality, their authenticity? Who are we to judge? Deep down, we all know that self-worship is not a good place to be, but it's the only place where all of these autonomous, God-silencing, Bible-bashing thoughts lead us.

Wherever You Go, There You Are

Kant's agnosticism is like an escalator to Nietzsche's atheism. On an escalator, you only need to take one step and you're committed to the whole ride up, or down. Along the way, you'll meet various versions of God, but when you reach the summit—or the basement—you'll wonder why you were ever looking for God to begin with, as you stare at the only object such a journey away from Scripture could ever lead you to see: a God-shaped mirror.

Nietzsche would congratulate the escalator riders on their liberation, but is the "authentic" life to which he calls them any better? It feels honest, but as a Roman governor once asked Jesus, "What is truth?" (John 18:38). It feels sincere, but who's to say we're not simply kidding ourselves? It feels brave, but what's courage except an ultimately meaningless sentiment? These haunting questions echo endlessly in a godless void.

Part of the reason agnostic pop culture and self-deceived self-worshipers in the church keep living by the rules of the ceiling of self, sometimes without realizing it, is the protection it seems to offer. The ceiling absorbs some of the blunt-force trauma of realizing that you are the closest thing to God you will ever know. Russian Christian convert Fyodor Dostoyevsky, who suffered horrifically at the hands of a government that assumed godlike power, notes: "If there is no god, everything is permissible." But instead of crying out "Cool!" it's more honest to just cry.

With God dead, morality and therefore moral restraint are baseless. Absent the great, indiscriminate equalizer that is God's law, humans assume godlike moral authority for themselves. Relationships are reduced to power struggles. Every interaction with others, no matter what the intent, is essentially an expression of what Nietzsche called the "will to power." More to say on that in chapter 5. For now, such struggles born of self-worship take a heavy toll on the combatants.

Here's the dark flipside of Jesus's commands and their intentional structure: self-worship feels fine for a while, but when we realize our inability to be truly and ultimately satisfied in ourselves, when we realize our incapacity to be God, it makes us desperate, and sometimes dictatorial, in our relationships with other people. We want godlike control in life, but we can barely manage our own lives. We want companionship, but it's just so hard to trust. Our hearts are powder kegs of incendiary insecurities. When someone sparks deep desires within us, we explode into a firestorm of irrational demands, consuming the person whose warming presence we craved.[47]

Nietzsche did perhaps the best, most philosophically consistent job possible of trying to face life without the ceiling and without a god ultimately any greater than himself. His writing, sometimes furious and in fits of inspiration lasting eight or ten straight hours, was truly courageous in that he battled intense physical sicknesses to get it done.[48] But if what he believed and wrote was actually true, and we take it to its logical end, then all of it, all of him, all of us, all of life, is ultimately just an often painful exertion of and toward emptiness. Trent Reznor sings in "Hurt" what it feels like to realize that all you are and do is epic futility. "Hurt" —doesn't that word describe our culture well?

Doesn't that word describe our culture well?[49]

Many people have gone godless because, for them, hurt has come at the hands of the Christian church, the place where they're supposed to find the love of Jesus. We'll explore that more fully as we go, but suffice it to say for now, Jesus hates many of the things that go on in his name as perpetrated by people claiming to represent him. Please see the next chapter on the obvious, painful follow-up question, "So why doesn't he do anything about it?" Suffice it to say for now, there is quite literally a special place in hell, a particularly intense judgment, awaiting these abusers if they never renounce their blasphemy, humble themselves, and turn to the Savior they've slandered. And on the question of whether such people should ever under any circumstances be forgiven, please see chapter 8.

Can a life consistently lived in self-worship lead anywhere else except hurt? As we'll think about in chapter 9, how can true love for someone else exist when the self is exalted as the standard of truth, meaning, and love? Can we worship ourselves and be selfless at the same time? This is schizophrenia on a cosmic scale, and we can't pull it off. We were never meant to try. The attempt will drive us mad.

There's so much in Nietzsche's outlook on life that's on point, so much that cuts through the self-serving bullgeschichte of arbitrary social customs and civic propriety hailed as the right and moral way of doing things. But instead of offering a way to get beyond the self, it doubles down on selfishness. It fails to turn its incisive criticisms on itself; it is never sufficiently self-critical because it rules out automatically the existence of any evaluative standard beyond the self. It admits what it is, hates what it is, but then relies on itself to carve out a better way forward, claiming to understand how life really is while raging against others who dare to do the same.

Nietzsche's legacy lives on in the sarcastic, suspicious-of-every-thing-except-the-self way of life common among deep-thinking, deeply jaded young adults in our culture. You know it when you see it, or feel it within yourself: it sees a potential enemy in everyone and is constantly on high, if not hyperactive, alert for an attempted philosophical takeover. Ironically, and instructively, those who pride themselves on being so worldly wise and wary find themselves plunging uncritically into relationships with people who seem to shine with the faintest glimmer of the truth and integrity that they otherwise mock as impossible. When those relationships flame out, the burn lasts. There's often a lot of hurt in the history of such volcanic souls, as it was for Nietzsche.

Compared to Nietzsche's pain-riddled life, Kant seemed to have a relatively carefree, happy one. But neither he nor Nietzsche lived to see the globe-spanning horrors of the twentieth century, to see the consequences and real-life refutations of their key teachings on morality and faith: when everyone wants to be God, the world burns.

For all his anti-establishment invectives, Nietzsche was no anarchist. Some have used his teaching as philosophical fuel for anarchy and even genocide—he's unfairly blamed for Hitler. But Nietzsche's writing leaves us with no reason not to go dark, except for the fact that his teaching presupposes that which it rages against. How can you have a legitimate sense of moral outrage against superficial, superstitious systems of morality if the very concept of morality is meaningless? Or, if a morality of your own creation is the only meaningful, authentic morality, how can you complain against other people who are simply doing the same thing but who happen to want to kill you as an expression of their victory over antiquated religious virtues?

Nietzsche's work is so helpful in flushing harmful elements of Kantian philosophy and its self-focused spawn from versions of the Christian faith that are full of it. It incinerates the ceiling of self, but has nothing greater than the self to offer in its place. Nietzsche's way of faith and life doesn't make us better; it just makes us bitter.

Radicalization, Down to the Root

When driving through a tunnel, have you ever played the game where you try to hold your breath until you reach the other side? Seeing the outside world just ahead of you makes you all the more desperate to breathe its air. But as long as you're in the dark, the game says you can't breathe. When you follow the rules through a long tunnel, you eventually get frantic. You start pounding on your seat and stomp-kicking the floorboards. Your eyes bulge and you grunt and squeal with wordless screams, willing the vehicle to move forward and much faster (at which point, if I'm the driver, I slow down). The longer you're without oxygen in the tunnel, the crazier things get and the more desperate you are to reach the other side.

As a culture, we've played the game of being our own gods, both the Kantian/theistic and Nietzschean/atheistic versions. But this game deprives us of God's truth, that which our souls need to breathe. We're getting desperate. We're going anoxic and getting angry, sometimes murderously so.

It's baffling that people are baffled when terrorist groups find willing recruits among the wealthy and privileged in the West, or when we witness the horror of yet another school shooting (see next chapter on these kinds of events). Our country's culture has always been quite comfortable with deciding whose human life is valuable enough to protect under the law, and with torturing, exiling, and even killing the undesirables. We routinely refuse to recognize the value of all human life and to respect all human beings, yet we're shocked and offended when someone feels the same way about us, or people we love. To paraphrase C. S. Lewis, we mock honor and are shocked to find traitors in our midst.

Spilling the blood of others feels like cosmic significance in an existence bled of it. Making others hurt feels like revenge against the gutting of souls that goes on in the name of peace and tolerance and compassion. It's calling the bluff of those who say that life has no knowable ultimate meaning, yet that we should all love each other and find our own way led by our own hearts, and that any anxiety and anger that results from being force-fed all of the above simply indicates the need for medication or institutionalization. "No shepherd and one herd! Everybody wants the same, everybody is the same: whoever feels different goes voluntarily into a madhouse."[50] Amen, Friedrich.

Some burned and burnt-out souls, already given to violence, will find whatever means they can to carry out their revenge against the hubris, vanity, and pontifications of the society in which they subsist, the ostracizing elitism against which the imprisoned energy of their souls is ready to lash out, desperate for any kind of escape and delighted at the darkness they'll unleash in what may be the last moments of their meaningless lives.

Scripture takes us deeply into such troubled souls (and unnervingly shows us the same potential for ruin and rampage in each of our hearts), and offers effective, though not exhaustive, answers. But beneath the ceiling of self, we've already ruled out such insights. So we'll continue, with every new and increasingly normal tragedy, to scratch our heads and wring our hands and ask, "Why?! Why?!" And as we'll think about in the next chapter, some will use such tragedies to redouble their denunciation of the God we long ago declared dead.

Thankfully, God's legacy remains somewhat intact in our culture; we feel the rightness of his commands when we're outraged that human lives we consider worthy of protection are attacked or ended ruthlessly. But as we'll think about in chapter 8, the longer we exalt ourselves as God, even generally nonviolent people will have less and less reason to think that murdering others, or themselves, is really much of a big deal at all. The offense we currently take and the sadness we currently feel is legitimate, but not because the core convictions of our relativistic culture require them.

The reason we're still around as a society, rather than as the ashen graveyard of a once powerful people, is that we tend to live in ways wildly inconsistent with what we claim to believe beneath the ceiling of self, or what we, like Nietzsche, believe once the ceiling has been burned down for us. We can literally thank God for these inconsistencies. But beneath the ceiling, we're continuing long into the dark; we're losing the power and will to keep stomping and screaming. We're feeling the gradual, generational suffocation of that life-affirming instinct that God built into humanity. Our helpful moral hypocrisy can't hold out forever.

Interview with the Satanist

For those courageous enough to critically question agnostic and atheistic cultural dogma, we can see gaping cracks in the ceiling of self. As the dust falls, we wonder if something isn't shuffling about up there trying to get our attention. We start to dig upward, trying to make contact, desperate to breathe even a bit of the air up there. But caution takes a back seat to spiritual hunger. We break through, reaching up and out, and we don't care what, or who, grabs back.

In our culture, death and darkness become attractive options to connect to something powerful, something beyond the weakness and emptiness of everyday empirical experience. Death and darkness become the closest things to life and light we can find. "So we stagger toward death with reckless laughter or deep, sad aching, and as we free fall we tell ourselves this falling sensation means we are alive. But the leap we took to get that feeling is a leap to our own destruction."[51]

Many years ago I sat across from a former satanist. He was an inmate at a juvenile detention center and we met because I and other undergrads from my *alma mater* were part of a Christian ministry team that visited the center every Sunday. Like most people, he was bigger than I was (and am). But this young man was a *lot* bigger. He leaned his hulking torso over in his chair so we could look eye to eye. He was politely uninterested in what I and the other Christian college students had to say about Jesus and the Bible, but I was utterly fascinated with his story.

He talked nonchalantly about having been a member of a group of self-identified devil worshipers, intentionally scarring his arms and running through fire with his friends. Though he was no longer part of the group, he didn't seem bothered at all that devil worship was part of his past. Surely I could shake some good Christian sense into him! "Didn't you realize that Satan hates you? That he wants to kill you?" His reply was simple, tinged with just a little of the condescending tone I deserved to hear: "Yeah, we knew Satan hated us. But he gave us power."

Satan and his demons do what they do out of sheer spite against God and the world he loves. They resent like hell the fact that they are not God and they do what they can to create hell on earth, offering their services to those who want nothing to do with religion based on divine revelation, but who, like my large, incarcerated friend, are desperate to experience something spiritual, something powerful. Ironically, we value autonomy so deeply that we refuse to worship the powerful One before whom the demons shriek in terror.

When Jesus presents himself as the light at the edge of our darkness, our lust for autonomy compels us to turn the other way, right back into the dark if need be. We'd rather wallow in hate and anxiety than give ourselves willingly to the one who can replace them with love and peace. Because if peace means bowing to Christ and surrendering our lives to him on his terms, we'd rather have war.

If God wasn't out there, and if he hadn't given himself to make reconciliation between God and people possible, then meaninglessness would make total sense; going dark would be seeing the light. But then again, in order to rage against life's meaninglessness, we have to have some deep sense that life *is* in fact meaningful and that it's just not living up to what it is and therefore should be. This is why some are drawn to darkness, why some seek it out as truth. Darkness would have no meaning without light; deception would have no meaning without truth. Though they're opposed to one another, leaning into the one helps you understand the other by way of contrast. But they're not equal powers in the universe.

The apostle John, a very close friend of Jesus, describes the impact of God's coming into the world: "The light shines in the darkness, and the darkness has not overcome it" (John 1:5). Lacey Sturm again: "Darkness can feel honest, and honesty can be beautiful and feel so inspiring. But darkness stops short of resolution. It's deceptive."[52]

The Bible tells us that the One who made life, and who therefore makes it meaningful, has also made a way to overcome our damning desire to replace him. Cosmic reconciliation, peace with God, is possible. And that's what really cheeses us off.

Another young man with a painful past spoke to me one day. He claimed to have come to Christ and was eager for his neo-pagan friends to do the same. Those friends met regularly at a local park, lush with forestry reminiscent of much deeper woods. They'd meet there to play with fire, literally, and to dance the night away with the dark spirits who inspired their revelry. The young man loved the fire-dancing itself, but didn't like the dark direction it always seemed to take. So one day he asked the ring leader, someone happily and respectfully tolerant of all kinds of spirituality, if they could incorporate Jesus into the supernatural festivities. The leader got deadly serious, and angry. "Don't you *ever* say that name around here again. If you do, you're gone, and don't ever come back."

Sometimes we want randomness and chaos more than we want reconciliation and closure. Sometimes the only thing we fear worse than being hurt is being healed.

We hate the pain, but it's familiar, and we don't know how we'd live without it. It's terrifying to even think about. Jesus knew this, and it's why he asked a paralyzed man what would seem to be a very stupid question: "Do you want to be healed?" (See John 5. Much more to say on this in the second half of this book.)

For people willing to be healed, the question becomes, "*What can save us and give us what we are restless for?* Not the world we live in and are rebelling against. That world can't fool us. And not the death we're plunging toward, the one we know nothing about. We just need the God who started life itself to tell us."[53]

We need the God in the room to speak up. The Bible tells us that God has done that. The Bible *is* that.

God Breathed

As a teacher, I appreciate when students put extra effort into their assignments. If a paper is carefully thought out and well written, I'll write an encouraging message next to the grade: "Outstanding!" or "Really well done!" or "There's no way you wrote this—see me after class!"—all statements recognizing especially good work.

I've read some truly brilliant student papers (and plagiarisms). Never, though, have I ever even come close to writing atop one of them: "This is the breath of God." I don't care how spectacular the work, or how much the student offered to pay me, I could never sincerely give that kind of praise to merely human words. It would be a ridiculously high compliment to the author, and (you would think) an outright insult to God. Yet the apostle Paul, in a letter written to his pastoral protégé Timothy, describes Scripture this way: "All Scripture is breathed out by God" (2 Timothy 3:16).

In Paul's day, "Scripture" was what we now call the Old Testament. Each Old Testament book was written by one or more flesh-and-blood, fallible human beings. But Paul had no problem calling these human compositions "breathed out by God." Did he have a low view of God, then? Hardly. Except for Jesus, it's hard to imagine a human being more utterly in awe of God than Paul.

Paul praises God as the being "who alone has immortality, who dwells in unapproachable light, whom no one has seen or ever can see" (1 Timothy 6:16). Kant would find that description eminently, perhaps even excitingly, reasonable. In his limitless reverence for God, Paul joined a long line of prophets before him who felt the same way. In their bones and in the depths of their souls, they felt something of God's universe-filling immensity, his boundless, unsettling majesty. Their hearts trembled at God's holiness, a word that mainly means *otherness*. They knew that God's ways were higher than their ways, his thoughts higher than theirs. Yet still, Paul calls the Old Testament, words written by humans, "God-breathed."

Though he had the Old Testament particularly in mind, Paul's description applies to the New Testament writings as well. Peter referred to Paul's writings by that same deeply meaningful term. He says that ignorant, unstable people distort Paul's teaching just like they do the rest of the Scriptures, to their own destruction (2 Peter 3:15–16). This is part of how we know that the authors of the New Testament, like those of the Old Testament, were quite conscious that their words were God's words to his people.[54] To them and to all the other biblical authors, the ceiling of self would have been an arrogant absurdity. They knew they were not the builders of truth and the makers of meaning; they understood that the only reasonable way to find truth and meaning in life was to look higher than themselves.

Have you ever trusted that someone else truly knows better than you do? It's humbling, but we've all had to do it in life. In some cases, we may have died if we didn't. Are you willing to explore doing that with Jesus? Given what Christianity has become beneath the ceiling of self, I'm asking these questions of Christians, too.

By and large, in our culture, it seems we would rather subject our lives, and therefore the lives of everyone else, to the tyranny of self-worship than to bow before the God Scripture proclaims, even though that God was willing to die to save us from the hell that self-worship is and spawns. But when we keep trying to distance ourselves from the author of life, what do we expect to get but the opposite?

We object: *No!* We can be different (or at least I can). This is the generation that will change all that! And we'll elect to power the people who really believe that, who really believe in *us*. So what if self-deification has never worked in history? We've never been as smart as we are now, never as open minded, never as tolerant of other views, never as trusting of the state, never as keen-eyed in spotting societal hypocrisy and the systematic deceit of religious systems, never as courageous in declaring and being who we really are and not letting anyone else tell us otherwise, never as scientifically advanced, never as capable of ruling ourselves and achieving peace. Who needs God when we've got us?!

Nope. Despite its being thoroughly discredited, Enlightenment-style pride has not died. But thankfully, neither has God. Nor is God afraid to speak.

Unlike the fictional timid boy emperor of Japan, the true God doesn't need a Westerner to give him the courage to speak up and assert his divinity, much less to tell him in an alleged act of praise why he cannot talk. His voice is indeed pure, but contrary to Kant's ceiling, and to Nietzsche's self-destructive explosion of it, he wants us to hear him.

The universe itself is one great big speech act of God, as chapter 1 of God's book tells us (and as we'll explore in chapter 5 of this one). God created by speaking, but he's gone further in letting us know who he is, and who we are as his most magnificent, but often maliciously confused creatures. He's spoken directly to us, in and through his word. The question is whether we're willing to put aside our delusions of godhood in order to listen, deeply and humbly, as the only one who deserves the title "God" talks to us.

As one Christian philosopher put it, "He is there, and he is not silent."[55]

4

Is the Bible Broken?

"Heaven turned its head,
Made to confess but digressed,
And left me alone in this mess."
—Second to Safety, "Esther"[1]

"I must have justice, or I will destroy myself. And not justice in some remote, infinite time and space, but here on earth so that I could see it myself."
—Ivan Karamazov

"A man's foolishness ruins his way, but his heart rages against the Lord."
—Proverbs 19:3

God isn't fixing this!" screamed the front page of the *New York Daily News* on December 3, 2015, the day after a living nightmare played out on the other side of the country. In San Bernardino, California, a husband and wife gunned down fourteen people at an office party that the husband had left earlier, enraged. The couple committed the murders in the name of Allah and were later killed by police after a high-speed chase and a high-powered shootout. These events are happening more frequently from sea to shining sea, and despite desperate pleas and prayers and unity-seeking public gatherings featuring songs like "God Bless America," many believe the guiding "light from above" has gone out.[2] Whether it was ever there to begin with matters less and less to people. It's not there now. We're on our own. God isn't fixing this.

In the aftermath of the San Bernardino slaughter, social media exploded with everything from rants on the political dynamics and public policy implications of the savagery to statements of sympathy for the victims' families. Some American politicians tweeted their assurances of prayer for those families, but others blasted such sentiments. Believing that stricter gun control is mandatory for preventing such violence, Senator Chris Murphy of Connecticut took aim at his pious-sounding political rivals. Cited in the *News*, Murphy mocked their posts as meaningless and, even worse, hypocritical: "Your 'prayers' should be for forgiveness if you do nothing—again."

What do you think of God and the Christian faith when you learn of another shooting, or other atrocities? Do you get angry, like Senator Murphy, at public leaders whose self-vaunted Christianity doesn't actually do anything to prevent society's suffering (especially if they appear more loyal to powerful political lobbies than the God in whose name they offer terse tidbits of comfort)? Have you ever felt like screaming at religious well-wishers in general like the *News* did? Something horrible happens, and the mere fact that it did screams to you that God either isn't there, or that he doesn't care, at least enough to have prevented it. Or maybe he's the Deist god after all, waiting upon Washington to pass particular prohibitions before he'll deign to act—"God helps those who help themselves."[3]

Whatever the explanation of why, the fact that "God isn't fixing this" couldn't be more obvious to you, and so it's maddening when someone wants suffering people to feel better because he's praying to a god who's either inactive or incompetent in preventing life's horrors. And anger downshifts to rage when someone takes to social media to provide that comfort, sacrificing all of ten seconds in his busy day to let the world know how wonderful he is for caring enough to offer pointless prayers on behalf of the bereaved. Nothing like social media for self-congratulatory expressions of sympathy!

Maybe you're willing to give the well-wishers the benefit of the doubt. They're sincere, but they're blind to the fact that they're invoking God not so much to make others feel better, but to make themselves feel better. And if blind faith in an invisible, inattentive God helps them cope with the harsh realities of life, you won't begrudge them. But for you, that blind, happy, easy faith isn't good enough. You want answers. If God is there and is not silent, then he's got some explaining to do. You want God to speak up about the condition of the world, or maybe to 'fess up and apologize for not fixing it.

Do you feel the same way about his involvement, or lack thereof, in your own life? When the X-ray comes back bad for you or someone you love? When the relationship falls apart? You might not be ready to declare God's death like Nietzsche did. But for all practical purposes, maybe even as a Christian, you're saying, "God may not be dead. But he's dead to me."

Faith No More

Have you ever voiced your soul's screams straight to God like a cosmic interrogation? Not content with the fact that "God isn't fixing this," you ask God: "*Why* aren't you fixing this?!" And all you get in response is deafening, maddening silence?[4] Maybe you've scolded yourself for asking such questions. What could be stupider than seeking answers from a dumb god dwelling in a deaf heaven?[5]

And then some obnoxious writer tries to convince you that God is *not* silent, and that the Bible is his voice. But for many who grew up with church as a big part of life but who now see life's pains through adult eyes, it's precisely their belief that the Bible *is* God's word that breaks their hearts, and begins to unsettle their lifelong faith.

They believe the Bible, eagerly, sincerely, fully—at first. And maybe for a long while. But then life happens. And keeps happening. All of a terrible sudden, the Sunday school stories seem childish, almost a mockery of the very adult problems they're facing.

They study history, they read today's headlines, or they simply peer into the pain of their own lives, and they start to wonder how much longer they should hold their breath in anticipation of real, satisfying answers from the book claiming to be God's breath. They fight hard and honestly to have faith, but they don't want to invest all their emotional energy in what feels more and more like a fairy tale. Fissures appear in the faith commitments upon which they stood firmly and happily in their youth. Gaps widen beneath them between Scripture and sound reasoning, between biblical claims and real life experience. Gaping holes in their entire belief system threaten to swallow them whole, so they walk away, hesitantly at first, from the idea that the Bible is in fact the word of God. At that point they might play around with various theories about *how* the Bible is God's word—anything but it's actually *being* God's direct word to us.[6] But once you've stepped away from the Bible's sense of its own truth and authority and application to real life, it's an easy (and rather philosophically consistent) exodus from biblical Christianity altogether.

Telling their Christian loved ones that they no longer believe isn't easy, but to them, the truth they've discovered, or rather, the falsehoods of Scripture they've uncovered, are just too compelling. Believing that the Bible doesn't adequately address life's biggest problems is heartbreaking at first, but then it starts to feel like freedom. It feels like you're seeing life for the first time as it really is. It's emotionally unsettling, but it feels intellectually honest. Like being a kid and realizing that you're growing up, there's that nervous feeling of discovering a truth you don't quite know what to do with. You're not even sure you want it. And as an adult, you realize you still don't *know* what to do with it and you know you don't want it![7] But life must be faced.

Growing up and out of faith creates lots of new questions, but at least now you can walk through life without being intellectually crippled by unreasonable faith and emotionally enslaved by the dictates of a dead god. Here, some who've left the faith adapt one of Jesus's most famous sayings, smiling with wistful sadness at the irony. Jesus said, "The truth will set you free."[8]

Certain scholars have risen like heroes among the newly but hesitantly liberated. Their work emboldens doubters to follow their instincts and their increasingly troubled consciences; it paves a smoother path out of the Christian community and calls shenanigans on the arguments that Bible-believing Christians have long used to explain (away?) the horrors of life; it steadies people teetering on the edge of unbelief for the leap off the fence and out of the faith. Those who never believed to begin with enjoy this work as well; it gives them scholarly-sounding reasons to keep staying far, far away from the faith.

Bart Ehrman is one such scholar. He makes the rounds of the late-night talk shows,[9] while Christian scholars who disagree with him are not as frequently sought out as guests.[10] Fair enough, some interviewees are more entertaining and engaging than others, and those shows are first and foremost businesses. Got to give the people what they want to hear, not necessarily what they need to hear if they're to be adequately informed on an issue.[11]

Ehrman writes on several theological topics, trying, as he sees it, to demythologize the Christian faith by discrediting some of its most cherished, time-honored claims. In *God's Problem*, a very personal work, Ehrman explains why he no longer believes in God. By and large, he blames the Bible.

Scripture just couldn't bear the scrutiny of Ehrman's serious, intellectually honest examination of human suffering. Throughout this chapter, we'll use Ehrman's work as a window into the similar views of other ex-Christians and outright atheists (and we'll think a bit about some of them, too). We'll focus mostly on Ehrman because he once believed, and because for him, the Bible became literally unbelievable.

Empty Sky

Ehrmans writes: "The God I once believed in was a God who was active in the world. He saved Israelites from slavery; he sent Jesus for the salvation of the world; he answered prayer; he intervened on behalf of his people when they were in desperate need; he was actively involved in my life. But I can't believe in that God anymore, because from what I now see around the world, he doesn't intervene."[12] As Ehrman surveyed the profound pain and horrific cruelty in the world, he realized to his deep disappointment that the God of the Bible just "isn't fixing this."

For Ehrman, it's not just that the Bible's description of God is unrealistic (a religious book could be forgiven that). It's that the Bible's account of God is so wildly inconsistent. Scripture's God is either a malicious schizophrenic or an outright fraud. Not only does God fail to adequately address suffering, he can't even keep his story straight when he tries.

> Different biblical authors...have different explanations for all the pain and the misery: some think that pain and suffering sometimes come from God as a punishment for sin (the prophets); some think that misery is created by human beings who abuse power and oppress others (the prophets again); some think that God works

in suffering to achieve his redemptive purposes (the Joseph story; the Jesus story); some think that pain and misery come as a test from God to see if his people will remain faithful to him even when it does not pay to do so (the folktale about Job); others think that we simply can't know why there is such suffering in the world—either because God the Almighty chooses not to reveal this kind of information to peons like ourselves (Job's poetry) or because it is information beyond the ken of mere mortals (Ecclesiastes).[13]

Considering the complexity of the topic—human suffering—writing these authors off as pretty much mutually exclusive is harsh and simplistic. Human suffering is not simple; there's really no area of study that doesn't touch it at some point. And as such, the topic has a complicated history of being addressed by people who lived in complex cultures and always in a complex world. So wouldn't you expect that a book that took more than a millennium to complete would have a decently nuanced approach to it? Couldn't it be that having many authors with multiple experiences over much time is an advantage in making a carefully considered, complex but consistent case? But Ehrman's given up on the idea that the Bible is a coherent, consistent, self-affirming whole.[14]

Like other scholars in his school of thought, Ehrman doesn't like to give the biblical authors that level of credit. They're just not sophisticated enough, even by the New Testament era, to have pulled off a correct, enlightened view of suffering—or God, for that matter—let alone to have combined efforts over so many years to create a credible, consistent analysis and explanation.[15]

Ehrman and others embrace what I'll call the "patchwork quilt" view of Scripture: the Bible is like a blanket made of wildly different fabric squares stitched together into a contained chaos of color and design; it's a hodgepodge of varied and sometimes mutually contradictory documents, with many of its books written much later than historically and traditionally believed and often not by the people whose names appear as the books' namesakes. Bottom line: the Bible is not to be trusted as the word of God.

We'll address the patchwork quilt view a bit more in chapter 7. The least we can say for now is that the biblical authors themselves, along with Jesus, did not share this view of Scripture as it accumulated through the centuries. Remember, Paul called the entire Old Testament the breath of God. But Ehrman doesn't put too much stock in Paul's view of things, ancient guy that he was with a hopelessly naïve view of the universe.

How could Paul *not* be misinformed about God, about ideas like the resurrection, the end of the world, and Ehrman's chief concern, human suffering?[16]

> That's how Paul thought—completely like an ancient person who didn't realize that this world is round, that it is simply one planet in a larger solar system of planets circling a single star out of billions of others....We have a different universe from Paul's. It's hard to imagine how he would have conceptualized his apocalyptic message if he had known what we know about planet Earth.[17]

The crazy thing is, it doesn't seem like Ehrman's trying to be condescending here. Sometimes he knows he is, but overall you get the sense that he's beyond the point of recognizing (or maybe caring about) his full-on display of what C. S. Lewis called "chronological snobbery." But if old is by definition and sometimes irredeemably ignorant, perhaps Ehrman should recuse himself from any further discussion on the topic of suffering (and everything else he writes about), because after all, he has no idea what we'll know about the earth or anything else in another century or so, let alone another millennium.

But no, he considers his rejection of God and the idea that Scripture is God's word to be so very carefully considered, so far more sophisticated and informed than the average Christian's— sadly, that may be true—and so compelling that he's absolutely certain that he cannot be certain whether a being such as the Bible's God even exists. The implication is that anyone who believes otherwise despite the level of suffering in the world is just engaging in ignorant, wishful thinking.

It's not that Ehrman thinks his own personal suffering is reason enough to dump the Christian faith. He says he's lived a very fortunate life. But as he relates one heart-sickening story after another, he explains that he's indelibly pained by the suffering of others. His work is a helpful reminder that we all should be.

But Ehrman acts as if he's the first, or among the few, who feels this pain so profoundly, and who also feels intensely the need to seek truth, and only truth, about it—as if the biblical authors (and Bible-believing Christians through history) were so blinded against reason by their recalcitrant religious faith combined with the unfortunate, inescapable idiocy of the time in which they lived,[18] that sadly, they just couldn't attain to the courageous, sufficiently informed and intellectually honest convictions he was compelled to embrace.

For Ehrman, the Bible's attempted explanation of suffering and exoneration of God for allowing it is a spectacular fail. It's a respectable fail, given the good things Scripture manages despite its being composed during such unenlightened ages. But for Ehrman, because the Bible does indeed fail and because millions of sadly unsophisticated people today[19] continue to look to that muddled tome and its mythical Messiah for truth and wisdom on that most important of topics, the Bible is an epic hindrance to honest faith and life.

Though Ehrman says he's not interested in deconverting anyone, he thinks you're far better off not trusting the Bible. You don't need the good book to recognize and work against evil in this life; you don't need faith in God to keep you from acting like a devil; and you don't need belief in a permanent afterlife to enjoy and improve the one-shot deal we have here in this world...Right?

Giving Up the Ghost

As we thought about last chapter, Nietzsche blasted Kant's attempt to have a Christian morality without the Christian God; he insisted that you cannot have one without the other. Taking his honest insight where it leads us, when you give up on the idea of God, and particularly the Bible's God, you give up far more than you realize. In fact, you give up everything, or at least the reason for anything. Let's start with the basics.

If there's no God, what are you? What am I? Sacks of surging chemicals, basically, with no reason to think otherwise. If there's no God, what is anything at all? How did anything get here, or why there is anything instead of just no-thing? If there's no God, what's the ultimate difference between an ingenious, world-changing idea and a fart? Both would merely be the byproduct of chemicals surging through a hyperactive human organ and exploding in a different form—nothing more. And both could make people suffer.

If there's no God, then everything that God is and makes possible—absolutes, ultimates, eternity, and if it's the Christian God, love—it all becomes baseless, changeable, temporal. It's all ultimately all about us, all stuff we invented. In other words, it's all meaningless.

Some would say, "But that's exactly what makes life so precious!" Wait. The truth (??) that there's no God, eternity, truth, beauty, etc., is precisely what makes life so precious? Well, it might make you want to hold on to life as tightly and as long as you can before you blank out into oblivion. But as we've started to think about, this idea tends to go the opposite way as people embrace it. And the objection doesn't work well on its own terms, because it basically asserts that it is life's inherent meaninglessness that makes it so meaningful. Some of the sharpest philosophers who inherited life below the ceiling of self realized in their day what nonsense this is.

Nietzsche said it would take a while for Western culture to realize the full significance of God's death, to realize that the universe had been turned upside down and set spinning. About halfway through the twentieth century, philosophers sometimes called the "Pessimistic Existentialists"[20] let the news settle in on them, and it made them sick. They wept, but not for God. Good riddance to God. They wept for themselves, over what they couldn't be without the God whose death the modern West so deeply desired.

French philosopher Jean-Paul Sartre famously called this spiritual motion sickness "nausea."[21] He wrote:

> The being of human reality is suffering because it rises in being as perpetually haunted by a totality which it is without being able to be it, precisely because it could not attain the in-itself without losing itself as for-itself. Human reality therefore is by nature an unhappy consciousness with no possibility of surpassing its unhappy state.[22]

In other words, it nauseates us to the core of our impermanent, accidental beings to desire an authenticity and independence that we cannot attain. We cannot be what we somehow know we are. German philosopher Martin Heidegger (1889–1976) called it "thrownness"—the unhappy realization that we are dominated by situations, people, and things outside our control and often contrary to our desires. We yearn for freedom to be what we want to be but are powerless to achieve it in a cold, impersonal world impervious to our influence. Having murdered our Maker, Western culture was flung into the wild, cold, dark madness of an accidental universe, empty of purpose and meaning.

For these philosophers, it seemed like God's ghost would forever haunt humanity, whispering to us of what we cannot be without him. This is what made those Existentialists pessimistic. They were all about the death of God, but they saw the implications of God's death clearly and felt them deeply. How do we both acknowledge God's death but also deal with our stubborn, searing longing to be significant—a longing the Existentialists thought was essential to being human? The dilemma is a double-edged blade plunged deep into our being: You want to rule your own life and define your own significance? Kill God. But kill God, and you kill any possibility of achieving any significance beyond yourself (or even *as* yourself, as we'll see next chapter).

But isn't that all a bit too bleak? Sadly, no.

If God was never there, and therefore if the God-sized lie that he exists (and demands that you live in certain ways) was lifted from humanity's back as the unnecessary cosmic burden that it was, wouldn't life feel so much lighter, freer? If the Christian religion really had been humanity's buzzkill, wouldn't the death of its god demand the greatest rave ever? With God dead, wouldn't we become so much better at living and at loving one another?[23] Apparently not. After the Enlightenment, instead of embracing a brotherhood of man,[24] we entered the era of the world wars.

(Self) Righteous Indignation

Throughout *God's Problem*, Ehrman shares story after heartbreaking story from the Holocaust and other human atrocities. Ehrman makes sure the evil and the horror and the senselessness of each terrible situation he describes sets in on the reader, and rightly so. These situations are beyond horrific. But Ehrman's point about how bad and horrible life is, especially the catastrophic events of the past 100 years or so, actually works against his argument that we don't need God to be good people.

Is it really a coincidence that the further along in time we get from God's Enlightenment-era funeral, the more we keep breaking world records for mass murder?

Despite this trend, Ehrman's outlook isn't as bleak as that of the Existentialists. After all, they were so seventy years ago. Ehrman writes: "My own suspicion is that...there is no afterlife, that this life is all there is. That should not drive us to despair of life, however. It should drive us to enjoy life to the uppermost for as long as we can and in every way we can, cherishing especially the precious parts of life that can give us innocent pleasure." Ah, but Ehrman uses a very important term here, a moral term—"innocent."

Some people derive great pleasure from causing other people pain and feel completely innocent, even morally justified, in doing so. Some people rack themselves with guilt over what others call innocent pleasures. It all depends upon their moral framework and who they trust to define terms like "guilty" and "innocent." But if there's no God, why feel guilty for pursuing what you find pleasurable? Isn't this the freedom we pried from the biblical God's cold, dead hand?

But when you give up the idea that the Bible is God's word, you also give up the ground, the soil in which the good things of the Bible grow—things like the command to treat others as more important than yourself, the command to meet the needs of the poor and to love all people. Even something as basic as "Please don't shoot up a room full of people" can't grow for long outside biblical soil. Though one belief system's prohibition against mass murder may seem to grow side by side with like-minded commands from another, the roots of these commands are worlds apart. The flower of valuing all life does not grow well in non-biblical soil.

Jihadi terrorists could agree: murder is wrong. But to them, every infidel deserves death, so killing them is not murder. You might say, "Exactly! Religion is what motivates these mass murders." Well, some religions do. But it's not as if organized religion has a monopoly on mass murder. Atheism-driven dictators have starved or slaughtered tens of millions of people, often their own people, in the name of their people's well-being.[25] Back during the Enlightenment, Denis Diderot's graphic declaration, "Men will never be free until the last king is strangled with the entrails of the last priest," pretty much said it all for the militant souls eager to be the Enlightenment's enforcers and executioners, the cutting edge of this great forward movement of freedom and tolerance, especially in France.

Albert Camus, Algerian-born, Nobel prize–winning freedom fighter and underground author of the World War 2 era, was an atheist who sincerely respected Christianity's historic engagement of the question of human suffering, especially as contrasted to the rising, lethally naïve faith in governments that claimed to champion the common people. "And as for the famous Marxist optimism! No one has carried distrust of man further, and ultimately the economic fatalities of this universe seem more terrible than divine whims."[26]

The truth is that we're all religiously motivated, whether or not we claim faith in a personal god. In 1961, in *Torcaso v Watkins*, the United States Supreme Court defined humanism as a religion.[27]

Human beings are inevitably and unavoidably religious. We are hardwired to worship, and the moral standards by which we choose to live reveal what god we worship, as individuals, as communities, and as a country. We'll get nowhere good led by "an assertive humanistic autonomy on which...it is not possible to build a culture worthy of the name, but only an inhumane civilization."[28]

To say that government works best when it's godless is to say that the government is God, with power over life, death, truth, morality, ethics, each and all of which are wrapped up in and the basis for every decision a governing authority ever makes. Where citizens have a say as to who rules them, it's always a struggle for power among warring religious loyalties. It's god vs. god, vying to control the state, territory, province, or nation through their respective worshipers. It's not organized religion itself that's dangerous; it's the god who's worshiped and what it tells its worshipers to do in its name.

For the self-described non-religious person, any standard of righteousness (or just "right" or "good" or "healthy" or even "productive") will inevitably be based in self, bound by the ceiling of self, or along Nietzsche's line of thought in which there's no ceiling, and no God above it, there's just self. Either way, it's all about us, I mean, me! This isn't meant to be snarky, but if you claim there's no higher authority, then any understanding of "right"—no matter how agreeable you think it ought to be to everyone else—is going to be, forgive me, self-righteous—in the truest sense of the term.

The self-righteous person—one who centers true and right on self, or a community of selves—can never say "ought"—or at least should—*ought!*—never expect anyone to care what he thinks people ought to do. "Ought" implies authority, ethical superiority, and in a world full of self-ruling selves, that just won't do. No matter what the ought-er thinks is right, others don't have to care, unless the ought-er has superior firepower.

Penn Jillette and other atheists claim that atheists have no "personal god." Not true. They see that god when they look in the mirror. There is no one in their lives whose word, wisdom, and authority trumps their own. And that means that the atheist has no basis except his own personal perspectives upon which to say, for instance, that the jihadist's god is worse than the object of his own self-worship, much less to say that the jihadist's god is "bad" or "evil." Destructive? Sure. But morally wrong? Who's to say, and who cares what the self-worshiper says? The jihadist serves his god, and the atheist serves his god, himself. Can't atheists just keep their faith private?

Jillette doesn't think so. He says it's time for atheists to stand and be counted. "After 9/11 we could no longer pretend that faith in God was harmless. The writing had been on the wall for awhile, but now the walls were a-crumblin' down and innocent people were dying. Thousands of innocent people of all faiths died in that religious terrorist attack—including atheists."[29]

But on September 11, 2001, it wasn't religion itself, but one particular religious ideology that launched planes full of terrified hostages at skyscrapers full of unsuspecting, caged, and doomed victims. Another outspoken atheist, comedian Bill Maher, has the guts and intellectual integrity to point out that, as stupid as he thinks Christianity is, it's not Christians who are flying planes into buildings.[30]

Similarly, prolific atheistic scholar Sam Harris points out what he sees as a defining difference between Christianity and Islam. Both religions boast holy books that they claim as absolute truth. Unlike Mohammed, Jesus did not spread his religion by the sword. In Harris's view, Christianity, mistaken as it is, is not inherently violent, whereas the Muslim faith, given the nature of its origins and initial spread across the world, can be credibly interpreted that way. More to say in chapters 7 and 8 on Jesus's relationship with the Old Testament, which Harris credits as possessing "the worst books ever written."[31]

Maher and Harris fancy themselves the few, the proud, the reasonable—in the midst of stupid religious people and atheists who should know better—and they ask people to agree with them on that basis. Can't we all just be reasonable? The problem is, each of us tends to think that we're the most reasonable person around, or that we know who is and everyone ought to trust that person, and that if people just lived like we wanted them to, things would be fine. But we have this pesky tendency to disagree with one another. You'd think after the Enlightenment failed to produce the glorious, death-defying humanity it promised, we'd give up on trying to make pure, self-consciously godless reason the standard by which humanity could move forward. But stubborn ignorance doesn't die easily.

William Lane Craig quotes Kai Nielsen, "an atheist philosopher who attempts to defend the viability of ethics without God." Nielsen writes: "We have not been able to show that reason requires the moral point of view, or that all really rational persons, unhoodwinked by myth or ideology, need not be individual egoists or classical amoralists. Reason doesn't decide here. The picture I have painted for you is not a pleasant one. Reflection on it depresses me….Pure practical reason, even with a good knowledge of the facts, will not take you to morality."[32]

For all his emphasis on reason unbound by the Bible, Kant realized that belief in God was still necessary as a basis for morality. But once he built the ceiling, separating God from his word, he set the stage for a bad breakup between reason and morality. God never meant human reason to try to function apart from his revelation of his own character. Reason and morality, deriving from God himself, come standard in humans and are meant to work together in tandem. God made us to love him, and each other, with all that we are. Jesus's recitation of the first and greatest commandment teaches that reason, rightly functioning according to design, has an essential ethical component to it. But when we separate reason and morality from the God in whom both are based, they cannot reach one another; they no longer require one another.

The biblical God, who calls us to love him with all that we are and as a result to love everyone as ourselves, unabashedly claims to be the best and only basis for morality, for true righteousness that would bless and bring peace to all people, especially the people who need it most.

The Kids Are Not Alright

The suffering that haunts Ehrman most, and rightly so, is that endured by children. When children are made to suffer, it helps us understand, to borrow and adapt a phrase, the evil of evil.[33] Children are young, defenseless, inexperienced, full of new life and endless possibilities—and if very young, untainted by too much experience in a blood-stained world. When they suffer, it's enough to drive a reasonable person out of her mind in rage against someone who could prevent it, but doesn't. Thus Ehrman's argument against the existence of the God of the Bible, who claims enough power to save the children, and compassion enough to want to stop their suffering, but who obviously hasn't. So Ehrman presses this raw nerve hard. As he should.

Among other sources of support, including nightmarish firsthand testimony from Holocaust survivors observing the torture and murder of children, Ehrman calls upon a legendary literary character to help him promote his anti-theodicy.[34] Ivan Karamazov is one of *The Brothers Karamazov*,[35] sons to a detestable father who is eventually murdered. This book of fiction by Russian author Fyodor Dostoyevsky (1821–1881) is a profound truth-teller. Nietzsche called Dostoyevsky "the only psychologist from whom I have learned anything."[36] Truly high praise!

Dostoyevsky's *Brothers* talk with one another about the deepest issues in life: God, eternity, hell, human suffering. No exaggeration, this book contains some of the most powerful, insightful, and incisive commentary on all of the above and upon the human psyche that's ever been expressed through fiction. No spoilers here. We'll just focus on the brother with whom Ehrman most closely identifies (and meet the others later).

Ivan rejects God, not with a malicious rage, but out of a deep-seated refusal to accept a world as unjust as God has allowed it to be. For Ivan, it's all about the children. After all but one of his horrifying accounts of child abuse perpetrated by some of society's cultured elite, Ivan tells of a little girl who is beaten and starved by her parents, simply for sport: "Can you understand why a little creature, who can't even understand what's done to her, should beat her little aching heart with her tiny fists in the dark and the cold, and weep her meek unresentful tears to 'dear, kind God' to protect her?"

Some say that God had to allow evil so that people could understand, experientially, the difference between good and evil. Here's what Ivan thinks of that: "Do you understand why this infamy must be and is permitted? Without it, I am told, man could not have existed on earth, for he could not have known good and evil. Why should he know that diabolical good and evil when it costs so much? Why, the whole world of knowledge is not worth that child's prayer to 'dear, kind God'! I say nothing of the sufferings of grown-up people; they have eaten the apple, damn them, and the devil take them all! But these little ones!"[37] Exactly, Ivan.

In his list of atrocities and his very right focus on the suffering of children, Ehrman makes a huge oversight—like, over 60 million people huge, the ever growing number of children killed in America, legally, since 1973. And that's just in the "Land of the Free." Ehrman writes: "We do not have to sit idly by while governments (even in strategically unimportant lands) practice genocide on their people."[38] Amen. So where is his call to end the genocide against the unborn? Ehrman is silent about them. Not once does he mention them, a glaring oversight in a book suggesting that if we just took human suffering seriously enough, especially that of children, we'd abandon faith in the biblical God.

The best possible reason for his silence is the essentially and extraordinarily deep and personal nature of this issue to the women who've had or have seriously considered having an abortion. This is the best reason to be cautious and compassionate in taking up the issue or deciding not to. Abortion is ethically complex. It's the right of a woman to control her body versus the right of the human being within her to live. And many of those pregnancies are attended by profound pain, strained relationships, fear, and desperation.

The women I know who've had abortions and with whom I've done counseling will tell you, the process of choosing whether to abort is so often saturated with lies, malicious lies, from organizations providing and in some cases eagerly encouraging abortions, lies that steal the attention of already pressured and scared women away from the reality of what, and who, is within them. The doctors who do the killing sometimes won't even look their patients in the eye, or listen to their screams to stop when they're overcome by the reality of what it actually is and means to have an abortion.

If more than ten or so young adults read this book, or even fewer, then someone reading will likely be very close to this issue, and might even be a woman who's had an abortion herself. If that's you, I can't tell you what an honor it is to have you read these words, and I can't imagine what any such words from any source stir within your soul as you read them, especially if they sort of sneak up on you unexpectedly. Please forgive any hurt this reading is causing. I'm simply trying to write truth as best I can. Here, I want to respectfully call out those who ignore this issue as they talk up their compassion for defenseless sufferers and those who express their umbrage against people they accuse of sinful passivity in preventing human suffering.

Ehrman's neglect of this issue is actually, however understandable as (presumably) a gesture of kindness toward women who grapple with it, a cruel oversight. It's catastrophic to his argument for self-made morality, partly because it overlooks not only defenseless children, but tens of millions of other humans, especially women, who suffer deeply before, during, and after their deaths.

As Ehrman's silence attests, our culture doesn't put abortion on its list of human tragedies and human rights violations. And that willful ignorance actively denies unborn children, moms, and dads who have no say regarding the life of their child, the dignity of recognition as victims of human rights violations. Scores of millions of children, and scores of millions of parents, are victims of the abortion industry, which makes scores of millions of dollars as it profits from the death of the defenseless. The expansion of abortion rights is heralded uncritically as a "win for women," but isn't it really more fundamentally a win for big businesses that thrive on death, that latch like parasites onto impoverished communities and minority populaces, and that perpetuate the hell of human trafficking and sex slavery by killing any children conceived, thus keeping female slaves ready for more sexual abuse in just the physical condition their abusers want them?[39] And how is the systematic decimation of human beings and communities a win for anyone?[40] Doesn't it rather indicate that we've all got some serious soul-searching to do as a society?

Some would say that because I'll never be in a situation where I'm forced to choose, that because it doesn't affect me immediately, my perspective on abortion is automatically invalid. "How does it affect *you*?" is a question often used to shut down discussion on this and other moral issues. Does it ever occur to us what a horribly self-centered view of the universe that question advocates?

Human trafficking in countries on the opposite side of the planet doesn't affect me immediately, but I can, and should, still voice opposition to it and do what I can to stop it. Life has become so thoroughly self-centered that the meaning of anything and everything rises, falls, turns, lives, and dies based on how it affects us. "How does it affect you?" is a disingenuous conversation-stopper, not a compelling moral argument.

I immediately concede that I can't be close to the issue of abortion like a mom or any woman at all can, or like a man who was or could have been vital to the life of an aborted child. For what it's worth, I'm close as a pastor and friend to moms and dads who have been victims of abortion, and many years ago I had the opportunity of ministering to a family headed by a woman who came to life in this world as a result of incestuous rape. I know none of that allows me to speak in the positon of a woman who's been forced to choose. But nor does anyone's lack of personal experience take away from the fact that when an abortion happens, a child—a human being—dies. That human being will never live in this world, and this death was certainly not the baby's choice.

One young lady who'd had an abortion told me that, when she came to the awful realization of what had happened, her family got angry at her for thinking that what happened was horrible. All of a sudden, their views about her body and her choice were more valid than hers! They didn't want to admit the truth she'd faced so bravely, that every image-bearer is priceless, unique, and irreplaceable.

Reading these words may have ripped open scarred-over wounds in your heart. This chapter, and this book, is all about the value of human life and of every human life, so this topic has to be addressed. I won't even come close to pretending to personally understand your situation, but I hope if you haven't already, you'll seek the love and wisdom and peace that only God, who gives all human life value, can give.

God gave the life of his own son so that you could know him as his own child, so that his justice could be satisfied regarding each and every instance of devaluing and disrespecting people and human life in general. Please see chapter 8 on this especially. The God who says it's wrong to devalue human life says that he wants you to come to him for help and healing. We shouldn't try to be wiser or more righteous than he is.

If you're close to this issue, please know that you are not alone. There are a growing number of honest, good-hearted organizations that are there to help. I'll mention an especially wonderful group that's so compassionately and carefully tended to the post-abortion needs of some good personal friends. Deeper Still provides these victims of abortion with the time and space and kindhearted, empathetic guidance from people who've been through it, to truly come to terms with abortion and its lasting effects, and to find honest help and hope and strength to move on in the aftermath. You can find contact information in this endnote.[41]

At the very least, this complex issue, and those affected so deeply and directly by it, could benefit from a lot more truth-telling on the topic, a lot more courageous action on behalf of all of its victims. But it's hard to courageously advocate for truth and life when one doesn't believe that ultimate truth can be known, and that the value of human life depends upon popular vote.

Ehrman believes that, despite our ignorance of why we suffer, we must still take action against it: "Our response should be to work to alleviate suffering wherever possible and to live life as well as we can."[42] He tries to end his book on a rousing note, to transform contentment-with-ignorance to action-with-purpose. But action based on ignorance can be, at the very least, misguided. Though some good can certainly be accomplished by a relatively baseless call to necessary action, the tunnel-vision fixation on *what* (people hurt other people, even children) and not also *why* (because people are self-worshipers and all of us have it deep within us) will leave many victims of injustice, including those who need us most, to languish and die in the dark periphery of our self-righteous view of life.

We have to ask: What gives value and meaning to any human life, and therefore to all human lives? Is a human life only valuable to the extent that powerful people upon whom the life is dependent want it to continue?

The abortion issue exposes the disingenuousness and dishonesty, or at least the damning inconsistency, of pop culture's cries for social justice and human rights. Why is one death, and even one murder okay, while another isn't? It all comes down to choice, and power. It's the privilege of the powerful over and against the defenseless, their human rights categorically denied because of where they live and the privileges they don't have. We claim to hate that stuff.

Margaret Sanger, the founder of Planned Parenthood, gave us a creed she thought society should live by: "Every child a wanted child." Those words glow like bone with deathly satanic subtlety. The expression sounds wonderfully life-affirming at first, as if it could fly on the banner of a children's rights advocacy group. But beneath the surface, murder lies in wait. It says, "Every child a wanted child," not "Every child IS a wanted child." Oh God, may that be true one day! But, no. The fallout of Sanger's words is, "Only wanted children should live."[43]

Social movements and political leaders who claim to be all about human rights and the autonomy of the individual often have no problem sanctioning the slaughter of the weakest and most defenseless human beings. Morality built upon or infected by autonomy will always leave the most defenseless humans helpless.

Childcare

Encouraging things are happening in the information age. Despite shrill objections from politically powerful thieves who prevent moms from making truly well-informed choices and who thrive on the cash flow from the abortion industry, truth is readily available for people who care enough to know what actually happens in abortion as well as the long-term physical and emotional toll the child's death takes upon the mother and others closely related to the pregnancy. By no mere coincidence, millennials—those masters of digital tech—are increasingly opposed to abortion.

Still, we've got so far to go, and many other human rights issues to address, before we can say that ours is a culture that values all human life. Without any moral grounding in any god greater than ourselves, our culture is not a fundamentally safe place for children in any age or stage of life.

Princeton bioethicist Peter Singer says it's fine to kill kids even after they're born. Christian apologist Larry Taunton writes that Singer "is the most philosophically consistent atheist I have ever met. Dangerously so….It is Singer's view that man is an animal like any other and that he deserves no special status among the various species. That is, he argues, a residual of Christian thought."[44] Too right on that last part.

Richard Wurmbrand, who because of his faith was tortured in Communist prisons, writes:

> The cruelty of atheism is hard to believe when man has no faith in the reward of good or the punishment of evil. There is no reason to be human. There is no restraint from the depths of evil which is in man….I have heard one torturer even say, "I thank God, in whom I don't believe, that I have lived to this hour when I can express all the evil in my heart." He expressed it in unbelievable brutality and torture inflicted on prisoners.[45]

Atheism is not inevitably murderous in its practical outworking, and sadly, Christianity as practiced does not always lead to life-saving. But atheism provides no deep reason not to be the monstrosity described above. It can provide no lasting definition of "human" nor therefore of what it means to act inhumanely. We may not think we need such definitions, but there are more than 65 million slain children in America and who knows how many around the world who could have used it.

The late Christopher Hitchens, prolific atheist and avowed public enemy of Christianity, and also Larry Taunton's good friend until Hitchens died of esophageal cancer, couldn't quite come to Singer's (consistent) conclusions about people being nothing but animals. "There is just something in me that is not prepared to equate a child with a piglet."[46] Amen.

Thank God, not everything that could happen to kids does happen when we embrace self as the center of our moral universe. And thank God, we still cry out by and large against most forms of child abuse, especially against kids being forced and manipulated into sex. But if truth-defining adults control terms like "healthy" and "forced" and "manipulate," then how much longer can such words provide protection for children, especially when we're still largely unwilling to use the words "human being" with reference to tens of millions of them? If we're holding out hope that we as a people are too reasonable and good to let things get worse for kids in our culture, we're crazy naïve.[47]

It's only based on the Bible that all human life can be declared consistently and unequivocally valuable and worthy of protection; only Scripture provides the sustaining principles that can protect all humans from harm and even murder spurred by societal redefinitions of "human" and therefore of human rights. We need the Bible's wisdom and restraint as, in the name of progress, we seem to be boarding a bullet train to terrible parts of humanity's past.

Blast from the Past

It's not chronological snobbery to look back upon the ethics of ancient civilizations and to find some seriously disturbing things, like rampant pedophilia and the marginalization of just about every defenseless member of society possible, namely, everyone except able-bodied, rich men of a societally favored ethnicity. But in that ancient world, against the abuse of any person, stood that book beloved by backward religious fanatics: the Bible.[48]

As we'll think about next chapter, Scripture establishes and affirms as absolute truth and inviolable principle the infinite value and essential dignity of humanity and all human beings. It does this on page one (Genesis 1:26–28). Somehow (call it divine intervention), this book rose out of and stood against cultures that would laugh at that idea, and whose economies depended upon the systematic abuse of human beings.

We often fail to appreciate just how radical Scripture's teachings on human rights actually are, and how revolutionary they were in the days they were written. In a staunchly and often violently patriarchal society in which men could divorce their wives for almost any reason at all (leaving them homeless and without real recourse for social survival, let alone progress), Scripture commanded Christian husbands to love their wives self-sacrificially and Christian fathers to deal gently with their children (Ephesians 5:25

and following). And guess who wrote those commands? That cave-man Paul! I know, right?! Paul even played his apostle card, while cheekily pretending he wasn't doing it, in order to convince a slaveholder named Philemon (for whom Paul's little New Testament letter is named) to treat his slave Onesimus no longer as a slave but as a brother. Onesimus was a fugitive slave, a criminal under Roman law, whom Paul had led to faith in Christ. Paul urged Philemon (but didn't command him—*wink, wink, nudge, nudge*) to treat Onesimus as he would treat the great Apostle himself, and to charge any of Onesimus's wrongdoing to him. Very Jesus-like of Paul. What a miracle, that such socially scandalous, humanly beautiful behavior could come from that slack-jawed, blockheaded Hebrew neanderthal! Nor was Paul's effort the exception to the rule of biblical ethics. This quiet social revolution came not *despite* Paul's allegedly crazy religious beliefs (like his belief in the creation story of Genesis, the resurrection of Jesus Christ, and that all Scripture is God-breathed) but *because* of them.

Paul's appeal to Philemon was a New Testament–era application of principles first articulated in the Old, specifically Old Testament slave law—which itself is a stunning example of counter-culture commands based on the inherent dignity of all humans. I know—that sounds strange. But if you read these laws in context and against the backdrop of the dehumanizing cultures in which they arose, and see how the Bible continually and pro-gressively worked these laws out into more mature form as time went by—it's striking how forward-thinking this ancient book has always been.[49]

Scripture demands that we treat all people like they were God's prize creations, because that's what they are.[50] James says we're not even allowed to cuss each other out! (James 3:9–10). These commands are absolute, grounded not in the shifting sands of self-made morality, nor in the inhumane dictates of another god, but in the character and changeless word of the true and living God who made humans the crown of his creation.[51]

If you're passionate about social justice,[52] please take note: biblical writers describe God throughout Scripture as the defender of the widow and the orphan (Psalm 68:5, Malachi 3:1–6, and James 1:26–7, among so many others). The writers mean this both with reference to actual widows and orphans and to the people they represent in society—the easily victimized. Other gods aren't like this.[53] None come close. God even gave the life of his own son to end the oppression, violence, and victimizing so prevalent in a world gone maliciously mad.

Historian Bruce Shelley expresses the essential uniqueness of Christianity: "Christianity is the only major religion to have as its central event the humiliation of its God." It's not just the mechanics of God's miraculously becoming human that are mystifying; what should also astound us is what the life and work of Jesus show us about the heart of God. God was humbly willing to be born into this torn world and to subject himself to its miseries, including murder. Why would he do this? To "fix this."

As we'll explore in the coming chapters, as soon as humanity plunged itself and the world into desperate need of redemption, God promised he would send a savior. Little did the recipients of that promise know that God would also *be* that savior.

The Old Testament chronicles the movement of history toward the arrival of that savior. God's worshipers got fuller and clearer previews as time went on. But still, they were always waiting. The New Testament tells us that this savior is Jesus, and that he will one day return to bring full peace to the entire world. So, except for the approximately thirty-three years Jesus was in the world, humanity has been in the constant posture of waiting, always waiting, for the fullness of God's "fixing this." The Bible tells us, so clearly that we can only miss it if we refuse to see it, that this is how history has been and will be right up until its end. This speaks directly to Ehrman's conclusion that the Bible's God had adopted a non-interventionist policy regarding human suffering and therefore does not exist.

Scripture tells us of real-life human beings who raged and wept at their circumstances, who cried out to God for his promised deliverance, and who waited, the vast majority of them dying in that wait, for the Savior to come. These people would understand Ehrman perfectly. His pain is nothing new, nor is it (by his own admission) anywhere near what they endured. They could have said—and sometimes did, right within the Scriptures—that God doesn't intervene in their time. Like Ehrman, they remembered the way God had intervened in the past (see Psalms 22, 42, and 73, especially). But unlike Ehrman, they allowed that history of salvation to form their view of the present, and to give them hope for the future.

We in the entitled, Enlightened West could learn from the pleading, humble patience of past peoples as we observe suffering that's nothing truly new to humanity, but which is new to us. We tend to be so ego- and ethno-centric, that we confuse the two: If it's happened to us, or at least in our time, why, it's the worst thing that's ever happened! And it calls into question everything previous sufferers held as truth in their lifetimes.[54] To call us out of a self-centered view of suffering, the Bible lets us look into the lives of patient sufferers, each of whom and all of whom let us know that suffering, and waiting, and God's faithful, sometimes frustrating actions and inactions, are what to expect in this world.

The Justice League

Jeremiah, "the Weeping Prophet," ministered during some of Israel's darkest days, the era of the Babylonian captivity. Babylon was a vicious foreign empire that conquered Jerusalem, destroyed the Temple—the place of worship and the heart and soul of the kingdom—and dragged so many survivors back to Babylon as slaves. Jeremiah lived through terrorist atrocities that would make ISIS leaders spontaneously detonate in masochistic bliss. God promised that one day he'd bring Israel[55] back home. He did, but not before many would have died as prisoners in Babylon, never in their lives seeing the salvation he promised them.

But then one day, some five and a half centuries after Jeremiah, after millennia of waiting, an angel appeared to a young lady named Mary and told her some very interesting news. She would carry within her the savior God had long promised. And about thirty years after the birth of that blessed baby, decades during which the Son of God lived unremarkably among his fellow Israelites, it was time for him to begin his public work as the promised Savior.

Jesus's cousin, a prophet named John, was more than ready. He had been preaching, "Repent! The kingdom of God is at hand!" (Luke 1). His fiery sermons were drawing huge crowds. He was baptizing people, getting them ready to meet their Messiah (which means "anointed one"), their true King. He even baptized Jesus, an unspeakable honor he was hesitant to accept. "I need to be baptized by you!" John said in worshipful protest (Matthew 3).

But the King commanded it, so John did it. The baptism marked the official beginning of Jesus's messianic ministry. Finally! Salvation, justice, freedom! But John would be horribly disappointed.

Time went on. Jesus didn't overthrow Rome, whose iron rule over Israel so many Hebrew people deeply and rightly resented. John kept preaching, eventually angering a powerful woman who quite literally wanted his head on a platter. She got her wish. John's last days before his martyrdom were spent in prison, in anguish. Nothing was going like it should have for the herald of the King of kings. Desperate, depressed, sunken in doubt, he sent word to Jesus, asking him, "Are you the one who is to come, or should we look for another?" (Matthew 11:1–15).

Like Ehrman, John could reconcile neither his personal experience nor what he saw in the world to the idea that the kingdom of heaven had come in Jesus. He was no longer sure that the Jesus he knew was the Christ he had preached. But Jesus responded to his message, and his words were straight from Scripture, which John knew well. Jesus told John that the miracles that only the prophesied Messiah would accomplish were happening. His faith was well placed. For all we know, his final words to John were: "Blessed is the one who is not offended by me."[56]

Jeremiah, John the Baptist, and so many, many others throughout Scripture wished in their day that things were different in the world and at times pleaded with God to do things differently. Even Jesus did that.

Just before he was betrayed by one of his own disciples, arrested and crucified, Jesus prayed in agony to God the Father for another way to save the world. "Father, if it is possible, take this cup from me" (Luke 22:42). What Jesus said next separates trust in God from self-worship; it expresses Jesus's internal choice of trust over treason: "But nevertheless, not my will, but yours be done." And it was.

Jesus willingly endured the death appointed to him, and rose again to life. With the rising of God's son, the kingdom of heaven had dawned.[57] But even then, some of his disciples were still not sure they'd seen the light.

In Matthew 28:16–20, the resurrected Son of God speaks to his followers. Matthew tells us that some of them worshiped Jesus, but "some doubted."[58] If the biblical authors were con artists, they could do a much better job selling their product to the unthinking masses. Why include that note about doubt right at the exultant close of Matthew's call to faith? Isn't it bad PR for Jesus? Why does Scripture tell us so often about the doubts of people who had a front-row seat to the faith-affirming supernatural events it describes? Because the Bible's authors were simply and honestly reporting what happened. These awkward moments in Scripture also let us know that God knows his truth is sometimes hard to believe, even when it's obvious and playing out right in front of us—and therefore that it's okay to struggle in our faith. Jesus honored a man who cried out to him, "I believe! Help my unbelief!" (Mark 9:24).

Scripture wants us to know that struggling to trust God's word is understandable, but that unbelief is not a function of intellectual integrity. At its heart, unbelief is not a decision demanded by rational thought; it's a refusal demanded by an autonomous will. As it has always done, unbelief, in its purest, most honest form, says to God, "I resent like hell the fact that you are God and I am not."

That resentment comes screaming to the surface when we or those we love suffer. And this is why God includes within his written word that "folktale" Job. Job (pronounced "Jobe," by the way) is my favorite book of the Bible. There's not enough space in this overly long book for a more detailed look at this man's life, but a quick overview is important because of Ehrman's dismissal of Job as moralistic lore.

Job Description

Job is such a literary masterpiece that it's understandable to question its authenticity as history. The dialogue is so profound that it's hard to imagine its happening spontaneously among people. As we'll think about next chapter, though, we have pretty low standards and therefore low expectations for human speech and the human capacity for spontaneous profundity. Other cultures thrived on that fancy speaky stuff. But that's for another book—many of them, in fact.[59]

Job's final chapters, starting with 38, contain a cosmic interrogation that God unleashes on a man who, body and soul, personifies human agony. Like a commanding officer dressing down a loyal soldier dangerously close to losing his nerve in battle, God thunders at his suffering servant, "Where were you when I laid the foundation of the world?" I won't spoil the rest for you here. Read through these questions, over and over, slowly, humbly, as if God is speaking directly to you, and see what it does for your soul.

At the end, Job knows he has no good answers, so he falls silent—a volume level we could all employ a lot more in our lives—and his soul is steadied. God's brutal, bracing, beautiful interrogation reminds Job of who's who in the universe. It rids Job of the hubris that still dwelt in his remarkably humble soul. And it reduces Job to nothing but the faith in which his humility and seemingly super-human endurance were rooted. Out of the crucible of his suffering comes the defining cry of that book, and of the whole Bible. "I know that my Redeemer lives. And at the last day he will take his stand upon the earth. I shall see him…though my skin and bones are destroyed, yet in my flesh I shall see God!…My heart faints within me" (Job 19:25–27). Job had faith in the coming Christ.

We'll revisit Job in chapter 7 and see that, from Genesis right through Revelation, faith in the coming Christ has always been the focal point of Christian faith, and it's the heart and soul of God's written word. It's what kept the biblical authors sane—realistic about how badly messed up life in this world is—while avoiding the pitfall of self-worship, which eventually destroys sanity, hurts the defenseless, and was the reason why the world went crazy to begin with. Every one of the biblical authors could have concluded, "God isn't fixing this!" But they didn't. Instead, they looked in faith, according to the Scriptures, to God's messianic intervention in the world.

Bart Ehrman claims that he's taking the Bible on its own terms, but his readers have grounds to wonder if even he believes that. His arguments are sometimes so snarky and easily answered from the very texts he criticizes, and especially from the combined Christ-centered testimony and trajectory of all of Scripture. Ehrman fails to see Christ in the Scriptures; so it's no wonder he fails to see God in the world.

How to Be Sad

The Bible's authors and the other models of faith it sets before us were real-life, grounded-in-reality, intelligent, flesh-and-blood people. Scripture shows them depressed, discouraged, angered, excited, overjoyed, contemplative, and all over the place emotion-ally—just like us. They're not the tub-thumping knuckle-draggers critics need them to be in order to sweepingly dismiss their argu-ments with such disrespectful nonchalance. They didn't write to answer all of life's deep questions to our satisfaction, but to teach us about and to prepare us to deal with life as it is, with ourselves as we are, and to know how we and the world itself can become what we should be.

Why did people throughout Scripture maintain their belief in a good, all-powerful God? Because they didn't really know how bad life hurts? No, Ehrman allows that they did. Because they couldn't possibly anticipate the devastating critiques Ehrman and others would one day make against their worldview? Ummm…no. Ehrman adds nothing new to the age-old discussion. Is it because the biblical authors couldn't be honest about God when they felt he was acting unlovingly and unjustly, or when he just seemed to be ignoring human suffering altogether? No. In fact, if a person really wants to complain to God about the condition of the world, that person should become a Bible-believing Christian.

God's book actually gives us "how-to" sections on complain-ing. There's a book in the Old Testament, attributed to Jeremiah, called Lamentations. But the biblical authors were not only com-plaining about God; they were complaining *to* God. Beneath their heartfelt pleas and protests, they understood that, as pained as they were at how and why God did or didn't do things, they were not he. And to them, the idea that they should deny God's existence because they didn't like how he did things was the very definition of foolishness.[60]

According to the Bible, we know deep down that God exists, and this explains the unease we feel at injustice, the very thing upon which so many blame their unbelief (Romans 1 and 3). C. S. Lewis was once a devout atheist. He eventually found that raging against injustice while denying the existence of God didn't make much sense. He writes: "My argument against God was that the universe seemed so cruel and unjust. But how had I got this idea of *just* and *unjust*? A man does not call a line crooked unless he has some idea of a straight line.…Of course I could have given up my idea of justice by saying it was nothing but a private idea of my own. But if I did that, then my argument against God collapsed too—for the argument depended on saying that the world really was unjust, not simply that it did not happen to please my fancies….atheism, in the end, turns out to be too simple."[61]

The biblical authors weren't simply anti-atheistic, however (Psalm 14). They didn't believe in just any god, whether an unscrupulous tribal deity or the distant, disinterested (and uninteresting) god of the Deists. They believed in a personal god who was himself good and who therefore made his creation good and expected good to flow from all of it, especially from the creatures made most like him. And this gets to something else the biblical authors believed, a truth embedded like a hornet's stinger in the depths of their being.

This truth throbbed every day in their souls. None of us owns up to this truth, at least fully, but the biblical authors knew they had to face it as they beheld a beautiful but bruised world that screamed in every detail that it should be and wanted to be healed. The biblical authors knew, because God's word told them, that they played a significant part in the essential pain of the cosmos. And they tell us that we did, too.

For all their alleged disagreements about how to best understand why we suffer, the biblical authors are all agreed: we have a deeply ingrained, instinctive, hell-bent belief that we are entitled to all the rights and privileges of deity. It was primal and pernicious to the point that, if God denied our divine rights, we'd take this world whose trials and travails we lament, whose pains prompt us to scream at God even when we claim he's not there—we'd take this world for which our hearts bleed—and we'd burn it.

"Who Killed the World?"

The Bible tells us that the world's miseries are far deeper than we'd ever accuse God of letting them be. But getting to the root of the world's pain requires some excruciatingly uncomfortable digging into our own souls, and we often feel above all that. As Jeremiah laments, "The heart is deceitful above all things and desperately sick. Who can understand it?" (Jeremiah 17:9). See why he was so popular?

In *Mad Max: Fury Road*, a haunting question is painted huge and desperate on the stone wall of a prison in the post-nuclear-war world. A runaway slave, pursued down the Fury Road by her psychotic enslaver and his army of anemic warriors longing for apocalyptic significance, puts the question to one of these "war boys" who'd snuck into her vehicle to capture her. He tries to explain why his master is a noble savior and not the self-exalting, raping wretch she knows all too well that he is (a none-too-subtle commentary on religion's appeal to the desperate and weak-minded, methinks). Before kicking him out of the vehicle, she screams the question from the wall, the question the film wants us to ask before everything goes all end-of-days for us: *WHO KILLED THE WORLD?* This question begins to answer the statement with which we began.

"God's not fixing this!" doesn't allow—or have time for—an exploration of why the world is in this condition to begin with. To protest that "God's not fixing this!" with integrity, we have to ask, "Well, who broke 'this' to begin with?"

Despite Ehrman's claims, the Bible is absolutely consistent in its explanation of the world's miserable estate. As if we weren't angry enough at God, the Bible blames us. We killed the world. And we keep doing it every day.

God spoke into existence an unspeakably beautiful world. The world and everyone and everything in it are God's (Psalm 24), and yet he gave it as a gift to humanity. Humans were to represent God in the world by ruling over, cultivating, and caring for creation as his most honored creatures (Psalm 8). There was only one part of creation that God kept out of our first parents' reach. For them, that was a deal breaker.

As we'll see in more detail later, desire for what God forbade slithered into the collective soul of humanity and became distrust, which became disdain. Proving that the forbidden fruit doesn't fall far from the tree, we perpetuate daily the same age-old rebellion. Every time we violate God's commands, feeling entitled to what he's forbidden, we kindle anew a fire that started long ago in a garden and burned the whole world.

As we'll see in coming chapters, this original rebellion against God was the inferno that started it all: all the pain, all the suffering, every bitter tear and bad news X-ray, every earthquake and every tremor of terror in any and every human heart—all the needless hurts you've ever felt—it's all afterburn. Because humans were put in charge of creation and were personally and vitally connected to it (Genesis 2:7), the world itself suffers from our rebellion (Romans 5).

Since "the Fall," humanity and the planet have coexisted in an achingly beautiful, but also just plain aching life—and often as enemies. Humans are always at war with one another, and doesn't it seem at times like the planet is taking revenge against its lapsed caretakers? Father Zosima, a wise, seasoned, and compassionate priest in *The Brothers Karamazov*, summarizes the world's pain and the posture of heart humanity must adopt if it's ever to be healed: "Everyone is responsible for everyone and everything."

Doesn't it just make sense that things are as bad as they are in the world, given that its highest creatures live largely in rebellion against the one who made it, and therefore against the very principles of life itself? To reject God is to ruin, well, everything.

The good news is that the world is not as bad as it could be, and that's because, broken as it is, it retains its essential identity as God's world. And despite Ehrman's thesis, God remains actively interested in it. Can you imagine how long ago we'd have nuked the place if God had abandoned it? But if we mean to prevent *Mad Max* from becoming a story based on real events, we need to confess our part in killing the world.

That Just Isn't Right

The Bible teaches that the evil we decry in the world begins deep within the human heart. Sin grows within, and if unchecked, goes public. What makes the headlines of the *News* always starts in the heart. Without heart-level disrespect for fellow human beings— whether the fire of unjust anger or the ice of indifference—there would be no murder. Jesus makes this point and includes other examples in the "Sermon on the Mount" (Matthew 5–7) as he presses God's law uncomfortably deep, judging not only our outward actions but our sometimes-secret inward motivations.

For you and me, our crimes may not have made headlines, but if we had a spiritual X-ray, what sinful stirrings would we see in our souls? Well, one might say, as long as it stays in the heart, it's fine. Really? That's a pretty low standard of righteousness. Even if we did all commit to just letting the good stuff out—putting aside that nagging problem of who gets to define good—who actually lives with such restraint?

Here's the irony beating within many a broken heart like Ehrman's: We call for justice, but we don't really want justice. We don't really want the end of evil. The selfishness that causes such suffering in the world is so tightly sewn in to the fabric of our being that its complete eradication would mean our complete eradication. Evil is not some abstract entity out there, some strange state of mind into which people sometimes slip for a break in the day's monotony. Evil is within. It gets personified in all of us. It's a part of who we are since our first parents left their first love and declared war against him.

We don't want to think that we're all that bad, but isn't it convenient that our criteria for good, or at least good enough, lets us look relatively fine while others stand condemned in our eyes? Again, self-righteousness.

It's very true that an unjustly angry thought against someone is far less of a bad thing than shooting up an office full of people. It's less of a thing, but it's the same thing, because it violates the same standard, God's standard. It's a difference of degree, not of kind. Both flow from an ungodly sense of entitlement and a disdainful view of a fellow human being. Why, when such evil is so easy for us, do we wonder what's so wrong with the world? And how can there be any doubt that we need a savior?

While we complain, sometimes quite understandably, that God doesn't care about justice, the reality is that God is far more concerned about it than we are. He's actually far more concerned about it than we wish he was.

About 400 years before Jesus was born, God's people were complaining that he wasn't sufficiently concerned about the evil going on in the world—the evil *out there*, committed by other people. Like Ehrman and so many others, they scream out, "Where is the god of justice?!" God responds through his prophet, Malachi: "I the Lord do not change. Therefore you, O sons of Jacob, are not consumed" (Malachi 3:6). In other words, *Do you really want me to deal with injustice? Then let me start with you.* God is not passive; he's patient. We think, "Okay, God is patient. But what is he waiting for?!" God answers us. He wants more time to be merciful.

God is not satisfied to deal with evil at the surface level, like mowing over weeds in the yard. God means to rip evil out of humanity and the world by its roots. But not yet. And there's a sense in which we can thank him for it. The apostle Peter writes: "Our Lord's patience means salvation" (2 Peter 3:15).[62]

Rather than eradicating evil and therefore evildoers—not good for us—God has given the life of his son so that we can instead be forgiven and changed deep within, saved. We can be spared the judgment that we, like the malcontents in Malachi's day, claim we want but could not endure. As we'll explore in coming chapters, salvation doesn't just rescue us, it recreates us; it renews us. Salvation sets us on a trajectory toward true righteousness and away from the self-righteousness that killed the world and continues to ruin lives.

Peter wrote to believers increasingly mocked and opposed for their faith. They were tempted to think that, despite the life and ministry of Jesus decades prior, the world would simply continue as it always had. Peter reminds them of what prior Scripture tells us: God will intervene; Jesus will return and bring in full what we really need but don't naturally want: righteousness. Real righteousness, God's righteousness, as revealed in God's law (verse 13).[63]

A Perfect 10

The reason why evil is so bad is that God is so good. Evil is defined by its departure from God's laws. Relating stories of the Holocaust, William Lane Craig writes: "One rabbi who survived the camp summed it up well when he said that in Auschwitz it was as though there existed a world in which all the Ten Commandments were reversed. Mankind had never seen such a hell."[64]

Reading the Ten Commandments (Exodus 20), especially as Jesus preaches them, is God handing us a mirror for our souls (James 1:23–25). Gazing into God's perfect standards, we immediately see our imperfections. Looking in the mirror can be excruciating, but we can't see ourselves accurately otherwise.

Lacey Sturm writes that it was only after she came to faith in Christ that she saw how condemning she had been of others, and how self-righteously she had been living.

> There was an order to my thought process, although somehow it all happened in the same moment. First, I saw *myself.* According to my own moral code, I had considered myself a pretty good person. Compared to the people I hated, I thought I was at least much better

than they were. But when you're standing in front of God, saying "I'm good," it's like saying "I'm tall" when you're standing in front of a mountain, "I'm big" when you're standing in front of the ocean, or "I'm old" while looking at the stars. The thought is absurd. I realized that I had no idea what good was, because up to that point I had not stood in the presence of the God who made the universe.[65]

If everyone in the world truly, from the heart, kept the Ten Commandments perfectly, we have to admit that things would be a whole lot better in the world. Violence, genocide, rape, human trafficking, the murder of people at any and every stage of life, stealing, slandering, and even the desire for others to suffer, would all die off and disappear. But we don't keep the full demands of God's law. We naturally prefer and pursue autonomy. God's laws are good, and in their goodness, they call out and demand autonomy's death.

Sturm goes on: "But in what I felt was my justified indignation with culture, I adopted my own set of rules. *I* defined acceptance, success, goodness, and beauty. I was just as guilty as the prude... the Christian, all those whom I felt had put their definitions on everyone else."[66]

If we're willingly blind to what's going on in our hearts, we'll be maliciously clueless about how to stop what's happening in the headlines. Given our daily refusal to live by God's law, it seems we're not quite ready for the evil in the world to end, or at least for our participation in it to stop. So between us and God, who's really the bad guy?

Many people blame God for his inactivity in preventing suffering, yet like Ehrman, also complain that God gets way too angry at sin. It's evident in Ehrman's handling of biblical texts that he thinks God overreacts to rebellion against him. That's like saying that an oncologist is overreacting if she's furious with businesses that make billions selling their purposely addictive, carcinogen-loaded products. We just refuse to see how deadly sin is and what our willing addiction to autonomy has cost us, others, and the world. For Dostoyevsky, this recognition was a game-changer in life. "But sin is not a failure of conditioning or an unwholesome idea. It is the major fact of the human condition. It was this fact that turned Dostoyevsky from…nihilistic revolutionary theories, to Christ and His Gospel."[67] Somewhat ironically, Ehrman rejects the worldview of the author who so clearly understood and so perfectly voiced Ehrman's views through his beloved Ivan.

Ehrman's work bears the marks of someone who's made his mind up irrevocably, but who at the same time wants to believe he's open-minded. Thus, Ehrman claims to be an agnostic, not an atheist. Penn Jillette, happy to be identified as an atheist, would call shenanigans on him. "Agnostic" answers the epistemological question of how perfect knowledge can be, but once you've said you're agnostic (which every sane person is), you still have to answer the theological question about your personal belief—and that comes down to "atheist" or "theist."[68]

Ehrman's work is plagued by a sad but instructive irony. As he's moved further and further away from belief in the Bible's goodness and trustworthiness, his work as a historian has been more and more suspect. He is now routinely called out by other scholars for just plain ignoring easily demonstrable facts of church history. Increasingly, his claims about Jesus and Christianity are doubtful to the point of being dubious; it's as if he's just making stuff up to substantiate what he wants to believe. Not good form for a historian. Ehrman is becoming what his work criticizes: someone who can't handle the world as it is, someone who needs myth in order to maintain his beliefs.[69]

God hasn't failed to give us enough reason to believe his claims in the Bible. It's not about evidence; it's about ethics. Ehrman and many others simply do not like, and have lost patience with, the Bible's God. But if dislike is sufficient reason for disbelief, then I hereby deny the existence of the New York Yankees. If the need for patience is reason enough to abandon hope, then generations of loyal Red Sox fans should have dumped their season tickets into the *habah* way before 2004. But the faithful waited, and were epically rewarded.

There is a fundamental, instructive irony in the kind of brokenheartedness that called Ehrman and other ex-Christians out of the faith. For them, the biblical God cannot exist because of the continual presence of evils that can only be identified as such by a biblical morality, and that only the Bible can equip us to adequately understand and consistently oppose. It's the confirmation bias inherent in unbelief.[70] Sometimes, the people who claim to be seeking and speaking the truth don't actually want to know it. As Jesus puts it, they don't have the ears to hear it (Matthew 11:15). At some point, a broken heart becomes simply a hard heart.

What If It's True?

What if, despite his being chronologically conditioned to be stupid, Paul (not to mention the other New Testament authors and the Old Testament writings upon which they build) was actually right about the resurrection of Jesus? He did claim to be an eye witness of the risen Savior (Acts 9, 1 Corinthians 15). But maybe that vision was just a stress-induced, hallucinatory by-product of culturally induced ignorance. How sad that, despite Paul's being one of the ablest scholars and philosophers of his time and a person who'd heavily influence world history, he lived long before the Age of Reason and thus never attained the intellectual maturity and ethical sophistication of post-Enlightenment thought. But what if, by some miracle, he was right? Are we willing to doubt our doubts? What if any of what he saw, what he believed, what he wrote, was actually true?

For Ehrman, it wasn't just human-on-human violence that forced him out of faith; it was nature-on-human violence as well. Paul understood both kinds of suffering firsthand. He'd been beaten and left for dead and he survived a life-threatening shipwreck after a horrendous storm at sea (neither of which he had to go through if he'd just kept quiet about his new faith in Jesus, whom he'd once hated with every ounce of his being—more to say later!). Paul writes not with the naïve platitudes of a well-wisher who's never really suffered, nor with the always suspect motives of a politician. He writes with the calm, kindhearted wisdom of someone who in every way knows exactly what he's talking about. "For I consider that the sufferings of this present time are not worth comparing with the glory that is to be revealed....the creation waits with eager longing for the sons of God to be revealed....the creation itself will be set free from its bondage to corruption to obtain the freedom of the glory of the children of God" (Romans 8:18–21).

Paul picks up on the theme from Genesis: humans destroyed themselves and the creation they were meant to rule in God's name.

Now, because of what Jesus did, things will be made right—first the humans, then the planet. It will take time, and patience, but righteousness and freedom are coming.

This hope is personified among the Karamazov brothers by Alyosha, an apprentice Russian Orthodox priest mentored by Father Zosima. He experiences something (no spoilers!) that draws him nearer to the Lord than he'd ever been or felt. And loving the Lord more, he loves God's bruised, beautiful world all the more.[71] After his experience in his monastery, he walks outside and into the night:

> The vault of heaven, full of soft, shining stars, stretched vast and fathomless above him. The Milky Way ran in two pale streams from the zenith to the horizon. The fresh, motionless, still night enfolded the earth. The white towers and golden domes of the cathedral gleamed out against the sapphire sky. The gorgeous autumn flowers in the beds round the house were slumbering till morning. The silence of the earth seemed to melt into the silence of the heavens. The mystery of earth was one with the mystery of the stars....Alyosha stood, gazed, and suddenly threw himself down on the earth. He did not know why he embraced it....But he kissed it weeping, sobbing, and watering it with his tears and vowed passionately to love it, to love it forever and ever....he was not ashamed of that ecstasy....But with every instant he felt clearly and, as it were, tangibly, that something firm and unshakable as that vault of heaven had entered into his soul.[72]

There are mysteries surrounding the way things are and why they're not another, better way—God-level mysteries. Pursuing them will drive you into the deepest, darkest labyrinths of mind-breaking reality, truth for which we don't have categories, or at least the capacity to contain. It's gold buried too deep, enticing but out of reach. God forbids it. As a species, we've never liked that, no matter how obviously incapable we are of mining such truth. But Scripture makes crystal clear that God knows the condition of the world, has done and is doing something about it.

Paul writes in Romans 8 that within us and the creation itself is a deep longing to be healed, to be free. Because of Christ, we know God will do this. "He who did not spare his own son but gave him up for us all, how will he not also with him graciously give us all things?" In the meantime, "Who shall separate us from the love of Christ? Shall tribulation, or distress, or persecution, or famine, or nakedness, or danger, or sword?...No, in all these things we are more than conquerors through him who loved us." Paul covers all the reasons we use to rage against God, so many of which he had personally experienced—he really had thought this through!—and says that believers are by their reconciliation to God through Christ, overwhelmingly triumphant in and over these miseries, just as Jesus, after being brutally murdered, defeated death itself and is alive forevermore.

Speaking of alive forever, think again of the children. Thinking about the little girl tormented by her parents, Ivan Karamazov says that any future and final judgment to come can't justify her suffering. Anything like what Paul writes about, even if real, isn't worth it. "It's not worth it, because those tears are unatoned for." But are they? Not if what Paul writes, and if what the whole Bible teaches about Jesus, is true.

What if these children, treated so cruelly in this life, killed so casually, are right now as you read growing up in heaven? Does that happen in heaven? More gold beyond reach! What if they're constantly in the presence of Jesus who entered this world as one of them? Jesus, who in his time among us held infants in his arms and blessed them, scolding his disciples for trying to prevent parents from bringing their children him (Mark 10:13–16)?

Admittedly speculation here, but what if untold tens of millions of children, discarded like trash in this world, make up a sizable portion of the untold multitudes the Scriptures say reside in heaven? Could this be the reason why that heavenly assembly described in the Bible's last book is innumerable (Revelation 7:9), and yet Jesus says that the way to God is narrow and that there are few who find it (Matthew 7:14)? I don't know, but I sure hope that's where those parallel truths eventually connect; I hope that's how heaven is and will be. The thing is, given God's character, given Jesus's interaction with children, and given God's uncomfortably complete dedication to justice and mercy as "the defender of widows and orphans," it might be much more than wishful thinking.

The least we can say is that it would be very much like the Bible's God to take the worst misery humans can inflict and to treat its victims to a bliss brighter than we could imagine. After all, God did this with his own son. Jesus was brutally murdered by his own people. It was the worst thing that's ever happened, followed within three days by the best.

Obvious as it is, it's crucially important to note that all of the arguments citing the existence of evil and suffering as sufficient evidence to disprove or sufficient reason to seriously doubt the existence of a good, all-powerful God have at least one thing in common: they all deny that Jesus is risen from the dead. The word of God says otherwise.

As surely as Jesus came the first time in fulfillment of God's written word, he'll do it again, bringing a justice as devastating as it is desperately needed. And for all who trust him and for the world itself, he'll bring not only the end of suffering, but freedom and peace far greater than disingenuous disbelievers demand, and far greater than brokenhearted believers could ever hope for.

We Could(n't) Be Heroes[73]

If you could eradicate from your heart every inclination of disrespect toward others, of unjust anger, of sexual greed, theft, slander, and envy in general (commandments 5–10)—if you could live a life free of all of that, even if no one around you wanted to and everyone around you hated you for doing it, would you?

If your answer is, "That sounds like hell," then, no offense, but please don't complain about the condition of the world. If you say: "That sounds like heaven, but it's impossible. I'd like to live like that but I can't," then you're feeling the need for the Savior the Bible says is real, risen from the dead, and returning, and who right now this moment offers you his life, to get you moving toward that life.

Hoping in him as we suffer and as we see the world in the throes of the same, we can say as we lament with Jeremiah, "My soul…is bowed down within me. But this I call to mind, and therefore I have hope: The steadfast love of the Lord never ceases…great is your faithfulness" (from Lamentations 3:20–23).

Don't lose heart. God is fixing this.

5

The Bible Is the Words of God

"They that have despised the word of God, from them shall the word of man also be taken away."
—C. S. Lewis, *That Hideous Strength*[1]

"She's walking on eggshells,
Biting off her tongue,
She's still searching for herself
But it ain't pleasing no one.
And none of you know her anyway
You don't even want to.
They aren't your tears, it ain't your pain,
So what's it to you?"
—Lacey Sturm, "I'm Not Laughing"[2]

Homer Simpson was hallucinating again. But this time he came by it honest. He wasn't drunk; he was suffering the psychedelic effects of ingesting several psychotically hot chili peppers. It was an acid trip that became a spiritual journey for the loveable lush. As Homer wandered through the surreal, he had a faithful canine companion to guide him. The dog could talk, which makes perfect sense during a mind-freak. After Homer completed his vision quest, he saw this same dog in real life. As he passed by, the dog spoke to him, "Hi Homer!" Homer was shocked, even offended. He looked back at the dog sternly. The dog caught on. "Oh, I mean…bark, bark!" Homer approved. "Damn straight!" he said, and he walked on, satisfied that real life had resumed its proper categories. Hopefully, none of us would be so easily satisfied!

If an animal, even a beloved pet, started to speak to us, then sanity would likely give us an ultimatum: "It's either me or this talking beast. You can't have us both!" All animals communicate in some way. Dogs bark. Cats purr—then they claw your face and spit if they're no longer pleased with you. (I'm more of a dog person.) Much as we may love our pets and animals in general, we are set apart from them in so many ways, most significantly by our way with words. Though some animals ape it, we humans have a monopoly on true, original, communicative speech.

God created the cosmos by speaking. We have no earthly idea what kind of language God used or even if it was vocalized as we would think of it. What the Bible's opening chapters make clear is that God made humans to be the creatures most like him, the ones who "image" him (Genesis 1:26–28). So God gave us a gift expressive of our exalted status in creation. "Speech...made us human, keeps us human, and in fact defines what human means."[3] Humanity is the crown jewel of God's creation, and language is the luster of that gem.

Like their divine creator and human caretakers, words are capable of life-altering, creative, and destructive power. Words are revealers and concealers; promise-makers and betrayers; supplicants and conquerors; creators and killers. Most essentially, words are communicators—ways to express what's deep within. Jesus tells us that it's "out of the abundance of the heart the mouth speaks" (Luke 6:45). Once our ideas climb into words, they can speed like an IndyCar into the hearts of other image-bearers, creating, continuing, or perhaps destroying relationships. Marriage vows are made of words; so are divorce papers. Words can carry the weight of the world, which makes sense if they're the means by which the world was created.

From a birth certificate to the engravings on a tombstone, human lives are all wrapped up in words. Words are so vital to humanity and human relationships that using them is always a matter of life and death.

"Killing Me Softly"

If you're anything like me—well, first of all, congratulations on that—but to my point: If you're anything like me, a conversation can feel like a struggle for survival, even if it's going well!

A talk with someone can be full of laughter and encouraging words, but afterward, do you ever feel like it was all fake?

Just meaningless niceties at best and at worst, a passive-aggressive attempt to soften you up for a hard, verbal smack to come later? Maybe you don't feel as vulnerable and defensive as I sometimes do in the midst of everyday interactions, or maybe you feel this way even more intensely. It's easy to let such feelings become unhealthy. But—and I know I'm biased—I think there's a certain amount of sanity in this slightly paranoid perspective. When we really think about it, life is a whole lot deeper than we typically give it credit for, and a whole lot more dangerous, too—especially when we talk to each other.

Words are combustible. They're like the old Ford Pinto—highly flammable vehicles that endanger human life with every use.[4] Our friend James dedicates much of his New Testament letter to calling out what we might call sins of speech (James 3). He says that the tongue, our speech, is a fire; it's like a spark that can set a whole forest ablaze.

In our day of expanding social media and increasing personal anxiety, our words have an unprecedented ability to burn. Heated words unleashed in cyberspace can find victims in their most vulnerable state: alone, quiet in their fears and too ashamed to reach out for help. The isolation they might already feel in life burns into them more deeply as the screen tells them that life would be so much better without them. These words are lies, full of hell's fire, but even if the victim knows this, they can create or reinforce such self-loathing that the victim decides to self-harm anyway, not to validate the cyberbully, but just to feel a different, distracting pain—or to stop feeling anything at all. As the Bible's book of Proverbs puts it, "Death and life are in the power of the tongue" (Proverbs 18:21).[5]

James tells us in James 1:19 to do a few counterintuitive things to keep us from overheating: "Be quick to listen, slow to speak, and slow to anger." As we put it in my house: "Pause, pray, and walk away." How many life burnouts could we prevent if we heeded James's counsel? But, like driving the speed limit when every other driver thinks it's time trials for the Indy 500, we think a "pause, pray, walk away" lifestyle would cause a devastating crash. Even if others slow down, we don't know what they'll do next. We might get sideswiped by comments from total strangers. *Who is this and why are they trolling me?!* Or a friend in our blind spot might suddenly slam into us with words we never saw coming. *Not you. I thought I could actually trust you*....Sometimes we're the ones with road rage, trying with our fiery speech to make other lives crash and burn.

Even if our words are carefully considered and kind, there is still something inherently violent about communication. Words change us. They force us to react, taking our lives in a different direction. The version of us that existed prior to encountering those words ceases to be, and will never be again.[6] You realize what this means, don't you? When people speak to us, *they are trying to kill us*. Okay, maybe not. But they are at the very least trying to make us different, forever. What's so wrong with us?! Who are *they* thinking that *we* need to change? Whatever.

The next time someone says to you, "Have a good day!" you should respond, "Don't try to change me, baby." Depending upon who assaults you with that kindness, you might want to leave out "baby." Better yet, keep it!—just to put the assailant off balance. We need all the linguistic defense mechanisms we can muster. One single, combustible word coming at us can change us in ways we never wanted or even thought possible. Dialogue is dangerous!

The life-and-death dynamics of worded communication doesn't have to result in paranoia, though. Instead, we could recognize and appreciate what a costly, consequential, and beautiful thing it is to converse with another human being. Words create instability, but God did not design them to make us insecure. As we'll see, God used words to create, structure, and stabilize reality, to give created life freedom within its forms. Words have God written all over them, and using them to benefit our fellow image-bearers expresses the heart of our humanity.

As we use God's gift of language to communicate, we humans are doing some serious God-level stuff.[7] And that raises some serious questions in the wake of God's alleged death and the silence that seems to confirm it: What are words in a world without the word of God? And because language is so integral to being human, what are *we* in a world without the word of God?

Power Plays

Words are powerful means of expression, but beneath the ceiling of self, they are merely expressions of power. Since God's death, words have become the purveyors and protectors of our godhood. In God's posthumous silence, our speech takes on divine significance, divine authority, and divine power. And we tend to like that. Like cosmic grave robbers, we're glad to take God's stuff now that he's gone. But it's as if the stolen goods were cursed. When we use God's gifts to deify ourselves, we lose everything we tried to gain by the theft. Ultimately, we lose ourselves.

When we're doing what I'll call from here on out our *godding*—acting as if we possess the significance, authority, and power of God—life becomes all about us. Godding poisons our use of words and the relationships we build with them. It's not that we're intentionally selfish all the time, but by adopting a way of life in which self is the standard of truth, right, authority, and beauty—all that God-level stuff—we get to the same place. And in becoming all about us, life becomes ironically, and horribly, impersonal.

Promise-based relationships depend upon trust, but the ceiling of self cuts us off from truth. How can trust exist without truth?[8] Down here, the best my words can do is express *my* truth; same for you and *your* truth. Notice, that's the language of separation. "My truth" speaks against any unity we could have as both of us believe *the* truth. "My truth" is also quietly hostile. Like we thought about in chapter 1, your truth and your beauty are only as truthful and beautiful as I think they are in *my* truth. Your value as a person depends upon my perception of you as a person. Put that in your wedding vows!

Despite our godding's natural tendencies, we might enter relationships with sincere and lofty thoughts of fidelity, honesty, and trust. And of course, lasting and loving relationships have been built beneath the ceiling of self. Some Pintos never exploded, but that doesn't commend their design.

Though our personal truths may get along, their foundations are fundamentally incompatible. I'm not you, and you're not me. Our truths are not the same. There's no truth beyond us to which we owe personal allegiance, so any terms of trust between us are constantly subject to change without notice. On a philosophical level, we feel just fine saying that we have no access to real moral truth. But then someone lies to us and we want blood. It's not lying in itself that offends us; we feel the right to do that from time to time. What really cheeses us off is that someone lied to *us*. How dare they?! Isn't this rather hypocritical? Yes, but we don't see it that way beneath the ceiling of self.

Hypocrisy is acting against what you claim is right. But down here, "right" and "I" are synonymous, so everything "I" do is by definition "right." I can break my word all I want to and still be offended when you don't trust me. But don't think for a second that you have the same freedoms. This is my world, *baby*. You're just living in it.

War of the Wor(l)ds

In our godding, we consider words to be "good" and "true" if they bolster our personal truth; they're "bad" and "false" if they belittle it. Down here, you can never say with any integrity, "It's not personal; it's just a different opinion." My truth is who I am, who I want to be, who I have every right to be. To say that I'm wrong isn't simply to reject an idea of mine; it's an all-out assault on my identity and worth. To criticize what I think or feel is to blaspheme, to incite my holy wrath. Beneath the ceiling of self, conditions are perfect for a constant, cosmos-shaking clash of the titans.

Down here, disagreement is a declaration of war. By offering a dissenting opinion, you might be genuinely trying to help me, sincerely offering gifts from the abundant self-defined goodness of your truthless heart. How sweet of you! But down here, your words are always your "will to power" destabilizing me, changing me, trying to convert me. It's always your truth trying to conquer mine.

This helps to explain the obnoxiously labeled "snowflake" mentality snidely attributed to American millennials. The irony is palpable when politically conservative talk show hosts bluster and storm against the "snowflakes," mercilessly mocking the younger generation, screaming that if they hear of just *One. More. Millennial. Meltdown,* their heads will explode. Seems those radio guys are a tad touchy, too. Stress and anxiety are statistically more evident among millennials, but raw-nervedness is not a millennial way of life so much as a cultural reckoning. It's not inherent within them; it's their inheritance.[9] Naturally, the crushing consequences of generations of godding weigh most heavily upon the young.

Stress Test

Do you ever walk into a room and instantly feel opposed? Judged, unwanted, or worse, just plain irrelevant? Life beneath the ceiling of self amplifies our insecurities. We become suspicious of the most innocent people—even writers!

Test your level of (dis)comfort with the following statements:

I wrote the words you are reading.
　　Okay so far? Let's proceed.
I wrote these words in order to make you think.
　　How's that? No big deal? K. How about this?
I wrote these words so that you would think in a certain way.
　　Getting a bit uncomfortable? Too late. Take this:
I wrote these words so that you would think like I do.
　　How dare I?!

This means that I think it's better for you to think less like you do right now and more like I do. Less of you, more of me. That's some good thinking right there! But before you get upset, it goes the other way, too. If you think I'm wrong—about anything—it means that you think my thinking is inferior to yours, that my truth isn't true enough or good enough for you. Wait, now *I'm* angry!

Maybe this all feels like overkill. We don't have to be this paranoid; our pursuit of personal truth doesn't have to mean all-out war all the time. In fact, maybe we can find where our personal truths agree and align them against someone else's personal truth we both oppose. Yeah, we could be allies! Maybe, but we can never really be friends.[10]

If the ceiling of self holds firm, then, despite appearances, perceptions, feelings and even physical touch to the contrary, true human connectedness is impossible. It's all images, perceptions, not reality. Or maybe, as more hardcore fans of the ceiling think, our images and perceptions *are* reality. But if that's just the way life is, then we might as well embrace it, right?

That sounds honest, even noble, but as we saw in chapter 1, to accept life on the ceiling's terms is to violate those terms. The idea that all we have is perception and not contact with reality[11] has to be, by definition, merely our perception. And if we say that our perception *is* reality, we've made the kind of ultimate statement about reality that our own view won't allow us to make. It's that self-defeating, suicidal inconsistency that eats away like termites at any thinking built beneath the ceiling of self. Any brave acceptance of its terms crumbles as we cry brokenhearted over lies trusted people have told us, as we shake with angry sobs because none of our relationships in life feel deeply real. Those tears are telling us the truth about the ceiling.

If the ceiling of self is legitimate, then friendship is a façade; community is a crock.[12] All we can do is fight hard to secure the most satisfying version of fake we can find. And that means conflict with other gods striving for the same. Gods are territorial and prone to get wrathful. They fight with fire and brimstone for what's theirs. At least at first.

After we scream it all out at someone during a sky-lighting burst of temper, we might feel a certain satisfaction as we hear the door slam. But then burning rage fades to cold fear. We realize that the other person is really gone and, if the fight was bad enough, might not come back. With enough of those experiences, or even one of them, we start to doubt our ability to ever truly and deeply connect with someone else again. We know we're combustible. We can't be trusted to keep it all together, and we're too terrified to really trust anyone else. Maybe getting burned by someone else is what sparked our rage to begin with. Suddenly, despite our desperate intentions and efforts not to, we find ourselves living exactly like the terrible people we swore we'd never be like, much less become. Godding is full of frustrating ironies.

After we burn out trying to avoid surrender to another god, we might find ourselves willing to yield to all comers. We let ourselves be used so that we won't feel useless. Afterward, when we're dismissed, we either wilt further, willing to be used again and again, or we choose war as a way of life. No more peace treaties; no more ceasefires; no more trusting; no more surrender...*ever*. Being a god is lonely, stressful work. And it's a burden we were never meant to bear.

We could call shenanigans on our godding, unearth and examine any deeply felt doubts about the ceiling of self and the suicidally inconsistent, separation-causing, instability-inducing ideas that breed beneath it. Or, we could double down on our alleged deity, blaming everything and everyone else—especially God—for life's pains and our failures to live successfully as gods; we can try to create a world where our will is power and our word is law, a world made right according to our personal truth. So far, pop culture has made a clear choice: the ceiling stays.

If the world is merely our perception, we might as well make like a lucid dream. Let's use our illusion[13] to make that world of our own. We'll defy and if necessary destroy any ideas, institutions, or people in our way. We shall have no other gods before us.

So how do we create our new world? The same way God created his. With words.

That's a Stretch

God used words not only to create the world, but to define, designate, and differentiate his creations according to what he made them and how he designed them to relate to one another. Genesis 1 makes statements like: "And God said, 'Let there be light,…and God called the light day." It tells us that God made the plants and animals "according to their kind." In Genesis 2, God lets the first image-bearer, Adam, share in some of that fun.

God brings the animals to Adam so Adam can name them something fitting God's design. It's quite a playful scene, like a dad introducing his son to the puppy he bought for him, smiling as the boy thinks about what to name his new buddy. Adam could not create, but he could describe and designate. Adam's authority was derivative and anchored within the reality that God established and all the rules by which God said it would run. In our godding, we're interested in all of the above. So we feel a lot freer in our wordplay.

Because we claim we can't know things as they are, we feel the right to decide what they are and to name them accordingly. We try to arrange reality according to our likeness and our likes. The subject matter we're most eager to define and designate is us, humanity. We've got to free ourselves from the categories that a dead God created for us. We feel the right, and increasingly we think we have the power, to make ourselves into whatever we think we really are, or want to be.

In our godding, we resist any attempt from others to categorize us, to limit and define us by their words. We let our desires define our true selves. Our feelings frame reality, and we expect others to adjust and address us accordingly. No need to submit our heartfelt longings to empirical data or moral truth. We can ignore the former and if the latter exists, we have no access to it anyway. Not knowing the truth has set us free! "Our culture has shifted toward a predicate of impulse release, projecting controls unsteadily based upon an infinite variety of wants raised to the status of needs."[14]

Though we don't have the tech yet to make everything we want possible, that doesn't stop us from declaring our definitions as fact by godlike words of power. If we say we are something, we are that something. Like God, our speech both announces and actualizes our creative will.

Language has always been subject to upgrade. In previous generations, we had "amazing." Today, we have "amazeballs." (You judge whether this is an improvement.) To declare and describe our true selves, we can simply update an old word or we can use the same old word in a brand new way.

I'll give you a sentence and then repeat it, word for word, but with an added emphasis on one word that will completely change its meaning, and therefore the meaning of the sentence. Here goes: "That dog is sick." And again, but completely different in meaning: "That dog is *sick*." The first means, "The canine animal suffers a malady." The second, "That dog is amazeballs! I want that dog!" If this book is ever finished, the example might be nonsense by the time you're reading it, thus reinforcing the point.

Whatever "sick" can mean by the time you read this, the ideas that "sick" can currently represent will remain the same. But beneath the ceiling of self, because we have no access to truth beyond it, we think *ideas* are just as flexible as the words that currently represent them. So to expand an idea, we simply stretch the word to fit what we want to add into it. But there are some ideas that can't stretch without snapping.

A white woman once tried to publicly identify as a black woman.[15] It seems her claim was a cunning response to literally getting caught in the act of a despicable masquerade game. She took sly advantage of a godding culture in which personal truth must never be criticized as false. But people weren't having it. Her effort was rightly recognized as supremely offensive.

But beneath the ceiling of self, what's the big deal? Especially if she was sincere in her feelings. If she says she's black, she's black.

She's a god! Her word is law, and her will is power. It's discrimination to tell her she can't be what she claims she is. Who are other people to tell me how to live my reality and my sense of self within it? What right does one community have to declare someone else an outsider? Right? Very wrong. African Americans, and everyone else, *should* reject a white person's claim to be black. But that freedom from redefinition is in serious jeopardy beneath the ceiling.

This racially charged incident reminds us that there is no true, lasting justice possible beneath the ceiling of self. An absurd affront to a people group will only seem absurd for so long. If popular opinion trends the other way, politically powerful thieves will seize the moment. They have no allegiance to truth other than their own, and no loyalty to people who cannot serve their desire for power. Down here, no social designation, no community, no people, no ideas, no matter how sacred, are safe.

To do serious godding, we'll likely have to unleash divine wrath against any person or institution that opposes us. We might feel bad about it, or we might have the time of our lives raining down vengeful judgment. Either way, we have to be willing to destroy because of the serious disadvantage we have in our efforts to create.

Because God—or something, maybe nothing?—beat us to the punch in creation, we would-be creators showed up when the world and everything in it were already here and acting pretty much predictably according to kind. So if we want to change things on the level of what they actually already are, then our creative work has to involve destruction—the reforming or deforming of what already is and what already works in keeping with its kind. In order to create the kind of world that welcomes us as rulers, we've got to go hellfire and brimstone on the structures, ideas, and people who defy our godding. It's for the greater good, though—the greater good being our godhood. Or rather, *my* godhood.

Thankfully, some ideas are beautiful and true forever. Word wars can't kill them. But debris from a devastating attack can bury a true and beautiful idea so deep that future generations might never experience it themselves. They may not know, except from stories old people tell, that buried in history beneath them is a once vital, beautiful part of life, something that they might have loved and without which they cannot truly understand who they are. Godding is neither just nor merciful, not even to children.

Beneath the ceiling of self, nothing is sacred except the self. Even when it comes to the most important relationships in the lives of the most vulnerable among us, godding wins out. There are no safe zones, no safe people, and no safe relationships. Beneath the ceiling, any word and any defined relationship it represents can be redefined, no matter how much it means to people, or to humanity itself.

There are many such relationship-bearing words that are marked for death by redefinition in our day, but I'll pick one example that's very personal. It's one of my favorite words in all the world: *Dad*.

Daddy Dearest

I will never forget seeing my fiancé walk down the aisle toward me during our wedding. Tears were streaming down her face—not the most affirming sight for a groom! But I felt fine when I learned why she was crying. Just a few minutes prior, her father was standing ready to walk her down the aisle. When she turned the corner from her dressing room and he saw her in her wedding dress, he got choked up. His eyes welled up, and she lost it.

My wife's dad (my kids call him "Papa") meant and still means the world to her. No one could replace him. But is her dad only irreplaceable because he was, and is, a really good dad? Is there anything inherently irreplaceable about dads, and therefore granddads, in children's lives? What does it even mean to be a dad? And who decides?

For most of human history, "dad" or whatever the equivalent in another language, has been a restrictive term. It couldn't stretch to fit just anyone. Yes, being a dad means much more than being a male who occupies an important place in the life of a child, but can it mean any less? Are fatherhood and motherhood merely social constructs, constantly subject to redefinition? If so, what do they actually mean? Beneath the ceiling, nothing. Nothing in any ultimate, true, fixed sense. So like I said, nothing.

Beneath the ceiling of self, no idea and no relationship is stable and fixed in meaning. And this is just a short step from meaninglessness.

But haven't we in our culture made "dad" meaningless anyway, by so many men's bad behavior in that category of life? That's more of a conversation stopper than it is a real argument against keeping "dad" a restrictive term. It's one of godding's favorite strategies in the word wars: cite the bad examples of a word/idea you want to change. That way, you show that the idea cannot be restricted to a certain kind of person, because look at how bad people of that kind mess it up! This maneuver is reinforced when we mention that other people can do for children what should have been done by the person who most naturally fits the word "dad."

Yes, when Dad is a deadbeat, it's good to be rid of him. And yes, other men can step in to help. A man might marry an abandoned mom and maybe, if—*and only if*—the child is okay with it, be called "Dad." And yes, there are homes without a dad in which children are genuinely loved and cared for. Thank God for these kinds of situations in which people step up as best they can to meet kids' needs as best they know how. But in all of these situations, the absence of the original dad is felt. At the very least, it creates questions in the heart of the child, questions that only cruelty would ignore as unimportant or dismiss as unenlightened.

Even if the child knows nothing about "Dad" except that he contributed to their existence, and even if that contribution took "Dad" less than a minute and he's never had more than a second's worth of serious thought about his kid, answering questions about who he is, or was, is intensely important to the child.

Such questions do not come softly and sit politely in our minds. They strike our souls like a hammer on a gong, shimmering within us and ringing with relentless, propulsive reverb in every part of our thinking and feeling. These questions have to do with who we are, why we are, and how we came to be. Our self-understanding is missing so much without these answers. Our self-development is driven by our relationship, or lack thereof, to the people who gave us our self.

At the same detention home where I met the Satanist, I had the privilege of interacting every week with young men and women from horrific home situations. Usually, Mom was still in their lives, doing her dead-level best to provide for and protect them with no help from Dad, whether or not he could be identified and chased down legally. The only thing some of the incarcerated youth knew about Dad was that he wasn't there for them. The only lesson they learned from Dad was not to let yourself care about people. You have to keep your heart closed to ideas and relationships that certain privileged people have, but that have been denied to you.

For others, Dad was someone who showed up once a month, collected a check, drank himself into a rage, and beat the living stuff out of Mom. And for some, Dad would have been around if he could, but he was also incarcerated, fighting a false conviction so he could get home to the family who needed him so badly. Whether the word "dad" froze their hearts, fired them up, or melted them, the idea always haunted.

Many of the youth could list the countless ways their fathers had failed them. But the abuse of an idea does not nullify the idea. Having no good dad did not make these young people want to redefine "dad"; if anything, it revealed how desperately they, and their moms, wanted a man who'd live up to the word. "Dad" represented a relationship so vital that the mere mention of the word sliced into their souls, cutting through a hard scar to reveal a raw wound in their essential personhood.

A wonderful woman who ministered to them, affectionately dubbed "Mother Hill," acknowledged the soul-shredding circumstances that brought many of these young men and women into existence. She would often say when speaking to them, "God had to get you here somehow."[16] By putting it this way, she acknowledged that something vital, often someone vital, was missing from their lives. She acknowledged their pain, but she also affirmed their purpose. Their existence, no matter how illegitimate the actions of those who gave them life, was sacred; their lives were a matter of divine appointment. But that truth didn't take the pain away, and she never pretended that it could.

A dad's absence in the life of a child is a vacancy not even the most heroic of mothers can fill, not because of a lack of sacrificial love, but because "father" is as closed a concept as "mother." Mother Hill knew that she was not these young people's real mom. The title honored her by recognizing that her actions came so beautifully close to a concept she couldn't personify in their lives without legally adopting them. She never tried to replace irreplaceable people in their lives, only to love as best she could from her position among them. Motherhood and fatherhood are defined relationships, irreplaceable relationships. But beneath the ceiling of self, that won't stop us from trying.

To free our thinking from unsophisticated and often religiously oriented ideas about parentage, ideas that repress adults and might make children think they're missing something if they don't have a "mom" and "dad" in the archaic sense, we first try to extend the reach of the words "mother" and "father." We can teach kids and culture as a whole that there's really no reason to be sad when children lack "mom" or "dad" in the old, dated sense of the terms. Thus, Elton John's partner had himself listed as "mother" to the child he and Elton adopted.[17] But as we saw with the phrase "black person," to stretch "dad" or "mom" to such proportions is to strain them to the point of rupture, to move them that much closer to meaninglessness. Hardcore godding sees this and says we should all save ourselves time and tears and just get rid of words like "mom" and "dad" altogether. In certain parts of the enlightened West, we're doing just that.

Oh, Canada

These topics are so personal to so many, and I truly want to be so careful. If possible, let's all take a step back to see what's speeding toward status quo in our culture's understanding of kids and family and ask a very simple question based on what we all say we want: is this really what's best for the kids?

Canada tends to be more cutting edge than America when it comes to the process of self and social redefinition. With a swift savagery that would make a ninja blush, lawmakers are slashing ties between time-honored words and essential societal relationships. One example comes from the province of Ontario (Canada's most populous province): Legislation called Bill 28 "removed the words 'mother' and 'father' from Ontario law, while allowing people to become parents through 'pre-conception parentage agreements' with up to four unrelated and unmarried adults."[18] Bill 28 was passed into law within two months, with no opposition.

By removing the words "mother" and "father" from legal definitions of parenting, Canadian officials are subjecting the relationships these words represent to all kinds of change. They're removing legal significance from motherhood and fatherhood, and this can't help but damage the personal significance of such relationships in society. If legal language becomes common language, reflecting and encouraging increasingly common practice, politicians have set the cultural stage for more and more kids to never know what it means to have a mom or dad, and for kids who do know to never be able to say "mom" or "dad" in any way meaningful beyond their personal experience.

Children won't realize until later in life what's been taken from them, the parts of their souls and self-understanding to which they were forbidden access. They will never discover aspects of themselves that only a dad could bring out and strengthen in his unique way, or that only a mom could call forth and cultivate in hers.

We've gone way beyond the good and necessary effort to help children not feel badly about themselves because they don't have both a mom and dad in the home. That's not their fault and they should never feel that it is, though some of them can't help but take on that guilt anyway. It's one thing, and a good thing, to tell a child that he or she will ultimately be okay in the absence of Mom or Dad. It's another thing, a dishonest thing, to tell that child that it's okay. It's not. It hurts, and it should.

Some hurts cannot be healed by any natural means; to disregard that is to dishonor the victim and to deny the importance of that for which her heart aches. Though our intentions may be kind in wanting to prevent kids' pain, pain is a signal that things are not as they should be. To no longer feel anything is not to be healthier; it's to be dead.

But, we think, if you remove the object of craving—in this case, an allegedly archaic, arbitrary, unnecessary aspect of parenthood—you'll remove the craving itself, right? Yes, but it's like trying to end hunger by eliminating food. Eventually, it will work. But what will be left of us when it does?

It seems that we're doing our best to bury concepts represented in the words like "mom" and "dad" so that more and more, generation by generation, the natural hunger within us for those relationships dies. In our godding, we're declaring vital aspects of human life—realities rooted not in arbitrary social custom, but tethered to why and how we exist—to be not that big of a deal.

Some would reply: "What or who gives you the right to define family and therefore what makes for a healthy one?" To which I'd reply, sincerely, "Thank you for asking that question." It's exactly the right question, and we don't ask it enough in the cultural war of words. These issues really do boil down to questions of authority, of who in life gets to be God.

If we claim the godlike authority to definitively answer such questions, we have to ask a painful follow-up: What, or who, are we willing to sacrifice in the name of our divine decrees and definitions? Isn't it so like false gods to demand the sacrifice of children?[19]

The Forever Family

"Dad" is a concept that runs deep in humanity and is deeply important to Scripture. God has chosen to reveal himself as "Father," *av* in Hebrew, *abba* in the Greekified Hebrew—especially affectionate terms. As we'll see in chapter 7, "father" was one of the most meaningful words in the life of Jesus, and the idea reaches back before his life in this world, before all created life and before time itself. The idea of "dad" goes way, way back.

We might say—well, God isn't a male so true fatherhood must not be restricted to humans who are. But that gets things backwards.

God accommodates our limited capacity for understanding as he reveals himself. Genesis 1 makes it clear that both male and female humans bear God's image, essentially and equally; but they express it differently, in ways unique to God's design in making different sexes. The redefinition of these categories of personhood means the undoing of the reason God chose them as categories by which he helps us to understand him. All of the analogies break down—there are obvious ways in which God as Father does not correspond to men as dads. But we have to honor the reason God chose the term to begin with. We must not redefine the term and then apply our new understanding to what God wanted to reveal of himself by the old. If we take this approach, then ultimately we define God and make the concept "God" meaningless. And that, of course, is exactly what we're after in our godding. It's the ultimate will to power. Kant's ceiling made this unreasonable power grab quite logical.

"It sounds questionable, but it is in no way reprehensible to say that everyone makes his own God."[20] From Kant, this is simply a statement of how life is. We make our own God in the sense that each of us has a system of perceptions about God that is not identical to anyone else's system.[21] And true, we cannot know apart from our perceptions, but it does not follow that our perceptions cannot touch truth, or, more to the point of what the Bible says and is: it does not follow that truth cannot touch us, and teach us. Our perceptions are not the prisons we pretend them to be as we seek freedom from God's word.

"Everyone makes his own God" is just one escalator step toward "everyone *is* his own God." In our day, we're sprinting down the escalator in the direction of our deity, with the ultimate goal of recreating the categories God created for us before we killed him. Categories like "dad" are the cages in which he's forced us to live for far too long. It's time for humanity to break free! And we in the West will show the world how it's done.

You would think that because "dad" is not a concept we came up with in the West, that we'd be modest about claiming authority over the term. But we're still high on Enlightenment pride and all the culturalism and racism that came with. Typical of the West's exalted view of itself, we've decided in our godding's missionary zeal to redefine family relationships for the rest of the world, to proclaim throughout the earth that "dad" isn't that big of a deal to children, societies, and civilizations. And "dad" isn't the only term we in the West think the world should forget.

In our quest to upgrade outdated words and delete disobedient ones from our cultural vocabulary (and the rest of the world's), we've sought to be rid of masculine and feminine pronouns, too. What are "he" and "she" but cagey social constructs, anyway?[22] Some of this effort comes from the good and right desire to destigmatize gender dysphoria, to enfold rather than ostracize people whose feelings and/or physical makeup do not match the category assigned to them at birth, or who don't fit easily and obviously into either of the binary sex categories. But destroying the concepts of masculine and feminine is another example of the "let's end hunger by eliminating food" approach.

The fact that God created humans male and female in no way whatsoever implies that issues of gender dysphoria or dysplasia make someone less human. God forbid! It simply means that these categories of human personhood are meaningful, and therefore so are the complexities that can arise within them. But beneath the ceiling of self, these variances are every bit as meaningless as the categories in which they don't easily fit. Resorting to nothingness, nihilism, is not a good way to help people belong. Why battle a debilitating sense of nothingness with more nothingness?[23] But we're going that way anyway. It's godding's only option.

We're trying to systematically undo everything God spoke into reality as recorded in the first chapters of his book, to alter creation's fundamental categories and label our work accordingly. But no matter what we name something, we can't create categories within humanity and the relationships appropriate to humans like God can. We can only unmake those things.

In the name of liberation, of the reclamation of our freedom from religion and other oppressive powers, we're stripping ourselves of vital aspects of our humanity, severing connections that run as deep as the reason and means of our existence. God created out of nothing, but our attempts to create can only result in nothingness.

We won't see that; we won't say that. It's all for our good, we convince ourselves, and for the good of our children! We want to make sure that our kids can experience fuller versions of the freedom for which we've godded so hard—the freedom to be and do anything they want to. And so earlier and earlier in their lives, we're forcing upon them the kinds of conversations and considerations many of us adults aren't ready for.

In the name of freeing children from repressive cultural archetypes, of establishing early their godlike right to self-define,[24] we're exposing them to ideas and issues that even the most mature adults haven't come close to figuring out—especially in the area of sexuality.

Little gods have so much to learn!

Puppy Power

When one of my boys was four, he told me something heavy upon his heart, a truth that burned within his young soul and demanded action. He just *had* to watch *Paw Patrol*.

This cartoon is named for its titular search-and-rescue squad, a group of puppies highly skilled in various valuable trades and led by their fearless human friend Ryder. Usually, when an emergency arises, Ryder will bark out orders (not literally) to his eager crew, calling upon the right canine for whatever the situation requires. Apparently, my boy took Ryder's orders personally. He knew he couldn't jump into the screen to join the rescue effort, but he figured the least he could do was watch to make sure it happened. My four-year-old put two and two together: If he doesn't tune in, people will die! With utter, adorable sincerity, my boy said to me, "Paw Patrol *needs* me."

These are cute delusions that for the most part parents try to correct gently, eventually. In our culture, the earlier the better. Kids face no shortage of people on screens trying to make them feel needed for all the horrifyingly wrong reasons. Sometimes, though, the people most responsible to protect kids by keeping them grounded in reality expose them to very adult issues that can't help but send their young souls spinning into all kinds of dangerous fantasies.

As we'll explore in chapter 9, almost everything these days is interpreted through the lens of sexuality, even one's essential humanity and personhood. So we think we spy within kids' natural curiosity and desire to touch everything their burgeoning sexual desires and patterns of sexual preference.[25] Whether by people or cartoon characters on the screens or by in-person authority figures in the classroom, kids are introduced to and immersed in matters of sex and sexuality at earlier and earlier ages. Kids can't get away from it all because we adults won't let them.

We encourage, or at least allow, young kids to listen to sexually explicit songs that glorify a predatory approach to sexual relations (often ignoring the lyrics ourselves). Clothing designers seem to want five-year-olds to dress tight, skimpy, and suggestive like they assume much older kids and adults want to. Children in our culture have no idea what's being done to them.

Oh, we say that we're not trying to force anything upon the kids. We just want to give them options, freedom to follow their inner feelings into outward behavior and life modifications. The earlier in their lives we can free them, the more time they'll get to live their lives as free people, right? So we offer ever-increasing personal identity options to kids at younger and younger ages, creating within their impressionable souls the thoughts and feelings that are interpreted by adults as demonstrations of the child's true identity—just more of the confirmation bias inherent in godding.

Why, oh why, do we forget just how impressionable kids are, how vulnerable to even the most outlandish ideas, and therefore how powerful our words are to them? It's a tyranny to teach them that they must explore and maybe even follow through on every impulse they have, especially sexually, lest they deny their true selves. In such a sexually suggestive culture, we need to guard the hearts of people so susceptible to the power of suggestion.

If I told my four-year-old that yes, unless he watched *Paw Patrol*, people would die, he'd believe me. If I told him that I used to play for the Red Sox, God bless him, he'd believe me! And if I told him that he might actually *be* a puppy, and that this would explain why he loves to act like one, why wouldn't he believe me? The mere suggestion would cause him to do some serious soul-searching.

I don't in any way mean to minimize or trivialize the real-life struggles for self-understanding we endure in a day of ever-multiplying options for self-identification. I'm just looking for an angle into conversations in which dissent to pop culture dogma is seldom allowed (and therefore seldom heard and considered), or in which dissent is expressed in threatening ways to questioning hearts. Christians have much repenting to do on that point. We'll get to that in chapter 9. At the very least, conversations so important and life-altering should be much more fully informed and much less rushed than they typically are.

You might object that issues of self-identification are often rooted in biology, whereas my examples only apply to normal cute kid stuff. But the objection doesn't quite hold. Life-altering decisions of identity can be made and surgically carried out without any reference whatsoever to biology, including neurology. Sometimes that's the point.

Besides, why, beneath the ceiling of self, is believing that I'm a dog so far-fetched? We're all variously evolved animals, right? And some people have decided that they prefer life as an animal, even a mythical beast, and have taken surgical steps to live this way. In our godding, scientific knowledge is only relevant when it serves our cause. Hardcore godding ignores all stats and studies that contradict our divine decrees. Because no matter what science or history or

God himself says, the real root issue remains: If I feel like it, maybe I *am* it. And even if I don't feel like it, if I want it, I should have it. A god can look, feel, and act like anything it damn well wants to.

In our godding, we feel we have to tell the little gods of all that they can be, and all that they might be without realizing it. From our standpoint and according to the terms of our enlightened deity, we've got to make sure that they are in absolute control of their lives—even if it kills them.

Pride in the Name of Love

There's nothing like godding to make us blind to how we're hurting each other, and to encourage us to ignore or rationalize godding-induced injuries as we start to see them. In 2008 it was announced that

> ...Ontario would publicly fund sex-change surgeries—elective procedures that do not improve mental or physical health outcomes for persons who experience gender identity disorder. Similarly, Ontario pays for puberty-blocking drugs and cross-hormone treatments, which can cause lifelong sterility. Such treatments can cost thousands of dollars per person per year. Yet studies indicate that chemical and surgical impersonation of the opposite sex is associated with negative health outcomes and high suicide rates, even in parts of the world that are considered the most "trans affirming."
>
> Paul McHugh, Professor of Psychiatry at Johns Hopkins Medical School and former psychiatrist in chief at Johns Hopkins Hospital says, "The idea that one's sex is a feeling, not a fact, has permeated our culture and is leaving casualties in its wake. The most thorough follow-up of sex-reassigned people—extending over thirty years and conducted in Sweden, where the culture is strongly supportive of the transgendered—documents their lifelong mental unrest. Ten to fifteen years after surgical reassignment, the suicide rate of those who had undergone sex-reassignment surgery rose to twenty times that of comparable peers"....
>
> Not content to fund "sex reassignment" surgery and cross-hormone injections, MPPs [members

of Canadian Parliament] voted unanimously in 2015 to prohibit alternative treatment methods for gender identity disorder. Bill 77 went from second reading to Royal Assent *in only three months*."

We know godding's got us when we demonize and when powerful thieves outlaw other options that might benefit some, if not many, sufferers.[26]

> These political power moves dictate
> medical policy in the name of political correctness, removing good options for parents and children. One such option was [put forward by] renowned child psychiatrists like Dr. Kenneth Zucker and Dr. Susan Bradley, who believe that encouraging children to be comfortable with their birth sex helps prevent long-term psychopathological problems. Dr. Zucker was removed from his Toronto clinic following Bill 77. More than 500 researchers and clinicians signed a petition in support of him. No matter.[27]

Remember, beneath the ceiling of self, truth doesn't matter. Words can't express it, so we don't have to listen to anything anyone says, no matter how much they know what they're talking about. It's not about truth; it's about power—and it's for the children! So if we love our kiddos, we should let them follow their hearts wherever they might lead, right?

Protective parental instincts kick in: "Well, not *wherever* their hearts may lead them." But why not? "We don't want them to get hurt." Well, who defines hurt? What if our child *wants* to get hurt? What if our child wants to die?[28]

Given our godding, and the fierce, reckless speed at which we're carrying it out among kids at earlier and earlier ages, we should expect that this is exactly what more and more of them will ask for—and not necessarily because they're in pain (see chapter 8 on this). Dying will just be a thing to do, and their right, because they are gods. And as a culture of youth empowerment, we've got to be all about letting youth chart the course for the future, right? How convenient! When we're the ones who filled their hearts and minds with our godding propaganda to begin with. Let them be free! Let them speak! Let them die. Most importantly, let them vote for us.

We adults are, both in our lack of knowledge and our stubbornness, very childish in these matters. Like children, we cover our ears and sometimes we will not stop screaming until we get our way. We don't care what studies will eventually reveal, or what they reveal now. We're continuing to teach kids that they can be anything, which, if true, means that they are nothing.

If there is nothing true and real beyond the self, it means that there is no true and real self to discover, nor even one to be invented. Unlike God, we can't make nothing into something, much less someone! In the end, and long before we get there, godding bleeds the self of meaning, truth, and power, precisely because it ascribes all meaning, truth, and power to the self.

(Not) Me, (Not) Myself, and (Not) I

Beneath the ceiling, our personal truth traps us within a world of our own making, a world that neither we nor anyone else understands, a world of fiction in constant flux. Pop culture observers are noting what's become the essential irony of our time: social media has revealed, and in some ways reinforced, just how alone we feel in life.

Philosophers were talking decades ago about the increasingly isolated self, "the lonely self," fading further away from "the disappearing other."[29] The greater our godhood, the greater the distance we create between us and others.

Sure, in this psychotically fast-paced culture of countless screens and unceasing sounds, it can be good to get away from it all. As one of my favorite fiction writers says through one of his characters, "Sometimes solitude is an unspeakable joy."[30] But beneath the ceiling of self, there's really no way to get away for some alone time. And that's because down here, it's always alone time. What godding gives us isn't solitude; it's solitary confinement.

Down here, we're walled off from reality. Truth floats around our words, disconnected and unreachable. And it's not just that we can't communicate *the* truth to one another. If the ceiling is real, we can't even communicate *our* truth to one another. If even God can't speak to people, why would we expect to do any better?

Every time we express ourselves—through words, art, even a facial expression—we're sending our personal truth on a suicide mission. It will never penetrate the other person's perception to "say" anything true. Our self-expression dies upon impact with the ceiling. The ceiling cannot exist above us without also existing all around us. Like a coffin.

The ceiling of self is meant to protect us from any truth higher than our own. But if all we have is our truth, *all we have is our truth.* To seek the freedom our godding offers is to be enslaved to its core principles. Belief in the ceiling of self entombs us beneath it.

And it gets worse.

The ceiling of self eventually suffocates our personal truth. If all we have is personal perception in our understanding of life, then all we have even of our own personal truth is merely our personal perception of it. This is the ceiling's most insidious irony. The ceiling of self isn't just set up beyond us and around us; it's set up within us. The ceiling cuts us off from ourselves.

Does this feel familiar? Sometimes, you don't even know if you really want what you want. You don't know if what you *feel* within is real, neither the feeling itself, nor the experience of it. The very idea of "you" drifts further and further away from you, fading further and further into the dark. You are beyond your understanding, beyond your reach. The ceiling promised you freedom to be yourself, but it's actually the ceiling that prevents you from knowing yourself.

Down here, we have no idea what a human being really is, and therefore of how much a human life is really worth. So we have no idea of who we really are as people, or of how much our lives are really worth. The God of the Bible says that we're his image-bearers, worth the life of his unique son to redeem us from our godding and bring us home to him, our truest father. But because God forbids godding, we're disposed to hate our first love. And that fundamental divide from the Creator separates us from the rest of creation, and the defining principles God built into it.

Godding dis-integrates us. Godding dislocates us from truth and distorts our perception of reality. It drags us away from God, others, the world, and ourselves. Godding is dehumanizing.

If we step out from beneath the ceiling of self and look carefully, we'll see signs all around us of our collective dehumanization and disintegration into nothingness. Naturally, the process of dehumanization is traceable along the lines of what distinguishes us as humans. We can see our demise in the development, or perhaps devolvement, of our way with words. "They that have despised the word of God, from them shall the word of man also be taken away."[31]

CUL8R

Diminishing language reveals diminishing humanity. It's no secret that rhetoric and writing are increasingly lost arts, but we're ready to abandon the use of words altogether. It's only logical: If we cannot reach others with our words, why speak or write to them? In fact, why use words at all when there's nothing they can really say? "We are probably witnessing the end of a cultural history dominated by book religions and word-makers."[32]

Have you ever seen a couple on a date, sitting at a table in a coffee shop, doing nothing but staring at and tapping their phones the whole time? On the bright side, maybe they're texting each other. One writes: ICU. The other: What? Need hospital? No, I C U. Oh, LOL. ICU2. Even when we're with someone we care about, we want to make as little eye contact and use as few words as possible to communicate. The screen is more vital to us than the living human being in front of us. "Athena," code name for a young lady with whom Dr. Jean Twenge discussed the social media habits of the "iGen," people born between 1995–2012, said, "I think we like our phones more than we like actual people."[33]

Terse words and digital communication in general have great benefits as "next best" personal interactions, but we seem to be texting our way toward a world in which we don't have to talk or even relate to one another at all. A reduced desire and a correspondingly reducing ability to communicate indicates a life going reclusive, shrinking into itself.

Our dying way with words is one crucial pain signal among many others we tend to ignore in our materially bountiful culture as we pursue deeply dehumanizing ways of life. Our increasing isolation and aloneness has us shaking, trembling together but cut off from one another. It may be our culture's death rattle before the oblivion that is the only possible outcome for a world of our making.

Thus did western man decide to abolish himself, creating his own boredom out of his own affluence, his own vulnerability out of his own strength, his own impotence out of his own erotomania, himself blowing the trumpet that brought the walls of his own city tumbling down and, having convinced himself that he was too numerous, labored with pill and scalpel and the syringe to make himself fewer, until at last, having educated himself into imbecility, and polluted and drugged himself into stupefaction, he heeled over…and became extinct.[34]

We're falling apart while speeding ahead, an already flammable vehicle shedding what safety features still work. We refuse to see it, but oh, can we ever feel that anxious unsettledness. It's all around us, and most disturbingly, it's deep within us. But we treat the distress signals as the disease itself, disregarding the system failures they're screaming about. Crouched into our Pinto, we're standing on the gas.

Bumpy Ride

Do you ever get a sense of motion sickness as you move through life? Not actual nausea—though that could come with—but an unshakable, unnerving sense of instability? Do you ever feel like "everything is too much"?[35] A constant bombardment of images and messages can certainly make us feel this way. But social media didn't cause the deep anxieties within and among us. A social media fast can cleanse and calm us, but it cannot cure our debilitating unease. Debilitation due to dis-integration is the eventual default mode of people and cultures living beneath the ceiling of self.[36]

For many of us, life is a constant, nervous trembling. Now that we've collectively turned a deaf ear to the divine speech that could calm it all down, it feels like life is always turned up too loud. At times, life's song might sound beautiful, but hearing it still hurts, especially if we really believe that "beauty" is just in the ear of the listener, that all of life's beauties are simply the sentimental perceptions of someone who might not even be real anyway, that someone being us. So it gets to the point where we feel that the only lasting reality and freedom life can offer us is death.

Life can feel this way whether or not we believe in the ceiling of self. It's the pulsing, pounding, pervasive vibe created by the cumulative mass of a culture that does. If someone's stereo is thumping with bass several cars over, you don't have to like the song to feel its concussive force, for your heart to buzz and your eyes to water. These days, anxiety is in the air. The collective anxiety of a culture can be breathed in and felt deeply even by those who conscientiously object to the culture's philosophical core and the anxiety-inducing principles and practices that rise from it.

It seems this is an unspoken, undiagnosed reason for the extra, otherwise unexplainable heaviness we feel in our souls these days in comparison to previous generations.[37] Given the dehumanizing, disintegrating conditions of life beneath the ceiling, it makes sense to feel so unsettled. It makes sense that we're simultaneously exhausted and buzzing with nervous energy. It makes sense that we're addicted to energy drinks! It's a hard time to have a soft heart. But that means it's also a time when such hearts can show us what our godding refuses to see.

We're so naturally reluctant to recognize our godding for what it is and does, much less to rebuke it as such. We bless the lie and curse its consequences. So we need sensitive hearts like yours to think deeply about what's happening—you already feel it deeply, perhaps in numbness—to understand its true nature and call shenanigans on the ceiling beneath which already hellish anxieties metastasize.

As much as life hurts sometimes, the greatest danger is that we would try to stop feeling altogether. When we've been hurt in the past, and when everything hurts in the present, it's so hard to believe that we can have and handle anything real, much less that any of it could help to heal us. We bring ourselves so close but we're afraid we're looking at reality through a glass, that to reach beyond ourselves is to shatter an invisible barrier and to bleed for the effort. But *this* is the lie: that we cannot touch what is real, that we cannot speak of it, or learn of it by way of words, by way of a book. The lie's consequences are a life of solitude without peace, community without connectedness,[38] movement without progress, speed without stability, all spelled out in shrinking, self-worshiping words that can't actually say anything. The Bible recognizes and rebukes the lie, and calls us to freedom from the dehumanizing world godding creates.

We can have real relationships, built on trust, based in truth. We can even remain intact when those relationships get troubled or collapse altogether. It really is possible to know and face life as it is, others as they are, and ourselves as we are. It's all possible because of someone Scripture tells us about, someone who holds all of life together, who doesn't change, who is good, and who lives forever. Letting us know once again how seriously God takes language, the Bible calls this someone "the Word."

A Joy Forever

Life's loneliness and painful instabilities, as well as its aching joys we wish would last forever, all beg us to listen to the deep, God-given, eternity-shaped stirrings within us, signals whose significance thieves are ever trying to downplay. "Nothing to see here! Just chemically induced sentimentality, the natural by-product of biological machines in motion. Let's move along now toward more enlightened chemical reactions." Forget them. Look anyway.

We're not meant to get past these stirrings, no matter how philosophically enlightened and scientifically sophisticated we fancy ourselves. One scientist wonders, as he looks back on years of dramatic advances in the study of the human brain, "why the 'Decade of the Brain' should have fallen so far short of explaining the mind."[39] The dogma that we are naught but biological machines appeals to our godding, but our basic composition as human beings says it's bullgeschichte. We humans were built to love life and to last forever.

Ecclesiastes tells us in 3:11 that God has set eternity in our hearts, and that he's made everything beautiful in its time. Not just efficient—but beautiful. And there's beauty *in* the efficiency! It's where "ought to be" meets "is." It doesn't just work; it works as it should, mature within its God-given meaning, fulfilling in its appointed time its purpose and design. It's a Pinto engineered not to explode, a computer that doesn't crash That's gorgeous! The aeronautical engineer who really loves her work remains awed that following certain mathematical principles with certain manufactured materials can literally make us fly. We discovered these principles; we didn't create them. We unwrapped them like gifts. Scripture lets us know that they come from a very personal God who wants his favorite creations to enjoy forever the beautiful world he created.

The apostle John starts his gospel where Genesis starts, and with the same words: "In the beginning." But John lets us look behind the scenes and shows us someone called "the Word" who was *with* God in the beginning. That the Word was there in the beginning means that the Word is eternal; that the Word was "with God" means more than we might think.

John tells us that it's through the Word that God created all things, which means that everything in the whole wide universe owes its existence and finds its essential significance, its form and function, its beauty and being, in relation to the Word. And that means us, which means that means you. And the Word is not some impersonal force. "With God" here is more closely translated "toward God," facing God, which throughout the Bible indicates familiarity and good relations. It's the language of personal love and corporate peace; it's God's own language of holy, holistic blessing (Numbers 6:24).[40] Through the Word, you are vitally and personally connected to everyone and everything else God made.

That the universe ever feels impersonal to you is one of life's most horrific ironies, evidence of the crime committed at humanity's beginning, which we'll explore more fully later. In life and in the world, you belong. As an image-bearer, you have a privileged position in it all. Our capacity for language tells this truth powerfully.

"Language is the major vehicle of human communication. Communication is the sharing of experience. If language is fundamental to human existence, it follows that the human sphere, the field of the personal, cannot be understood through organic categories, in functional or evolutionary terms. It means, in other words, that men are not organisms. *The exploration of the structure of this personal world, and the discovery of the categories through which it may be coherently conceived is the task set for philosophy in our time...*"[41] This task is to explore the implications of John's more detailed telling of what Scripture says with its very first words.

So why does John choose "Word" to designate this eternal, beloved, personalizing, unifying person through whom God created all things? Because, back to how we began this chapter, words are revealers, means of connection and communication. John tells us that the Word has revealed God (verse 18).

The Word expresses the abundance of God's heart, especially his love for his image-bearers and the world he made. God loved the world and us so much that he sent the Word into the world as one of us, in order to save us. Verse 14: "The Word became flesh and dwelt among us." That's Jesus.

"In the beginning was the Word, and the Word was with God…" and then John writes possibly the most significant clause ever penned: "and the Word was God." Yes, John absolutely means that about Jesus. He makes sure we know he means it.

Like the rest of the New Testament, John's gospel was written in Greek. In Greek, you can move words around for the sake of emphasis. So John brings "God" up to the front of the sentence to make his point in the strongest, clearest possible terms. We ought to read it like, "…and the Word was *God*!!!"

If this is at all confusing, thank you for paying attention! John's confounding words are a window into the Bible's teaching that the one true God exists as a trinity—Father, Son, and Holy Spirit. As we'll see next chapter, that inscrutable truth has some major explaining power in life. For now, we can focus on another of Scripture's mysterious but clearly taught truths: the Word, Jesus, is fully God and fully human.

As we'll see in chapters 7 and 8, Jesus completed the work God the Father gave him to do. Jesus earned as man what he already owned as God: the world and everything in it (Psalms 2, 24, Matthew 28:18–20). So now, Jesus represents us to God and God to us; he reconciles us to God and reconnects us to one another, the world, and ourselves. This is what the gospel offers us. "Gospel" means "good news," but our godding doesn't take it as such.

Bigger Than Jesus?

In our godding, we're aghast that God would give all power and authority in creation to a human being who is not us. Our sometimes unrecognized resentment toward the Word made flesh is revealed in the Jesus-like things we think and say about ourselves. In our godding, we say "I am the truth" (John 14:6). And when we claim the right of self-definition, we're essentially saying of ourselves what only God can say of himself: "I am that I am."

This sentence translates God's chosen name for himself, which indicated, among other things, his self-existence, and therefore his right to self-define. It's also the name by which he revealed himself as his people's Savior (Exodus 3:14). Jesus not only spoke this name out loud—which in that day was blasphemy and merited death—but he, a true human being, applied it to himself. We know he knew the significance of those words, and that his enemies did, too, because when he spoke it in reference to himself, they tried to kill him (John 8:58–9).

Descartes's "I think, therefore I am" should have been more informed by God's declaration "I am that I am." Unless God is, we are not. We want to self-define, but self-definition can only come from self-existence. We do not exist in and of ourselves, so someone else has a definitional say in what and who we actually are. That's what it is to be created. Them's the breaks.

Scripture calls us from page one to recognize our creaturely dependence, ultimately upon God, and to find our true significance in him. We belong to God; by embracing this through the word, we'll find our belonging in the world. As we'll see more fully as we go, we embrace our true identity by trusting God's words. As Jesus once said in a prayer, "Your word is truth" (John 17:17).

Jesus's way with God's words set him apart as more than a prophet and more than a mere man. All the prophets before Jesus made it absolutely clear that they were speaking God's words, not their own. It was always, "Thus says the Lord" (and sometimes implicitly, "Don't blame *me*!"). But when Jesus spoke God's word, it wasn't just, "Thus says the Lord"; it was "I say to you" (Matthew 5–7).[42] Jesus taught as one with divine authority. He declared God's word as his own to interpret, preach, and apply. That just wasn't done! But Jesus could back it up. The Word was with God and it was obvious that God was with Jesus (John 3:2).

Jesus was once out on the sea with his disciples, and he was also out in terms of consciousness (Luke 8:22 and following). A true and tired human being, Jesus was profoundly asleep in the back of the boat, even as a monstrous storm swept up and put the world on spin cycle. His disciples, despite being seasoned fishermen, were terrified. They woke him, accusing him of not caring that they were dying. (We tend to do that to God.) Jesus went to the front of the boat, and told the storm to be still. And it did. The winds ceased and the sea became like glass. And that, even more than the storm, really freaked the disciples out. "What kind of man is this, that even the winds and the waves obey him?" Word.

Notice that Jesus chose to calm the storm by speaking. God created the world by speaking, so he can calm the world the same way. What's true for the world itself is true for God's favorite creations: it's only by God's words that we can be at peace.

Jesus said that all other human beings were guilty of godding, even the religious authorities (!), and that they needed to turn away from their sin and turn to God, and that to get to God they had to go through him (John 14:6). As Jesus made these claims increasingly clear and backed them up with his actions,[43] his enemies' anger mutated from irritation to hate to homicidal rage to malicious insanity.

When Jesus raised someone to life (John 11), his enemies decided to put Jesus to death. Good thinking! But such is the insanity of godding. It can witness the miracle of life but only see a threat to political power. It sees supernatural might and decides to flex on it.[44] We're so committed to our godding that, even if we saw an indisputable miracle happen right in front of us in the name of Jesus, it wouldn't convince us to worship the true and living God.[45]

One popular way to disregard what Jesus said about himself is to deny the possibility of the miraculous at the outset of any study of Jesus's life. C. S. Lewis writes: "Whatever experiences we may have, we shall not regard them as miraculous if we already hold a philosophy which excludes the supernatural....if the modern materialist saw with his own eyes the heavens rolled up and... had the sensation of being himself hurled into the Lake of Fire, he would continue forever, in that lake itself, to regard his experience as an illusion and to find the explanation of it in psycho-analysis, or cerebral pathology."[46]

We're way too stubborn to be convinced of the truth by a spectacular supernatural verification. Something transformative needs to happen to us. We need to see the truth with eyes not blinded by godding. This vision comes by way of God's word. "In your light, we see light" (Psalm 36:9).

Scripture shows us life as it is, ourselves as we are and as we're meant to be. By looking in faith to God through Jesus, we mature within our God-given meaning and become our truest selves.

I know this is a huge and maybe even hurtful claim, and I'd never make it unless the Bible did, unless Jesus did. Here goes: unless you know him, you don't really know you.

To know God, we need to know the words that express his heart. Jesus says that these words are our life and sustenance (Matthew 4:4). Genesis 2:7 tells us that God breathed into man the breath of life, and Paul says that Scripture is the breath of God. That's not to push a thematic connection beyond its bounds, but God makes it clear in so many ways from so many angles that his words are vital to us. They form us, feed us, and as we'll see in coming chapters, they free us. One twentieth-century Christian martyr put it this way: "Only those who have been placed into the truth can understand themselves in truth."[47]

Augustine, one of Western history's most influential thinkers and writers, and a Christian, asked a profound question: "Who has the art and power to make himself?"[48] It's a rhetorical question that implies bad news for our godding.

Our godding removes our true significance from our sight and causes us to gaze instead, first in worship and then in horror, upon a fabricated self, ever diminishing and dying beneath the ceiling of self. Heirs of generations' worth of godding, we've never loved ourselves, or loathed ourselves, more than we do today.

In the light of the word, we need to take a good, hard, humble look at what our godding has done and is doing to us, to younger generations, and to the world. When we confess what we've become, we're ready to learn who we are.

A Smashing Good Time

The Bible shows us the path between narcissism and nothingness. As we start out in this world, we are by nature a bunch of Lokis.

Loki is my favorite character in Marvel's *Avenger* films. Brilliantly played by Tom Hiddleston, the demigod is entitled, sarcastic, and deeply resentful of any superior power. It's good to meet a kindred soul.

As we first meet him, Loki's angry at his god-father Odin and looking for a weak world to rule. So he comes to Earth. But the Avengers oppose him. In one of my favorite movie scenes in any movie ever, Loki tries to intimidate the Hulk—intimidate the

Hulk!—the ridiculously muscled result of gamma rays gone bad, whose calling card is his uncontrolled and uncontrollable rage. Loki prattles on with simpering indignation about how tired he is of opposition from beings so obviously inferior to him; he's grown impatient and he calls the Avengers, including the green beast of fury, to bow before him. "Enough of this. I am a *god!*"

Hulk's had enough. He grabs Loki by the ankles and makes him the hammer in an apocalyptic game of whack-a-mole. After smashing the god around the room, Hulk leaves him lying in one of the many new Loki-shaped indentations in the floor. Stunned, Loki stares vacantly upward, wide-eyed and wondering what the Hulk just happened to him. Having put Earth's would-be ruler in his place, the sated monster stalks away in dismissive disgust, saying with a snicker: "Puny god."

Sometimes it takes a powerful monster in our lives to remind us of what we're not. Life's unalterable tragedies declare immediately what our self-made traumas declare eventually: it is our deity that is fraudulent, not God's. Enlightenment pride tried to flex on life's horrors and got floored, not the least by the wars we made as we vied for divine supremacy in the world. Insufficiently humbled, we keep trying to be gods, but life's monsters keep winning and showing us what we're not.

"Puny god" is actually a great description of what we humans truly are. It rebukes our delusional pride but it's also a reminder of our real greatness. We are not God. He is the Creator and we are the creatures. He's infinite but we're finite; he's the perfection of goodness, truth and beauty—we're…well, not. But nor, as we've thought about, are we totally unlike him. The Word, who is both God and the most blessed human ever to live, the one who bears his image perfectly, teaches us how to flourish most fully as God's favorite creations. He does this through the written words he's given us.

Love Letters

Thieves in our day like to teach us that words can't really, truly communicate, that we can never break through one another's perceptions to achieve truly meaningful communication. (They use words to teach us this.) True, the work of words is always incomplete. But it's not always incompetent. It's a bad artist who blames a brush for a lousy painting, and it's a bad writer who blames words for failure to communicate. Blue duck shunning scampi synapse. See? Not the words' fault. And it just might be a thief who bewails the inability of words to communicate meaningfully, but who sells lots of books doing it.

Because of the living God and the word, words work. Right now, this very moment, through the medium of words, you and I are actually communicating. There is a bridge between our perceptions by which we have reached some mutual understanding; a relationship has formed. It's not perfect. But clearly, it's possible.

And there's more good news. If we can communicate, we can relate, which means that relationships are possible. The triune God is big on relationships. He wants his favorite creations to be more than mere allies; he wants us to be friends.

The Word is the bridge by which we can and do actually relate to one another, the connection between us. He is that which we have most deeply in common, the unspoken language written deep within. He is the constant in our conversations that keeps them from decaying into chaos. And to let us know that this is all true, he gave us a book.

There's something about a word being written and not just spoken. Writing seals into permanence statements that take only seconds to speak. Written words immortalize the message they carry, which is why it's such a fitting compliment to God's eternal, living word that it would be committed to writing.[49]

There's a note I have tucked into the little green Bible I almost always have with me. "Dad, I hope you have a good day at work. Love, Calvin." That note does not apply to any other human being on the planet, nor will it ever. These letters have stamped time, pressing into it something that goes beyond it, a relationship real and not subject to redefinition, one that will last no matter what happens to me or my boy. It's a relationship that reflects a preexistent reality applicable to people in every age and place, yet into which my boy and I step uniquely, claiming our special possession of that which is common to humanity. All of that and more, communicated through big, adorably crooked letters on a tattered page, written words that mean more to me than I could ever possibly say.

Last chapter we thought about Paul's description of Scripture as "God breathed." You'd think Paul was referring to spoken words, and many of the written words of the Bible started that way. But Scripture is, by definition, written. Paul is letting us know that the written word of God is every bit as much God's word as what God had spoken directly through the prophets of the past. Peter (2 Peter 1:19) thinks of Scripture as an even better and more reliable witness to Jesus than what he saw with his own eyes.[50] To say "it is written" when citing Scripture was to appeal to final, absolute authority, the authority of God himself. "These three words settled matters for Jesus and the apostles. If Scripture said it, then God said it."[51]

Jesus once made the same point by asking a religious group we'll think about later a strangely worded question. Referring to Exodus 3, Jesus asked, "Have you not *read* what God *said* to you…?" (Matthew 22:31). Jesus considered that written text to be God's own voice. *So according to Jesus, if you've read Scripture, God has spoken to you.*

Maybe your experience with the Bible has been anything but personal, or personal in a very bad and painful way. God's written words are so powerful and so personal that their abuse is devastating; there's no counting the number of people who've been abused in the name of Jesus and biblical faith. As I was writing this chapter in a coffee shop, a dear elderly woman asked me what I was doing. I told her that I was writing a book about the Bible, largely for people who've had no experience, or a very bad experience, with it. She responded immediately, "You can count me in that second category." She'd been reared in a repressive, psychologically abusive "Christian" background. We had a heartbreaking conversation. At one point I asked her, "Can you in your mind disassociate the things done to you in the name of Jesus and the Bible from Jesus and the Bible themselves?" She said, with sadness and resolution, "No."

One of my deepest hopes for this book is that it will help people do what she, at least so far, couldn't do: separate the soul-crushing behavior of some Christians and their fraudulent claims to know and teach the Bible, from the soul-freeing person of Jesus himself, and the life-giving words that all tell us of him.

This book is about approaching the Bible and understanding it on its own terms. Taking the Bible on its own terms begins by understanding that all of these Spirit-filled words are from the mouth of God and are written to tell us about his son, the Word.

This is what the Bible is: *God the Father authorized a biography of his Son, and he commissioned the Holy Spirit to write it.*

The first part, the Old Testament, tells us that Jesus is on his way; it prepares the people through whom he'd come, the Hebrew people, and all hearers and readers of the Hebrew Scriptures, for his arrival. The second part of the Bible, the New Testament, tells us, "He's here!" It tells us of his life's work in this world to save it, and that he's coming back.

The Bible's closing book chronicles a series of spectacular prophetic visions John sees of what has been, what is, and what will be. In Revelation 21, John sees that the risen Christ is presently working against the godding that unmakes us in order to make all things new, to bring all things to the fullness of what they really are and are meant to be. God wants us to know for sure that all of this is actually happening, that it will absolutely come to be. So an angel says to John in his vision, "*Write this down,* for these words are trustworthy and true" (verse 5).[52]

God's gone on record with all of this. He's put it in writing. He's given the life of his son to make it real. And that's the best way we know it's all true. We can trust his promises because he's given us his word.

6

The Bible Is the Story of Us

"We're not lovers,
We're just strangers
With the same damn hunger—
To be touched, to be loved, to feel anything at all."
—Halsey, "Strangers"[1]

"It is not good for man to be alone."
—Genesis 2:18

My generation doesn't have its great story yet." She sat in my office, a freshman in college and one of the brightest, most perceptive students I've ever had the privilege to teach. In fact, after she took my section of a particular class that fall semester, she ditched it so she could take the honors section in the spring, which I did not teach. As if having me as a teacher wasn't "honors" enough! Whatever.

In addition to being academically astute, she was kindheartedly sensitive, and riddled with anxiety. We often discussed our angst-ridden culture and its concussive effects on all of us, especially upon people already hardwired to have a soft heart, whose perception of the world's pains is heavy-laden with deep empathy. This young lady was (and is) such a person. In the midst of our many conversations, a theme developed. We somehow got to talking about stories, and how our day and age is lacking in great ones.

There are lots of popular stories in our day, and some really good ones among them. Dystopian stuff has been big for about ten years as of this writing, along with tales of gothic horror, neo-paganism and zombie apocalypses. Kind of lets us know how we're feeling about life these days. But what has there been lately about which many people could really geek out, and then do so again in twenty years when it is rereleased in whatever media form is trending then? What stands out as something that's not only well-executed and cleverly expressive of our day's dominant philosophies—such as *The Walking Dead* and *The Avengers* franchise—but something that, rising from them, also transcends them? Will the 2010s and '20s produce anything about which we can say, "Wow. This is genuinely great. This is truly creative. It's new and it's gonna last"?

Quality artistic output ebbs and flows within civilizations. But because all humans bear the image of God who created a beautiful world, artistic creativity will last as long as humanity. We humans *need* to process and express life artfully. God created through the word, so life consists of eternal principles at play in time, of humans and other creations bound together in advancing a living narrative. Story is built into our beings as image-bearers. Among God's creations, it is our unique privilege to recognize the storied structure of reality and to consciously, even joyously, participate in it. Image-bearers love to hear and tell stories, and we love those who do it artfully for us. But our deliberate detachment from our Creator, our effort to unmake the conditions and categories that God built into creation—it's all taken a severe toll on the beautifully human work of art. Being unmade is making us uncreative.

Writer's Block

It's hard for a culture to produce a truly great story if it believes that "greatness," like beauty, is just in the eye of the beholder—nothing real, nothing transcendent, nothing, well, great. Without a belief in the fundamental connectedness and coherence of all things, it's hard to write stories that make sense of life. Some stories try to tell us that there are no transcendent truths tying all of life's details together; but they are, in that very effort, trying to tell us "the truth" about life. Would randomness ever recognize itself as such and feel the need to explain itself?[2] And without a belief in knowable moral absolutes, it's hard—or at least hypocritical—to write stories that tell us how we should live.[3]

God built his moral character into his image-bearers, and even into creation itself. It's by connecting to God's character that life and human lives thrive. Psalm 89:2 sings, "Steadfast love will be built up forever; in the heavens you will establish your faithfulness." Creation comes with a way that things have to be done, in love and faithfulness to the truth, so that things, and people, don't disintegrate. Jesus, the word made flesh, is the way creation reconnects to God and reintegrates with itself. Truly great stories awaken our hearts to ache for the connectedness and completeness that only the word can provide.

Some stories incite that ache by making us laugh till it hurts. Good comedy is a gift from God. Typically, what makes us laugh is a carefully executed, slightly exaggerated expression of true-to-life scenarios. Something normal but just slightly off can be hilarious (or horrifying). The familiarity draws us in, but the view from another angle makes it compelling, showing us more than we've ever seen, and sometimes more than we want to see, of how humanity (dys)functions in life.[4]

Good stories help us understand and enjoy our humanness,[5] but story can also be used to degrade it. Lots of stories these days, especially in the comedy genre, contain lots of smut but precious little smarts. Any fool can make fun and reinforce base sentiments.[6] It takes an artist to make us think in new, bigger, and deeper ways about life, and an especially gifted artist to make us double over in smiling agony while we learn.

Good stories of all kinds open our hearts unthreateningly and give our souls some exercise, without our realizing that we're getting a good workout. But beneath the ceiling of self, we've got nowhere good to go with the strength we gain from art whose beauty, creativity, greatness, and truth defy the ceiling's principles and call our souls upward. The ceiling of self keeps us from stretching in our humanness, and this stunts our growth as storytellers.

Oh, the Humanity!

For stories to be more than mindless fun, and especially if they aspire to the level of great art, they need to have lots of what we often call "the human element"—even among aliens! Episodes 1–3 of Star Wars proved that, in storytelling, glossed-up sights and sounds are no substitutes for compelling characters, human or otherwise. Art nearly died with the advent of Jar Jar Binks. It was a close call, and this probably explains the vengeful glee with which Lego Star Wars and *The Simpsons* violently dispatch Binks in their use of Star Wars material.

The need for the human element spans the genres. Shoot-'em-ups aren't nearly as compelling when we don't care who's getting shot. Romantic comedies—well, some genres are irredeemable, so never mind. But if a film, maybe even a romantic comedy, is full of humanness, then two people sitting and talking in a non-computer-generated room can make for great cinema. Utterly non-human characters become compelling as filmmakers lead us in our very human desire to understand the strange creatures. *Arrival*, starring Amy Adams, is a brilliant example. See, I'm not a hardened cynic about contemporary culture! But I am a self-congratulatory one, because that exception in the world of pop art makes my point. What makes this story of alien invasion so compelling is its beautifully human heart.

Adams's character tries to build a linguistic and emotional bridge to aliens who've suddenly arrived all around Earth, and whose motives for doing so are unknown. It's all about the stuff God built into the human heart and experience: communication, contact with others, relationships across time and space, and the valuing and protection of human life and the world itself. The CGI is the most effective kind—it doesn't let you know it's there. *Arrival* is also a deep meditation on the fear of the unknown, on loss and our relationship to time. Whether or not it can be deemed a truly great film, it reaches high and with great integrity in that direction, calling the audience to come along and have their eyes and hearts opened to great human thoughts, themes, and struggles. That's hard to do in an age that defines greatness, truth, and beauty according to the individual, godding self. That definition kills creativity.

Here We Go Again

Without belief in timeless truth, it's hard to write compelling new fiction. Maybe this is part of why there are so many reboots in our day. It was wise of Spiderman to sling a web the Avengers' way, pulling himself up and away from forced reboots every time he managed a sequel on his own. Sadly, some reboots seem to be creative bankruptcy hiding behind nostalgia. When we're the standard, we run out of ideas. We can't top what we've already done, and we don't believe anymore in the fixed meaning of virtues that inspired us beyond ourselves back then. Sometimes we reboot to download contemporary moral values into tales of the past.

Every generation likes to update old tales. But when godding gets creative, storytelling looks upon the past not so much with an artist's eye for new possibilities, but with an editor's eye for correction—and, if necessary, deletion.

In our godding, we believe it's our divine prerogative to write a future fit for our redefined humanity. To do that, we need to rewrite, to unmake, the past. Like Kylo Ren in *The Last Jedi*, we believe that, to become what we're meant to be, we need to forget the past. And in some cases, we need to kill it.

Like forced programming updates from certain computer companies, our godding demands that classic stories be updated to ceiling-of-self specifications, whether those stories or their fans want it or not. Some rebooting efforts simply and kindly attempt to make the old stories we love a part of the new world we're trying to make. Usually, the characters just don't fit. In an artist's mind, that friction could spark a fascinating tale of time and culture clash. But that would require that we let the characters be themselves. And whether in real life or fictional stories, our godding doesn't like to live and let live.

When we (post)modernize and therefore rewrite beloved characters of past stories, we steal artistic capital from their original writers. Something essential gets lost, if not murdered, in translation. We force the gutted forms of richly human, transcendent characters to lurch about in our stories, awkwardly serving our preferred politics and sociology.[7]

In both Kevin Costner's and Russell Crowe's Robin Hood jaunts, Maid Marian is a precursor to Wonder Woman. She's a ninja[8] and a crusading soldier, respectively—contrary to more classic portrayals of the lady who steals the heart of the Prince of Thieves. But strangely, both of the Marian remakes are eventually saved by Robin. And Robin, at least the Russell Crowe version, is a man. So the story's internal integrity is shattered and the feminist point fails to be made anyway. A classic story suffers from clumsy attempts at politically expedient revisions that end up insulting the cause they're promoting.

No worries if a new story features Marian as the marauding heroine of the story, but that would require the integrity to admit that she's not really Maid Marian, but a new character we've created. And if so, cool! Wonder Woman is a great story in itself, and doesn't have to leech from, much less kill, other stories to be so. But in our godding, we can't leave well enough alone because we don't consider the past to have treated our modern priorities well enough.

Emma Watson felt the need to amp up the feminist street cred of Belle in *Beauty and the Beast*, as Belle and her father, a properly enlightened man better than his times, struggle against toxically masculine bigots. This might be overcritical, but it seems that when her Belle gazes kindheartedly upon the townsfolk of her ordinary, provincial life, there's an unintentional twinkle of condescension in her wistful eyes, as if she's pitying the poor dears who surround her, stuck as they are in their smallness and insignificance. Watson definitely wanted her Belle to ring—sorry—more true to contemporary feminist sensibilities. She thought progressivism was in the character's DNA.[9] Interesting idea. And it raises a crucial question not often heard in the sound and fury of radical efforts to reboot real life as well as fiction. What gives us the right to say what's truly "progressive" in our recasting, and sometimes redefining, of characters?

Who decides what proper femininity looks and sounds and thinks like? And aren't these forced anachronisms at least a little insulting to the characters (and their creators)? At what point do we disrespect the unique personality and even the personhood of the characters we try to recast in our image? If we want to preach (post)modern politics and its god, the tyrannous phantasm of the autonomous self, why not just write a new "tale as old as time"?

It can be thrilling to see a new actor take on an old role, but that role establishes boundaries beyond which the actor cannot roam without becoming another character altogether. For anything to remain what it is, its boundaries must be respected. But we're all about breaking boundaries, which ultimately leads to breaking ourselves and our stories down to the point where there's nothing true still standing, and nothing meaningful to say.

Intelligence, compassion, bravery, and lethality do not discriminate according to sex. That truth can be powerfully and honestly proclaimed in new, well-told stories as well as respectful, rather than reproachful, treatments of beloved, timeless tales of the past.

The Force Awakens—and even better, *Rogue One*—just told compelling stories having female leads without having to make a fuss about it. One film critic wrote that *Awakens* was "quietly making history."[10] Maybe in terms of American cinema that's true. The Hollywood industry is rarely as egalitarian, and hardly ever as feminist, as it commands its audience to be.[11] But when it comes to promoting powerful female leads, God's story beats any Hollywood script. The Bible's been cutting edge on that point for nearly two thousand years.

Lady Killers

Pop culture is presently focused from all angles on promoting feminism,[12] trying to write a proper future largely by understanding the past as "her story." The effort gains moral momentum from the rise of misogynists to high political power and their being outed in a film industry that's long been silent about their abusive behavior. So let's stick with the theme of femininity for a bit as we continue to think about art, stories, and humanness.

At the very beginning of human history, and on the very first page of Scripture, God stipulates the essential equality of men and women. As we've thought about, God made both male and female humans in his image. This means, to use the fancy philosophical term, that women are the "ontological" equals of men. The Bible provides the best and really the only true, consistent, and lasting basis for an understanding of humanity (anthropology) that honors females as they should be honored, respecting their differences from males but letting us know immediately that the differences between the sexes are not matters of essential worth, dignity, and value. Pretty good for a book often considered to be the misogynist's field guide to life.

Scripture tells of women as respected rulers of nations, as saviors and assassins, prophets and teachers,[13] and most significantly, of one particular woman as the mother of God.[14] God-incarnate's first relationship with mankind was with a woman. Mary carries God in her womb, holds God in her arms, and leads God by his hand. Her soul is pierced three decades later as she watches her divine son dying on the cross, fulfilling the purpose for which she brought him into the world.

Popular Christian commentary on current controversial topics can feel artificial, and thus awkward: "The Bible is totally relevant to today's culture. It has strong female characters, too!" I get it. But isn't the Bible's straightforward presentation of its understanding of humanity and its practical application to life more genuine than Hollywood's subtly condescending and ironically man-praising efforts?[15] Misogynist ignorance is better confronted by absolute truth than by contrived fiction.

Some of Christ's closest and most significant followers were women. John tells us that Jesus, who expresses God's heart perfectly, chose a woman named Mary as the first image-bearer to see and talk with him following his resurrection (John 20:11 and following). In fact, Scripture features the testimony of Mary and other women as part of its case that Jesus actually did rise from the dead. If the authors of the New Testament were lying about a living Jesus, they would *never* have included the testimony of women in their accounts. In those days, the words of women had no public credibility. Their testimony wasn't even admissible in court. Undaunted, the biblical authors defied convention and the principles of contemporary jurisprudence in their witness to the risen Christ. They kept these women's eyewitness accounts front and center, not to make a sociopolitical point so much as to just tell what happened, regardless of who will be offended at the message, or the messengers.

Although the gospel writers weren't trying to be social revolutionaries, their happily highlighting the significance of women as Jesus's disciples did make a revolutionary social statement. In a day of utter and sometimes brutal patriarchy, the Bible stands out as respecting, honoring, and featuring women in some of its pivotal passages. This is a window into how Scripture effects, and has effected, good social change in the story of humanity.

Scripture-based social change is not typically instantaneous, and biblical truth about humanness sometimes arises in the midst of, and its particular expression is colored by, cultural conditions of shocking misogyny and bigotry. As we saw with Paul's treatment of a runaway slave, God's liberating truth interacts with the cultures and time periods in which it was originally written in a way that is both sophisticatedly aware and sublimely subversive of their dominant dehumanizing elements. But wisely, it doesn't always incite immediate change.

When someone is weaned away from a powerful narcotic that's destroying him, the break from the substance can't be too quick or abrupt, or the traumatic transition itself could kill him. So, too, God through his word progressively and patiently leads his people, from Genesis to Revelation and throughout history, to freedom from the godding and the systems of godding that dehumanize his favorite creations.

Our godding encourages us not so much to explore our humanness, but to redefine its essential principles by defying God's definitions and prescribed boundaries for human identity and behavior. We invent categories of human personhood and therefore of community, elevating individual personal life preferences to the level of ontological personhood and creating social groups of people who feel similarly. Feelings become definitional of identity, so there can be as many identities as there are surging feelings within us. Of course, these identities are always subject to modification or change, because so are our feelings. But if every category of life is fluid, then it's all a wash.

Our efforts to explode allegedly cagey categories of humanness are leaving us with no solid materials to build a truthful anthropology. And that brings us back to our troubles as storytellers and would-be writers of the future. How can we fill our lives and stories with humanness, when we've made it our goal to make humanity meaningless?

You Can't Say That!

One of the reasons we love a good story, and art in general, is that it carries us beyond ourselves, allowing us the mercy of time outside our own heads. Art is all about what we could call "moreness." It gives voice to the internal scream gone silent beneath the ceiling of self, but which still rattles our bones, that we are more than biological machines. There is "moreness" to art because there is "moreness" to us! Art influences our perception of the world, and in doing so helps us understand that the world is more than our perception of it. That we recognize the "moreness" of the world means we have a special place within it.

Beneath the ceiling, we think we're trying hard to find ourselves and our place in life. But are we willing to deal with what honest investigation might discover? What if what we find denies our godhood and forces thoughts that make us stumble on the path of self-definition? What if a work of art—a song, a speech, a book, a painting—suggests truth we refuse to accept? We might not even deign to give it a look or a listen. We might start a public protest against it, calling it hateful and demanding its banishment from the public square. We don't want another challenge to our deity; we get enough of that from everyday life.

The less willing we are to reach beyond ourselves, to risk confronting truth that might change us in ways we don't want to be changed, the less creative we become. Not coincidentally, it's the kind of fear that religious fanatics are accused of mongering: we refuse to even hear an idea contrary to our dogmatic beliefs. Godding sees no truth higher than the self, so it becomes the ultimate enemy of uncomfortable, deeply provocative ideas. Godding silences the deep stirrings within us and stops our ears against any voice from beyond us. And that is so exactly the opposite of art!

Well, we say, art is about self-expression! It's beautiful when what it says is true to who you are. Yes, amen, and let's hear it for authenticity! But if self-expression were enough for truth and beauty, then every Facebook post would by definition be great literature.

The artist knows in her soul that "moreness" is what art is all about. Good artists know that, despite the demands of the ceiling of self, there are standards for art, rules for what counts as good. Some art deserves to be criticized for its unartfulness. Good art touches timeless truth, causes our souls to pause, to ponder, and to stretch and grow in our understanding of life—including our understanding of what and who we are.[16]

Art is inevitably, inextricably engaged in matters to which the ceiling of self forbids access. "For aesthetics, the chief question concerns in what sense art may be conceived to embody being, meaning, and truth. Defenders of the autonomy of art argue rightly that it should not be compelled to serve some extraneous moral, and certainly not political, end; its task is to serve reality as it distinctly perceives it. But that raises the question of reality…"[17] Which, beneath the ceiling of self, we cannot know.

Down here, our perception does not merely link us to reality; it is reality. So all art can be is relatively true, relatively beautiful. We create some good stuff, but we choke out its infinite capacity for "moreness." Down here, absolutes are unknowable; virtue is socially contrived; beauty is in the eye of the beholder. The principles of the ceiling of self comprise the perfect plot for the murder of the arts. They encourage the death of the humanities because they render humanity mechanistic and meaningless.

Filling our souls with lesser art beneath the ceiling of self is killing our craving for, and ability to produce, great works of art. As my student said, "My generation doesn't have its great story yet." Thankfully, she didn't stop there. "Well," she thought for a moment, "with the exception of Harry Potter." *Yes* and *amen*. Love me some HP![18]

A Good Boy and a Bad Man

Reading together through J. K. Rowling's Harry Potter series has blessed my family with some of our most treasured times.[19] In case you've not had the deep pleasure of reading these great works of fiction, I'll try to avoid spoilers.[20]

In the very first book, a major bad guy tells Harry what the biggest bad guy, Lord Voldemort, taught him. "A foolish young man I was then, full of ridiculous ideas about good and evil. Lord Voldemort showed me how wrong I was. There is no good and evil, there is only power, and those too weak to seek it."[21] Ha! Consider the source. And that, of course, is Rowling's point.

Evil considers itself to be in the right, and what makes right but might? But in her opinion (and Harry's), evil is wrong no matter how mighty it is.[22] Good exists and is measurable, definable, knowable, and worth fighting for, even if it costs us everything. Without this moral framework to ground these soaring stories, Rowling's inspired writing would fall far short of the heights it reaches, if not altogether flat.

What draws us in and keeps us turning the pages of these relatively new classics is the beautifully written human element:

authentically human people (and other sentient creatures!) moving a plot that doesn't just touch but seizes and stands upon transcendent moral truth in its explication of love versus hate, good versus evil, selfishness versus self-sacrifice, and friendship versus the forsaking of others. If none of that is real, if it's all just perception, would this fictional story hit so close to the heart and, in creating a magical world, feel so true to life?

And, we can't ignore the story's emotional substructure: as a very young boy, Harry is cruelly deprived of his mom and dad. If the principles of life beneath the ceiling of self are strictly adhered to, this most poignant pathos is rendered pathetic. Beneath the ceiling, the essential tragedy of Harry's loss is that it was neither Harry's nor his parents' choice to be torn apart from each other, not that it's in and of itself tragic to be without a mom or a dad. Thankfully, there's still good fiction like this to gently, perhaps even unintentionally, remind us of precious, humanizing truth.

By going all fanboy on Harry Potter, I am most emphatically *not* trying to hijack Harry in the way Christians sometimes seize upon popular art in order to politicize it, or worse, to Christianize it. An artist's use of themes that loom large in Scripture does not imply Christian intent, nor does it imply endorsement of a biblical worldview.[23] Christ-figures and themes deeply important to the ministry of Jesus abound in popular stories through history, but any progress along paths of Christian ideas stops dead as soon as we hit the central truth from which all truly Christian ideas come and to which they lead: Jesus is Lord.[24]

Harry Potter does mine explicitly Christian themes deeply,[25] especially in its final volume, which makes extensive use of Paul's statement about the future effects of Christ's resurrection from the dead, "The last enemy to be destroyed is death" (1 Corinthians 15:26). And while it's not for me to say what Rowling believes about the Bible and Christianity, she does a brilliant job of taking readers pretty far down the paths of Christian virtue, of values that make sense and can only be maintained based upon a biblical anthropology.[26]

As the series progresses and Rowling develops the character of Voldemort, we learn more of what she considers despicably evil. Voldemort is completely self-absorbed; he exists for his own glory and sees everyone else as merely means to that end. Even his most psychotically, sycophantically loyal servants are not allowed to get close to him. He mocks and publicly shames them, sometimes immediately following their most heartfelt expressions of praise. He believes friendship is foolish and beneath him. He's the perfect example of godding consistently lived out, seeking and exercising godlike power to make a world where his will is power and his word is law. And to make his god complex complete, he wants to live forever. He's more than willing to do whatever it takes to achieve immortality, even if it means murder, many times over.

Rowling presents murder not only as horrible, but as inhuman and self-destructive.

The irony of Voldemort's life is that his efforts at self-exaltation, though they gain him great power, essentially diminish him. What he gains toward immortality he loses in humanness. His self-centeredness, his deliberate isolation from others, and his insistence on his self-sufficiency are all seen, in significant agreement with the Bible, as essentially inhuman, even demonic. There's even a significant link between Voldemort and snakes!

Through all of its characters, human and non-human, magical and non-magical, and in the wildly imaginative world Rowling creates as the stage for her very human drama, the Harry Potter series makes great and good statements about what it is to be human. Harry Potter teaches us that an amoral world is a mask for a murderous one, that to be human is to pursue truth higher than the self, and if necessary for the sake of others, to pursue it at great personal cost. The story reminds us of the goodness of life without the ceiling of self.

The principles that Harry Potter champions are those written by God into creation's story. They're universally applicable and broadly applauded throughout the world, not because they're vague enough to fit everyone's way of life, but because they derive from a single source common to all of us.

This living being is "big" enough to be the one in whom we all "live and move and have our being" (Acts 17:28)—whether we recognize it or not—and yet of such specific character qualities that his code of ethics cannot be lived out among people for very long if they're disconnected from him. The Bible tells us that human history is the story of our forsaking our first love and of God stepping into history and human flesh to bring us back home.

The Story of Us

God's book refuses to be thought of as just a good story, or even the very best of stories and compilations. It claims to be *the* story, not only good, not only true-to-life, but morally and absolutely true. And this is why, unlike Islam, for instance, Christianity's holy book invites translation and is just as much God's word in Spanish, Dinka, Chinese, or English as it is in the original Hebrew (Old Testament) and Greek (New Testament). God wants people everywhere to know the story of life, who he really is, and who we really are as human beings.[27]

Ever since philosophers have been philosophizing, and every time we've wrestled with questions of how we as individuals fit into a world that's much larger than we are, we've been struggling to understand the relationship between the "one and the many." That relationship is at the bottom of every deep question of belonging and every surface level complaint that says, "This makes no sense!" We recoil in frustration when something in life just doesn't fit the story we think life should be telling. We humans are immersed in and sometimes overwhelmed by questions of relatedness because we bear the image of God, who tells us on page one of his book that he is *both* one and many. The one true God has always been a social being.

Although the details don't develop until later, the opening chapter of God's book gives us a serious teaser-trailer about the complex nature of his being. As we've thought about, John says that God reveals himself through the word. So God's creative speech recorded in Genesis 1 is his drawing back the blinds just a bit to give us an early glimpse of his son. In verse 2, we're told that the Spirit of God was "hovering" over the face of the waters. The Hebrew word translated "hovering" conjures the image of a mother eagle's protective, attentive posture over her brood.[28] So in the first three verses of the Bible, all three persons of the Trinity make their debut. It's a modest if not minimalist introduction to Jesus and the Spirit, but it sets the stage for dramatic details to come.

This explains what God means later in the chapter as his work of creation nears its summit. God says, "Let *us* make man in *our* image."[29] If there's only one God, who's the "us"?

Scripture ascribes truly creative power to God alone, not to angels or humans or anything else. Here, the one God refers to himself in the plural, and he keeps doing it throughout Scripture, advancing an idea only hinted at in Genesis 1. In Isaiah 6, God seeks a servant to spread his word and refers to himself in both the singular and the plural: "Whom shall I send, and who shall go for us?"[30] Isaiah responds, "Send me!" In Isaiah 61, we have the words of the Messiah, about seven centuries before he comes into the world (biblical prophecy is like that, especially in the Psalms), speaking about his ministry and the source of his power to accomplish it. "The Spirit of the Lord God is upon me, because the Lord has anointed me." Once again, all three persons of the Trinity are present in a biblical text. As Scripture progresses, the idea of the Trinity becomes increasingly clear, sharpening to crystalline clarity in the words of Jesus.

In Matthew 28:18–20, just before the resurrected Jesus returns to heaven, he commissions his disciples (very much like God commissioned Isaiah), to bring his word to the world. He wants them to make more disciples by teaching people all that he's commanded, and baptizing them in the "name of the Father and the Son and the Holy Spirit." Notice, it's "name," not "names." One God, three distinct persons. And in the original language, there's a cool thing happening that emphasizes the fundamental unity of all three. It's "the name of the Father *and* of the Son *and* of the Holy Spirit." To Western eyes, the "ands" are redundant, but in the Greek, they're crucial. They serve like linguistic hitches between cars in a word train. They allow the main words/cars to remain distinct but not separate from the other words in the linguistic locomotive, emphasizing both the individuality of each word and the indivisibility of the whole they together comprise.[31]

And lastly for now, within Scripture each person of the Trinity is called God. Jesus accepts worship from his followers (John 20:28, Titus 2:13); no mere prophet would do this, nor even unfallen angels. When prophets and angels do something supernaturally spectacular, and when onlookers understandably fall down to worship them, these servants of the Lord freak out and tell them to get their worshipful attention back where it belongs, to God alone (Acts 10:25 and following, Revelation 19:10). Jesus never turns away such worshipful attention. He also teaches his disciples to worship his Father (Matthew 6:9 and following).

A particularly sobering scene in the book of Acts shows us the deity of the Spirit. A husband and wife named Ananias and

Sapphira are struck dead because of their bald-faced hypocrisy and deception in pretending to give more money to the needy than they had actually given. Peter accuses Ananias of lying to the Holy Spirit and says, "You have not lied to men, but to God" (Acts 5:4).[32]

The word "Trinity" is not actually in the Bible, but it represents well the Bible's mysterious but clearly taught truth that the one true God exists eternally as three distinct persons, each of whom is fully God, and there is one God. Though inexplicable, this most essential truth of reality has some major explaining power.

All of created reality is an expression of God's own essential, eternal interrelatedness. God wanted his creation to have integrity—all of its constituent parts holding together and relating to one another to form a diverse, unified totality. God's triune nature is where we must look to begin to understand, and to explain, us.

Love Will Keep Us Together

It's time for me to invent another word. God is all about what from here on out I'll call "Withness," by which I mean interrelatedness, togetherness, and relationship. Remember John 1:1: "The word was *with* God." There was once perfect "Withness" between God and humanity, through the word, and Jesus came to restore and even improve it. This is why Jesus is also called Immanuel, "God *with* us" (Isaiah 7:14, Matthew 1:23). We'll see next chapter how God's desire for restored Withness takes shape within Scripture in the form of a promise, and how this promise is the key to understanding every passage in the Bible. True to God's nature, the "Withness" essential to his being, and which he seeks to share with us (John 17), is very personal.

John wrote three New Testament letters, known simply and straightforwardly as 1 John, 2 John, and 3 John. First John 4 contains a stunning statement about God's essential being. John tells us, "God is love." John did not say that love, defined however we like, is God. No. God, as proclaimed and described in Scripture, as personified in Jesus—is love. The Withness for and in which the triune God created the world is a loving Withness.

This loving Withness is what we walked away from so early in our history; the ceiling of self institutionalized that tragic separation. In our godding, love is by, for, in, and of the self. Though it may try, love ruled by godding cannot get beyond the self. Love as the Bible defines it, however, recognizes and reaches out for the other, who ought to recognize and reach out for us. Bearing the image of the God who is love, we were never meant to live in the world our godding creates, the world of the lonely self.[33]

The desire for loving Withness is definitional of being human. It burns in the deepest recesses of who we are. Great stories like Harry Potter excite that most vital human impulse; they gently touch that most exposed and vulnerable nerve, having clandestinely cut through the calluses our godding forms over it to protect us from divine truth. Loving Withness is what we hurt for when the silence falls around us and the whispers start within us. It's the divine signature on our being. The stories that artfully feature loving Withness speak to us with timeless eloquence. In a fallen world, we receive them with painful rapture. The desire for loving Withness is the primeval ache of the human heart.

A Voldemortish, self-centered life breeds aloneness and brings others into that inhuman pain. Because humans are based in loving Withness, aloneness—not simply solitude, but deep aloneness—is dreadful.

Whether ours is a chosen aloneness, or one inflicted upon us by the selfishness of others or the tragedies of a tumultuous world, aloneness is, fundamentally, not good. God said this from the very beginning. He could have stopped making humans after he created the very first one. After creating Adam, God said that all he had made was very good. Then he said, "It is *not* good that man should be alone" (Genesis 2:18, emphasis added). So God made woman, another human being, an ontological equal named Eve. The first two people would become one in the world's first marriage. There's all that diversity within essential unity stuff again! Out of Adam and Eve's marital love would come the rest of humanity, but because of their rebellion against God, a humanity stricken by and willfully living out the aloneness-inducing lies of godding.

After enduring one loveless relationship after another, we might give up and call loving Withness a cruel fantasy. And then along comes a glorious story like Harry Potter, to let us feel it as we grow to love deeply human, well-written characters, to warm our frigid hearts to its possibility in real life, to let us know that, no matter how hard we try to pretend otherwise, we need it. We can only be who we really are, who we're meant to be, together.

Deeply human stories remind us that the ceiling of self is fake, and they gently shake the walls of separation among us. But only God's word made flesh, as we're told of him in God's story, can make those walls come tumbling down.

Can I Get a Withness?!

It's no coincidence that the age of self-definition is also the age of the lonely self. "When individual self-contemplation becomes the basis of the self, rather than the relation to the divine and human others on which our reality actually depends, the self begins to disappear."[34] The ancients understood this. Plato realized that God wanted humans to be vitally aware of the existence of other people and things beyond the self, that "without…the knowledge of objects without us, man himself would not be man."[35]

The "objects without us" to which we're most personally connected, of course, are other human beings. Every one of us resulted from the union of two other human beings; whether that union was born of love or violence,[36] in the bedroom or the lab—we all had a mom and dad, even if they never met, and if we've never met them. God had to get us here somehow.

Once we're here, our selves take shape in the sea of "objects without us" in which we constantly swim. Esther Meek puts it memorably: "We should see personhood itself as interpersonal."[37] A vital part of our interpersonal personhood is our essential connection as image-bearers to God's world.

As we grow up in the world, in the midst of created natural wonders, so many splendid "objects without us," we get to take it all in like no other creature can. As God's image-bearers, we get to stand back and study animals in their natural habitat, to lie down and gaze at the stars, to sate our souls on the goodness and grandeur of everything from the smallest subatomic particle we can't see to the farthest star we can, and to smile at it all, the glory of the triune God glinting in our eyes. And then that Being speaks to us.

This is how the Bible works with and within the world. All of creation tells us that God is there. God is not silent; we've got the volume turned down. It's not that God overlooks us; it's that we sometimes don't recognize his gaze. Our godding dims our eyes and dulls our hearing to what creation constantly shows and tells us: that the eternal God, who makes all things beautiful in their times, is there. So we need the specific details of just exactly who this God is, to understand life as he sees it, life as it actually is. And that's why he gave us Scripture.

God's word cuts through the fogginess we might feel as our souls awaken and start to stretch beneath the ceiling of self, as we start to wonder what we're missing, what unrecognized realities are shaping us and the world. Given the condition of the world, it's easy and right to assume that not all of those unseen realities are friendly.

Just a few chapters into his book, God tells us of the most hostile, unseen influencer of the world. This being's lies led humanity away from the loving Withness we had with God, and he's active in our day as well, coaxing us further along the path of isolation in the age of the lonely self.

"I Love the Way You Lie"[38]

In a fallen world, God's is not the only gaze set upon us. Someone else is watching, and Satan's look is more of a leer. We see in his snake eyes a distorted reflection of who we really are. Satan offered our first parents an alternative tale to God's story about us. Our self-perception is fed either by the truth God tells us or the lies Satan sells us. For the vast majority of human history, we've been inclined to trust the wrong storyteller.

Jesus calls Satan "the Father of Lies" (John 8:44). We'll examine the Savior's struggle against Satan in chapter 8. For now, we'll focus on the first lie Satan told humanity. It's become life's deepest lie, the one we want to believe most: that we're autonomous, that we are or are entitled to be God.

This lie leads us away from God, from everyone else, from ourselves, and from creation itself, and into all the separations we've thought about. Our separation from God is like a deep crack in a windshield; it spider-webs out into countless other separations, combining to bring us closer to collapse. Expect no sympathy from the devil. Satan will call you a god and then gut you, leaving you to die alone. Autonomy leads to aloneness. Our greatest desire yields our deepest dread.

So many of our deepest anxieties and most disquieting thoughts come down to this one: "I don't want to die alone." Or the related misery: "I feel so alone I want to die." Loneliness can be the deepest pain of dying; it's an especially intense experience, ahead of time, of what death is and brings: separation.

Even if a dying person is surrounded by loved ones when the time comes, her last sight in this world the tear-filled eyes of those whom she knows love her so genuinely, the separation still comes. Death hurts so deeply the loved ones left behind. It can be good and right to let someone go, but death itself is never good. It's the culmination of decay; it's not life's original design.

Death causes separation even in the one dying, as soul leaves body and enters a mode of existence about which God tells us little in his word. Paul tells believers that to be away from the body is to be present with the Lord, but that even so, being without the body is not essentially good. The body is "home." Jesus came so that we can be with God forever, body and soul, in a world made whole, no longer dis-integrated by death, forever (2 Corinthians 5:1 and following). Until then, on every level of our humanness, death tears apart what God joined together.

Really good stories make us hunger and even hope for loving Withness beyond this life. Ah, that's kids' stuff, says our cynicism. Well, it might be the stuff of great children's literature, but that's not because it's kids' stuff. The best kids' books are not childish.

Harry Potter's dealing with death is complex. Though characters come to terms with the departure of their loved ones, death is still treated as an enemy. The longing to defeat death is childlike, not childish. The image of God within us longs for what's good and just, what's true and beautiful to last forever and knows that it should. But since humanity's dawn we've listened to the lies of one who ever courts us toward darkness and death.

Have you heard this one? "You are a burden, and life for everyone else would be better without you." Beneath the ceiling, under the devil's tutelage, we either believe that others are too much of a burden to bear, or that we are too much of a burden for them to bear. But here's part of the goodness of admitting that we're not God! The fact that we are fundamentally unable to define ourselves is a lifesaver.

You cannot define yourself, and so this means that, no matter how intensely you may feel otherwise, you are not a burden. You are an image-bearer. Image-bearers are not burdens, but we do have serious baggage. Jesus was willing to carry all of it for us, to crucify it so it can't hurt us or others anymore, and to give us new life, begun in forgiveness and always growing toward freedom. Satan loves to watch us writhe in our aloneness, and he's thrilled when we beg for more of the separation-inducing stuff he sells. But when Jesus saw us in our hell, he wept.

Slaying the Vampire

When Jesus arrived at the funeral of his dear friend Lazarus, his soul was increasingly troubled as he saw the mourners in their agonized bereavement. He didn't tell them, "Hey, it's all good! I'm going to raise him from the dead!" Jesus joined them in their tears. When he saw where his departed friend was laid, he lost it.

Christ's tears were not a few trickles quickly brushed away in embarrassment. The savior about to defeat death sobbed as he saw its effects among those he loved. Some observing him remarked, "See how he loved him!" (John 11:35-36). Indeed.

What must it do to Christ's heart as he sees us turning so quickly to death, going the hellish, lonely way of our godding? Truly believing that we are burdens other people shouldn't have to bear? "For a moment he seemed choked, and a great sob rose in his throat. He gulped it down and went on, 'There are some here who would stand between you and death. You must not die. You must not die by any hand, but least of all your own. Until the other, who has fouled your sweet life, is true dead you must not die."[39] This is from *Dracula*—see what I mean about great stories!—and is spoken by Van Helsing, the wise, skilled, faithful friend of Mina Harker, a woman whom the vampire, kind of a Satan figure, is trying to completely possess. Dracula is undead, and Van Helsing, in his halting, sometimes imprecise English, says he wants the blood- and-soul sucker to be "true dead"—really, fully, actually dead—separated and gone forever from this life and this world. Death is not inherently good, but it's good to desire it for beings ceaselessly committed to evil.

Satan's true death is coming; he'll be forcibly and forever separated from the world. In the meantime, we owe him some serious hate. As we'll see in chapter 10, hate is a legitimate, necessary thing in this life, when properly, not self-righteously, directed against the devil and his murderous work. Scripture teaches us to recognize Satan's work within the world and within ourselves, and to deeply hate and courageously oppose it. But as much blame as

Satan deserves for life's pains, we've got to own up to the ways we keep giving his old lies new life.

As we return the devil's gaze by believing his lies, he smiles as our lives collapse beneath the burden he's convinced us to carry, the godding we keep strapping on our own backs every day.

As we first start to feel the gravity of our godding and to recognize the blame we deserve for its consequences, it's difficult but crucial to recognize the difference between what the Bible calls "godly grief" (2 Corinthians 7:11) and what we might call "godding grief."

Godly grief mourns the causes, not just the effects, of our sin. Godding grief refuses to recognize the causes and stubbornly continues to do grievous things. Satan seizes upon this self-righteousness, and if we're not careful, he'll take good mourning and lead us into the lonely, desperate night of self-worship. Because we're easily deceived, Scripture teaches us what godding grief isn't as well as what it is.

Godding grief is not the fearful doubting we do when what we want doesn't work out; it's the Voldemort-like certainty that others need to suffer so that we can live as we choose. It's not the honest, scared questioning of what is true and right when we hurt; it's the dishonest decision, masking itself as moral courage, that nothing is true and right except what we want. It's not the soul-crushing disappointment when the one you love chooses someone else; it's the jealous fire that makes you see red everywhere and ready to hurt and kill. It's not the deep pain of unrequited love; it's the desire to control the object of your affection because you so deeply fear rejection. It's not the bitter song you write when your relationships fall apart; it's the text you send that threatens suicide if someone you want won't submit to your demands. And of course, it's the carrying out of any of the above that redoubles and spreads to others the agony of our unrepentant godding.

Godding grief takes form in the constant and growing feeling, gnawing at your bones, that your failures mean you just don't have what it takes to be loved. We put all the stock of our personal significance into what others think of us, especially the ones from whom we crave love the most. We drive ourselves mad in the effort and Satan mocks us—"You're a god! And yet, people hate you so very much. Hmmm…"

Ideally, our inability to be the gods Satan claims we are would make us seek truth from someone worthy of the title "God." Oh, beneath the ceiling, we'll talk about God; we'll even claim to be searching for him, longing for him, crying out to him—anything and everything except acknowledging that he's already here and that he's spoken.[40] The problem isn't that we need to search for God; it's that we need to submit to him—to which our godding responds, "Well, then. Let the search continue!"

In some of his last words to God's people, the prophet Moses called Israel's bluff, one that in our day sounds like this: "If only God would just show himself to me! Then I'd believe!" Moses says, "For this commandment that I command you today is not too hard for you, neither is it far off....The word is very near you....See, I have set before you today life and good" (Deuteronomy 30:11 and following). Moses calls them to life, to know and love and serve the living God.

God's word is near you as well, and he calls you, too, to life—everlasting, true, free life. But Satan's deceit lies nearby as well. Moses calls the people to life and good and warns them against the alternative, death and evil—Satan's specialties.

As God's life-giving truth comes near us, Satan sees an opportunity to twist it into his own insidious lies, laced with irony. Satan calls us gods, and then tells us that we can't possibly live forever.

Memento Mori[41]

The Father of Lies adds deceit upon deceit. He says to us, "You're alone. You're a burden," and then he makes his closing argument by telling us, "And you're terminal." His lie is that the story of our lives ends in annihilation, or who knows what. Notice how we can see the root for nihilism in the word annihilated. It's to make into nothing. Satan would love for us to believe that aloneness is all, and all becomes nothing.

Beneath the ceiling of self, we're encouraged to live like gods precisely because of our mortality. The lies follow logically: *There's no God—no eternal, living being—so you are nothing of the sort. You have no soul, so you can and should do anything you want with your body.* The ironies abound!

Scripture tells us that immortality is built into God's image-bearers. C. S. Lewis writes, "You've never met a mere mortal."[42] But due to Satan's work in the world, especially in the West, many of us grow up never being prompted to doubt the ceiling of self's legitimacy, so we never search for knowable truth beyond what the ceiling lets us see. Living beneath it as the thieves say we must is as natural as breathing. So the idea that we might actually have a significance not confined beneath the ceiling of self can come as quite a shock.

My friend Rosaria writes and speaks on issues of identity, having come to faith in Christ in what she calls a "train wreck conversion," one that upset and upended so much of what she thought about life and her ontology as a person.[43] She's a first-rate scholar, academically credentialed to the hilt on her subject matter, so it's no mere coincidence that some of her most intense and meaningful encounters come on college campuses. She's especially effective at schools that are unabashed bastions of ceiling-of-self thinking. Dens of thieves. Rosaria insists in her presentations that humans are far more, and worth far more, than humanism, agnosticism, and its more mature brother, atheism, preach that we are. To many of the students she meets, the thought is a lightning bolt.

The idea that we are more than biological machines comes out of nowhere and sparks fire. It sheds sudden, shocking light upon their lives. It illuminates, for one shining moment, the lies lurking in the darkness in which they didn't fully realize they were living. They'd certainly felt the darkness, but they'd never been given a reason why they should consider it dark, and possibly false. Then, suddenly, they catch a bright glimpse of truth that's always been near, but which thieves have mocked as impossible and thus kept hidden in plain sight. They don't want the darkness to settle back in, not before they've seen the rest of what that blast of light started to show them.

Rosaria says it's so hard to leave these conversations, to leave just when new, vibrant self-awareness starts to shine. As a foster parent, she knows what it is to give a young child away, uncertain of what will happen to this precious person, what ideas will shape the child's future, what ideas will be allowed to take root in the child's soul, and what truth will be snatched away by thieves. But contrary to the hellish, allegedly merciful but actually murderous logic of pop culture, it is absolutely worth it to bring young life out into the world, cruel as the world can be. Every new life is a shining light against the darkness. And sometimes we're well into our lives before we realize just how alive we really are.

After one such life-sparking encounter on a college campus, one of the students, clearly shaken, called out to Rosaria as she walked away, "Wait! You can't leave! What do I do now that I know I have a soul?!"

C. S. Lewis writes, "It is always shocking to meet life when we thought we were alone."[44] Indeed. Especially when that unexpected life is your own.

What's My Name?

Great stories gift us with a deep sense of our "moreness" as humans, and they deepen within us our longing for permanent loving Witness. They help us explore and experience the depths and the heights of our humanity, and they hint at our essential nature and true origin, truths that thieves say we can never know. But if we question the ceiling of self's integrity, we start to realize that it's not just certain ideas, things, and experiences that have been stolen from us beneath it. It's that we, WE, have been stolen. We've been robbed, and we've been stolen, from ourselves and from everyone else who ought to know us as we really are.

The English literary artist G. K. Chesterton writes,

> We have all read in scientific books, and, indeed, in all romances, the story of the man who has forgotten his name. This man walks about the streets and can see and appreciate everything; only he cannot remember who he is. Well, every man is that man in the story. Every man has forgotten who he is. One may understand the cosmos, but never the ego; the self is more distant than any star. . . . We are all under the same mental calamity; we have all forgotten our names. We have all forgotten what we really are. All that we call common sense and rationality and practicality and positivism only means that for certain dead levels of our life we forget that we have forgotten. All that we call spirit and art and ecstasy only means that for one awful instant we remember that we forget.[45]

A millennium and a half before Chesterton, Augustine wrote about the life for which we humans naturally long. He wonders in his *Confessions* whether it resides in the memory,[46] a holdover from humanity's first days spent in peace with God, an undefinable but definite notion of lost identity and belonging. "No one can deny that he has felt this way, it is therefore found in the memory and recognized when the words 'happy life' are heard."[47] Sherlock Holmes deduces something similar: "There are vague memories in our souls of those misty centuries when the world was in its childhood."[48] The memories aren't clear enough to be called recollections; they're more felt than seen or heard in the mind, but good art draws those feelings out and sets them before us in a form beautiful and painful to see. Chesterton writes, "There is a road from the eye to the heart that does not go through the intellect."[49]

Our souls awakened, feeling our immortality if only in the longing for it, we're brought before the one who made us, and who made us to last, who knows and can give us our truest selves. In God's story, he tells us our name.

We may not find within the Bible the particular assembly of letters by which we're typically known—try finding Rutledge!—but Scripture absolutely spells out our souls and invites us to read all about us.

Revelation symbolizes this truth as the risen Christ promises his people a new name, one that represents their true selves as found and fulfilled in him (2:17). By coming to God through Christ, we get ourselves back. God gives us back to us. By the word, we remember, and we become, who we really are. Much more to explore on recognizing and becoming our new and true selves and how the Bible is crucial to all of it. For now, we can summarize it in the words of my friend Rosaria: "God's story is my ontology."[50]

The Never-Ending Story

By taking us deep into our souls and high above the ceiling of self, great stories encourage and enrich our exploration and understanding of life and our humanity. But their greatness is derivative, and therefore limited. Harry Potter is a truly great story, but not even Harry's magic can guide us as far into the truth as our most definitional desires call us to go. Childlike questions such as "Why?" begin to surface in our souls, and all the great stories but one begin to leave the path, unequipped to climb the heights ahead. No matter how far great stories travel alongside God's words, a turn upward always comes. And a choice has to be made.

Either we go back and backward into our godding, hiding beneath the ceiling of self in our alleged inability to know real truth, or we follow where those stories (sometimes unwittingly) point us: beyond themselves to a place higher than humanity, into the presence of the living God, where our godding is not only questioned, but confronted with the truth. Only Scripture can guide us here.

God's words not only guide us through life (Psalm 119:105), but are his means of freeing us from enslaving lies and forming us in the truth (John 17:17, Hebrews 4:12).

The Bible is truth, and truth artfully told. If we take it seriously and travel its pages, we'll journey through some treacherous and terrible territory, passages that force us to reckon at the deepest level with our godding, that bring us face to face with our enemy and with ourselves as burdened beneath his lies. The Bible does to us what good art, good storytelling, is meant to do: it'll make us laugh, scream, cry, pump our fist in excitement, or shake it against God in anger. As we'll see next chapter, there are some passages of God's book that seem to be just plain ungodly. But as we go, we'll see how utterly, and often uncomfortably, true to life Scripture is. We'll see why, if we really mean to be us, we need to hear and to believe—and as James would tell us, to do—what God says to us through his written words.

In God's story, the character you might be most surprised to meet is you.

Within the pages of God's book is the real you, just waiting for you to arrive. Augustine wrote: "For a long time I have burned to meditate upon your law, and therein to confess to you both my knowledge and my lack of wisdom, the first beginnings of your enlightenment and the last remains of my darkness, until my infirmity is swallowed up by your strength."[51]

Learning who we are as humans, we can learn who we are as particular human beings, and how to live human life to its fullest and freest, together.

7

The Bible Is a Book...?!

"The essential thing 'in heaven and earth' is apparently ...
that there should be long obedience in the same direction;
there thereby results, as has always resulted in the long run,
something which has made life worth living."
—Nietzsche, *Beyond Good and Evil*[1]

"For one and only,
For one so lonely,
Faith creeps slowly over me."
—Sia, "Jesus Wept"[2]

It's the one childhood nightmare whose clutch on my heart I could never shake. It fingered out to touch every raw nerve in my soul, made a fist, and gave that bundle a hard, root-ripping pull. When I woke up, I felt like something in me had shifted, given ground. Fears that had apparently dwelt below the surface within my soul were now unearthed and undeniably in front of me. I remember being frightened when I awoke, but more sad than scared. I came back to reality in a state of silent surrender to a fear I knew could never be buried again.

There was no story to the dream, just discordant images sleep had woven into a seamless scene. I was standing, presumably on dry ground, but alligators were teeming about in the water in front of me. On the other side was my dad. He was laughing. But not like, "Oh my, son. What have you gotten yourself into now? Here, let me help." It was laughter as if he was enjoying my fear. I saw a glint in his eyes that I'd seen in real life. I'd wondered what it meant, and the dream told me it meant something terrible. The dream told me that I could not trust my father.

What the dream suggested was so powerful that I could no longer see real life but through the lens of my nightmare. It made no sense in my life, but nor could that fact stop me from looking at Dad with suspicion. *What am I missing? I don't want to be a fool; I don't want to believe lies. I don't want to trust someone who's not worthy of it, no matter how much he's proven beyond a reasonable doubt that he loves me.* Fear is such an able writer of fiction.

Whatever fears I'd harbored now had a form, an image, and from that point on in my life, sorting out truth from fiction became complicated. It was one of those unhappy maturations in child-hood, one more unwelcome entrance into understanding the true nature of real life, and real people.

Early on in relationships, especially as kids, we idolize people. Eventually we see the cracks in the images. Even in the best of father/child relationships, the kids sadly come to realize that Dad is not a superhero. In the worst of them, it can take a deceived child a long time to realize that Dad is a villain. These possibilities were now before me. The only option no longer available was the one my heart craved the most—that Dad was perfect and that he could do anything.

My dream told me that there was a severity to my dad, and maybe some darkness. At the very least, he was keeping some stuff in the shadows. I was realizing that there was so much I didn't know about him, and that some of it might hurt me. It goes that way as we're getting to know God, too.

If some walk away from the biblical God because of the con-dition of the world, others walk away from him because of the content of his word. For some Christians taking their first steps in faith, loving nearly everything they hear about God their heav-enly Father and especially about Jesus his son, reading (all the way) through God's book brings some unhappy maturity. Sometimes a particular passage stares at us like an image we know we'll see in our nightmares. We stare at God's book, wondering if God is really like his book says he is, and sometimes hoping desperately that he's not.

Learning about a father's past can be a deeply unhappy mat-uration.[3] Some passages in Scripture make God seem profoundly ungodly. (As we'll see, perceiving this disconnect is crucial to wrestling through such passages without having to tap out of the faith.) We read in Scripture about what God has said and done in the past, things not only bizarre, but just flat out bad—especially, it seems, in the Old Testament. Maturing Christians think, "Do I really need to believe this about God? If so, do I even know God? Whom have I put my trust in?"

The Scriptures suggest a severity, a darkness to God the Heavenly Father that can frighten his children as they get to know him better. At the very least, God definitely keeps some stuff in the shadows.

The Reveal

John tells us that in God "there is no darkness at all" (1 John 1:5)—no moral darkness, that is. But there is oh-so-much mystery to God. Beneath the ceiling of self, we take that truth and run with it into all kinds of lies, especially the allegedly liberating lie that God cannot speak or be known. But there's a difference between what is unknowable and what is knowable but not fully explainable. "To say that something is mysterious is not to say that nothing can be said of it."[4] And probably more often than we'd like to admit, our struggle with a particular truth is not that we can't know it, but that we don't want to.

In this book, we won't enter (at least directly) into some of Scripture's most troubling passages. And that's because I'm a coward. But also! It's because this book is about creating a conversation with Scripture, not having all of them. Before we get into the toughest talks we'll have with our heavenly Father, we of course need to be mature enough to speak the same language, and it really helps to have known him long enough to trust the heart from which his hard words come. As Jesus teaches, we come to know God as Father through him (John 14:6). All of God's hard words come to us and must be understood through the Word, who expresses God's heart perfectly.

Learning to see how Scripture takes us with every word to the Word incarnate, we learn the language of our Father's heart.[5] We'll focus a lot in this chapter on how Scripture teaches us to interpret Scripture, and apply it especially to those biblical texts we wish we'd never seen. (I'll refer to some really good work that's been done on these passages, and a number of sources can be found in the bibliography.)[6] But instead of engaging multiple dark passages, we'll go to the very darkest.

My pick for Scripture's darkest passage is neither arbitrary nor random. Scripture sets us up to see it as the worst of the worst, the darkest of the dark, because the Holy Spirit means for us to see the rest of God's book in the blazing light to which this passage's pitch-black yields if we're willing to walk through it.

If you're familiar with the Bible, you might be thinking right away of Christ's crucifixion. Good call; our passage has everything to do with that. But as with everything else in the New Testament, the crucifixion narratives depend upon and draw directly from material in the Old Testament. Our passage is from the Old Testament and the man who bears its burdensome truth lived long before Jesus took up his cross.

The text shows us God acting with almost unspeakable cruelty, afflicting this man with possibly the worst suffering described in the entirety of the Old Testament. And it seems that God is laughing at his pain, or at least making sport of it. Much like Christ's crucifixion but so long before it, it's hell ordered from on high in heaven.

Father Figure

In Genesis 11, the Holy Spirit introduces his readers to a pivotal figure in his book, Abram, whose name God would eventually change to the more familiar "Abraham." Abram and his father's household, for all we know based on the Genesis narrative, were living a standard-variety life of paganism when the true God disrupted it all and made him one of history's most significant human beings.

Very similar to the way Jesus calls his disciples to himself in the gospels (see Luke 5:27–28), God just tells Abram one day to pick up and move, to leave the life he's known and the gods he's worshiped in order to know and worship God exclusively. As is God's prerogative, there was no negotiation. God said "Go," and Abram went.

Whether he realized it or not, Abram was learning something crucial to the nature of the God who called him: God is both Savior and Lord. His saving work doesn't ask our permission to operate. Well, that doesn't sound very gracious! Maybe not. But sometimes life-saving work needs to be rude that way. God doesn't ask for our permission to do his saving work any more than a lifeguard consults a drowning man dead set on saving himself.

God's saving grace is severe and deadly serious, because it cost the life of his son to provide. God began to make this clear to Abram in increasingly dramatic ways. In Genesis 12, God tells Abram that he has huge plans for him: God will make him into a great nation; peoples will come from him and all nations will bless his name. Most personally, and most significantly, God promised that Abram would have a son, a boy of his own to begin the generations of people to come from him. God's words to Abram were not simply plans; they were promises. So God made a covenant with Abram and sealed it in blood.

To make a deal back then, especially a covenant of life-and-death significance, sacrificial animals were used. The animals were cut in half—yes, gross—and from there, the covenant-making people would "cut a deal." The halves of severed animals were lined up, creating grisly parallel borders with a path between them. The oath-makers would walk that path as a way of saying, "If I break my word, my life is forfeit. May what happened to these animals happen to me." Seems extreme to us,[7] but at the very least we can tell how much honor and honesty meant back then, especially to God.

God could have let his word stand on its own, but this bloody covenant ritual would give Abram even more reason to trust his word as truth. Abram arranged the animals as God commanded him. The scene was bloody death; Abram had to chase off birds of prey gathering for a feast. Then God caused a kind of unconsciousness to come over Abram, a dark and dreadful sleep deeper than normal dreams can fathom, but perfect for a prophetic vision of God's blood-earnest faithfulness to his word. In the vision, Abram saw the ceremonial setup, but he did not walk the promise-making path marked by death. God did.

Abram saw a torch passing between the animals. The fire, as it often did in the Old Testament, represented the presence of God.[8] In cultural terms Abram would understand, God was telling him, "You can trust me. I swear on my own life that I will keep my promises to you. If I break my word, may what happened to these animals happen to me."

God was teaching the father of the faith a truth vital to God's own faithfulness, something he emphasizes throughout his book and that goes to the heart of his saving grace. God's promises depend upon God, not the recipients, to fulfill. God swears by his own name. He cannot deny his own character. He swears to his own hurt and remains true to his word (Psalm 15). Think of that! God is not above his own word. He never makes a promise and then says, "You know what? I'm God. I don't have to do that." Abram was learning what King David, whom we'll meet next chapter, would write in Psalm 138:2: "You have exalted above all things your name and your word." God's word and his reputation go hand in hand; though frequently attacked, they are unassailable.

God's good promises did contain some very bad news. Abram learns that his descendants would be slaves for four centuries in Egypt, but that God would bring them out and into a land of their own, and the plans for all nations to be blessed would go forward. It seems impossible that Abram wouldn't wonder why his descendants' slavery was necessary. Why not just bring the good without the bad?

We don't know how much God told Abram, but Genesis lets us know very clearly and very early that, from its first occurrence, human godding had gone immediately septic and killed the world. There was no man-made cure. Pain and suffering make sense in a world like this. What's stunning is that God doesn't stay above the fray, aloof in his righteousness and looking down with contempt upon the creatures who killed creation.

Abram learned that God would rather die than fail to bless the creatures who cursed him and wanted him dead. This God was not to be trifled with, but he could be trusted. His heart toward his world was kind.[9] Abram was taking the first steps of faith under the watchful care of his God.

But how was Abram to know that his God had the power to back up his promises? Promises on a scale that big, no matter how sincerely given, would require nothing short of almighty power to accomplish. But the God of Abram was no tribal deity, no minor god with limited power and jurisdiction. God had all power in heaven and on earth. And that's exactly what God showed Abram next.

Show Me a Sign

As we arrive in Abram's journey of faith at Genesis 17, we've reached a seminal point in all of Scripture. By now, every major biblical truth has made its debut,[10] and together they're starting to take Christlike shape. God was about to give Abram the clearest preview yet of the coming Messiah.

As he does several times in Scripture, God changes his worshiper's name to something that more fully identifies the worshiper with God and his promises. From then on, Abram—"exalted father"—would be known as Abraham, "father of many peoples."

To call Abram to a deeper commitment to God's correspondingly more detailed covenant, and to symbolize and seal the substance of that promise, God tells Abram to be circumcised and to circumcise all the sons that would come from him (Genesis 17:11). The covenant still involves cutting! And this time, it's really personal.

By connecting his promise to a ceremony that cut close to the source of human reproduction, God was telling Abram that he and his descendants would be committed to the true and living God and his promises with their very lives and throughout their generations. God would get this started by giving Abraham and his wife a son of their own. Abraham thought God was delusional, or joking. He and Sarah were way beyond baby-making age (verse 17). No worries. With this God, all things are possible.

In verse 1, God reveals himself as *El Shaddai*, God Almighty. This God makes nature the servant of saving grace.[11] God would bless the infertile couple with a boy of their own. Sarah laughs at the idea, too, so God tells them to name the boy Isaac, which means laughter. God does indeed have a sense of humor.

These were good tidings of great joy, ultimately for all people. But in the years to come, bright family joy would suddenly go pitch-black. A new command from God would envelop faithful father and promised son in deepest shadow. Now, at last, we're ready to approach Scripture's darkest passage.

With Fear and Trembling

In Genesis 22, we read: "After these things God tested Abraham and said to him, 'Abraham!' And he said, 'Here am I.' He said, 'Take your son, your only son Isaac, whom you love, and go to the land of Moriah, and offer him there as a burnt offering on one of the mountains of which I shall tell you.'"

Genesis 22 should bother Bible-believing Christians a whole lot more than it tends to. People familiar with Abraham's story know that he is spared his miserable duty, that Isaac survives, and that the whole situation points us to Jesus, who actually did give his life as a sacrifice. Somehow, their knowing that this story points so clearly to Jesus dampens the fire they're meant to feel as the narrative builds. That dilution is spiritually dangerous. God forbid that seeing Jesus in a biblical text would lessen its impact!

If we're not feeling the burn of particular passages of Scripture, then either we don't understand what those passages are saying or our faith in God has gone numb. We're standing on white coals and feeling just fine. It's not right; we're missing something in our relationship to the text and therefore to the God who breathed that fire out.[12] As we come across Genesis 22 in the natural, unfolding narrative of God's book, we can't get to Jesus yet. We're not meant to. First, we have to feel Abraham's pain.

This early narrative fire burns away all trite and trivializing efforts to understand and apply difficult biblical passages. *Dude. This is so intense of God. I think he's teaching me that I've got to give my best to him no matter how much it costs me, just like Abraham did. Wow. I'll seriously spend like at least five more minutes in devotions tomorrow.* Treating biblical texts as moral object lessons—"moralistically"—is unintentionally self-absorbed, and it takes our attention away from the fact that Abraham and Isaac actually went through this. Would we drive by a car wreck, seeing mangled metal, crying people and ambulances everywhere, and think—"Wow. This happened to teach me not to text and drive"? That might be a very good take-away lesson, but the wreck's significance is not centered on us. Our first thoughts need to be with the devastated souls who endured it.

This passage also burns like a gaudy neon sign in the face of people looking for reasons to write off God and his book. *Here you go. If you choose, you can see all your worst suspicions about God, the Bible, and the Christian faith confirmed right here.*

But for those in between, people who know their need for God and are willing to learn from him, but who are bewildered and heartbroken at what they're learning about him, this passage is a crucible. On the other side, when followed faithfully, is life-saving, world-saving truth. But you won't get there unsinged. You're not supposed to.

Danish philosopher Søren Kierkegaard (1813–1855) wrote about his own fire-walk through this passage. A devout Christian and one of Western history's most profound thinkers, Kierkegaard was in some ways modern-era Christianity's last strong breath of biblical faithfulness before it nearly suffocated beneath Kant's shiny new ceiling.

In his day, Kierkegaard noticed among Christians and non-Christians alike a growing admiration for philosophy and a growing disdain for theology. Anything smacking of "book religion" was thought uncouth and unintelligent while philosophy and its emphasis on autonomous human reason was hailed as the way forward for humanity. Kierkegaard's work forged a hard, faithful path in time between Kant's sophisticated naïvete about autonomous reason's moral possibilities and Nietzsche's brilliant but poisonous pining for a morality-incinerating anti-Messiah.[13]

The great Dane wanted a deeply considered, actively practiced Christianity.[14] No cheap and easy approaches to the word of God—either by arrogantly dismissing it or flippantly embracing it.[15] Kierkegaard found his champion in Abraham.[16] Kierkegaard rightly but modestly asserted his ability to comprehend even the most complex philosophies and philosophers of his day. But, he wrote, "*When I have to think of Abraham, I am as though annihilated.*"[17] The strength and foresight of Abraham's faith left Kierkegaard in stunned disbelief.

Abraham personified the honest struggle we thought about in chapter 4: engaging a God whose particular activities or inactivity can drive us mad, and yet whose innate goodness and justice form the only moral basis upon which we can stand in protest against him.[18] As we've thought about, when these standards are not rooted in God, they shrivel up and die the inevitable death of redefinition. Suddenly stricken by God's awful command, what could Abraham do? There was no greater power and no higher moral authority to which he could appeal.

Should Abraham have just turned the knife on himself? Kierkegaard notes: "He would have been admired in the world, and his name would not have been forgotten; but it is one thing to be admired, and another to be the guiding star which saves the anguished."[19] Because of God's previous promises, Abraham knew God had bigger things in mind for him and his son.

Besides, Abraham's sacrifice of himself would have spared him pain, but would also have added inestimably to Isaac's. And if God Almighty was going to require Isaac as a sacrifice, how could Abraham prevent it? So Abraham did the most unthinkable, brave, and selfless thing he could in a place where every exit led through hell. Like someone who gains lucidity in a dream, Abraham begins to take the nightmare into his own hands. He resolves in his shattered heart to obey and to do the deed himself. His son would die at God's command, and by his hand. Abraham gave himself and his son to the unwanted will of a severe God who kept so much in the shadows.

One truth shone clearly through the darkness, though, one we could only guess was in Abraham's heart if we hadn't read past Genesis 22. But it'd be an educated guess based on what we already know of the God who makes nature the servant of saving grace. God could and would move heaven and earth to keep his promises.

God had promised that, through Isaac, Abraham would father many nations, and Isaac had no kids. Although Almighty God could make kids appear out of nowhere and attribute them to Isaac, it seemed that this God liked to accomplish the impossible within the framework of what he'd created, bringing life not randomly, but rising from ordinary conditions that could not naturally produce it. Isaac himself was proof. So, Abraham apparently got to thinking. There was hope.

We don't know how quickly this ray of hope dawned in Abraham's heart, but we do know it shone with a warm logic. Hebrews 11:19 tells us that Abraham "*considered*"—you can see in this Greek word what becomes the English word "logic"[20]—"that God was able even to raise him from the dead." Biblically defined faith is not about what's unreasonable; it's about what's unseen (Hebrews 11:1).

It was a perfectly reasonable matter of deeply considered faith for Abraham to believe that he would get his boy back. Faith approaches God on God's own terms, and trusts God to be true to his word. But moving on that trust isn't in the same galaxy as easy. Faith is a fight. Abraham's trust in God's faithfulness and power is precisely what made it so immensely difficult for him to obey God.

This is the real reason why we, like Kierkegaard, should be thunderstruck at Abraham's obedience. "I bow seven times before his name and seventy times before his deed."[21]

If there was nothing beyond death, then Abraham should have followed his son into the darkness. If God was all talk about his power, then Abraham could have gambled that God couldn't make him kill his son. If God was powerful enough but couldn't be trusted to keep his promise, then Abraham should have run with his son as far and for as long as they could, before God pinned the boy down, put the knife in Abraham's hand, and forced it into Isaac's heart. If Abraham didn't trust God on any of these levels, any of those reactions would have been reasonable and would have made the situation at least somewhat more bearable. Because at least, in some way, he and his boy would go down while fighting this apparently malevolent, capricious god. But Abraham opted for none of the above. He believed God with what Kierkegaard called "the faith that made it hard for him."

Very early in Scripture, Abraham personified biblical faith. He was confident in God's power and content with God's providence. He was confident in what God could do and content with what God would do. Abraham didn't know how long it would be before he got his boy back, but it couldn't come quickly enough.

Though we can infer Abraham's resurrection-hope based on prior passages, it's important not to get ahead of the narrative, much less to use the resurrection as an anesthetic for a text meant to pierce us. The passage wants us to walk with Abraham through the valley of the shadow of death, to the mountain where God said his son would die.

Three Days in Hell

If Abraham had simply been a man of his religious times, in which human sacrifice was normal if not common, God's command may not have bothered him too terribly much. Or at least, it wouldn't have surprised him. And as we read his reaction to God's command, we might think that Abraham was just like his polytheistic peers, just doing his duty to a bloodthirsty tribal deity. God gives this soul-cleaving command, and what do we get in verse 3? Not, "And Abraham wept and cried out, 'Lord, let me take his place!'" No, it's just, "So Abraham rose early in the morning."

Scripture is often understated in its storytelling; only readers careful enough to pay attention to the details of the whole story can feel a narrative's full weight.

Based on what Genesis has already told us, we know that Abraham's suffering was, as Kierkegaard put it perfectly, "superlative at every point." By this point in the narrative, it's obvious that Abraham's deepest desire was for a son of his own. It was normal fatherly longing, enhanced within a culture and era that especially prized sons, and amplified by God's promises to provide a boy of historical proportions with a supernatural backstory. We're meant to know all of this by the time we read God's command. The minimalist description of Abraham's response is intentional; so is the painfully detailed description of the divine words that wrecked him.

God's command cuts into Abraham's heart as a dad, and it twists into his growing faith in God. With each added phrase of the command, God pushes the knife deeper: "Abraham, take your son…your only son…whom you love…" When we've read and cared about all that's come before, we realize that Scripture wants us to feel this plunging stab, too. The narrative keeps referring to Isaac as Abraham's son, even when it doesn't need to.[22] Verse 3 again: "Abraham…took two of his servants"—nameless in the narrative—"and *his son* Isaac." The way it's worded, God's command touches with its dagger's point both our sympathy for Father Abraham and our fears about God the Father.[23]

God's command instigated a slow-motion nightmare Abraham had to move through in waking life. Kierkegaard calls our attention to the time between God's command and Abraham's lifting of the knife: *"These three and half days were infinitely longer than the few thousand years which separate me from Abraham."*[24] Growing in his understanding of God, this was the unhappiest of maturations for Abraham. Yet, exemplifying with excruciating integrity the faith that hails him as its father, Abraham moved forward.

Abraham moved moment by moment toward a death more fearful than his own, into the shadowy territory of a God who commands loyalty more fundamental than Abraham's loving, protective instincts for his own son. What's more, God seems to press the point every chance he has to make it hurt. To cap it all off, the narrative opens by telling us that God designed Abraham's torturous odyssey as…a "test." What the Faith?!

Bad Imaging

God's PR is horrible here! But hang on.

If we take the Bible's commentary on itself seriously—that it really is God's word and words—then something literarily and artistically strange is happening in this passage. Viewed with moral vision borrowed from God's own book, this narrative paints God very unflatteringly. But God is the artist!

The Bible is God's worded self-portrait. He wrote the words that make us want to write him off and to reject biblical faith as absurd. But in good art, when we examine an apparent absurdity more closely, it sometimes reveals unrecognized, actual absurdities in us.

The Bible loves irony. Its method of truth-telling fits every age and people, yet seems almost especially designed for our culture—we who so aggressively pride ourselves on self-awareness and are therefore so easily self-deceived. As Jesus says to such a group in his day, "If you were blind, you would have no guilt. But now that you say, 'We see,' your guilt remains" (John 9:41).

Here with Abraham, God mirror-images himself, as if inviting us—baiting us?—to think our absolute worst about him. Judge him by the best and highest standards of righteousness we've got and call him the criminal we secretly suspect he is, and that we so desperately need him to be in order to justify ourselves. Scripture loves instructive irony not because God loves to belittle us with sarcasm, but because we need to really see ourselves. That's not easy for people so adept at and addicted to false self-imaging. We need self-reflective vision from another angle, from a source of light we can't dim and whose resolution we can't manipulate as its sharpness shows us as we are.

We could view Abraham's test and the narrative's description as just more evidence that God's book isn't worth bothering with. Or, we could do what good artists want us to do with their work: we can take a longer, more serious look, opening our hearts and minds to what the piece might teach us, maybe even about ourselves, as we take in the artistry on its own terms rather than judging it harshly by the unknowingly arbitrary and sometimes self-congratulatory standards of our own moral and aesthetic demands.

Thankfully, the Bible gives us its terms of interpretation very early on, not even halfway through its first book. The Bible teaches us how to interpret the Bible, and it uses Abraham's story as its most instructive tutor.

The Bible Tells Me So

We so easily forget, and some biblical scholars deliberately ignore, the fact that the Bible is a self-interpreting work of literature[25] (thus the brilliant, anticlimactic title to this chapter!). Something so obvious it's forgettable about interpreting the Bible: every verse is surrounded by other verses, which are parts of books, which are parts of God's book as a whole. So, to understand a particular passage we're staring at, we need to employ what I like to call in my classes "the plop principle."

This poetically delicate title derives from what happens when a rock drops into a pond. The impact creates bigger and bigger circles in the water beyond it. So, too, in order to understand any passage of Scripture, we need to start close to our problematic passage and work our way into bigger and bigger circles of text beyond it in all directions, until the circles touch the Bible's first and final words.

As you look more broadly at Scripture and dive into the details of what you see, you discover deep connections within, similarities of style and content, even when the authors are separated by centuries. You begin to see the growing, developing, refined expression of the essential truths the Bible was written to proclaim. Though it doesn't matter much to their modern-era critics, the biblical authors would not at all agree with the patchwork quilt concept of Scripture: *Pffft. What did the biblical authors know about what they were doing?! If only these modern critics had been around back then to help biblical authors understand the true nature of their work!*

In addition to Scripture's constant cross-referencing of itself, and Jesus and the Apostles commending the entire Old Testament as Scripture,[26] perhaps the most powerful demonstration of the Bible's fundamental unity is the proclamation and development of a promise, one that God's promise to Abraham serves to advance and that explains why God puts Abraham front and center early on in the book about God's promised son. This promise is the Bible's thesis statement, and it doesn't begin with Abraham. A good writer, the Holy Spirit, gives us his thesis statement early, all the way back in Scripture's third chapter.

As we'll see in more detail next chapter, Genesis 3:1–6 tells us how we killed the world. It takes God all of eight verses after that archetypical atrocity to promise that he would save it, and to begin to tell us how.

God first speaks this promise to Satan, who'd taken the form of a serpent and whose lethal work in the world was just starting to unfold. The devil learns in this promise that his days are already numbered. From verse 15: "I will put enmity between you and the woman, and between your offspring and her offspring; he shall bruise your head, and you shall bruise his heel." Explains everything, right? No, but it sets the stage for everything that follows.

In so many ways, Genesis is the book of beginnings—hence the name. By design, each of the Bible's major truths begin here. Just like children, they don't arrive fully grown. One theologian compares biblical truth to an acorn.[27] If you hold an acorn, you're holding an entire oak tree; it just hasn't developed yet. But given the right kind of soil, enough rain and sun, and a whole lot of time, the seed develops. We get a sprout from the ground, a trunk, branches— eventually, what you could once hold weightless in your hand you cannot budge with a bulldozer. So, too, with biblical truth.

The truth we get in Genesis is shadowy, vague, and sometimes just strange. But as it moves on into Exodus and plays out in the rest of ensuing Scripture, that truth develops in detail until we're presented in Revelation with the literary equivalent of a magnificent oak. This is part of why there's so much Old Testament imagery, especially from Genesis, in Revelation. It's the same truths, fully matured, spectacularly displayed. The Bible knows what it's doing.

God says he will put hostility between Eve and Satan, like separating the addict from the dealer, and between their respective offspring.[28] Yes, God speaks of Satan's offspring—yuck! Again, it's a "What the?!" kind of moment, inviting a closer, more careful look at surrounding Scripture.

When Scripture refers to people with language like "the offspring of," it's often associating those people not with particular parents, but with a way of life they personify. So Jesus, drawing upon Genesis 3:15, calls his enemies the children of the devil— not because they're a freakish hybrid of demon and human—but because, in opposing God's son, they were believing the devil's lies and doing the devil's work (John 8:44).

Significantly, Jesus was correcting his critics' malicious misconception that their genetic relationship to Abraham (and their self-assessed, sterling obedience to God's law) gave them a right relationship to God. Jesus taught that it was not Abraham's DNA, but only Abraham's faith, that could do this. Genesis 15:6 tells us, "Abraham believed God, and it was credited to him as righteousness." Jesus's critics did not believe what and how their forefather did, so they were not his true sons. In their self-deceit and self-righteousness, they were the spawn of Satan.

We'll revisit these kinds of seemingly confusing but actually clarifying expressions and passages in our final chapter as we wrap it all up. For now, when confronted with scriptural strangeness, remember to take the Bible on its own terms. When you find yourself staring, don't forget to plop!

The promise in Genesis 3:15 tells us that the woman's offspring will win a decisive victory over the serpent. His foot bruising (or crushing) the serpent's head calls to mind the victory parades of ancient civilizations. The conquered ruler takes a walk of shame through the capital city of the victorious king. At the end of his humiliating march, he bows before his enemy, now his king. The victor places his foot on the neck of his once-great opponent, who is now merely his servant. "I own you. Your kingdom is over and you have no authority here" is the message. Next chapter, we'll see how Jesus did this to Satan.

As he crushes the serpent, the promised conqueror's heel is bruised. It's as if the snake twists around and bares its fangs. As the heel pushes down and presses the victory, the enemy's fangs pierce upward. The victor sustains a devastating wound in his win. Ages before the cross, we know that the Christ's victory will be complete, but costly.

Promises, Promises

Revelation 12 gives us a vision that encapsulates the age-old struggle of the woman and her seed against the serpent. A dragon tries to kill a woman's newborn child and is enraged as she's rescued and carried away with her little boy. You can see in this vision either a portrayal of Eve and her as-yet-unnamed offspring or of Mary and Jesus—and you'd be right both times! The second option complements and completes the first.

Biblical prophecy often has multiple fulfillments over time, and the Bible lets us know when it's happening. Like wave after wave hitting the shore from the same body of water, God sends into history and records in his word smaller fulfillments of his promises, preparing us for the big one on the horizon, the history-shaking tsunami that hits with the arrival of God himself into the world.

Abraham was a semi-tsunami that God sent to history's shores. With him, the promise rooted in the garden of Eden begins to grow and take shape, speaking of the loving Withness that God would bring back into the world through the conqueror of the serpent. In Genesis 17, the promise breaks the surface and shows the form it will take as it matures through the rest of the Bible. As spoken to Abraham, it's often called "the covenant of grace."

The covenant of grace is a threefold promise. God says, "I will be your God; you will be my people; and I will make my dwelling among you." Beginning with Abraham, this elevated, more specific form of God's essential promise of salvation begins to branch out into the different books of the Bible, each telling us how it was playing out in history, how God preserved and advanced it and the Hebrew people through whom the Christ would come.[29]

Let's take a flyover look at this promise as it runs like a deepening river through the course of Scripture. The wording varies, but the more deeply you look into God's word, you'll begin to see this promise everywhere, even in the subtle details. We'll see just a bit of that subtlety in this sampler list, a teaser for the treasures that await those who dig deeply into God's trove of truth.

Genesis 17:7: "And I will establish my covenant between me and you and your offspring after you throughout their generations for an everlasting covenant, to be God to you and to your offspring after you."

Exodus 6:7: "I will take you to be my people, and I will be your God, and you shall know that I am the Lord your God, who has brought you out from under the burdens of the Egyptians."

Exodus 29:45–46: "I will dwell among the people of Israel and will be their God. And they shall know that I am the Lord their God, who brought them out of the land of Egypt that I might dwell among them. I am the Lord their God."

Jeremiah 30:22: "And you shall be my people, and I will be your God."

Ezekiel 36:28: "You shall dwell in the land that I gave to your fathers, and you shall be my people, and I will be your God."

And on into the New Testament!
John 1:14: "And the word became flesh and dwelt among us."

As we thought about in chapter 5, the word is Jesus, and "became flesh" is his incarnation. Notice John's use of covenant of grace language: "dwelt among us."

And now for some of those subtle details. In the Greek, "dwelt" is "tabernacled." The word "tabernacled" among us. Exodus gives so much literary space to the description of the tabernacle, a big ol' tent, that it's typical to stare at those texts, and then skip quickly past them. But the tabernacle was supremely significant to God's people. It was the place where God would meet with them, resplendent in his glory, as they journeyed to the Promised Land. It's where he dwelt among them (Exodus 40:34). By telling us that Jesus "tabernacled" among us, John proclaims Jesus as the ultimate dwelling place of God's glory and the fulfillment of all those seemingly tedious tabernacle texts in Exodus. John writes in verse 18, "And we beheld his glory, glory as of the one and only, who came from the Father, full of grace and truth."

And now from Paul:
2 Corinthians 6:16: "For we are the temple of the living God; as God said, 'I will make my dwelling among them and walk among them, and I will be their God, and they shall be my people.'"

Notice: God's dwelling place, his house, is his people! It's another biblical prophecy both/and. As we'll explore much more fully in our final chapter, God's dwelling place is Jesus, and as Paul puts it in Colossians 3:3, believers are "hidden with Christ in God."

The covenant of grace is in Revelation, too, with a cool twist to the wording that really shows the Bible's fundamental unity in its essential message about Jesus. Hold that thought!

The covenant of grace gets us past the staring contest with Scripture. We can ask of every passage in the Bible, "How does this passage advance that promise?" "What does this passage teach us about Christ who fulfills this promise?" Looking at Scripture this way doesn't answer all the questions each passage raises, but it does answer the most fundamental question of why the Holy Spirit put that passage there in his book to begin with. For instance, it tells us why the Bible has a book within it that doesn't even mention God. (?!)

Esther is the story of God's behind-the-scenes work to preserve the Hebrew people from genocide. No Hebrew people, no Messiah. Esther's connection to the covenant is vital. Her courageous work is pivotal to the survival of the people from whom God's son would rise.

Esther's saga shows us that God is very active in history; his unseen hand guides all that we see playing out in the world, as the "major prophets"[30] like Isaiah and Jeremiah alert us to. This is why the Bible has so many genealogies in it.[31] Those long lists of unpronounceable names are historical records of God's faithfulness in human history, his ensuring that the seed of the woman would ultimately come through a young virgin named Mary to crush the head of the great dragon.

Paul helps us to see it all coming together. In Galatians 3:14, he tells us that the blessings of global significance promised to Abraham come to Gentiles (and Jews!) who trust in Christ. In verse 16, Paul recalls the promise God made to Abraham and to his offspring, telling us that the offspring ultimately in view is the Christ. Jesus knew this.

The Sermon on the Mount is Jesus's inaugural address as the Messiah. Every would-be prophet in Israel was measured by his fidelity to the writings of their greatest prophet, Moses, who led Israel out of slavery in Egypt, gave them God's law, and wrote the first five books of the Bible. So Jesus tells his audience in Matthew 5:17–18 that he did not come to abolish the law or the prophets (shorthand for the whole Old Testament). So far, so good. Tell us something new, Jesus! And he does. Jesus says he hasn't come to abolish Old Testament Scripture, but to fulfill it—every letter and every little detail, down to what we'd consider the dot on the i and the cross on the t—and therefore to fulfill the covenant of grace. So Jesus not only agrees with Moses's writing, he's the one about whom Moses wrote. To believe Moses (and the rest of the Old Testament) is to believe in Jesus (John 5:46, Deuteronomy 18:18).

In Galatians 3:29, Paul says that those who have faith in Jesus Christ are children of Abraham, "heirs according to the promise." Christ fulfills the covenant of grace. He is "God with us," and those trusting in him are inseparably identified with him. His story is their ontology.

Now that we've got the means to get past the staring contest with Scripture, we can see more clearly the significance of Abraham's suffering, and why it was Abraham who had to suffer this way.

Conscientious Objection?

As you thought about Abraham's willing obedience to God's terrible command, did it strike you as uncomfortably similar to what prompts religiously motivated murders? The holy warrior says, "God told me to do it. Despite my misgivings, my weak faith, I had to honor him, because he and he alone is true and right."[32] Isn't that also the secret sauce in totalitarian politics, just substituting government for God? The greater power commands me to do something for the greater good; I must obey! This mentality could conceivably rationalize any atrocity. And what if Abraham was having a bad day, or was mentally addled, hearing voices and attributing them to God who must be obeyed in all things?[33]

Once again, this is where Christianity stands ethically apart from other theistic religions and from statism, humanism, or any other "ism" to which people pledge their allegiance. No other god or social system has demonstrated goodness in such earth-shaking fashion. The Christian God is the very basis, and the only basis, for what makes us cry out against his command to Abraham.

The question always comes down to God's essential and rightful authority over all human life (Genesis 1, Psalm 24:1), to the issue of who defines the terms "good" and "evil," and to the recognition that God can and does use that which is morally impermissible (according to his own commands) to accomplish his righteous purposes. As another of Scripture's famous sufferers told the people who sold him into slavery—his own brothers!—"What you intended for evil, God intended for good" (Genesis 50:2).[34]

But if you're Abraham, what do you do when God, whose character is what defines messed-up things as messed up and yet who keeps so much stuff in the shadows, commands you personally to do what he forbids? That's messed up! This is where the covenant of grace, even as Abraham had experienced it so early in its surface-breaking development, lets us see in the dark.

We have to acknowledge Scripture's shadows and respect God's right to keep stuff within them, but we need more than the acknowledgment of mystery to move ahead with faith in a God capable of giving the hellish command he did to Abraham. We need something objective and unchanging, something that, no matter how badly a deranged disciple hallucinates, will call out his homicidal intentions as evil and command him to cease and desist. Better than a something, we need a someone. And that's Christ, of course.

Jesus, who came into real time and space and history, whose tomb is empty, stands as the crucial and defining difference between faith in the true and living God and godding in all the secular and religious forms it takes. He's the focal point of faith when God and the world and life don't make sense. Christ's coming into the world is the significance and meaning of the extraordinary situations God's scriptural servants like poor Abraham had to endure. (Thankfully, Abraham's ordeal was extra extraordinary!)[35]

As their lives play out in the biblical narratives, God's servants can't see the resolution. They have to feel the stress that comes with learning to trust a God who keeps stuff in the shadows. Those who came after Abraham had more light through which to see than he did, shining brighter until the coming of Christ in whom those situations and Scriptures find their ultimate, essential significance. So Abraham's ability so long before Jesus to see light in the dark is especially stunning; it's like he had night-vision goggles.

Without anywhere near the amount of truth we have about God, let alone our detailed knowledge of how this would turn out and how it points us to Christ, Abraham seems to perceive truths only partially revealed but which are enough to move him to follow this God, with his son, into the dark. What he did not know at that point was that on the other side of the darkness, he would get a stunning view of the light of the world.

Proud Papa

As we look to their fulfillment in Christ, the words and the wording of God's command to Abraham reveal God not as torturer, but as mourner. Seen in the light of Christ, God's words express more than a millennium ahead of time his own fatherly grief.

After Jesus's baptism, God the Father speaks from heaven his affection for his son (Matthew 3:17). Think of God's command to Abraham while you read God's commendation of Jesus. "This is my beloved son, with whom I am well pleased." Combining this wording with what we find in other, related Scripture, we have: *This is my son, my one and only son, whom I love, and I hereby authenticate and approve his ministry. My beloved son has my blessing to go and give his life for the sake of the world* (John 3:16). On that day, Jesus began a three-year public ministry, the shadow of the cross looming ahead of him. His whole ministry as the "man of sorrows" (Isaiah 53), and, really, the whole of his life, was Abraham and Isaac's three-day journey to death. Unlike Isaac, blissfully ignorant of what was happening until the terrible time came very close, Jesus knew the whole way with dreadful certainty who the real sacrifice was, and that there would be no last-minute reprieve.

Oh, but still, why put Abraham through this?! Yes, God spares Abraham the pain of fulfilling the command, but the pain of those three days must have lasted the rest of Abraham's life, like the headache that won't go away after the concussion. The trauma is done, but hurt lingers and unsettles your sense of life; it can still blur your vision. As he looked in resolute, growing faith to his heavenly Father, I wonder if there was ever a narrowing of his faith-filled eyes in suspicion, or at least a wincing that said, "Oh no, what now?" But always, the book of Hebrews tells us, Father Abraham moved forward in faith.

Abraham seemed to understand that the ordeal with Isaac was no stunt. It was a statement. It was a living, flesh-and-blood prophecy and a tangible focal point for faith in the unseen God and his promise to provide for the world's salvation.

Testing, Testing…

Okay, maybe it wasn't a stunt, but doesn't the text say it was a "test"? How cruel is *that*?! Crucial to letting Scripture interpret Scripture is letting the Bible define its own terms.[36] God "tested" Abraham for the same reason you'd run a fleet of tractor trailers over a new suspension bridge: not because the bridge's structural integrity is in doubt, but because you want to demonstrate its strength.

It's not that God didn't know what Abraham would do. Remember the plop principle. David writes in Psalm 139, "Before a word is on my tongue, O Lord, you know it altogether." Abraham's actions demonstrated the genuineness of his faith. James is one of Abraham's biggest fans. He cites Abraham for support in his famous argument that "faith without works is dead" (James 2:21 and following).[37] Abraham modeled true faith for all his children who'd come after him. We need to learn from Father Abraham.

In Abraham's heart, his first love was first. He understood that Isaac, like all of creation, belonged to God. Abraham knew that everything he loved and treasured and hoped and believed—in short, everything good about Abraham, his life, his son's life and life itself, could only rightly be attributed to God. So, too, for us.

Every person we love has a significance beyond their relationship to us. They do not belong to us, but we are to love them. God is the one who commands it. All parents give their kids over to ideas or principles that function as gods in their lives. We teach our children and love them. And we recognize that they might one day give their lives in the service of the god we've taught them to honor, or perhaps the god they've chosen despite our hopes. Abraham gave his son over to his God, the God who gave him an excruciating command for an extraordinary purpose. In so many ways, Abraham's obedience paved the way for the arrival of God's own son into the world, not least as a visceral picture of what God would do to save it.

God's love for the world is tested and genuine; he did something about it. It makes sense that, of all people, the father of the Christian faith, the man who'd become a blessing to the whole world, should be the one to undergo this awful test. This is part of why God calls Abraham his friend (James 2:23). Abraham did what good friends do; he shared as much as he could in his loved one's pain. But still, God was in control of all of this. Why would God treat a friend like that?

Mother Teresa, her own soul in shreds as she surveyed the human suffering she gave herself so entirely to alleviate, said in eminently understandable bitterness: "If God would treat his friends better, he'd have more of them."[38] She sounds like Jeremiah, and as we'll see, like David in many of his songs. But those prophets knew there was more to it.

Jesus didn't give his life to die in the place of a bunch of God's friends, which would sort of make sense. He gave his life for us who, by our nature, are God's enemies—for people like you and me naturally addicted to our godding and who, despite what it's done to the world, to us, and to those we love, still feel entitled to it. So yes, we can ask: why would God treat his friends this way? And God gives true, but not exhaustive answers. But to be honest, we should also ask: Why would God give his son for people hell-bent on godding, for people who hate and would murder his son, people who in the West's modern era danced on his grave, drunk with pride, and who in our era still have the gall to complain about him as we experience the awful hangover? Why would God treat his enemies like that?

In Genesis 22, Abraham walked into death's shadow and was taken into something holy, a visceral sharing of God the Father's own experience in loving and saving the world. It was devastating, and it must have exhausted everything in Abraham's soul. But shouldn't we expect something like that when a person, a sinful creature, has such familiar dealings with a being worthy of the title "God"? Friendship with God can never be casual.

What a View!

The Christian faith is friendship with God. In a fallen world, as Abraham shows us to superlative degrees, that relationship is hard, and it hurts. But Christ teaches and shows us that his Father can be trusted, always. God wasn't playing games with Abraham, because God wasn't playing games with the life of his own son. Every sympathy we feel for Abraham should lead to thoughts of God the Father, not staying as sympathy, but stretching like dawn into awe. Every scream of protest in defense of Abraham is actually a shout of praise to God the Father, who actually did what he prevented Abraham from doing. Next chapter, we'll see very specifically why such awe-ful action was necessary.

Having walked a bit with Abraham and battled alongside him in the valley, we can see with the eyes of well-informed, hard-fought faith the view from the top of the mountain. From its glowing, dizzying heights we can see all things in the light of the risen son.[39]

We don't know how much Abraham understood of what would come from him and his ordeal with Isaac on the mountain. He probably knew more than we give him credit for; we're sometimes chronologically snooty with people in Scripture, especially

Old Testament people. We do know that, in the midst of the shadows, in which are hidden the impenetrable mysteries of life, the unknowns behind our deep anxieties, Abraham carried within his soul a hope strong enough to allow him to part from the boy who was his very heart. Abraham looked forward to the resurrection. And after three days of grieving his son's death ahead of time, he learned that God himself would provide the true sacrifice necessary to fulfill his gracious promises (verse 14).

Could Abraham have known that it would be God's own beloved, promised son who'd come into the world to save it, that God-incarnate would be torn upon the cross like those animals in his dark, dreadful vision? Could Abraham have known that, within three days, God's beloved son would rise from the dead, triumphant over sin and death and hell, to build the globe-spanning family God had promised to him?

There's good reason to believe, especially after Abraham got his boy back, that from that mountain the father of the faith could see much of what was to come, and perhaps much of the Redeemer who was to come from him and his boy. Jesus said to his critics, those sons of Satan, "Abraham saw my day, and he rejoiced" (John 8:56). Job saw it, too, and he likely lived before Abraham.

Job peered with Christ's light through the future's shadows and saw all the way to history's final day. As we thought about briefly in chapter 4, in the midst of his living nightmare, Job cries out, "For I know that my Redeemer lives, and at the last he will stand upon the earth. And after my skin has been thus destroyed, yet in my flesh I shall see God" (Job 19:25–26).

Job believed that he would stand in the presence of his Redeemer, his torn soul healed, his rotting flesh resurrected. He's insistent. In *this* body I will see him! And though no name is given, Job knows this Redeemer whom he'll see with his own eyes, this righteous One who will vindicate him body and soul before God. This Redeemer is God himself. "I know that my Redeemer lives... in my flesh I shall see God."

Seeing Is Believing (But Not Seeing Is Even Better Believing)

Paul saw the resurrected Christ, and he served as an apostle alongside other eyewitnesses like Peter and John. Just twenty or so years after Jesus rose from the dead, Paul writes in 1 Corinthians 15 that Jesus appeared to as many as 500 people at once after his resurrection. And Paul adds a note that lets us know how serious he is that Jesus is alive, that Jesus's resurrection was no metaphor, no collective hallucination of grieving people, and certainly no lie.[40] He tells us that most of those 500 people were still alive. In other words, go ask the eye-witnesses yourself! Having one or two available eye-witnesses is good for an attorney's case. Having at least 251 is juridical ecstasy.

Ah, but what about for us? We weren't there to see Christ alive from the dead. And if we're going to risk this much—risk ourselves and give ourselves to life-altering ideas we naturally hate but whose essential goodness is hard to deny—it'd be nice to see some proof that it's all real, that he, Jesus, is real. None of us wants to waste our lives on what might prove to be a wishful thought, or a cruel lie. Very understandable. Very reasonable. Once again, the Bible has us covered.

Jesus said, "Blessed[41] are those who have not seen and yet have believed" (John 20:29).[42] But he doesn't stop there. Just like with Abraham, God sealed his promises regarding what is unseen, by that which can be seen. This time, though, it's not as personally painful to participate in the signs and seals of the covenant of grace.

Before Jesus died, he instituted a practice in his church that would continually, tangibly remind people of his resurrection. The night he was betrayed, he observed the "Last Supper" with his disciples. Jesus took bread and wine and gave them to the disciples. Using the same kind of covenant language God used to instruct Abraham regarding circumcision—"This *is* my covenant"—Jesus speaks to his disciples: "This bread is my body, given for you. This cup *is* the new covenant in my blood. This do in remembrance of me" (Luke 22). Paul lets us know more of what the Lord said that night. "For as often as you eat this bread and drink this cup, you proclaim the Lord's death *until he returns*" (1 Corinthians 11).[43] The Lord's Supper lets us taste and see, physically feel and experience, the covenant of grace. It's a visceral reminder of Jesus's very real life, very real death, and very real resurrection. Eating and drinking in faith, we have sealed to our souls the truth that Jesus is risen from the dead and He is Lord, and that's he's returning. It's Jesus's gift to us of something tangible to bind us to what is, for now, intangible.[44]

Baptism does the same kind of thing for those who are entering God's family. It's something we can see, something we can touch that reinforces and seals into our souls the word, the promise, the covenant of grace. These sacraments don't stand alone. They confirm and strengthen our trust in that which is our soul's food, the written and preached word of God. And it's this word to which Jesus constantly refers us.

After Jesus's resurrection, he met up with two depressed, disgruntled disciples. They didn't know Jesus was alive, and Jesus kept himself from being recognized as he talked with them. Their messianic hopes had died with Jesus; they didn't realize that, according to the Scriptures, the Savior would be killed and rise within three days.[45] They hadn't paid close enough attention to their father Abraham.

Jesus calls them out for their lack of scriptural savvy: "How foolish you are, and how slow of heart to believe all that the prophets have spoken! Did not the Christ have to suffer these things and then enter his glory?" So Jesus, in what must have been the best Bible study in history,[46] "beginning with Moses and all the Prophets...explained to them what was said in all the Scriptures concerning himself" (Luke 24:27). Jesus found himself in the Scriptures, and he expected all who knew them well to find him there, too.

You have access to these very same Scriptures that Jesus opened to his dim-sighted disciples, and you have far more of God's word because we have the New Testament as well. We can, and must, see even more clearly that Jesus and the promise he fulfilled are on every page[47] of God's book, from first to last, from Genesis to Revelation.

"He Saw Reality and Thought It Was a Dream..."[48]

As a result of Jesus's finished work, we read the covenant of grace again in the Bible's closing chapters, this time not as prophecy, but as fully realized reality. From a passage we looked at in chapter 5:

> And I heard a loud voice from the throne saying, "Behold, the dwelling place of God is with man. He will dwell with them, and they will be his people, and God himself will be with them as their God. He will

> wipe away every tear from their eyes, and death shall be
> no more, neither shall there be mourning, nor crying,
> nor pain anymore, for the former things have passed
> away. (Revelation 21:3–4)

Notice the change of verb tense. All up until this point in Scripture, the promise had been: "I *will* make my dwelling among you." Now in Revelation, "Behold, the dwelling of God *is* with man." Jesus is Immanuel, God with us. Based on the work Jesus did when bodily in this world (he remains with us by his Spirit), John sees the day when God and all of his people are fully together, when there is no more separation between us and God, at all. No more not seeing the object of our faith. No more separation between our souls and bodies at death. No more fractured relationships, no more broken promises, no more broken world, no more suffering, because no more sin. This complex book of prophecy that closes God's book has a very simple message: Jesus did it. He is risen from the dead and he is Lord. Loving Withness, accomplished. And he is returning to apply to the world the full effects of the work he's already finished.

Until then, in this life, God keeps much in the shadows. God says to our knowledge what he says to the seas: "Thus far shall you come, and no farther" (Job 38:8-11). Dr. Dan Estes sums up Job's thoughts following God's illuminating, humbling interrogation: "What I know now is that I do not know, but I know that God knows…and that is sufficient."[49]

Job sounds like David in Psalm 131: "My heart is not proud, O Lord, my eyes are not haughty; I do not concern myself with great matters or things too wonderful for me. But I have stilled and quieted my soul…like a weaned child is my soul within me. O Israel, put your hope in the Lord both now and forevermore."

God the Father calls us to childlike faith. As we thought about in chapter 1, it's not that children are unintelligent. It's that they trust, and their lives depend upon being led by someone trust-worthy. As Abraham shows us, the Lord is absolutely that.

Of Tears and Trust

Imagine a little boy in an examination room in the ER with his dad. Scary people in scrubs surround him, talking in hushed tones, looking at monitors and then looking back at the boy, deep concern on their faces. No one is explaining what's going on, at least in a way he can understand. All he knows is that he's in pain and he's scared. But Dad is there, so it will be okay.

Then, one of the scrubby people comes close, and she's holding a needle. The boy's pulse starts pounding and, despite his burning fever, he breaks out in a cold sweat. But Dad's here. No way will he let that needle-wielding maniac touch him. She approaches with a look in her eyes that says, "I'm so sorry..." The boy looks to Dad with frantic eyes—*hit her!* But instead of punching the nurse like he should, Dad places both hands on the boy to hold him still. The boy screams, his heart pounding wild with fear and now anger at his alleged protector. A cold sensation against his arm, prepping him for the stick, and the needle goes in. And it hurts. He bawls, having lost all confidence that Dad will protect him from pain.

There's not one rational explanation, no matter how true and realistic, that can convince this child that what just happened to him was good, much less that it saved his life. He wouldn't, couldn't, and doesn't want to believe it. But there are certain truths he knows, and to these he clings.

He opens his streaming eyes and looks at the man who just let him suffer, who's now embracing him. The boy continues to cry on his shoulder, feeling the strength that could have prevented his pain, letting loose still more sobs. None of his questions answered, unable yet to comprehend what just happened or why it needed to. "It's okay," Dad says. "I'm here. I love you and I won't leave you." That much the boy knows; that much he believes. He trusts his father.

As we'll see next chapter, Jesus trusted his Father this way, though knowing far more than the little boy in the ER about what his father was doing and why.

But why doesn't God just give us more information to go on as we try to trust him? Why not let us see just a bit more into the shadows? Jesus understands our desire to know more so we can trust more. But instead of supplying all the truth we want from God, he points to himself as the truth by which we know and can trust him (John 14:6).

On the night before he died, Jesus said to his beleaguered, bewildered disciples, "I still have many things to say to you, but you cannot bear them now..." (John 16:12). Jesus never deceives us; he spares us truth that's too heavy to bear. That God keeps things in the shadows is mercy, not malice. In the same passage, Jesus tells his disciples, "Let not your hearts be troubled, neither let them be afraid" (14:27). "Believe in God; believe also in me" (14:1).

Into whose hands are you commending your heart and its heaviest thoughts? Upon whose cosmic shoulder are you crying? Have you convinced yourself that there's no one there for that, and that only the weak-willed and small-minded look for such a being? Do you consider yourself open to the question, but not to any answers—dogmatic in your agnosticism?

Two more questions and then I'll stop the interrogation— for now! Who are you trusting to tell you the difference between what's knowable and what's impenetrable mystery? Who are you trusting to tell you truth? God has given us the Bible, to tell us the truth we need to know, the truth we can know and bear now.

In calling us to Abraham's faith, Jesus is not calling us to believe anything he doesn't believe, and certainly not calling us to endure anything he hasn't endured. We'll think about his unique suffering next chapter. Jesus's trust in his Father was superlative, and it's the very best reason for ours.

Abraham was an early light in the darkness, a guiding star pointing us to the true light who was coming into the world (John 1:9). Abraham is the father of the faith; Jesus is the founder. Abraham was the patriarch: Jesus is the perfecter (Hebrews 12:2).

8

The Bible Is the Book of Life

"He beheld man's depths and dregs, all his hidden ignominy and ugliness. His pity knew no modesty: he crept into my dirtiest corners. This most prying, over-intrusive, over-pitiful one had to die. He ever beheld *me*: on such a witness I would have revenge— or not live myself."
—Nietzsche, *Thus Spake Zarathustra*

"What I need is a good defense,
'Cause I'm feelin' like a criminal.
And I need to be redeemed
To the one I've sinned against,
Because he's all I ever knew of love.
Let me know the way, before there's hell to pay;
Give me room to lay the law and let me go,
I've got to make a play
To make my lover stay,
So what would an angel say?
The devil wants to know."
—Fiona Apple, "Criminal"[1]

A good friend of mine was strolling with his dog through the woods when his canine companion suddenly spotted a rival animal. The dog took off after his nemesis and eventually cornered it against a tree, where the scrappy beast put up a nasty fight. My friend caught up and called his buddy away from the battle. The pooch obeyed, but he wasn't happy about it. As they got further from the scene of the fight, the demoralized dog was whiny and anxious, a deep internal struggle clearly vexing him. My friend stopped and said to him, "You want to go back, boy, don't you?" It was like the dog smiled. "Go." His buddy bolted back to the fight he just had to finish.

What are the fights in your life that, forgive me, dog you like that? The ones you can't stop thinking about, leaving you antsy and anxious? What are the failures that haunt you, the do-overs you'd do in a second if you could just go back and try again? When it comes to the pains of the past, something primal within us longs to atone for our failures, to finish our fights. We hunger for redemption.

To redeem means to get back something of what's gone, maybe something we gave up in a moment (or a decade) of bad judgment. God's image within us wants redemption from our moral failings. We're haunted by the fights we lost when we gave in to selfishness and fear and our hearts yearn to help the people we've hurt. Our conscience calls us to pay the moral debts we owe to God and our fellow image-bearers. But then, as usual, our godding fights back.

They started it! If they hadn't done this, we wouldn't have done that! But in those rare moments of honest, sober, quiet self-reflection, we realize that, at least for some things, we really are to blame. *NO!* says our godding. *We did what we had to, and they deserved it.* We try to justify ourselves—*ha! as if we needed to!*

Our godding is all ears to friends who tell us what amazing people we are and who couldn't care less about listening to the people we've hurt. We lap up the diagnoses of counselors who say that feeling guilty is our real problem, and that if we feel we owe God something, it's a straight-up psychosis. But getting rid of guilty feelings doesn't mean getting rid of guilt.

It's absolutely true that, sometimes in life, we really are the victims. In the tangled mess of human conflict, it can be terribly hard to know which guilty feelings we've earned and which ones we're not meant to bear. But in some things, much more than we like to admit, we are most definitely the perps. We've got legitimate guilt and no legitimate excuse.

Our godding naturally suppresses what we know in our souls to be true, and conditions beneath the ceiling of self allow us to go pro in self-deceit. If truth is going to get by our defenses down here, it's going to have to hit hard. This is where God's law drops in for a visit. And crushes us.

The Ten Commandments, especially as Jesus preaches them, drop on us from so much higher than the ceiling of self. They're an uncompromising standard strictly interpreted by a judge who cannot be bought off. When righteousness like that breaches our self-righteousness, we not only fall far short; we fall apart.

God's law locks our sights on our unpaid ethical debts, upon the fights we lost and keep losing to our godding. Just when we think we're gaining ground against it, our godding claws back all the more viciously. A scrappy beast is never more vicious than when it's cornered.

The more we battle, the more our hearts are besieged by previously unrecognized but now undeniable examples of our godding. How can we win a battle against ourselves? And even if we could, we could never undo the damage we've done to others. We're defeated and demoralized. We can ruin ourselves, but we can't redeem ourselves.

We could call it an unfair fight, curse God, and double down on autonomy, suppressing those stirrings within that call us higher than the ceiling of self but sound cruel because we can't scale those heights. But if we do what's harder, and humbler—if we accept both the impossibility of self-redemption and the illegitimacy of self-righteousness—then something beautiful and counter-intuitive happens. Hope for redemption opens before us, and we see Someone there who's willing to stand in our place and take up our fights.

Oh yes, you know where this is going.

Save Us, Superman! (And Then Leave Us Alone)

Biblically, redemption involves not only getting something back, but giving yourself up in the process. Your debt gets paid, but you get purchased! Jesus pays the moral debt we owe to God and simultaneously purchases us for him. There's no redemption if we don't renounce our godding. Jesus means to free us not just from the eternal consequences of godding, but from godding itself.

Even as Christians, learning what redemption really means might make us want to jump off the Jesus bandwagon. We don't naturally want to be redeemed; we just want to be rescued. We don't naturally want a biblically defined savior; we'd prefer a superhero.

Superhero films have been wildly popular this century. If we're into it, we have our favorites and there are likely some superheroes we think aren't so super. When my oldest son was eight, he weighed the merits of Superman and concluded that the Man of Steel is pathetic. Just one of the many reasons I'm so proud of my boy. Superman has it all—ridiculous strength, X-ray vision, the ability to fly, a full head of hair—Oooooo! It's all so easy for him that he's hard to respect. Batman is more like it. Batman has to earn his glory. There's a sense of realism there. Batman could happen, and I hope it does. And that's why—forgive me, Justice League fans—he and Superman should never be in the same story. But no matter what their stories, superheroes all have something in common we tend to really appreciate.

Superheroes are like us, but superior in some way. They excite our imaginations about life just beyond the normal. They make us wonder what it's like to fly or to have a full head of hair well into one's thirties. But for all their spectacular powers, they all agree to operate beneath the ceiling of self. We love the good guys for letting us live like we want to and swooping in for the rescue only when our godding gets out of hand, or when crazy powerful titans like Thanos decide to pay Earth a visit. Superheroes transcend us, but they don't try to transform us. We love them for this. Jesus is not like that.

The apostle Paul tells a group of Christians in a place called Corinth: "Do you not know that your body is a temple of the Holy Spirit within you, whom you have from God? You are not your own, for you were bought with a price. So glorify God with your body" (1 Corinthians 6:19–20).

The Corinthian Christians didn't realize fully enough that following Jesus meant walking away from their former way of life, which was all about sexual indulgence. As we'll think about more fully next chapter, our sexuality involves some of our deepest intimacies and our most intense internal drives, so it makes sense that it's the field of life on which we'll fight hardest to have total control. Undaunted, Paul tells the Corinthians that the risen Christ[2] is their Redeemer, their Savior and Lord, and that his law must rule all of their affections and activities.

Can't Jesus relax a little and let people do *some* godding? Nope. Jesus calls us to renounce our godding, not just to rein it in a little. But doesn't Jesus say he came to set us free? Yes and amen.

But in our godding, we don't want freedom. We want autonomy. We confuse autonomy with freedom in the same way we confuse superhero with savior, rescue with redemption. Though we hate to admit it, freedom demands what autonomy disdains: restraint.

Freedom allows flourishing within defined boundaries. For a rose to bloom, it has to be grounded in good enough soil, receive enough rain, and soak up enough sunshine. We might respond, "Rules are fine for flowers. We're human beings with wills and wants." Yes, and some of our wants will destroy us.

Imagine a dad walking on an ocean pier, holding the hand of his increasingly restless toddler daughter. The boards beneath them creak and groan as they walk further from the shore, and Dad decides it's time to pick his daughter up and carry her. Daughter's not having it. She tries to pull away, enticed by the waves and wanting to take a dive. In her mind, she can handle it. She's got her floaties on, so what could go wrong? Dad knows what she's thinking and he sweeps her up in his arms even as she kicks and screams her outraged protest. But if Dad really loves Daughter, shouldn't he honor her freedom, her deeply felt, sincere desire to show her strength and play amid the waves? Does Dad really have the right to restrain her in this way, to keep her from following her heart? Of course he does!

Dad knows what Daughter doesn't: that, despite her screaming insistence to the contrary, she can't handle what her heart wants. In this case, love restrains; love restricts; love does not respect the desires of the other. Despite his daughter's rage, Dad holds tight, and she lives. There is no earthly way she'll be convinced of it, but in her father's arms, she's truly free. It's his right and responsibility to keep her from certain of her heart's deepest desires, even if she hates him for it.[3]

There's just no avoiding it: for human life and the life of the world itself to flourish, certain laws apply. The Bible accuses us of breaking them all. Our redemption begins by pleading guilty.

One of the Bible's most prominent people, King David, gives us a perfect example of this painful, freeing plea.

A Royal Pain

David was Israel's greatest king—a legendary warrior, poet and musician who grew up a commoner and a shepherd. He wrote many of the Bible's songs, the Psalms, and some of them are personal confessions of his sin.

In Psalm 51, David confesses to crimes that ripped his and another family apart and would result in the fracturing of his kingdom. Two lesser kingdoms would form, Israel in the north and Judah in the south, and both would fall to pagan powers. This was the backstory of Jeremiah's miserable ministry to Judah. When kings live as a law unto themselves, the consequences for their royal subjects are catastrophic.

David's crimes included adultery and murder. While one of David's soldiers, Uriah, was away with David's army fighting the king's war, David quite uncharacteristically stayed home. He eyed up Uriah's wife, Bathsheba, and slept with her. A child was conceived. To cover up the child's true paternity, David summoned Uriah back to the home front to enjoy a bit of leave time and hopefully to sleep with his wife. Uriah obeys the king's summons, but refuses to go home to his wife. He says it would be disrespectful to his fellow soldiers still in the field and away from their families. In this situation, Uriah proves to be twice the man (at least) that Israel's greatest king was.

Insufficiently shamed, David tries to get Uriah drunk. If Uriah's sense of honor drowns, the morally stalwart soldier will finally go home and David's sin will remain a secret. But Uriah just falls asleep under the influence, drunk but still duty bound. Out of options, the king sends his noble servant back to the field, carrying sealed orders for David's general, Joab. Hoping Uriah will be killed, David commands Joab to send Uriah to the front lines and to pull the other soldiers back when the fighting gets fierce. It works.

When David hears of Uriah's death, he thinks he's won his own personal war to keep his sins from public scrutiny. Through all of it, David willfully forgets that God is watching, or at least that God doesn't play favorites—see James 2 on this—even if the sinner is the great king who'd served God so faithfully and courageously until then.

God sends a prophet named Nathan to confront David, but with a soft approach very similar to the way Jesus subtly convicted societally powerful people of breaking God's law.[4] The prophet told a story.

Nathan's tale was a tearjerker that struck all the right soft spots in David's heart and personal history; the clincher called forth David's kingly rage. There was a poor man who raised a little ewe lamb as a family pet. A rich man lived nearby and wanted to prepare a meal for a recently arrived guest. Instead of picking from his own numerous flocks, the rich man took the poor man's beloved pet and made mutton chops of it. David goes apoplectic: "As surely as the Lord lives, that man deserves to die!" God's prophet replies: "*You* are that man!" David disintegrates. The fictional story discovers the truth; the self-deceived, self-righteous king is exposed and undone (2 Samuel 12).

In his confessional prayer, David writes, "Against you, and you only have I sinned, and done what is evil in your sight" (Psalm 51:4). But hadn't David hurt so many people? Yep. And Psalm 51 is his public confession. Though he doesn't give details in the song itself, the situation is well known and even written into the song's introduction. And the fact that this confession comes through a psalm ensures that David's betrayed people would know his sincere sense of guilt and shame. The Psalms were written for public worship services, so every single time the people sang the 51st, they'd remember their hero's fall and his broken heart.

David, of all people, could have done some serious godding here and claimed exemption from guilt. *I was just following my heart. Happiness is truth—especially for a king! Laws are for lesser people; we who rule them are exempt.* (Sound familiar?) In David's day especially, a king could have called it all his royal prerogative, lived as if he'd done nothing wrong, and claimed that the fallout from his behavior was beneath his dignity to face. But David didn't. His was godly sorrow, not godding sorrow.

David felt and accepted the consequences of his crime, including those that devastated his own family. The child he'd conceived with Bathsheba died, and one of David's other sons eventually incited a revolution against him and died in the process. David's heart would be shattered over and over; he'd made his own life, and the lives of so many others, miserable. But he made no excuses; he owned his guilt. He knew he needed redemption. And stunningly (scandalously?), David found hope that redemption was possible, even for him. This was because David knew why his behavior was wrong to begin with.

As he writes in verse 4, David knows that his crimes can only be considered truly awful because they were committed ultimately against the God who gives human life meaning and dignity, whose life-preserving commands express the goodness of his heart.[5] David's confession does not callously dismiss his victims' pain; it appeals obediently to the one whose standards make that pain worthy of protest and tears and who calls sinners to repentance (verses 13 and following).

The Bible wants us to be angry at David. But we can't be upset if all David did was violate *our* code of conduct. We can say we don't like what he did, but beneath the ceiling of self, we can't condemn it as wrong. That's judging, and our culture's judgment on judging is that it's wrong. The only basis for right behavior, and therefore the only basis for righteous indignation at bad behavior, is God and the law he's given.

But if God is really all about law and order, and David is undeniably guilty of the most serious of sins, should God have forgiven David? (2 Samuel 12:13). Please be careful with your answer.

Because God's law comes straight from his heart, to break one of his laws is to break them all. A heartbreak is total; it doesn't happen by fractions. James helps us again: "For whoever keeps the whole law but fails at one point is guilty of breaking all of it. For he who said, 'Do not commit adultery,' also said, 'Do not commit murder.' If you do not commit adultery but do commit murder, you have become a lawbreaker" (James 2:10–11). Looks like David is doubly damned. But if James is right, it's not just double—it's total. And so it is for us.

David knew his soul needed deep cleaning, not just a surface-level wipe down. He leads, "Have mercy on me...wash me...cleanse me..." He knew that God wants truth to reside in our inmost being, for sincerity and lack of self-deceit to define the deepest parts of who we are (verse 6). God's law searches us out to that level, and no human being comes up clean, with the exception of one. This is why Jesus can be our Redeemer.

Jesus is unstained by our godding. He is not self-righteous; he's righteous in himself. He can pay the debt we owe to a relentlessly righteous God. But that raises another question, one that maybe you've had about the relative rightness of God's forgiving anyone based on what Jesus did: how is it right to forgive someone based on someone else's moral achievements? It's a really good question. So good, in fact, that before we answer it, we need to amplify it.

To understand the magnitude, let alone the rightness, of Jesus's redeeming work, we need to fathom the true depths of our need for it. Scripture tells us that our corruption as God's fallen image-bearers is not merely individual. The loving Withness that God built into creation was horrendously twisted into its mirror opposite form: a fundamental Withness, a corporate complicity, in the godding that killed the world. Our guilt goes back to our beginning, and to *the* beginning.

Enter the Dragon

In the garden of Eden, Satan assumes the form of a serpent and speaks to Eve (Genesis 3). At this point, people like to mock Scripture for telling us of a talking snake. I understand. I scream when I see snakes. Like we thought about in chapter 5, it'd be a total mind-freak if the serpent I'm screaming about actually spoke. But creation was brand new at that point. Who was to say that snakes didn't talk, or that language-adept beings couldn't speak through them?[6] Lots of details in the creation story are left out, but what God wants us to know is clear: the cunning subtlety of a serpent fit Satan's plans perfectly.

Satan was an angel, and apparently the original God-hater. He and other angels, at some point after creation, declared war on God and were cast out of heaven for their attempt to dethrone him (Revelation 12). Satan's revenge was to ruin the perfect peace between God and his image-bearers. The devil introduced our first parents to something their souls had not yet experienced: discontent.

God had given our first parents exalted status in a world of ceaseless wonders, so they would have absolutely no reason to attempt a cosmic power grab unless they began to believe that they deserved more, and that God was holding out on them. Otherwise, God's image-bearers would continue in blessed bliss. Satan couldn't stand the thought. But how to break the bond between the Creator and his most beloved creations? Easy. Go after that which binds them together. Get the image-bearers to question God's word.

Satan begins his inquiry: "Did God really say that you may not eat of any tree in the garden?" He's not trying to make sure he understood God correctly. *Is this what God really said? I want to be sure God is quoted accurately.* Not at all. This is subterfuge. The King James Version of the Bible, with its old-school, hissy "th" suffixes and its stately structuring of the English language, really captures the slithery feel of Satan's question, "Yea, hath God said...?"

Eve responds with God's command (and possibly a bit more),[7] "We may eat of any tree in the garden, but from the tree that is in the middle of the garden we must not eat of it, or touch it, or else we'll die."

"You will not surely die!" Satan says. He calls God a liar, and rather than laughing at such a silly idea or getting angry at such an evil one, Eve is intrigued. Her silence says, "Keep talking. I like where you're going with this."[8]

Remember, it was by God's speech that the universe burst into being. He said it, and it was. His word gave and sustained life. So there was no reason to believe that he spoke anything but reality, truth. When our first parents began to drift in their hearts from God's life-preserving law, it threatened the freshness and vitality and unfolding wholeness of the creation, a world integrated and at peace through God's word. To question God's word, his word, and his words—is to question his character.

God's integrity is a constituent part of created reality. If God lies, creation goes kaboom. It wouldn't be surprising if, when Adam and Eve began to doubt God's truthfulness, the world began to tremble. Like a calm and content baby, happily surveying her surroundings until she hears a sudden crash. She tenses hard and begins to shake, her eyes frantically searching for a danger she cannot see or understand. Creation should have been terrified at the world-shaking thunderclap of humanity's distrust of the Creator. But then again, what was terror? What was there to fear? The world was about to learn.

By questioning God's word, humanity exposed its jugular. The serpent struck.

The Cosmic Killjoy

Satan continues to impugn God's character. "God knows that in the day you eat of it, you will be like him." *God is an egomaniac! He's holding out on you. You could be just as great as he, and you deserve to be, but he won't let you. Eve, you could be powerful. You and your hubby could rule the whole world, no exceptions, and no one—except me, of course, but don't think about that—telling you what you can and can't do, what you can and can't be. Go on, Eve. Taste your freedom.* And she did. And she gave some to Adam, and he ate, too. And in the garden, on that day, we all died.

David affirms this in Psalm 51:5 by confessing himself sinful from the point of conception. In other words, we are sinful by nature. We begin life alienated from God, a separation so severe that Scripture calls it death (Ephesians 2:3–4).[9] Ever since that power grab in the garden, though we continue to bear God's image, godding is our natural bearing. As any parent can tell you, children need to be taught how to do what's right and selfless; they've already got wrong and selfish figured out.

Satan attacks any suggestion that our godding is not good for us. His argument has always been: You don't need to be redeemed; you need to be released!

Satan got our first parents to willingly think of God as someone he is not—a cruel tyrant. And that caricature has been encouraged through history by Christianity's harshest critics, including one we've met before.

Reading Nietzsche is like reading Satan's thoughts in the garden expounded and unfolded. (I don't mean that as an insult—and I don't think Nietzsche would have taken it as one.) They seem to think of God similarly; at least they describe him similarly as they willingly overlook clear truths and emphases within God's word so they can focus with contextless tunnel-vision on some and completely distort others.

In the garden, Satan's words draw a cartoonish version of God: an insecure deity with a dangerously fragile ego, which he protects with empty threats of death. Nietzsche takes out his literary crayons in the modern era and puts his artistic twist on Satan's sketch in the garden:

> Every sin is a slight to his honor—and no more. Contrition, degradation, rolling in the dust—all this is the first and last condition of his grace: in sum, the restoration of his divine honor. Whether the sin has done any other harm, whether it has set in motion some profound calamity that will grow and seize one person after another like a disease and strangle them—this

honor-craving Oriental[10] in heaven could not care less! Sin is an offense against him, not against humanity. Those who are granted his grace are also granted this carelessness regarding the natural consequences of sin. God and humanity are separated so completely that a sin against humanity is really unthinkable: every deed is to be considered *solely with respect to its supernatural consequences*, without regard for its natural consequences; that is what Jewish feeling demands, for whatever is natural is considered ignoble.[11]

This is satanic thought at its purest, which translates to human thought at its most poisonous. Don't we want to think of God this way? *God doesn't care about me and how I've been hurt. If he's there, he's far away. The only time he comes close is to tell me to beg forgiveness for following my heart and being who I really am—as if I'd actually want to be one of his people! They treat others so hatefully and feel so righteous in doing it; they call out other people's sins and feel just fine about their own moral stains. Hypocrites and cowards, the whole lot of them!* Sadly, it'd be crazy to deny the credibility of these criticisms in many cases. There have been many Christians whose personal actions or public "ministries" portray God just as the devil wants the world to see him. More to say next chapter.

For now, notice how Nietzsche takes a truth—God is profoundly offended by sin—and twists it in a direction the Bible never goes: God couldn't care less about the damage sin does to his creatures. As we saw with King David, sin is indeed first and foremost an offense against God. But even a casual view of commandments 6–10 shows that God is very concerned about how we treat other people. It's precisely humanity's closeness to God's heart that makes sin damning and deadly for the creatures made most like him.

Listen to just one example of God's pleading through his prophets with his stubborn, self-willed people. He says through Ezekiel, "As I live…I have no pleasure in the death of the wicked, but that the wicked man turn from his way and live; turn back, turn back from your evil ways, for why will you die, O house of Israel?" (Ezekiel 33:11).

Our godding brought death into the world. How can walking away from the one who is and who gives life yield anything but that bitter harvest? God wants us to live. To really live means to live lawfully. Since the garden, and increasingly beneath the ceiling of self, we'd rather be dead.

Die and Let Die

Even if our lives are not a matter of public record like David's, the most hidden, covered-up, secret motions of our souls rat us out when God's law gazes upon them. God knows it all, and that drove Nietzsche nuts.

"He beheld man's depths and dregs, all his hidden ignominy and ugliness. His pity knew no modesty: he crept into my dirtiest corners. This most prying, over-intrusive, over-pitiful one had to die. He ever beheld *me*: on such a witness I would have revenge— or not live myself."[12] This is the heartbreaking cry of a creature who hates that he's got a Creator.

God's law is that intrusive, that invasive. Nietzsche admitted that God's gaze was not a look of cruelty, but of pity. And that made it worse. Pity can enrage us; it feels so condescending. But the problem is, in many ways, we're pitiful! God does pity us; he won't pretend, as we do, that we're independent and authentic in ourselves. God tells us the truth, in love. Satan deceives us, and we love him for it. And that's the nasty truth of human nature since the fall: We prefer Satan's lies to God's love.

"Eating the apple"[13] still feels enticingly scandalous—for now. But once we've seized it and explored the most extreme versions of a once scintillating and scandalous pleasure, what then? What happens as we experience the compounding dissatisfaction, the desperate agony of an "ever increasing desire for an ever diminishing pleasure"?[14] Life becomes little but pain and unsatisfied longing. It only makes sense that these days, more and more people are seeking a quick and early exit to beckoning oblivion.

Others want to stay around and fight as long as they can for expanded godding rights, shaking a defiant fist in a dead God's face for reaching out from the grave to rule us by his book. Cultural dogma demands that we mock and despise rules that hold us back from exploring and experiencing our hearts' desires. We think it's wrong to restrain gods; we feel duty-bound to reach for that which God's book forbids.

But have you ever considered questioning that script?

Whom does all this rejection of God really serve? What's Satan doing in the garden except exalting himself as God and making slaves of God's greatest creatures? His work isn't about human empowerment; it's about human enslavement. It's not about living life to the fullest; it's about getting us to love and seek death.

By getting our first parents to question God's word, and therefore God's character, Satan turned everything in creation on its head, and set in motion all the painful ironies that fill life in this beautiful, bruised world. Satan made our first parents think of their privileges as a prison. By promising them life and power, he introduced them to weakness and death. His strategy still works on Adam's offspring, and he's happy to make tactical adjustments as necessary, just like he did in the modern West.

In the garden, there could be no doubt that God *had* spoken. The question Satan raised was about what exactly God said, and why he said it. The ceiling of self was built on the idea that God had never spoken; it answered with a firm "no" the question of whether God could or would want to speak to us directly. It's the same venomous question, "Yea, hath God said…?" but it bit doubly deep. In the garden, ignoring God's word by blatant disobedience led to undesired death. Beneath the ceiling, treating God as if he's dead has led to a greater desire for our own permanent demise.

We in the West have a front row seat to watch how the murder of God is playing out. Though there's still plenty of anger left, we're moving from rage against God to resigning ourselves to the idea that he's really gone. We're moving from the scream to the sigh. We're no longer in the anti-Christian phase of life; we're in the post-Christian phase.[15]

Those who'd moved on from God a long time ago, and young people growing up with God's death as the unquestioned ethos of their existence, are living the half-life between God's death and the rapidly growing desire for their own. "We are all statistically more likely to kill ourselves than we were ten years ago."[16] It's as if we're saying, "Now that we've gotten over God's death, we can finally get on with killing ourselves." For many in our godding culture, death is the new life.

Lacey Sturm was once completely convinced that she'd end her own life. Her childhood was marked by deep, traumatic pain within her immediate and extended family, including the murder of her three-year-old cousin. She rejected thoughts of truth and light as dishonest and blind.

> And being honest felt so much closer to being right. But eventually the shadows of darkness overwhelm and actually become part of you—that's what happened to me. Then it turns into a thirst for sadness. And it bends and twists into a very dark, animal-like thing, as if the sadness has given birth to an evil so sly and cunning that it seeps in and suddenly you're contemplating death, like I was. Or cutting. Or puking your food out all the time.[17]

Today's death wish is not always the bravado-laced "live fast, die young, leave a good-looking corpse" of previous generations. It's not always a desire for eternal glory by means of a spectacular burnout staged and caught on camera-phone; it's sometimes just a desire to be done. It can happen quietly, alone, unnoticed, and anywhere. We're transitioning from the hard, perennial difficulty of figuring out how to live to the new difficulty of figuring out why we should. What's the point, especially when life is full of so much pain? Or even if life feels beautiful and mysterious and full of wonder, many people think it's all the more beautiful to leave it on a high. Suicide increasingly comes with a smile.

Sometimes that smile is a wicked one. From vampires to cannibals, we're increasingly fascinated and even sexually aroused by the danger of devouring, and of being devoured. Sometimes the smile beams from someone in perfect health but who's decided that she's had enough.[18] Either way, it seems that death is the part of life that interests us most. Death is no longer just the inevitability lurking and looming in the recesses of our thinking. Death is now our default mode. It's something we desire, and increasingly, it's something we demand.[19]

It's always been within our natural power to end our own lives. But now we feel entitled to that death, to have other people pay for it and to have people we consider properly equipped do the actual killing.

For some, it's not so much the desire to die, but the desire to have that right—again, not simply the ability, but the right—as in the state-sponsored, state-enforced guarantee. If death is our right, then we are due compensation of some sort if it's denied to us, and other people can be forced by law to provide it for us.

The West is being swept up in a tidal wave of persistent, aggressive demands to recognize and enforce people's "right to die"—access to doctor-assisted suicide, not only at times of great suffering in the midst of a diagnosed, terminal illness, but any old time at any young age we want. As we saw with the Enlightenment and the philosophical and theological forces at play in Western Europe at the time, major, society-shifting and -shaping ideas are once again "hopping the pond," traveling from Europe to find a home in the United States and Canada. As of this writing, Canada has just legalized euthanasia and is rapidly approaching Sweden[20] as the most "liberal" right-to-die society in the world.

But maybe, as films like *Million Dollar Baby* and *Me Before You* teach us, life really isn't worth living if it can't be lived fully on your terms, or someone else's.[21] If someone is a successful athlete but suffers a devastating, career-ending, life-altering injury, and she decides she can't live any longer without the fans' applause, suicide's a good way to go.

Or, if someone has a physical handicap, is loved romantically by someone else, but realizes that he's holding her back from having a fuller relationship with a more able-bodied person, why shouldn't he just do his love interest a favor and off himself? It'll be great. We'll celebrate the self-sacrifice as the very essence of romantic love. We'll put a sweet soundtrack to it, and self-inflicted death will enjoy the fame and appreciation it deserves in our society.

Can you imagine Valentine's Days based on this view of love? "This year, give your Valentine the gift that lasts forever: your death!" At this point, card companies probably wouldn't go for it. Too edgy. But maybe they're not enlightened enough. There's a growing market and money to be made. Are we really that far from the day when greeting card companies start selling suicide notes?

Isn't it beautiful—all this freedom? NO. It's hellish.

Both of the films mentioned assume that life is only worth living, for you or someone else, if all your body parts are working well and your partner is getting everything she wants out of you. Human life in that case is not inestimably valuable; it's cheap. And when we remember that so many people in the world struggle with severe physical limitations, it's a shockingly heartless dismissal of their full significance as human beings in themselves, and of their infinite value to other image-bearers.

God placed the desire for survival like a fire in the human heart. We were meant for life, *everlasting* life. Death, though everywhere all the time throughout history and the world itself, is actually unnatural to us and to the world. It's not by design, and it's why, when our hearts are thinking clearly, the death of someone we love shakes us, especially when someone leaves us by suicide.

Suicide still saddens society, for now. It still baffles many in older generations, while more and more younger people see it as just a thing to do, maybe *the* thing to do. It would probably shock most older adults to know just how commonly and casually suicide is discussed among young adults as a viable if not inevitable end for their lives.

That people feel free to discuss these issues openly is good; some who harbor suicidal thoughts are terrified to mention it to others, especially older adults. More than they fear ending their lives, they fear the scandalized eyes with which loved ones would look upon them if they admitted their feelings. Please, if you have these thoughts, speak up—don't give in to the fear that would keep you silent. I've listed in this endnote some wonderful, understanding resources.[22]

Getting used to suicide is a sure sign that as a people, as a culture, we're dying. Well, maybe the deadening of that instinct for life demonstrates that life really is pointless after all. Maybe it's time for the human story to end, for our species to exit Earth's stage. Maybe this is just how it should be? How it has to be? Hell. No.

The weakening of a vital organ doesn't demonstrate its purposelessness. It makes us realize just how important that body part is and how serious the disease must be that is shutting it down. So, too, the weakening of the will to live, the increasing inability to exult in the glory of living, should let us know that something is deeply wrong within and among us. Something has infected us, something venomously hostile toward life, toward the stirrings we learn to suppress in our souls, toward all that we and the world itself were meant to be. In the dark beneath the ceiling of self, Satan has sunk his fangs deep into the postmodern West.

Jesus came to heal humanity's snakebite, to expose Satan's lies, and to liberate us to live and love life in a way that's superlative at all points. Jesus came to provide redemption, and freedom.

This life-loving freedom begins by taking a humble, honest look at the law of God, not through snake eyes, but through the eyes of the dragon slayer.

Love Hurts

The essential satanic lie is that freedom and compulsion are opposites, that love and law are enemies. And sure, some laws are unloving and some forms of compulsion are nothing but cruelty. It all depends upon the source and the aim of the rules in question. And whether we realize it or not, we've likely all experienced, and deeply enjoyed, mutually complementary combinations of love and law, freedom and compulsion. Here's how.

Is there someone in your life whose smile hits you like a force of nature? It doesn't matter where you are or who you're with: if that person locks eyes with you and grins, you're done. You can't help but beam back in return. Perhaps when you realize what's happening, you bury your face so no one, especially *that* person, will see how flushed it is. But think about those precious few seconds before self-consciousness kicked in and you felt you had to hide your feelings. In that small space of time, you felt eternity—time was moving and your heart was pounding, but it was all somehow timeless, undying. You felt fully alive, fully conscious, but not yet self-conscious about it. You were unashamed, unafraid, sincere, open—you were shining. If only for a moment, you were free. And yet that freedom came by force—gentle, yes, but irresistible. When that gale-force grin hit you, your inmost being came storming to the surface, honest and free. You couldn't help it, and in that situation, it's good to be helpless.

This happens to me when I see my daughters smile. Their smiles are symphonies. They take me out of myself and leave me beaming in blessed, unself-conscious sincerity. In a split second, they can draw my deepest affections to the surface for all to see. I'm powerless to stop it, and I have no desire to. In the presence of something so wonderful, vulnerability is a virtue. Weakness is strength. Confinement is freedom. There's a way to describe the sweet ache of that forced freedom: it's called being captivated.

This is how Jesus felt about the law of God. God's law drew out the depths of his being and held him spellbound, day and night (Psalm 1). He loved it, lived it, and died to fulfill its righteous requirements. He wept when people rebelled against it. He even sang its praises as he sang Scripture's songs, the Psalms.

Significantly, the longest single passage in all of God's word is the 119th Psalm, an acrostic that scores the praise of God's law according to each of the twenty-two letters of the Hebrew alphabet, suggesting the totality, the completeness and moral perfection of God's commands. David wrote this song, but as we've seen, he fell so far short of his own claims. Jesus came to keep God's law as the true King, the rightful and morally upright Ruler that David, and Adam before him, failed to be. Jesus kept this law, flawlessly, from his heart. "I delight to do your will, O my God; your law is within my heart" (Psalm 40:8). He never failed David's words; he fulfilled them (Hebrews 4:15).

Though morally spotless, Jesus sang confessions of sin like Psalm 51.[23] He understood that sin incurs death (Romans 6:23), and he understood and identified himself with sinners (Isaiah 53). Though we've done such shameful things, Jesus was not ashamed to stand alongside us, and to stand for us (Hebrews 2). He resented neither the law nor those whose rebellion against it would cost him his life.

Our godding despises it, but Jesus had no problem with the law's insistent intrusiveness. God desires truth in the inmost being. And that's exactly what the law's prying eyes always found in Jesus.

Why did Jesus so deeply love such a demanding law? It's not just because he was a law-and-order kind of guy, blindly following rules because, well, those are the rules! There are lots of stupid rules on the books. Jesus loved God's law because it was good. In it he heard the familiar voice of someone he loved and trusted, the one whom he calls, and wants us to call, Father.

Trust Issues

The love between God the Son and God the Father is mutual, infinite and eternal. The Father proclaimed his love for his son with that Isaac-esque proclamation at Jesus's baptism. And Jesus is just as delighted with his Father, as he shows by singing and fulfilling his Father's law. "Oh, how I love your law!" (Psalm 119:97)

How many sons sing the praises of their fathers' house rules? Some forlorn, fatherless children might actually do that if they were taken in by a father who loved and was there for them. In that kind of household, kids come to know that, though their father's rules are restrictive, they're given in love. Jesus knew this of his Father's law.

Every human being alive now and who's ever lived could agree that God does or says things that shred our hearts. Count Jesus in this category. But Jesus stands out among all of us for never doubting God's goodness and righteousness in the midst of his pain. He prays just before he gives himself over to the authorities who'd commission his crucifixion, "O righteous Father, even though the world does not know you, I know you" (John 17:25).

Love and trust for Dad do not always join hands in the heart of a son. So many boys and men can't help but love their dads forever, but they wouldn't trust him for a second. One of the reasons we hold on to our autonomy even when we admit the mess it tends to make of our lives is that, unlike Jesus, we don't know who we can really trust to lead us to what's true and right. It can be so, so hard to really, truly trust.

Even if we take the hard step of admitting that someone has rightful authority over us, it's another huge leap of the soul to actually trust that powerful person. We might feel like it's a form of (undesirable) suicide to subject our thoughts to that person's review, and even worse to seek their approval, and worst of all to invite their correction. What little of ourselves we feel we have left might scream from within and beg us not to take that one final, terrible step beyond acknowledgment of authority and into trust.

Trusting feels like a gamble, and the stakes get higher depending on what we're giving over to someone else. Scripture calls us to give everything—every last thing—all that we are, have been and will be, all that we want and need, nothing held back, to God. Having "all-in" love for God means trusting God unconditionally, unlimitedly, and unreservedly (Proverbs 3:5–6). Terrifying, isn't it? Even as a Christian.

But isn't there also something so appealing about it? Wouldn't it be wonderful to trust like that? There are times when you do, when trust is instinctive, and you're not afraid.

Think back to that special someone's force-of-nature smile. When you're captivated, someone or something from outside reaches deep within you; the sometimes-wordless conversation between our souls and the source of their transport is perfect, and full of peace. These moments are ruled out by the ceiling of self, which bars access to anything good beyond us, but we don't care. For those moments, we forsake and forget the ceiling. They're just too good, too pure to miss for the sake of philosophical consistency. In these times of trust, we're not looking to be treated like gods. We're happy to be humbled; we're longing to be led.

Jesus trusted God's law this way, because he loved and trusted his Father this way. He fulfilled the first and greatest commandment; he was all-in. And this is what made him what even many non-Christians might regard him to be: the most loving, compassionate, selfless man who's ever existed. It makes sense. Jesus says the second great commandment is like the first: all-in love for every image-bearer. Good laws, loving laws: the blueprints for full and abundant life, love, and freedom for all of us and the world itself.

Of course, we have the capacity to be captivated by the wrong things. And we've already thought a lot about the ease and dangers of self-deceit. Some would consider Jesus naïve for his complete love and trust in his Father, a sign of weakness or a lack of intelligence. But aside from the awkwardness of claiming to be spiritually stronger and smarter than Jesus, or to know God better than Jesus did—fairly ambitious claims to make, especially if we clear our hearts of chronological snobbery—we're once again faced with the fact that Jesus's two commands, which sum up God's ten and upon which Jesus says the entire Old Testament depends (see Matthew 22:37–40), are unwaveringly and uncompromisingly good. The Ten Commandments are sometimes called "the ten words," ten serving very significantly in Scripture to indicate completion.[24] Those ten words reveal the perfect goodness of God's heart.

This is why the law is so invasive and uncompromising. God's boundless heart holds, and his all-seeing eyes find out, every secret in the universe. So his law searches out and finds the smallest moral faults, the tiniest deficiencies of love. His relentless desire for justice expresses itself in what sound like over-the-top penalties for thinking and acting unjustly. But contrary to popular opinion, God's law is not only about what we cannot do.

Every "thou shalt not" has its positive flip side. So if we're not even to be unjustly angry at another human being, we *are* to do everything we can to act, speak, and even think in life-giving ways toward that other person. Sounds like love! And this is why Satan hated Jesus so much.

When Jesus redeems people, he frees them from the guilt of breaking God's law, reinvigorates the image of God that they bear, and begins a renovation that brings them increasingly up to code according to God's loving law. Jesus was ruining the hard work Satan had done since the garden. The devil couldn't stand it any longer. The Savior had to be stopped.

Satan attacked and killed humanity in Eden. His attack against God in the flesh would take place not in a lush garden, but in a barren wilderness. The results were, well, quite different.

Round Two

After his baptism, Jesus went on a fast. Believers sometimes abstain from eating to spend especially intense time in prayer, feeling viscerally their dependence upon God for life and sustenance. If they're particularly burdened, they might fast for a day or more. Jesus did this for forty days. In one of the Bible's biggest understatements, Matthew tells us that after these days, Jesus was hungry (Matthew 4:2).

Seeing the Savior at the point of starvation, Satan seized his opportunity. "If you are the Son of God, command these stones to become bread." *Jesus, what are you doing to yourself? What's the point? Claim your divine rights. You don't need a hunger strike to prove you're God's son. All this suffering is so far beneath you!*

But Jesus refused. He responded, "Man shall not live by bread alone, but by every word that proceeds from the mouth of the Father." This answer deeply offended the prince of demons.

Not only did Jesus refuse Satan's slyly sycophantic suggestion, but he cited Scripture as the reason. Satan was able to get Eve and Adam to question God's word and resent his rules, and this was when they were in paradise, well fed and doing just fine—perfectly, in fact. And here was Jesus, nearly dead from hunger, alone in an arid land, the weight of a wrecked world upon his shoulders, with seemingly every reason in that world to question the integrity and goodness of the way God was running it, not least his deathly design to save it through his own son's unimaginable suffering—and still, Jesus quite literally would not bite. And that's because Jesus saw the hook beneath the bait.

Jesus says in John 4:34 that his food is to do the will of the one who sent him. The Savior wasn't being overly spiritual. He was truly human, and humans have to eat. But more basic than that most basic human instinct to physically survive was Jesus's soul-deep commitment to doing his Father's will. Exactly the level of commitment he needed in order to endure the cross.

For Jesus to live any part of life on his own terms and not on the terms stipulated by his Father would be to repeat humanity's original rebellion all over again, to act as if God was anything less than fully true and trustworthy. And just as Eve demonstrated in those horrible moments, to believe that God is untrustworthy is to believe that Satan is worthy of trust. Jesus knew differently. Whenever Satan presents his case against God to Adam's offspring, he's always hiding something. And that's because he's always after something. How compelling do you find his arguments?

It's only through the eyes of God's word that we can see what Satan's hiding, and it's only by trusting God's word that we can prevent him from getting what he's after. He's hiding his inability to provide you with what you want, with what he offers you: godhood. And he's hiding this inability in order to get you to worship him as god.

Satan tried a second time to lead Jesus away from following the word of his Father (Matthew 4:5–7). But very Abraham-like and even better,[25] Jesus kept moving ahead, faithfully, not straying to the right or the left of his Father's straightforward rules (Deuteronomy 4:2, Joshua 1:7). After his second spectacular fail, Satan put all his cards on the table.

Satan showed Jesus all the kingdoms of the world and said that he would give them all to Jesus, if he would only fall down and worship him (verses 8–9). *All right already! Just do what Adam did, will you? Take all that love and trust and loyalty away from the God whose plan for you is literally killing you, and give it all to me!*

But didn't Jesus, if he was really God, already own all those kingdoms? Yes. It seems Satan was offering to remove his influence from the world, as if to say to Jesus: "You can earn your crown without suffering the cross!" But Jesus came to beat Satan, not bow to him.

Jesus needed to earn as a man what he already owned as God. And to do this, he had to die—not from starvation, but nailed to a cross as a substitutionary sacrifice, bearing our sin and guilt. And to be an acceptable sacrifice, he needed a spotless record when it comes to sin. Adam represented all of humanity and failed to keep God's law. Jesus would keep it, and represent all of fallen humanity who'd find forgiveness and redemption in him. This is why Jesus is often called the second Adam. Human sin wrecked the world, so human obedience would save it. It's just that this human would also be God (Romans 5).

In a very real sense, Satan ultimately didn't stand a chance. But that doesn't mean he wouldn't do all he could to hate and hurt God's son along the way. A scrappy, nasty beast is never more dangerous than when it's cornered. Though in one way Satan did not want Jesus to go to the cross and bear the judgment due our godding, in another way he must have lusted for that day to come. Satan seemed to understand that the cross would mean his defeat, but it was also an opportunity to unleash hell on the Son of God himself. And he wouldn't miss that for the world.

The crucifixion was "the point where evil, including the violence and terror and the nonhuman forces that work through creation, had become truly and fully and totally itself."[26] But during those dying hours, Jesus's affection for his Father never fled him, even though he felt that the Father had forsaken him. The Savior screamed from the cross, "My God! My God! Why have you forsaken me?!" These were the perfect, and the prophesied, words to express his agony as the sin-bearer. These words open Psalm 22. Jesus fulfilled God's breathed-out words until his dying breath. Enduring hell, the Son of God remained faithful to his Father's word.

"Though He Slay Me, Yet Will I Trust in Him..."[27]

Jesus's question from the cross was sincere, but he knew its answer. Jesus was forsaken by the Father so that we would never have to be, so that you would never have to be. The essential pain of Christ's cross was not the indescribable physical suffering—though that cannot be underestimated. It was the unprecedented agony of aloneness. On the cross, Jesus experienced something he had never known in timeless ages past: the Son in whom the Father was so pleased felt his father's displeasure.

Jesus felt the death that sin earned, the separation from God's loving favor and protection. He felt the weight of his Father's silence. But he knew all of this was coming. He knew it was right, and righteous.

For many atheists, agnostics, and ex-Christians, and many Muslims as well, a God who would do this to his son is unworthy of worship. Bishop John Shelby Spong, who claims for some reason to be a Christian, calls it "cosmic child abuse."[28] Once again, it doesn't seem to matter enough to change the critics' minds that Jesus completely disagreed. You'd think that disagreeing with a person whom they'd likely regard as one of history's top ten or so most significant people, and doing so regarding the subject matter of his indisputable and inimitable expertise, would give them pause. You'd think.

The Scriptures prepared Jesus, as much as he could be, for the world's darkest hours, during which he'd hang between heaven and earth to bring God and his image-bearers together again. Psalm 22 was written about 1,000 years before Jesus came into the world. David describes a time of personal agony, using poetic exaggeration that described Jesus's pain literally. Long before crucifixion was invented, David describes himself as surrounded by mockers, enemies who've pierced his hands and his feet. Still loving, still trusting, Jesus's dying words were yet more Scripture. Just before his soul left his body, Jesus cried out, "Father, into your hands I commit my spirit" (Luke 23:46, citing Psalm 31:5).

Jesus did it. It was finished—all that was necessary for anyone to be redeemed. And to show his continued love for and approval of his son and the magnificent work of salvation his son accomplished, and to bring all his sons and daughters home, God raised Jesus from the dead. Jesus earned as man a right standing before God, and in that standing, the resurrected Christ puts his arms around all who trust him for redemption, who believe that he is who God's word says he is, and who give him their lives accordingly. Paul says that Jesus was raised to life for our justification (Romans 4:25), our being declared righteous in God's sight through trusting in Christ's finished work.

And that brings us back to the really good question we had to amplify before we could answer. How is it just that we, guilty by association with Adam and guilty by our own daily godding, could be forgiven, much less declared righteous, based on what someone else has done?

Both Sides Now

If God is really all about law and order, and if our godding really does deserve and bring death, then how can redemption be right? How can one person, even if morally perfect, atone for the moral faults of another? Paul was very concerned about this, too. So was the apostle John. So were all of the biblical authors whose writings contributed to the story of God's reconciling the world to himself in his son.

To redeem genuinely guilty people, it seems like God would have to go schizophrenic, pitting his inviolable justice against his limitless mercy. But God decided from eternity past that mercy and justice must meet together, neither dishonoring nor diminishing the other. And it was through the sinless life and in-our-place death and resurrection of Jesus the Christ, God with us, that they could.

In God's conflict with his godding image-bearers, the Word (fully God) made flesh (fully human) can represent both parties equally. Jesus agrees with God's law that sin earns death, and he advocates on behalf of sinners seeking forgiveness and redemption. And it's not as if God the Father had to be convinced against his will to provide redemption. He's the one whose love for the world sent Jesus into it (John 3:16).

Because of Christ's spotless obedience to God's law, Paul tells us in 2 Corinthians 5:21 that God made Jesus, who committed no sin, to be a sin offering for us so that we could have a right standing before God. Jesus gets our sin and we get his righteousness. As Paul puts it in 1 Corinthians 1:30, Christ *is* our righteousness. This is the vision that dried Jeremiah's tears—or maybe made him weep with joy! (Jeremiah 23:6).

Paul writes in Romans 3:26 that God is both just and the justifier of the one who has faith in Jesus. John agrees, writing, "If we confess our sins, God is faithful and just to forgive us our sins and to cleanse us from all unrighteousness" (1 John 1:9). Notice,

John doesn't write, "God is faithful and *merciful* to forgive us for our sins." That's true, but that's not John's point.

John writes that God is "faithful and just"—righteous—"in forgiving us our sins and cleansing us from all unrighteousness." In Jesus, God provides a forgiveness that does not defy his justice, but that establishes it (Romans 3:31). All who come to God through Jesus Christ can be assured, can know for certain, that they are forgiven, that they have a right standing before God. They've sought God on his terms. Their redemption is not only a matter of divine mercy; it's a matter of divine justice.

And contrary to Christianity's harshest critics and its worst hypocrites, God's true children desire to honor and love their Father by loving and blessing all image-bearers, and the world itself. Those are God's house rules.

Redemption frees our hearts to love to their fullest. Jesus says that the person who has been forgiven much will love much (Luke 7:47). Our godding keeps us from recognizing just how much we need to be forgiven. God's law shows us, and points us to the one who fought for us the war against sin and self, the war we could never win. We can't undo the past, but giving our lives to the one "who inhabits eternity," and who gave his life to bind up and heal what's desperately broken in life, is the best thing we can do for those we've hurt in our godding. Jesus sets us free so we can really love, lawfully love, all image-bearers—including ourselves.

How much we need that love, and the life of true freedom to which it leads—we who are so surrounded by death!

Life Sentences

Living in a culture already immersed in death and diving deeper still, it can be tempting for us to give up hope for fuller, freer life. Maybe your past is so painful, your present filled with so much fear and loneliness, you think the only way out is to prevent your future. Please think about this one truth, deeply, if even for a few moments: you are alive.

Maybe you've been the victim of other people's sin, and fear and shame and self-loathing are like breathing for you, and you're not sure you want to breathe anymore. Your life might feel like a hellish mess right now, but you're alive in the midst of the mess. And that is good, and right, and beautiful. Please do not

ever—ever—give in on any level to the lies, from others or yourself, that tell you otherwise.

Falsely accused of his father's murder and likely facing years
of hard labor in Siberia as a result, the third Karamazov brother,
Dimitri, is nevertheless at peace. He tells his Christ-loving brother
Alyosha of the joy that's drenched his soul since he stopped living
for himself and found his way back to the Lord. Alyosha visits
Dimitri in prison, and Dimitri can't contain himself: "I seem to
have such strength in me now that I think I could stand anything,
any suffering, only to be able to say and to repeat to myself every
moment, 'I exist.' In thousands of agonies—I exist. I'm tormented
on the rack—but I exist! Though I sit alone in darkness—I exist! I
see the sun, and if I don't see the sun, I know it's there. And there's
a whole life in that, in knowing that the sun is there....all these
philosophies are the death of me. Damn them!"[29] Philosophies like
the ones coming to full, hellish flower in our day, the ones that say
that we're the rightful rulers of our lives, and therefore of all of life,
the ones that keep us trending and tilting toward death as the only
meaningful aspect of life.

Please turn from all that noise and chaos and untruth and
instead look to and listen to the image of God that you bear, urging
you to live. And listen to Jesus's voice through his Scriptures, which
are the words of life.

Beneath the lies we're tempted to believe—that life without
God is better, or that life without us is better—the truth remains:
life itself is beautiful, and every human life bears God's image
and is valuable beyond description and price—and you are no
exception.

To see that, you have to see yourself through the all-seeing eyes
of the God who got you here somehow, who knows you exhaustively, intrusively. Sometimes that divine look comes through the
eyes of someone else who sees what God sees.

If Looks Could Kill (Then Maybe They Can Save!)

Lacey Sturm was going to commit suicide. She knew it as fact.
But on the day she planned to do it, a series of events unfolded that
led her to a church service. On her way out, a man gently spoke to
her. He was from the church but she didn't know him. He looked
at her, tears in his eyes, with unnerving Christlike compassion. She

didn't really know what that was or looked like, but there it was, in that man's eyes.

"This strange man held me in place with a look that conveyed his genuine, humble, selfless love for me. And I couldn't go anywhere, because I didn't know this man and was completely perplexed by why and how he could love me."[30]

He told her things about her life that he had no way of knowing; he cried for the lawless things that had been done to her and those she loved in her young life, creating so many scars on her soul and setting her on a collision course with a death that, until this very strange situation, she had craved. He lamented the lawless things she was doing, too, culminating in her plan that day to take her own life. He pleaded with her to give her life to the God who'd made her, who'd seen her suffering, who'd been there without her knowing it as she cried herself to sleep at night. God beheld her, but up until that point in her life, she'd been unwilling to look to him. The man asked Lacey if he could pray for her.

She was at a crossroads. She could have told the old weirdo to back off and to take his prudish, pushy religion with him, with its repressive rules about right and wrong and its cruel god who'd allowed such horror into her life. Up until that point in her life, she probably would have. But this moment was different. She was captivated. Her life exposed, her deep pain brought so uncomfortably but somehow lovingly to the surface, she shocked herself by agreeing to his request. And he prayed to God, calling God his Father.

"Heavenly Father, wrap your arms around this girl whom you created, like the loving Father that you are." Lacey writes: "As he prayed, a great warmth wrapped around me. I felt a sense of holiness I had never felt before in my life, like God was embracing me. It felt familiar. It felt like I was finally home."[31]

The Book of Life

You might think, "Well, that was a nice thing that happened to Lacey. But no one's ever done that for me." Are you sure?

It's no accident that you're reading this book. And I don't claim to have anywhere near the significance in your life that the older gentleman did in Lacey's. But this book is written to help take you to the same place he led her, to help you understand the language and personalize the word of the Father who'll gladly receive you as a beloved child come home.

God's word is his looking upon us with that knowing, frightening, maddening, calming, captivating love; Scripture is his speaking to us about himself and about us.

When silence falls around you and the whispers start within you, will you let the Lord's voice, his word, join the conversation? Are you willing to allow his word to identify and speak against what lying whispers tell you in their soft-spoken, satanic malice? Will you trust that God knows better, and that he knows you best?

Yes, God's word is revealing, uncomfortably at times, but it sees and discloses reality. Yes, God's law is intrusive, but he's no intruder. When David wasn't trying to hide sin, God's perfect knowledge calmed and stabilized him. In Psalm 139, he writes, "Lord, you have searched me and known me. You know when I sit down and when I rise up. You discern my thoughts from afar.... you hem me in, behind and before, and lay your hand upon me. Such knowledge is too wonderful for me. It is high, I cannot attain it. Where shall I go from your Spirit?"

David, who had been racked with guilt and had begged God not to take his Holy Spirit from him (Psalm 51:11), now realized that God isn't going anywhere—and that's because he's everywhere! "If I ascend to heaven, you are there. If I make my bed in the depths, you are there. If I take the wings of the morning and dwell in the uttermost parts of the sea..." (Psalm 139:8–9).

These words serve equally well as expressions of frustration or faith, of panic or peace—*I can't get rid of him!* versus *He's always there for me.* It all depends upon your heart's disposition toward God, whether you believe and trust his word.

The Bible brings us to a crossroads. Where godding balks and asserts its phantom autonomy, faith bows and confesses God's rightful reign over us. Our sin separates us from him, but he sent his son to buy us back from the slavery into which we sold ourselves through our first human father. To be redeemed is not only to be bought back from a cruel master; it's to be brought back to a loving father. We even get a big brother in the process!

To be redeemed is to be related to Jesus, not just as a servant, but as a sibling. Hebrews 2:11 tells us that he is not ashamed to be called our brother. David basked in this brotherly love. He was redeemed. Despite all he'd done, he knew he was loved. Do you know this about yourself? Will you trust that it's true, coming from the Word of God?

When we trust, we feel like we're giving ourselves away, or at least some of ourselves, and maybe giving it up for good. That's scary. It's also inevitable.

We've all got a god. Our god is the idea, the person, the system of values for which we will, if forced, forsake all things. Our god is that in which we find our true selves and the terms by which we feel we must live, and by which others must accept us. Our god is that for which we're willing to be rejected by those we love, or often is the reason why we're willing, and sometimes eager, to reject others. As we'll think about next chapter, our god is who we trust to answer the question we all have of ourselves: "Who am I?"

Jesus says, "The one who loses his life for my sake will find it." He's not talking about being martyred, though untold numbers have died throughout history for refusing to renounce him. He's certainly not talking about suicide. He's not talking about the end of living; he's talking about the beginning of real life. He's talking about you with no ceiling.

Home, Free

Right now, this moment, you are alive. You are like the living God. You may have done things that you believe are worthy of death, but redemption is possible. And through Christ, redemption is morally right. Christ finishes your fights for what's real and true and good, and teaches you to face the rest of your life's battles in his strength.

Being redeemed is not only to be owned by the Lord. In a very real sense, it's also to own him. God gives himself to his redeemed people as *our* God. Paul identifies Jesus as the one "who loved me, and gave himself for me" (Galatians 2:20). David writes, "O God, you are my God" (Psalm 63). And as the author of the Song of Solomon puts it: "I am my beloved's, and my beloved is mine."

God has bound himself forever, willingly, to his redeemed people. As he gazes upon them with that relentless, all-knowing, unnerving, and constant compassion—he's captivated. He's a redeeming God, so the objects of his redeeming love draw out the depths of his being. Jesus loves bringing people home to his family. "Behold," he says with joy, "I and the children God has given me" (Hebrews 2:13, 12:1).

Jesus says in John 10:10, "I came that they may have life, and have it abundantly." Trust him. He's the Lord of life, and he wants you to live forever.

9

The Bible Is the Book of Love

"In Catholic school, as vicious as Roman rule,
I got my knuckles bruised by a lady in black.
I held my tongue as she told me,
'Son, fear is the heart of love,'
So I never went back."
—Death Cab for Cutie, "I Will Follow You into the Dark"[1]

"Perfect love casts out fear."
—the apostle John, 1 John 4:18

Have you ever had to tell your loved ones something about your-self that you knew would devastate them? The fear can be paralyzing, especially if you know that their disappointment will be of biblical proportions. This fear and the religiously driven rejec-tion that can follow is a sad and common tale among those who've come out in their sexuality.

It always hurts when loving Withness collapses between peo-ple; the pain is excruciating when it comes with the added cruelty only religion can bring. To many, God's word encourages fear and intolerance. Biblical strictures, especially concerning sexuality, seem to foment every kind of phobia, teaching hatred in the name of holiness. And nowhere are God's tyrannical, puritanical[2] laws more egregious than when they dictate who, what, and how we're allowed to love. It's in the pursuit of love that many abandon the God of the Bible, or have felt abandoned by him.

Some people feel just fine with the Ten Commandments, until they read the fine print of how these play out in Scripture's teaching on human sexuality and sexual relationships (Romans 1). They feel a terrible choice creeping up on them between God's commands and their heart's deepest desires. If things fall apart with God, it leads to painful separations from loved ones who insist that, in life and love, the Bible rules all. The people coming out feel they have to be willing to part ways with God and anyone who won't love them for who they really are. So they speak their hearts.

For some, courageous confession meets condemnation crashing down with heavenly force, heavy with threats of hell in the future and accusations of betrayal in the present. Sometimes the response doesn't include condemnation—yet—but it does include plans for conversion therapy. The one coming out thinks, "I just want to be true to my heart, to live life on my terms in a way that might actually make me happy—that's all! I'm not a bad person and I'm not trying to hurt anyone!" The shame that comes when such conversations go badly has led people to take their own lives.

As we've seen especially from our friend James, Scripture forbids cruelty and disrespect in any of our doings. But even when loved ones respond softheartedly, out of obvious love for the one coming out, it still of course hurts deeply to be told that God doesn't agree with your way of life. It feels like divine hypocrisy, like a knife in the back with God's hand on the hilt—*if you exist, you made me this way!* For those coming out, what pushes the stabbing pain straight into their hearts is the feeling that God and the people promoting his book are rejecting not only their personal choices, but their essential personhood. It's not just disagreement; it's disavowal. It destroys loving Withness. How can there be peace between people when one rejects the other's personhood?

That these breakups are painful is, in a sense, good. It demonstrates real love in the relationship. A heart has to be open to be broken. But what if some of the pain might come from posturing on both sides, from unintentional, unnecessary, and self-aggrandizing moral stands born more of pride than principle? Bridges will definitely be burned, but maybe we don't have to set fire to the whole city.

Here's a crazy thought: this experience of relationship disintegration could actually be a point of connection between those who believe that the Bible requires certain sexual norms and those who reject those restrictions as repressive and bigoted. Here's how.

Frenemies

I cringe whenever I hear conservative or libertarian political pundits say, referring to any sexuality but hetero: "As long as they don't bother me, I don't care what they do in their bedroom"— as if sexual preference is simply a matter of sex acts performed in private, and not something that colors our whole world and orders our priorities. It's a condescending view of a very complex dimension of personhood, and it's certainly not the Bible's view. The Bible understands how deeply these issues run, and to everyone's frustration, it labels much of what we consider essential to our personhood as sinful. We are complex creatures! No sin is a one-off behavior.

Both parties in a dispute over sexual ethics are uncomfortable with what God says about *something* in their lives, and that's because both parties are human beings. God demands moral perfection of his image-bearers, and only Jesus aces the test.

Scripture confronts Christians who pride themselves on promoting "biblical sexuality" for the godding they act out as if it's essential to their personhood. Never mind for now the fact that biblical sexuality is not coterminous with heterosexuality;[3] sexuality is complex. Though the Bible draws hard lines and gives clear definitions, it recognizes and addresses the nuances, and never does it posture the way some of us Christians do—self-righteously satisfied with proper form in relationships and ignoring all kinds of abysmal private dysfunctions and outright disasters within that form. Nor does the Bible restrict its invasive, impossible demands to issues of sexuality.

Here's a command that cuts us all to the heart: "Do not worry about *anything*." Paul writes that in Philippians 4:6, after admitting in 2:28 that he's really worried about something![4] Recalling one especially grueling stretch of missionary work, he says that he despaired of life itself (2 Corinthians 1:8). But there it is, a command from God's heart through Paul's pen. Don't worry. About anything! Ready to punt God's book across the room? How unrealistic is that?! Hold that thought. We'll come back to it toward the end of this chapter. For now, we just need to feel how deeply God's commands reach, not only into our hearts in general as we thought about last chapter, but even into our essential personhood.

If we can read God's law, especially as Jesus preaches it,[5] and feel untouched by its invasive reach, unoffended by its demands that we do things we're clearly incapable of doing and that we submit to moral strictures that we naturally interpret as violations of our natural desires and rights—then we aren't reading it right. So, both sides in a confrontation over biblical sexuality can sympathize with one another about how demanding God's law really is. And there's more room for sympathy, even empathy.

Both sides have drawn hard lines in life in the name of love and loyalty, in the pursuit of truth and personal authenticity. Both agree that real love accepts the other person for who the other person really is. But they disagree about who gets to define who we or other people really are.

Jesus ascribes that authority to God and the law through which God makes his moral demands. Jesus also claims that authority personally. As God, Jesus gave the law. As man, he fulfilled it. Now, he mediates his authority as the God-man right back through his book. Here's a bit more of what the resurrected Christ told his disciples before he returned to heaven:[6] "All authority in heaven and on earth has been given to me. Go therefore, and make disciples of the nations, baptizing[7] them in the name of the Father and the Son and the Holy Spirit and teaching them to obey all that I have commanded you."

The Bible communicates Christ the King's nonnegotiable commands for humanity, and Jesus tells us that those who trust his word and live it out can expect rejection from family and friends who want the Bible to quit getting all up in their business (John 15:18–19). Paul says to his pastoral protégée Timothy that "all who desire to live a godly life in Christ Jesus will be persecuted" (2 Timothy 3:12). Untold numbers of Christians have been murdered because their relationship to Jesus was essential to their personhood. To deny him was to deny themselves. As Paul writes in Colossians 3:4, the resurrected Christ "is our life." So Paul and other martyrs were willing to die for him. They've also been willing to do what might be harder: live with the consequences when friends and family force a choice between Jesus and them.

Not all Christians yet understand personal rejection for the sake of Christ, so as applied to Christianity in the contemporary, wealthy West, this line of thought might seem particularly absurd—maybe more like a martyr complex. But historically, hate and rejection come standard with the faith. It was after Jesus told his disciples that he would be murdered in Jerusalem that he said to them, "If anyone wants to come after me, let him deny himself and take up his cross daily and follow me" (Luke 9:23). There's a cold logic to it: if they're following Christ and displeasing powerful people in doing so, Christians can reasonably expect things to go about as well for them as they did for Jesus.[8] Yikes. But it makes sense. To follow the Lord is not only to denounce your own godding; it's to denounce everyone else's, too. And everyone else doesn't like that.[9]

Burning Straw Men

We all want the freedom to be the people we really are. Recognizing this can help warring factions humanize each other. Maybe the mutual recognition that "it's personal," instead of inflaming antagonism, could actually cool it off a bit. We could recognize how deeply one another's beliefs run, and handle one another with care accordingly. Where conflict is inevitable, it's the part of peace-seeking people to try to minimize casualties. We can start by being honest with one another, and honest about one another.

The ninth commandment forbids slander (Exodus 20:16). No matter how much we think a lie to or about someone can help us, truth must be honored and we must honor our fellow image-bearers by speaking it in humble, self-effacing love (Romans 13:9). Honoring God's image in others also requires us to give the benefit of the doubt to those with whom we disagree, and to acknowledge and affirm the best in what they say and do. The Lord requires these acts of love,[10] so Bible-touting Christians must give them especially close, obedient attention.

For example, I've heard Christians refer to agnostics and pretty much anyone who identifies with "postmodern" thought as moral relativists, even moral anarchists. They think that to be a "non"—someone who does not identify with a particular organized religion[11]—by definition means an "anything goes" approach to life. They ask, genuinely puzzled, why any non-Christians want to do anything good. "Given what you believe, what's the point?"

They seem to miss the condescension (and perhaps unrecognized self-righteousness?) in the question. Ironically, this accusation insults the image of God found in everyone.

It's certainly fair to ask about the basis and boundaries of people's ethics, whether they're self-referentially consistent and sustainable; and that's what the befuddled believers are getting at. We all want to find within ourselves, and without reference to God, the reasons for our goodness. It's fair to question whether this isn't ultimately circular thinking. But to be dumbfounded about or to dismiss out of hand the genuinely good and helpful things done and desired by non-Christians is to insult their fundamental identity as humans, which is to insult the God whose image is that identity.[12]

In reality, no one believes "anything goes."[13] None of us really thinks that all understandings of humanity have equal moral validity—otherwise we would never assert a contrary opinion about anything. We know that these matters in particular are personal, and that there are wrong and hateful ways to think about them, even if we disagree on how to define "wrong" or "hateful." Each of us assumes and treats as knowable absolutes—or at least as nonnegotiables—certain ideas about humanity. These ideas cannot be "proven" scientifically; they have to be assumed.

We all begin our understanding of ourselves as humans, of human personhood and human relationships and human rights with an assumed answer to a crucial question: what does it mean to be human?[14] That question takes us immediately to God-level stuff.[15]

I Gotta Be Me

The heated battles over personhood and sexuality are fundamentally religious conflicts. "It's who I am" is a direct result of "It's who/what I worship." Scripture sees it as God versus god(s), God versus godding, God's law versus autonomy, just like it's been since the garden. Whether our god is simply our desires and we know it, or whether we give our god another name or no name, this god will have a law and we'll consider our god's teaching on humanity to be gospel truth. We will praise this god as the ruler and regulator of human life and love and preach its doctrine against all infidels. I know it seems unfair to apply "god" language to beliefs that deny the existence of any such being, but we show our godding when we act as if our understanding of human love is nonnegotiable truth that only the bigoted would reject[16] (especially when we simultaneously deny that absolute moral truth is accessible).

Let's think about a statement that pop culture holds sacred: "love is love." It sounds simple to the point of being self-evident, so those who challenge it are called haters[17] (heretics?). But does this statement really honor love and protect lovers?

"Love is love" attempts to say that love is something transcendent but commonly experienced, something essential to humanity and not subject to religious strictures. You can love anyone you want and express that love sexually. But even there, there are boundaries, right? If so, there must be a higher standard—dare we say a law?—that governs love. So, does "love is love" really honor the idea of love, or does it render love and lovers prey to any idea or action, no matter how unloving, that simply claims the name?

How many victims of abuse have been told by the abuser, "But I *love* you!" James would go apoplectic at this, and the other biblical authors are with him.[18] A claim of "love" has certain standards to meet if it's a claim worthy of the name. Clearly, some people who claim to "love" are liars. Some liars are self-deceived, having learned no higher standard for love than the self. But self-deceit is still deceit. Love has boundaries, rules, laws. The question is who gets to define them.

There are terrible things done in the name of "love" that deserve the strongest possible condemnation. But in our godding, all we can ever say is that such things are terrible...for now. Because if we say there is something inherently, always, terrible about them, we've admitted the existence of a knowable, unconditional moral standard higher than we; we've admitted that the ceiling of self is a fraud and that no matter how deeply and sincerely we feel a certain way, it doesn't make that way good and right and true.

We know there are deeply felt desires within us, very natural to us, that tend toward destruction. We can all acknowledge that we've loved some very unlovely things in life. Our loving them could not redeem them; it showed that our affections were in need of redemption.

At least on a very practical level, we admit that certain desires, no matter how natural to us, are not healthy. My desire to set fire to the car double-parked in a crowded lot is probably a teensy bit overkill. (An anonymous threat letter tucked beneath its wiper blades will do just fine.) Pop stars tell us we're perfect just the way we are, but that feels more and more like desperation, not truth. Besides, how do they know? We know we need to get better. But then we get scared.

We have certain desires that we want to keep out of bounds and untouchable. We think, "No, please—not that! That's me! That's who I am! If you take that away from me, I'm done. I'm over and I might be tempted to make it official." So we maintain the right to distinguish between natural desires we're willing to ditch and ones we wouldn't trade for the world because it would feel like selling our souls.

But when we make ourselves the sole standard of what's good and right in love, we lose something of love, and we steal something from the beloved. We forfeit the transcendent quality of love itself and we diminish the inherent significance of that beloved someone.

For love to have meaning, it must exist beyond the jurisdiction of self-definition. If the self wants to participate, the self must submit. Beneath the ceiling of self, we're not being drawn out by and falling in love with someone else. Captivation[19] as we've thought about it isn't really happening. If that someone or something we love has no fixed meaning beyond what we ascribe—if the beauty of the beloved is only in our eyes and the beloved's power over us only a matter of our perception, then we're just loving ourselves. "Love me some me" becomes all life is.

We're not God. Our loving something does not make or define it as lovely. And that's really good news! If you don't love me—what?!—that doesn't make me unworthy of love or unlovable.[20] Same for you. You may not be loved in the way you deserve, but you are worthy of love and eminently lovable. But for that to be true, something higher than the ceiling of self must dictate what constitutes lawful love and, therefore, true loveliness—what in life is worthy of love and what kind of love is best for us to have for the beloved. Otherwise, "love is love" is nihilism.

Out of the Shadows

If we want to say that our love means something beyond ourselves, then we have to take some terrifying steps into the light of a law higher than we,[21] or "I."[22] Coming out from the dark beneath the ceiling of self, it can hurt our eyes to adjust to the light. But once we're ready to look, we might be happily surprised to see what Scripture actually teaches about love.

No matter how badly we think the Bible botches the topics of love and personal freedoms, remember: this is the book whose divine author claims to actually *be* love (1 John 4:8). For some people, that's an irony. But let's not miss the statement's significance. This is God declaring his own ontology. And therefore it's his declaration of the essential nature and practical priorities of his image-bearers.

We've thought about Jesus's summary of the Ten Commandments: love God with all you are and then love your neighbor as yourself. Two commands. But notice, there are three targets for your love: God, others, *and yourself.* Jesus tells us to love our neighbor as ourselves, not instead of ourselves.

Loving others is to be as instinctive and important to us as our own self-preservation. God wants self-preservation to be important to us! So everyone's covered by God's command to love. As we'll see next in our final chapter, this command also covers animals and the planet itself. God's law is perfect, complete, in its call to love.[23]

God calls us to make every single thing we do and think a matter of love, down deep even to the level of how we know and understand anything. Jesus says to love God with all your mind. Isn't that rather beautiful? All our knowing is to take place in the context of loving.[24] For God's favorite creatures, truly learning is truly loving.[25]

A child exploring the world naturally loves to discover and to understand everything around her. Has there ever been a child foraging the forest or digging into the sandy beach who responds to all that unfolding wonder by saying, "Awww, crap! *Another* new thing?!" In God's heart, knowledge and love, understanding and affection, go hand in hand. We see this especially when God tells us what it really means to know his word.

Paul urges Timothy to prevent contentious people from distorting apostolic teaching; their desire for controversy destroys its intended result. "The goal of our instruction is love, from a pure heart and a good conscience, and an un-hypocritical faith"

(1 Timothy 1:5).[26] To know God is to love God, and that loving knowledge is proved genuine as it leads us to follow God's law, which covers the world in its loving embrace. John writes, "This is how we know that we have come to know him; if we keep his commandments" (1 John 2:3). Jesus says, "If you love me, you will keep my commandments" (John 14:15). *Complete love is the goal, and God's law is the guide.*

As we've seen throughout the book, the sequence Jesus gives as he summarizes God's law is crucial; it provides priority and stability to our loves. As we love down the line like Jesus shows us—God, others, us—our hearts are strengthened, steadied, and focused. Rooted in our first love, we can branch out fruitfully into the other loves God requires of us and by which God forms us. So much confusion and so many unnecessary pains and separations in life come because we get Jesus's sequence exactly backwards.

You've Got to Keep Them Separated

Every human life is a world, and each of us is a world at war. We battle ideas and people outside of us, but we're also profoundly conflicted within. We're a civil war, a house divided against itself, full of warring instincts, intentions, and impulses all battling for supremacy in our hearts. Yet our godding wants to base our understanding of love in this world at war. It wants to begin with this swirling cosmos of conflict as our moral constant. Is this really such a good idea? If we start our understanding of love with the Originator of the concept instead, we learn not only to love in the right order, but to rightly order our loves.

As we should expect from the triune God who is love, there are related yet distinct kinds of love within the beautiful complex of loving Withness. Understanding these distinctions is crucial to a right and healthy self-understanding.

In *The Four Loves*,[27] C. S. Lewis distinguishes and shows the relationships among what he calls Affection, Friendship, Eros (erotic love),[28] and Charity (an older word for unconditional, action-oriented, self-denying love). Lewis doesn't pretend that his taxonomy and analysis are gospel truth about love and its various kinds and expressions, but he recognizes that, for all of our loves to survive as true, we must maintain their distinctiveness and make sure the Lord rules them all.

When we suppress our first love, we deprive each of our loves of the power of their distinct nature and the focus of their designed trajectory. It becomes easy for them to stray beyond their designated jurisdictions. When that happens, our relationship statuses get "complicated."

Our loves are like runners on the track. They need to stay in their respective lanes for the race to run well. God's law defines those lanes. In our godding, we feel entitled to jump the gun and to let our loves cross the lines, especially when it comes to one runner in particular—Eros.

In our culture, we've given Eros special privileges and powers that, ironically, have led to his downfall. We look to Eros as the truest indicator of how free we are to be ourselves. In our godding, we claim the right to have sex with anyone and everyone we want. In the hookup culture, being sought out for sex is proof that our godding is going well. But the more sex is spread out among partners, the less potent and self-affirming it is.

This is part of why biblical commands concerning sex are so restrictive, and why sexual promiscuity was so severely punished in Old Testament civil law.[29] *The severity of the sanction indicates the value of what the law protects.* Stealing a candy bar might get you fined. Stealing guns and ammo gets jail time, because suddenly human lives are at stake.

Sex and sexual desire are powerful to the point of life and death. Without it, there would be no human life beyond our first parents. Lack of sexual fulfillment makes some people want to end their lives. Unable to get the sex they desire, they believe they're not fit for love, and that makes them feel that life is not worth living. We've made our relative success or lack thereof in pursuing sex an indicator of our worth as people, or least the determining factor in our sense of personal fulfillment. We've considered sex so crucial to having a fulfilling life that we now think of sexuality as a matter of human ontology, essential personhood. As Philip Reiff puts it, our culture "expects too much of sexuality."[30]

At first glance, our culture seems to worship Eros. Explicit sexual imagery abounds and enslaves millions. But Lewis says that's not Eros. He gives the name Venus to the selfish, objectifying, animalistic approach to sex so often seen and glorified among us. God says that erotic love, within its proper lane, runs good and right, powerful and beautiful toward the beloved. God's law forbids sexual greed, often called lust.[31] Erotic love and lust, Eros and Venus, are not synonymous. God commends Eros and condemns Venus.

Lust respects no boundaries. It credits itself for what's desirable in the other person and objectifies, distorts, disrespects, uses, takes, plunders, and eventually abandons when "the thrill is gone." Lust and love can combine in a destructive hybrid in which one is confused for and equated with the other.

Confusion comes easy among us because we're all about crossing boundaries and, if sexual desire or discovery demand it, obliterating them. Strangely, we wonder why we're not able to build solid, sustainable romantic relationships out of smithereens.

It's one thing to have a "best friend with benefits." That's what marriage should be. But we're seeking the benefits package everywhere and as early as possible, in regular friendships and casual acquaintances and even if we don't particularly like the person we're sleeping with. Sexual activity is just the thing to do. It's the standard for social legitimacy, so young people feel pressure to get in "the game" at younger and younger ages. It's just as the original spoiler of humanity would have it.

Off to the Races!

Satan loves to rip out the tender roots of blooming sexual desire and toss them into the scorching heat of a hypersexualized culture. We spy his work as educators teach kids the latest popular theories on sexuality as if they were God's own truth—and this before they graduate elementary school![32]

Satan's influence is also seen in our giving kids easy access to sexually explicit sights and songs. These screened and auditory images deceive; they incite envy and self-destructive thoughts as they call us to worship glossed-up people of exaggerated sexual prowess. And as they boast of glorious erotic experiences, kids learn to crave and pursue sexual conquest rather than loving commitment.

Under the Enemy's influence, pop culture perpetually mocks virginity and laughs at abstinence. Sex is always right out there as the constant unspoken possibility; it's so commonplace that we sometimes say it "just happens"—which, of course, is a ridiculous lie. "Just happens" describes a sneeze, not sex. As quickly as it might end, sex is never that quick to begin, at least in real life. But life increasingly imitates art.

It's a clichéd scene in movies featuring romantic relationships, even the relatively squeaky clean ones: two characters make eye contact across the room and the scene flashes immediately to their physical entanglement. Not even enough time to say, "Gesundheit!" In dating, sex is often the first and immediate consideration between two people, the inevitable end to which all words and activities are merely means. Might as well get right to it, right?

It's a nearly forgotten thought and it's mocked when it's remembered: God reserves sexual intimacy for marriage. The very idea of waiting for pleasure is profoundly offensive to our godding. I want, I deserve, I am owed, and I will have whatever pleasure I want to have...NOW!!! And of course, having no restrictions is most appealing in the stage of life when we feel we ought to be the freest, when we vastly overestimate our capacity to bear life's heaviest burdens and joys.

Combine that core philosophical commitment with raging hormones in young gods; complement the natural impatience and entitlement of youth with constant encouragement to explore sexual desires and to forsake religiously based caution; provide access everywhere and at all times to sexually explicit media and even apps to solicit "casual" sexual encounters, and the climate is ideal for a perfect storm of human destruction, for a natural human disaster.[33]

Loving Withness is at the core of our existence; it's ontological and so our hunger for it is primal. Sex is meant to be a particularly rapturous expression of loving Withness, and we naturally want the most pleasurable experiences we can have in life. With no real reason for personal restraint—we're gods!—the compulsion toward sex is overwhelming. For some people, it's unbearable. Sometimes it turns abusive, toward others and self. We haven't been taught to order and prioritize our affections before we're tossed into the frenzied waves and rapid sea changes of culture's obsessions and controversies concerning sexuality.[34]

Scripture tells us to take our time with loving Withness. If something is good and true, it will endure; it will grow naturally and its maturity is worth waiting for. When it comes to Eros, we'd be wise to listen to the lovers in the biblical book Song of Solomon.

Borderline giddy in anticipation of her marriage and the intimacy that comes with, the lady teaches her fellow maidens— young adults, not kindergartners!—"Do not awaken love before its time." This must be important advice; she gives it three times in the course of the book.[35] And the fact that she has these conversations suggests that they were typical in her community of faith. The maidens had loving, protective mentors.[36] As we'll see in a bit, the book of Proverbs, a tutorial on practical life within the covenant of grace, is full of such conversations.

When the covenant community lives according to God's commands, children are taught early to guard their hearts and to be patient as they grow into life's mature beauties and intensities. They're taught to trust in the Lord with all their heart as he makes everything beautiful in its time (Proverbs 3:5–6, Ecclesiastes 3:11).

In 1 Corinthians 13, Paul writes what is perhaps the most famous and beloved description of love. Love is "kind; it does not envy or boast; it is not arrogant; it is not rude or self-seeking; it is not easily angered; it keeps no record of wrongs. Love does not delight in evil but rejoices in the truth. It always protects, always trusts, always hopes, always perseveres; love never fails."[37] Ah, but I left out what Paul puts first on his list. Love's first attribute? Patience.

Just like with God's law in general, none of us measures up here. Paul's words describe an objective reality, rooted in God's essential being, into which we step and in time learn to walk with surer footing and greater endurance. Only Jesus fully lived a 1 Corinthians 13 life, and that makes sense, because God is love.

If we took God's definition and descriptions of love to heart long before our loves want to walk (or sprint like mad) into sexual specifics, wouldn't our hearts be so much freer when the time comes to experience them? So much better prepared to really engage and enjoy the loving presence of another person, in whatever context of love that person lawfully belongs?

The Lord truly knows us. He knows what is good for us to understand and to experience, and when it is good for us to understand and experience it. His word guides our loves to be beautiful and powerful, true and free, in their time.

Animal Attraction

Lewis notes that Eros in its best form isn't strictly about sex; it's about being "delightfully preoccupied," what we've called "captivated," with the beloved. Eros does not need to be there at a relationship's beginning. This is crucial to know for people who want marriage but who despair of its possibility because while they're very attracted to a potential spouse's character and personality, sexual attraction, for whatever reasons, just isn't there—yet.[38]

As delightful preoccupation increases, Eros can rearrange the relationship's dynamics and bring a formerly unfelt and therefore unforeseen intensity and pleasure that augments the happy, mutual, and perhaps platonic captivation already present. But that's just it— it's delightful preoccupation *beyond* the self. That's where the Bible takes us first in its teaching on love, but our godding, because it sees self as absolute, can never really get there. So, true Eros has a difficult time doing his work of pleasure.

Lewis calls Eros the king of pleasures, but says that the most intense experience of Eros is a by-product of the beautiful experience of being with the beloved. Beneath the ceiling of self, we cannot know beyond our perception, and the value of the other consists primarily of how the other makes us feel. So our godding tends to value sexual activity more than it values the one with whom we share it. As Lewis puts it, "Sexual desire, without Eros, wants *it*. . . . Eros wants the Beloved."[39]

Since Lewis wrote in 1960, it's become commonplace to refer to the beautiful, mutually life-giving act of sex as "it." We seek "it," and the person with whom "it" feels best is the person we want to be with forever—for now. "It" is also the name for a demonic clown in a classic Stephen King book. Demonic clowning is probably an apt description of our culture's sexual ethos and antics. It's satanic to lie about and cheapen a loving Withness that marks us so deeply and, in many cases, leads to new life. And speaking of fallen angels…

Lewis writes that Eros, if not ruled by God, either dies or becomes a demon. It's easy to spot that demon's violent, corrosive presence in abusive relationships. The attraction between potential lovers is powerful and immediate. And like the quick cut to the love scene, before they even learn each other's last names (or first?!), they've already been to bed. Some genuine,

Venus-defying affection, admiration, and appreciation might be there and might develop. But with an errant Eros unchecked and in control, the relationship ebbs and flows, flames up then flames out—daily, probably. Inability to sustain the sexual high, to maintain the physical heat, forces cold lovers to realize that there really isn't much else to their relationship. Once again, self asserts itself. Now, it's all about survival and not being made a fool; it's all about control.

Having rushed into animalistic intimacy; having sprinted past affection, friendship, and far away from "charity," having bolted wild-eyed past true Eros and into the vicious jurisdiction of Venus—reckless urgency and the tyrannical commands of a corrupted Eros begin to rule the lovers. There's no time and space for love and peace to grow between the concupiscent combatants. And they'll be damned if they're going to give up the other to someone better looking, someone the other has been eyeing up for a while now.

Eventually, one party withers and wants out. But it's too terrifying to walk away or even to talk to anyone else about the hell the relationship has become. Eros become Venus reigns like the devil in lawless romantic relationships, "mercilessly chaining together two mutual tormentors, each raw all over with the poison of hate-in-love."[40]

These relationships cut deep and cause dangerous confusion. When one partner's insecurities go violent, the victim, right in the midst of painfully obvious powerlessness, will often try to become the abuser's savior. In our godding, it's easy to develop a Messiah complex. The victim says it's worth the pain to help the abuser confront personal demons and become a better, freer person. But as the Bible teaches throughout: There is only one Redeemer, and we are not he. The well-intentioned Christian cliché, that we need to "be Jesus" to people, is dangerously naïve.

Jesus is the only human being whose Messiah and God complexes are accurate. When he lifts us up from the pit of our godding, our redemption can't help but bless those we kept trying to drag down to its miry depths. The Lord sets us on the solid ground of his word and teaches our loves to walk and then run toward their rightful recipients in the protective lanes of his life-giving law.

Sex Is Not the Enemy[41]

Despite popular stereotypes, following Christ does not dull, much less delete, our passions. God commands us to love with all that we are. He joys in creating truth in our inmost being, uniting the warring affections within us. He shepherds us toward faithfulness and truth in the totality of our being as we give to others the particular kinds of love his law says we owe them. Jesus leads our loves along paths of righteousness toward their purest forms and most powerful expressions.

In karate, you learn that putting the maximum amount of undistracted force into the smallest possible space is the best way to make your target explode—and in class, you get to try it on people! A proper punch comes loaded with the compressed force of your full body weight, flying true on two knuckles like a laser-guided missile right into one square inch of your victim's body—actually, *through* that one small spot. Your true target is behind what you hit; this ensures that your punch doesn't put on the brakes before impact. And then, BOOM. Eyes bulge and lungs expel their contents (bowels, too, if it's a really good hit). It's beyond awesome. Even when you're on the receiving end, as I've been many, many times, you have to respect the technique and execution. You give a respectful nod as you gasp and crumple, vowing silently to block or evade next time and realizing that this won't stop hurting for a week.

Similarly—sort of—God's law teaches us to focus each of our loves, and to dedicate to them the power and conviction of their truest form. God's law guides our loves toward their proper targets and teaches us to love with the full force of our hearts, aiming ultimately to make contact with a standard beyond the human object of our properly focused affection, so that the impact upon the beloved will be profound, perhaps leaving the object of our affection breathless. It's beyond awesome.[42]

In marriage, when our affections are aligned and in order, when Eros is properly humbled and focused, and therefore at his most potent, physical intimacy can be truly profound in its intensity and pleasure. "It" happens in keeping with what it is, and that's why "it" is really only itself in marriage. It's a perfect complement to the marriage covenant, a complete, unrivaled, and unreserved giving of oneself to and the receiving of the same from the beloved. In God's moral economy, that's pure pleasure. And there's a sense in which God calls the married couple a step further in intimacy. The physical expression of Eros "obliterates the distinction between giving and receiving."[43]

As God said at the beginning, "For this reason a man will leave his father and mother and be united to his wife, and they will become one flesh" (Genesis 2:24). God designed this oneness to seal and to keep secure a covenanted relationship based on mutual love, trust, compatibility, respect, and fidelity, all grounded in the true and living God who is love. It's in this covenant construct that Eros can go lawfully, wonderfully wild.

God wants spouses to be so singularly dedicated to one another that they don't even think lustfully about someone else (Matthew 5:28)—no sexually greedy leers in the direction of those who don't belong to the marriage covenant. Our godding looks at such laws and says, "Repressive! Boring!" Godding wants the fire of forbiddenness, not of faithfulness. But if we're honest, it's easy to see the hellish consequences of sexual greed. What's difficult is living with them.

How many marriages have been ruined by a spouse's pursuit, online or in person, of "the other man" or "the other woman"? And often in the name of love, or at least pleasure. Adultery is just good adult fun, right? Especially if it's just in the mind or what we see on the screen? No. God forbids it because God is good.

God's law mandates patience, respect, self-control, and a deep personal investment in the feelings and needs of the beloved. That's very attractive to the partner: *The other person waited for, is only interested in, and won't be involved sexually with anyone else but me? That's freakin' hot!* Our godding naturally hates exclusivity, but exclusivity is rocket fuel for Eros. When we're shown that kind of devotion, we feel safe and are eager to do the same for the one we love.

God designed sex to complement and increase trust in the marriage covenant. Faithfulness yields pleasure and pleasure encourages faithfulness. Sexual intimacy beyond these bounds can't help but diffuse the life-giving, soul-strengthening pleasure that sex is meant to bring within marriage. Proverbs 5 makes this point vividly.

Keep Out!

Like many of the Proverbs, chapter 5 is a father pleading with his son to heed his counsel; this time it's about "the other woman."

"Keep your way far from her...lest you give your honor to others and your years to the merciless" (verse 8 and following). But God's law is not all about saying no. Every no has a positive yes implied, and vice versa.[44] Turning away from the fool's gold of godding means turning toward the life-affirming treasures of godliness.

There's some serious yes the dad tells his son to pursue instead of adultery. "Let your fountain be blessed and rejoice in the wife of your youth....Let her breasts fill you at all times with delight; be led astray always in her love." In other words, with body and soul, go for it! The married couple should be infatuated and satiated with one another. When spouses are wanted bad like this by their partners, to the exclusion of anyone else, it means really good things for their sex life, and that's good for every aspect of their lives together. And when physical intimacy doesn't go so well, the trial and error, letdowns and do-overs in this context can be truly good adult fun—because there's trust.

Neither partner is comparing the spouse to someone else, a real "other" or an imaginary one—not in the present nor in the past, nor in some horrible hypothetical future like Proverbs 5 warns against. The burden of measuring up to the beloved's previous partner(s), let alone an utterly unrealistic fantasy, is crushing. It creates constant insecurity, suspicion, and fear.

John tells us "Perfect love casts out fear." Instead of igniting jealous rage and withering worry about what better lover the other might be contemplating in the wake of an unsatisfying interaction or a period of abstinence, bedroom blunders can leave husband and wife smiling at one another, and even laughing. Better luck next time, and lots of loving Withness in the meantime.

None of this is to suggest that it's easy and the highlights are frequent. That's why they're called highlights. But with the stage properly set, with the time necessary to rehearse and the patient endurance necessary to learn their respective roles well, the players can get better and better with their parts. Ahem.

When they pursue truth and not envy-inducing fiction (see the tenth commandment), God opens the eyes of the faithful couple to appreciate the beauty that's before them in their beloved, to learn to want and pursue and have and hold the beloved, and to have God's blessing in doing so unabashedly. Both partners feel wanted, because they actually are—and feeling wanted makes one feel beautiful. Beauty is not in the eye of the beholder, but desire's glow in the eyes of one who loves with exclusivity affirms and empowers the loveliness of the beloved.

When that desirous gaze lacks the glint of greed, it says to the partner, "You are objectively beautiful, not just an object." Within that look—the love it expresses and the love to which it leads—there is safety, peace, exhilaration, and satisfaction. Whether or not the beloved feels worthy of such adoration, the beloved can be certain that he or she is desired and adored, and can trust in the context of truth and faithfulness that he or she is desirable and adorable.

As with martial arts, so it is with love. We pursue but we don't attain perfection, and sometimes we get the stuff kicked out of us in the process. We need practice, and there's always room for improvement and, when we act unlovingly in any way, for repentance. Between lovers in covenant with the God who is love, real forgiveness can happen and real peace can bloom because their relationship is based upon the ultimate act of reconciliation and reestablishment of trust. That's what marriage is ultimately all about.

Paul writes in Ephesians 5 that marriage is meant to picture the loving, forgiving, self-giving relationship between Jesus Christ and his redeemed people. In verse 33, Paul sums up the duty husbands and wives owe one another: "Let each one of you love his wife as himself, and let the wife see that she respects her husband."[45] Despite what we try to convince ourselves these days, Paul's commands touch and are meant to heal raw nerves in the souls of men and women, husbands and wives. Each partner meets the deep needs of the other, both of them submitting to Christ, their loving Lord, who shepherds their union to a mutually fulfilling, radiant picture of his own life-giving love for his redeemed people.

Sorting through the mess that godding has made of our loves brings deeps pain. There's so much to unlearn about how our souls and bodies are meant to work as we give and receive love. Sometimes we'll despair of the whole process. But then the true nature of love, a longing for the good of the other and to be a means of supplying that good, can take over. Remembering that we're not here in the first place for ourselves, but for God and for others, resets our priorities and can push us through the pride-swallowing work necessary to love well and to forgive much, and to receive the same from others.

No Regrets?

As always, our godding won't go down without a fight. It doesn't see the need for forgiveness. If you want it, take it. Do what you want and don't apologize for who you are.

Perhaps you've seen a meme that says something like: "Don't ever regret your past decisions. Because at one time, it's what you wanted." Quite possibly some of the worst advice ever given. It's perfect ceiling-of-self thinking, which means it's perfect for self-destruction.

Our desires are not always good, so our decisions based upon them are not always good.[46] Our desires need redemption.[47] As David prays in Psalm 51:10: "Create in me a clean heart, O God."

Denial of the past doesn't do us any good, nor does pretending that something terrible was great simply because we wanted it. When the realization of personal truth depends so heavily upon the suppression of truth, it should tell us that something is off in our pursuit of authenticity.

The Bible always calls us to honesty, to facing life as it is. And there's no glossing up some of our past desires and decisions—they were just straight evil or at the very least self-deceived, perhaps stubbornly so. The originator of the meme sounds like someone processing a rough past. But to say that we shouldn't regret something just because we once wanted it is to ascribe all power, authority, and glory to our personal cravings. Yikes. Imagine how bad it would be for the world if we had power to sate all our cravings!

Maybe the meme expresses our coming to terms with the way we let someone hurt us. We can't accept that we gave someone a chance to do something terrible to us—*again*—so we just redefine the terms and say it was okay because we wanted it. But we know better, and the meme's consolation is barely a Band-Aid for what's hemorrhaging in our souls.

Our godding is supposed to be all about personal power—nobody tells me who I am! But ironically, it sets us up to be the hapless victims of people who know how to spot and take advantage of self-deceit and the resulting lack of true self-respect. The more we reject God's truth about who we are and therefore how to respect one another, the less we're able to tell when we're being disrespected. We might mistake the flattery of a sociopath for the affirmation of a friend. When our souls are glutted on godding, we get lazy, bleary-eyed, and unable to spot the predators lurking about. And by the time we realize their true nature, we're too out of shape to run. But hey, to be hunted is to be wanted, right? It's so sad when we settle for this, and only self-deceit says not to regret it.

In our sexual relationships, some of our most painful mistakes and deepest regrets come in the context of sexual relations. On this field of life, deep insecurity meets deep desire. We're vulnerable, even if we try to prove our strength by making it a onetime encounter of animalistic aggression. Despite attempts to move on and pretend otherwise, physical intimacy always leaves a mark upon our souls. These marks don't disappear. There are no second chances at first-time experiences, and our sexual experiences stay with us like no others. Touch can't be taken back.

If we start to sober up from self-deceit, Satan quickly serves up more lies to keep us under godding's influence. Godding says we don't need redemption; its subtle, mirror-opposite form says we're beyond it.

Because the past cannot be changed, the Enemy has an easy time convincing us that it's a prison. We might desire what God says about sexual relationships and relationships in general, but then we think, "Stinks to be me. That's great for others, but I'm so far beyond any of that it's not worth getting my hopes up."

"This is who I am!" often means "This is what I want!" But not always. Sometimes it means, "This is my life sentence." The past can't be undone, so we think we can't be put back together.

We think in our despair: *How can I get myself back when I've given so much of myself away? How can I get my heart back so I can give it away in love?*

Only God can do this. God does do this. God *loves* to do this.

Prison Break

God can't "forgive and forget," as we think of it. By the way, neither can any of us. We can forgive, but unless we undergo mental trauma, past hurts don't leave the mind.[48] In redeeming us, God doesn't pretend the past didn't happen; He deals with it decisively so that we can actually move on among people we've hurt and who've hurt us, and know that it's morally right to do so. Because of Christ, and through Christ, making forward progress in life by seeking reconciliation, by giving and accepting forgiveness is not only possible; it's a moral imperative.

As David's repentance taught us, we need to endure the consequences of our actions. Redemption doesn't erase the past, and the forgiveness associated with it doesn't in the strictest sense erase our guilt. Redemption gives our guilt to Jesus in exchange for his righteousness. Our guilt is gone, "crucified with Christ" (Galatians 2:20). His resurrection means that his siblings' sin and guilt are "true dead." If we're reconciled to God, then real, true, and effective reconciliation can happen among us. And it must happen. If a relentlessly righteous God can be reconciled to relentlessly rebellious creatures, then no human, and no human relationship, is beyond redemption.

In the resurrected Christ, real, vital relationships can rise from the ashes of burned-down partnerships and burnt-out souls. Redemption results in what Jesus calls being "new." We'll explore "newness" in our final chapter, but it's important to say here that being a new creation in Christ means that our guilt no longer claims us, and it's no longer ours to claim. It's not ours anymore, so it's not us anymore!

Satan doesn't like how "new" looks on you. He'll do everything he can to convince you that "new" doesn't suit you, that there is no freedom from your past, and that you can't live without particular desires Jesus means to renovate as a result of redeeming you. But remember the Corinthians.

For them, what Scripture calls "sexual immorality" was not only a way of life; it was a way of worship. And it was really difficult for them—impossible for them, actually—to understand and implement the totally foreign system of sexual ethics Paul called them to live out. Impossible for them, but not for God through them.

Paul asks, "Do you not know that your body is a temple of the Holy Spirit, whom you have from God? You are not your own." (1 Corinthians 6:19). It's a redemptive statement of ownership against which our godding rages. But think about it. How much do we love it when someone we love says to us, "You're mine"? The Lord says this about his people.

Paul is saying to the Corinthians, "You are God's, and God is with you." The sexual sin with which they identified, body and soul, didn't own them; it didn't define them. Paul writes, "And such *were* some of you. But you were washed, you were sanctified, you were justified in the name of the Lord Jesus Christ and by the Spirit of our God." Paul is saying, "*This* is who you really are. You're new. You're free."[49]

The Lord says this about you if you'll trust in his son. "You are mine and I am yours. I am with you, and no one can change that. You're safe, even from your past. You're free now to be the truest you."

As our lives take shape along the lines of God's loving law, we grow out of our past like a kid grows out of old clothing.[50] At one time, we wore it and were known by it. Maybe it made a social statement—a declaration of independence or of war. But now that clothing just doesn't fit us anymore. We'd be foolish to deny its significance as our history, but it can't contain all that we've become.

Keeping the Scars

The irony is obvious when Jesus says that, to find and gain our lives, we must deny and ultimately die to ourselves (Luke 9:18 and following). But this is not mere wordplay. Following Jesus leads to the death and eventual departure of aspects of ourselves we thought were ontological. But that's precisely how and why we can be free from our past!

The self to which Christ calls us to die is a false one, a malicious fiction told by our godding. It's true that godding is an essential part of us in that we've never been without it (Psalm 51:5). So wouldn't God's getting rid of it mean his deleting essential aspects of our personhood and personality?[51] Wouldn't the removal of our godding dull the sharp and defining edges of our personalities, which, though they can cut, make us who we are as individuals?

Redemption does kill individualism, and that's a good thing. But killing uniqueness of personality is not good, and God does not do that.[52] Jesus has a way of bringing peace and common purpose to us without diminishing our distinctiveness as individual human beings. The triune God is very good at combining diversity with fundamental unity, and making it all a matter of love.

But what about the lasting marks our godding leaves upon our souls and bodies? Horrible as these can be, aren't they a vital part of our true selves? Definitely...sort of. Godding is like a congenital disease. It's part of us, but it wants to destroy us. If there were a life-giving cure for such a disease, wouldn't we take that medicine?

But still. We might bid good riddance to godding as its perpetrators, but what about our status as its victims? We're supposed to remember our roots. Some of the roots in our past were rotten, but they fed our self-formation in deep ways. We might fear that following Christ means forgetting vital, formative lessons learned and convictions forged by the deepest pains in our past.

This is where it helps to distinguish between our history and our ontology, between what's happened in our lives and who we really are at the core of our being. Our history is essentially us in that we cannot change it. It was what it was so it is what it is. Jesus doesn't redeem the past, but he does redeem the person who lived it. And he gives that person a new life like his own.[53]

Being new in Jesus, we retain what godly strength we gained as we endured the traumas of godding, but we're increasingly rid of the godding itself. As we follow Christ in this life, the Holy Spirit through Scripture does within our souls the intricate, delicate work of a surgeon. He cuts godding away from the loves vital to us without killing them in the process. As they recover from mercifully traumatic spiritual surgery, they grow in the strength they were designed for.

And even more than having a soul like that of Jesus, the Bible tells us that believers will get a body like his as well. When Jesus appeared to his disciples following his resurrection, his body was what the Bible calls "glorified"—impervious to death because it's no longer subject to the miseries of sin that merits it (Romans 8:16–17). But the marks of Christ's crucifixion remained. Some healing had obviously taken place. He no longer looked like he did upon the cross, battered and bloodied, barely recognizable as human. And yet to demonstrate that he was still very much flesh and blood, not some disembodied spirit, Jesus kept his most defining scars. He retained at least enough scarring in his hands, feet, and side to show that he'd been crucified (Luke 24:39, John 19:34). The prophesied marks of Christ's most essential pain did not disappear. Touch can't be taken back.

Yes, that raises all kinds of questions about our resurrected bodies, some only semi-serious. Will my glorified body be at least 5'9"? Probably not; that never was part of my past. How about a full head of hair? I had that! Still doubtful. But as it is with Jesus, it seems we'll keep some reminders of what formed us in this life. Whatever scars we keep from life in a fallen world, the wounds will be cleansed of godding's poison. We'll be able, like Jesus, to bear these marks in our resurrected bodies as testaments not primarily to the pain we suffered, but to the life and victory that followed.

Godding has influenced every single human life there's ever been, but that does not mean that it is essential to humanity. Three humans started life in this world uncorrupted by godding, and the first two didn't make it. Adam and Eve fell, but the second Adam stood strong. So humanness cannot be thought of as ontologically, essentially, sinful.

Jesus proves, and makes possible for us to experience, that sin is not definitional of human personhood. Nor, therefore, is anything the Bible calls sin definitional of us as particular people. Even when it comes to our deepest desires, as hardwired into our humanity as they may currently be, "natural" and "essential" are not synonymous. In the resurrected Savior, we are neither doomed nor defined by our godding, even though it was powerful enough to kill the world and is as natural to us as breathing.[54]

True—walking away from what we feel defines us is about as easy as rising from the dead. But that's why Scripture calls coming to Christ a resurrection, even prior to the one that will unite glorified body and soul forever at Christ's return. Paul writes in Ephesians 2: "And you were dead in the trespasses and sins in which you once walked...following...the spirit who is now at work in the sons of disobedience....But God, being rich in mercy, because of the great love with which he loved us...made us alive together with Christ."

Hope That Disappoints?

Because of what Jesus did in this world, it's all the more crucial to ask the kinds of critical, dangerous questions forbidden beneath the ceiling. And because Jesus is alive, we know there are life-giving answers.

Does deeply felt desire always correspond to true personal identity? No. Thank God! Well, then, what are the loves most essential to us, most definitional of us as human beings and as particular people? Once again, the resurrection teaches us.

The most essential loves are those that last beyond this life. The resurrection will complete our newness. We'll finally be free of the godding that killed the world. We'll also lay aside some very good things, but no essential things, from this life. Apparently, sex is one of them.

Matthew places Jesus's summarization of the Ten Commandments right after his teaching about marriage (Matthew 22:23–40). Jesus gave this lesson on marriage in response to a snarky question from his not-so-loyal opposition.[55]

The interrogator was one of the Sadducees, a religious group known primarily for its denial that physical, bodily resurrections could happen or ever would. Trying to publicly humiliate Jesus, he asks:

> Teacher, Moses said, "If a man dies having no children, his brother must marry the widow and raise up children for his brother." Now there were seven brothers among us. The first married and died, and having no children left his wife to his brother. So too the second and third, down to the seventh. After them all, the woman died. In the resurrection, therefore, of the seven, whose wife will she be? For they all had her.

You can almost see the condescending smile, an allegedly superior intelligence toying with an inferior—and a little smirk at the end with the implied mention of sex. *Riddle me this, Rabbi! Here's a sordid scenario that proves how silly it is to believe in the resurrection.*

The questions reveal shallowness in the interrogator's understanding, not in the belief he's mocking. The Scriptures clearly taught that one day, humanity will rise from all its graves for the final judgment. Martha, the sister of Lazarus, knew this and confessed it at her brother's funeral: "I know that he will rise again in the resurrection on the last day" (John 11:24). (Little did she know that she wouldn't have to wait that long to see her brother again!) Jesus responds as he always did, affirming the Scriptures and their vital relationship to the true and living God.

At first, Jesus doesn't jump on board their allegedly sophisticated trick question. He just tells them that their beliefs, which gave rise to the question, are bunk. "You are wrong, because you know neither the Scriptures nor the power of God." Old Testament Scripture really does teach the resurrection, and God really does raise the dead. But then Jesus condescends to answer their inquiry. The master teacher, Jesus uses their snarky question to reveal a sublime truth.

> For in the resurrection they neither marry nor are given in marriage, but are like angels in heaven. And as for the resurrection of the dead, have you not read what was said to you by God: "I am the God of Abraham, and the God of Isaac, and the God of Jacob"? He is not God of the dead, but of the living.[56]

The Bible views sex and marriage as ethically inseparable, so that means no sexual relations in heaven. What Jesus says may sound like very bad news, especially for married people who really love and enjoy each other. It really depresses me personally. But then I remember: like every human except one, I have a very dim view of the brilliance to be when time meets eternity, when godding dies for good and we dwell in the immediate presence of God, our first love.[57]

As displayed by Jesus's critics, ignorance or outright unbelief leads to so many trite, crass, or dismissive thoughts about life beyond death. Martin Luther said that we understand heaven like an unborn baby understands the outside world. In this life there are intimations of that place, but we have a hard time processing even these. We feel the pull to our true home in those sublime, captivating moments of life. But we just don't have categories for it other than the descriptions God gives us in Scripture, which are so often symbolic—partial, metaphorical pictures of what we cannot yet comprehend.

In many ways, God's law is a more precise preview of what will be than the images we get from the future-forecasting biblical prophets. Peter describes the "new heavens and the new earth" relatively straightforwardly as the place where "righteousness dwells" (2 Peter 3:13). God's Ten Commandments tell us what that righteousness looks like lived out, fully present and all-pervasive. It looks like love.[58]

It seems that Eros will one day take a final bow, perhaps to a thunderous standing ovation. Or perhaps he'll make a quiet exit, humbly recognizing the approach of a loving Witness far greater than even he could provide, a loving Witness that his former worshipers sought in him but could never find and one that he gave his devoted but circumspect fans reason to anticipate. Either way, Eros will have played his part well, at least when he was led by God's law.

In the meantime, as we hunger and thirst for loving Witness in our frenetically paced, hypersexualized culture, we need to pay closer and more biblically tuned attention to the kinds of love that God says will last forever.

Bosom Buddies

We've focused so much on Scripture's teaching about sex because it's the form of loving Witness that we tend to worship in this culture. But really good, satisfying love in this life is not limited to what God designs for marriage.

Despite the way singles are often treated by popular church culture—you *must* get married!!—and the way singles are often treated by popular godding culture—you *must* have sex!!—the Bible lets us know that there is so much more to love than sex and marriage. Scripture also lets us know that marriage itself is not for everyone.

Paul, writing as a celibate single, lets us know that his way of life has serious advantages, including an undivided focus in serving the Lord. The celibate single person lacks nothing essential in relationship to God, and therefore lacks nothing essential in relationship to other people, and nothing essential in the ongoing process of self-formation. Not all of us are meant for marriage, but each of us is meant for a form of loving Witness that we talk about all the time but perhaps seldom deeply understand and implement: friendship.

As our souls wither and our bodies lose their vitality through the worshipful perversion of Eros, our other loves can't help but suffer. Beyond our sacrificing honesty and credibility within "the game," we also give up precious time and the ability to focus on the cultivation of real, true, life-giving friendship.[59]

Sure, we have peers we use as counselors, people who affirm us in our partying and hold our hair back as we're puking out the night's intoxicants. Some of our peers, the true friends, might even have the courage to question our godding, knowing full well that they're risking the friendship by doing so. But how sweet would it be to have a friendship that's not fundamentally about damage control? This is not to say that friends shouldn't be there for one another; it is to say that friendships defined by putting out fires are easily extinguished.

In the day of the lonely self, true friendship is hard to cultivate. It's even hard to recognize because we're so quick to spy sexuality in almost every expression of affectionate interest. It's easy to forget in our culture that not every impulse of love and attraction toward another person is sexual.

I remember a sermon in which the preacher, who would not mind being identified as an old-school good ol' boy, made remarks about a painting of *The Last Supper*. Unlike da Vinci 's legendary version, the apostle John was pictured reclining, nearly horizontally, at the table, his head resting upon Jesus's chest. The preacher fussed and fumed. "That's not what happened! Jesus was no sissy!" But there's a big problem for this preacher's pontification (and the terrible view of masculinity it implies): Scripture tells us this is exactly what John was doing, and that Jesus had no problem with it (John 13:23).

There was no reason to have a problem because this is how Middle Eastern meals happened during that day, how the furniture was set up, and how the diners interacted. Meals were a big deal back then; people relaxed and took their time to eat and talk (!!). The table was set low so that people could really spread out, practically lying down, while eating. This put them in close proximity to one another, so John really could have been, should have been, in this position with Jesus. There was nothing sexual about it. His being there instead of the other disciples certainly indicated a personal closeness to Christ,[60] but it was a culturally normal and utterly platonic familiarity. Despite the preacher's scandalized shock at the painting, the picture of masculinity it presented was perfectly biblical. "Toxic masculinity" has many expressions in our day, and its antidote, biblical masculinity, had many expressions back in those days.

Soul Mates

Before David became king, he had a best friend named Jonathan, the son of the current king, Saul. Their friendship was loving and intimate and we might immediately take that to mean that they were lovers. Admittedly, their interactions raise questions, but we have to remember that we're reading these texts with eyes trained early to see sex everywhere. We're like the dog in *Up!* when he sees a squirrel. Long eye contact? Secret lovers! We need to see biblical narratives as they grow within the native theological and sociological soil of the time.

Starting in the Old Testament book of 1 Samuel 18, Scripture repeatedly tells us that Jonathan loved David as his own soul. At one point, Jonathan strips himself of his robe and armor in David's presence—to give it to David as a pledge of friendship and as practical protection for the battles he knew David needed to fight against Israel's enemies. And when Jonathan realized that his father's jealousy of David was irrevocably homicidal, he and David wept and kissed one another. But the kissing here is Hebrew, not French! And when David later learns that Saul and Jonathan had been killed in battle, David composes a lament for them both. He writes of Jonathan: "Your love for me was extraordinary, surpassing the love of women." We think, "Come on, now! They were clearly lovers and that's an admission of their affair!" No, they weren't, and no, it really isn't.

Especially given the sexual strictures of the Old Testament law, and the fact that the Bible is not squeamish in letting us in on people's sexual secrets—remember David and Psalm 51[61]—there's just no contextually honest way to view David and Jonathan's friendship as anything but that. Friendship can be expressed in ways that make hypervigilant people point and scream "Sexual!"—but that scream can say more about the squealer than it does the perfectly platonic behavior being tattled on.

In that culture, friendly affection was physically expressed. They didn't have the inhibitions typical of some Western Gentile cultures. Good friends loved one another body and soul, and with David and Jonathan, their entire friendship was a self-consciously covenanted matter before the God who wrote all those restrictive rules about sexuality. David's lament for Jonathan was composed for public use; he ordered that it be taught to the people of Judah. This means that the people of Judah would find nothing scandalous about his celebration of the love he had with Jonathan. Contrast this with David's very heterosexual, very sinful relationship with

Bathsheba, and for which David's family and the entire kingdom suffered horrifically. David's relationship with Jonathan was godly; his relationship with Bathsheba was godding. God treated both according to their true nature. In his holy word, God memorialized the former and condemned the latter.

The texts that, to a hypersexualized culture, suggest erotic love actually show us how little we understand the other loves, how much we're missing in our idolatrous obsession with Eros. Friendship can, and should, run very deep, and can meet deep needs for loving Withness. Lewis writes: "Those who cannot conceive Friendship as a substantive love but only as a disguise or elaboration of Eros betray the fact that they have never had a Friend."[62]

Generations of girls have grown up in America holding hands and kissing, sometimes even on the lips. It was considered cute and not at all sexual in nature, much less a prelude to sex when their bodies matured. Paul, who calls the Corinthians away from unbiblical sexuality, commands believers to greet one another with a holy kiss (Romans 16:16).

In general, so much of what we immediately ascribe to sexuality can simply be an expression of what Lewis calls "appreciative" love. Appreciative love can acknowledge and appreciate the physicality of another image-bearer. And when our appreciation does focus on "sex appeal," we can recognize that someone is sexually attractive without getting sexually greedy in our thoughts, without desiring to have with them the kind of relationship and encounter that God's law forbids.[63] We can gather from Scripture's descriptions of both David and Saul that they were dreamy studs, but the biblical authors weren't trying to incite lust in their readers (1 Samuel 9:2, 16:12). We've lost such distinctions and discretion, and with them the deep capacity God gave us for appreciative love. As a result, we've forfeited and missed out on so much of the loving Withness we're meant to enjoy with one another.

Making sex the default lens through which we view everyone diminishes our ability to really know and appreciate other people for who they are, and to receive from them the kind of loving Withness that might provide some personal clarity within a confusing and confused culture of reckless, relentless sexual chaos, and maybe even lessen the loneliness we feel in the midst of it all.

A Forever Friend

Having a good friend doesn't mitigate the desire for sex, but hanging out with and listening to wise, selfless counsel from someone who genuinely loves us can keep us from the dangerous places we go when our felt desires are unfulfilled. God says to us in love, "Above all else, guard your heart" (Proverbs 4:23).[64] A good friend helps us keep that watch, even when we wish they'd look away and let us do what we want. That kind of friendship reflects the self-denying, protective love of the truest friend we could ever have.

As we have seen, marriage reflects the greater, eternal reality of Christ's relationship to his church. But marriage is neither an exhaustive nor an exclusive picture of the Redeemer's relationship to his people. Jesus is a faithful husband, and he's also a true friend—our truest Friend.

As Jesus prepares his disciples for his imminent death, he tells them how dear they've become to him. From John 15:13 and following: "Greater love has no one than this, that someone lay down his life for his friends." Jesus calls his followers his friends! He's not forgoing his claim to be their Lord, and that's exactly what makes his statement staggering. But it shouldn't surprise us. As we saw with Abraham, God has a long history of calling his followers his friends.

How good is it to have a friend who truly knows you, who truly loves you, who truly enjoys being with you, and who will always tell you the truth! As our truest friend, Jesus leads us along sometimes frightening but always freeing paths of righteousness, and he never leaves us behind or loses sight of us. He's walked that way before us, and is with us as we follow him.

In Jesus, our loves begin a journey toward their completion. We won't see that perfection in this life. But God promises to keep us moving in perfection's direction, until Jesus returns and God completes the good work he's begun in us (Philippians 1:6).[65] On that day our loves and our lives will be complete—not completed, but complete. On that day, life and love get really good. Until then, the Lord is with us as we deal with dysfunction, dis-integration, and dysphoria of all kinds, as is the norm in a fallen world.

Though we're on our way toward perfection, the process won't be perfect, nor painless. Sometimes in following Christ, we relapse badly into godding. We willingly dive right back into the depths from which Christ raised us. It creates a doubly crushing desperation: I can't live without Jesus, and I can't live faithfully with him! But God is faithful to us. And this is another reason for the marriage metaphor.

High Fidelity

Nowhere in Scripture is the truth of God's relentless faithfulness to us proclaimed more poignantly than in the Old Testament prophecy of Hosea. Hosea depicts God as a faithful husband with reason to be jealous as his people pursue other gods. In some of Scripture's harshest language, God calls his people out for their constant whoring (?!). The cringe-worthy language is precisely the point. Stop selling yourselves! You're too valuable to act as if you're for sale! Be mine and I will love you for all you're worth.

As God compares his worshipers to a prostitute, he's disparaging the dehumanizing act of giving our intimacies away for money, not denying the inherent worth of the people who sell themselves. Jesus particularly sought out people enslaved both to sexual sin and the economic system that fed and profited from that enslavement. Some of them were among his most loyal followers, and some of them figured prominently in his genealogy. A woman named Rahab, a prostitute when we meet her in the book of Joshua, is Jesus's ancestor.[66]

Our godding runs so deep that, even when we begin to understand how good the true God is for us, we still look around for a more ego-satisfying offer. This wandering grieves God, and his willingness to forgive it shows the depths of his love. To make this point, God tells the prophet Hosea to marry Gomer, a woman bound to be continually unfaithful to him. So he does. And she is.

Hosea keeps going after her, trying to keep their marriage intact. He suffers the shame of public ridicule—obviously he's not man enough for her; she goes after other guys every chance she gets! He pledges his undying faithfulness to her, and he proves it by his continual pursuit of his faithless bride, relentlessly loving her into her true identity in his family.

Hosea and Abraham could compare notes on miserable ministries; God called them both to personal agony in his service. The same Christ-centered dynamics that defined Abraham's pain were operative in Hosea's miserable ministry. Again, it could seem petty and cruel of God, like a dad who forces his son to method-act his lousy day at work. "I'm going to burn your Hot Wheels cars! Then you'll know how I felt when someone double-parked in my space!" But no. It's God giving flesh-and-blood examples, the tangible demonstrations we cry out for when we doubt his presence and love.

By reading Hosea, God's people get a gut-wrenching glimpse of what it means to really love, and what it means that God really loves them. They also learn that God really knows them and his love is unchanged. Our hearts are indeed harlots; we leave our first love on a daily basis. Still, God is there. Still, God pursues. The prophets God tasked with these awful assignments gained a visceral, personal understanding of the stunning self-denial to be shown by the coming Savior. They were, in Paul's words, knowing Christ in the fellowship of his suffering (Philippians 3:8 and following).

The prophets who had such miserable ministries understood viscerally and very personally what the ministry of the Messiah would be, that he would give himself to the uttermost for the sake of his beloved, and that his faithfulness was undying.

When we trust that Christ loves us this way, that he'll never leave us or forsake us, we want to reciprocate. Having been forgiven much by the self-sacrifice of a relentlessly faithful Savior, our hearts open more and more to love much. Paul describes his captivation with Christ: "For the love of Christ controls us, because we have concluded this: that one has died for all, therefore all have died; and he died for all, that those who live might no longer live for themselves but for him who for their sake died and was raised" (2 Corinthians 5:14–15).

Paul was especially captivated with Christ because Paul was once a violent persecutor of Christians (Acts 7–9). But Jesus redeemed him, forgave him, freed him, and even gave him a new name. Paul used to be Saul, feared enemy of the church. Now he was Paul, beloved son of God and brother in Christ. Paul did the only reasonable thing in response to such transformational love: he gave his life fully to his Lord, offering himself as a "living sacrifice" (Romans 12:1). And in this self-denial, he found his true self.

Paul writes, "I am crucified with Christ, therefore I no longer live. Jesus Christ now lives in me. And the life that I live in the flesh I live by faith in the Son of God who loved me, and who gave himself for me" (Galatians 2:20). John self-identifies this way as well, referring to himself in his gospel as "the disciple whom Jesus loved" (20:21). This is not narcissism, nor is it a comment about the other disciples! It's a simple, humble, awestruck statement of personal ontology. *Jesus loves me. This is who I am.*

John calls all believers to the joy of their ontology. If you know the Lord, or come to know him, that's you, too. John writes: "See what kind of love the Father has given to us, that we should be called children of God; and so we are. The reason why the world does not know us is that it did not know him. Beloved, we are God's children now, and what we will be has not yet appeared; but we know that when he appears we shall be like him, because we shall see him as he is. And everyone who thus hopes in him purifies himself as he is pure" (1 John 3:1–3).

God's child. In Christ, that's who you really, truly, fundamentally, essentially are.

And it's also who you're becoming, as you set your heart upon the return of your Redeemer.

The Christian life is the graced process of becoming practically who we already are positionally. A child is never *more* her father's daughter, but she sure can become a lot more like him. So, too, with the children of God. Jesus, our eldest brother in God's family, has earned us a right standing with God. From a position of standing, we can learn to walk.

Paul writes, "Walk in love, as Christ loved us and gave himself for us" (Ephesians 5:2). And then Paul goes on to describe, in the language of God's commandments, the life of holiness—in sexuality and all areas of life—to which the Lord leads us. It will not be an easy walk.

And now we're back to where we began this chapter, to the terrible and sad fact that loving Withness brings division, that declaring who we really are can be devastating to the people who thought they really knew us.

Just a few sentences after Jesus calls his disciples his friends, he says, "If the world hates you, know that it has hated me before it hated you" (John 15:18).[67] Sometimes following the Lord means treading a terrifying path away from the kind of loving Withness we once shared with friends and loved ones who continue to go after another god.

Our First Love

When loving Withness collapses between people it hurts badly enough, but it's even worse when that cutting apart comes with the added cruelty that only religion can bring. It's scary to have deep, honest conversations with people you love when they might not like or approve of what's going on down deep. And it's downright terrifying if their disapproval might crash down upon you with the hellish force of godding.

Where there can be less violent battles in the worship wars, we need to pursue peace. But religious loyalties run very deep, and our dogmas are uncompromising. No matter how softhearted and clear-headed our actions in society may be, they're always rooted in some-times unseen, below-the-surface religious convictions, in particular ways of thought and life to which we ascribe divine authority. Our chosen god will abide no rivals and won't stop until its reign over the world is total. We see this in the way cultural gods aggressively proselytize kids and therefore future generations. The question isn't the size and scope of our respective gods' ambitions. The question is which god is true, and which divine law is truly just and good.

Whether we love him or hate him, at least Jesus is upfront with his claims of authority and his ambitions. He makes his plans for world conquest clear. Thinking of God's promise to Abraham, and the fact that he fulfills it, Jesus sends his followers, his friends, into all nations (Matthew 28:18–20). As we'll see next in our final chapter, it's a worldwide march for love, peace, and human whole-ness that will bless the planet itself.

Following Christ may sound terrifying, and it might well cost you much of what you love and value in this life. But it's also the best and truest way to love and honor the very people you're afraid to disappoint, because you'll be loving them not simply in your own truth, but in *the* truth.

So much fear and pain and lack of peace in this life all comes down to: "I just want to be who I am. I want to love and be loved in keeping with who I really am." God wants exactly the same thing for you.

As the Lord leads us by his word, knowing us and loving us, he repeats one particular command more often than all the others. What do you think is the most repeated command in Scripture? "Knock it off!" perhaps? No. It's "Don't be afraid."

As you give your heart to your first love, you'll find the courage to live as who you really are. Perfect love casts out fear.

10

The Bible Has a Soundtrack

"Lead me not to temptation,
Hold my hand harder,
Ease my mind.
Roll down the smokescreen,
And open the sky. Let me fly.
Then I need a release from these troubles of mine
Fix my feet when they're stumbling
And well you know it hurts sometimes
You know it's going to bleed sometimes…"
—The Killers, "Sweet Talk"

"Before the gods I'll sing your praises…"
—Psalm 138

Music can be a kind of salvation. Certain lyrics, tunes, styles, and artists just really get it; they get *us*. A song can sum up our souls and sweep us along in its otherworldly flow to a place with no location, but which is undoubtedly home. Music is where our hearts can open like a rose to face and feel whatever life rains on us. That so-right song can drench our souls like a cold, soaking downpour, or soothe us like a warm and gentle shower, soft as summer's tears. Or, when life's coming undone and so are we, it can hit like the hard-water assault of a hurricane. Whatever we need to feel to be whole, or to express our emptiness, music can take us there. Music can be captivating.

Just one note from a song that gets it can make us smile and say, "Yeah." When certain beloved beats start up, we're tapping our feet and nodding our heads. It's not just enjoyment; it's affirmation. And it applies to all ages.

One of the cutest things on earth is a toddler who hears a song that gets her; she smiles bright enough to light a city block, gets to nodding and maybe gets her whole body into it—*This is my jam*!! And even if we're older and not among the head-nodders, we might find our souls blissfully lost at sea, riding the glorious swells of a centuries-old classical composition. We sit back, look up at the ceiling or perhaps close our eyes as we take a deep, satisfied breath. "Ahhh…" Tears may come—from grief, gladness, or who knows why?—as we feel the aching joy[1] of imminent personal contact with a transcendent realm.[2]

One of the Bible's most obvious features is one whose significance we tend to miss. It's like standing right next to a skyscraper—we don't take in the immensity of what's right in front of us unless we step back and look up. Then the view is staggering. When we step back to survey the contents of the whole Bible, we find music everywhere.[3] And right there in the Bible's heart[4] is an entire book of songs—the Psalms. The obvious but staggering truth here is that each of these songs, because they're Scripture, is God-breathed.[5] God is a musician! God is a songwriter.

The Psalter (all the Psalms together) has been called "a little Bible."[6] So in the final chapter of a book all about connecting personally with Scripture, we'll spend a lot of time on these songs that summarize and so uniquely personalize the word of God.

That God created music, that he created humans to be musical, confirms all the more beautifully just how personal this God is, no matter how far away he feels. God speaks to us through words, and some of his words are music. In this way, the idea that music can be salvation is literally true.

Permission Granted

We've thought about how and why Scripture and the Christian faith can feel so terribly, even abusively, impersonal. I've talked with so many Christian teens and young adults who've been made to feel that their passions and personalities—let alone their deep questions and doubts—have no place among properly believing, properly behaving Christians.[7] Not all of their churches are unfriendly; no doubt many older members would happily try to help if the young people among them would take their hearts off silent mode. Sometimes they do speak up. But often, the older

Christian responds with a knowing but unintentionally dismissive smile—like an auto mechanic as you mimic the horrifying sound your car has been making—and cheerfully recommends a good theology book. Problem solved! At least for the older believer.

The increasingly lonely souls in these churches have been told over and over (and over) that they need to understand the Bible. Yes and amen. We all do! But it's one particular characteristic of God's book that proves pivotal for them as they begin a personal exodus from the church. Somehow they discover, like a sunburst in their darkening hearts, that the Scriptures understand *them*.[8] To their heart's rapture, they begin to realize that biblical Christianity is bigger and far more welcoming of different kinds of people and personalities than what they've experienced in particular Christian churches.

I was having lunch with one such young man, a former student and now the frontman of a local rock band. He told me that when he was growing up, his questions, his eccentricities, his kind of music, his intensely introspective nature, and his deep struggles with depression and anxiety had him feeling like the odd child on the periphery of God's family. He'd wondered if God wanted him in the family at all. Then one day he was at a friend's house, sharing the sad conclusion he'd come to: he needed to shut off those parts of his personality that just didn't play well in daily life and among the Christians he knew. His friend's mom simply said, "No, you don't. Be different." He was thunderstruck. He said it felt like... then I interrupted him and said, "Permission."

"Yeah!" he said. I wasn't trying to be rude by interrupting. It's just that I knew exactly what he meant. We hear "be different" all the time in pop culture, ad nauseam. Be different, just like everyone else! But this encouragement came from a Christian household that knew him very personally. It wasn't permissiveness—do and be anything you want! That's godding. It was permission, from people who loved God and his word. It was freedom. Today, this young man loves and is avidly following his Savior, feeling God's joy in his work as a musician.

Truly biblical faith doesn't repress our personalities and God-imaging passions and creative powers; it releases them. It unearths and helps us understand what God has personally placed deep within us. All of God's words can do this, but God gave us some words specifically designed for it. The Psalms together comprise an "anatomy of the human soul."[9]

You'll find within these holy lyrics every soul-deep inclination and feeling we can experience in this world. From calmed repose to blinding rage, from fierce joy to bitter grief that not only rejects easy answers but refuses any resolution, to self-defying courage and commitment to live justly in the midst of rampant unrighteousness—the Psalms express the human heart in various stages of spiritual maturity and at all points of the human experience. "Here the language of the Bible comes to meet the very thoughts of our hearts before these can even clothe themselves in language and we recognize that we could not have expressed them better than the Spirit has expressed them for us."[10] The Psalms *get* us. They let the true us come to freedom and fullness, holding nothing good and necessary back from us as we grow in God's grace and offering nothing cheap and easy as we sing God's praise.

David's Psalms can be disturbingly intense, switching with sudden violence from light to dark, like a gentle breeze over the salt sea shifting split-second into tempest.[11] Sometimes David is calm like a baby just nursed (Psalm 131) and sometimes he's shrieking in very adult agony (Psalm 22). His artistic ranginess reflected the wild range of emotions and experiences in his remarkable life. Because of his frequent refusal to shift smoothly between emotions, some critics think David was mentally deranged.

Good artists seem off to those who aren't turned on by their work, who can't appreciate its depth, and who maybe don't want to face what it's saying—perhaps about them! Of course, accusations of mental derangement also apply to psychopaths, and bad artists can develop a martyr complex when people don't like their stuff. So we have to be careful. But if nothing else, there's no way you could accuse David or the other Psalmists of inhibition in their art. For artists who feel like the Christian faith wants to lock up their image-bearing gifts, the Psalms sing a sweet song. The Psalms are all about freedom.

The Psalms are God's permission to express honestly our truest, deepest selves—you don't have to hide your heart from God!—and they're God's most personal means of forming us in full humanness. Among God's other words, the Psalms are uniquely powerful and personal because they are simultaneously God's words to us and our words to him. By divine design, the Psalms simultaneously speak *to* and *for* our deepest selves. The Psalms express the abundance of God's heart and the abundance of our hearts, together.

That's why they were so perfect for Jesus.

Redemption Songs

The combination of divine and human in God's songs has Jesus written all over it. The Psalms are not only God-breathed, but even more specifically, Paul calls them the word of Christ (Colossians 3:16).[12] These songs spoke to and for the holiest of souls, the most beautiful and robustly human heart there's ever been. The Psalms really *got* Jesus.[13]

As Jesus did his Father's will in this life, the Psalms captivated him. "Our Lord himself, who had a perfect religious experience and lived and walked with God in absolute adjustment of his thoughts and desires to the Father's mind and will...found his inner life portrayed in the Psalter...and in some of the highest moments of his ministry borrowed from it the language in which his soul spoke to God, thus recognizing that a more perfect language for communion with God cannot be framed."[14]

Communion with God, loving Withness, is what we humans were made for and it's how we grow into our true selves. It's what Jesus lived and it's what he provides for those who trust him. The Psalms are vital for this formation. As we believe and sing the songs the Holy Spirit composed, the Holy Spirit composes us.

God is, in every way, the original artist; and the Psalms invite us to think of him as a musician. The divine composer can take an original concept through lots of musical twists and turns that would, in less capable hands, destroy its artistic integrity. God does this with his image-bearers. As he did with Jesus, God can even use the way others have hurt us—like an inferior band corrupting a classic song with their attempted cover—and use that pain to produce a final product that's absolutely true to the original, but which is somehow more authentic, more itself. The Holy Spirit's final, remastered production is a heart like that of God's son, perfectly tuned to the unique personality of the particular image-bearer.

The heart of Jesus is fully formed in love, so his heart is the one in which humanity sees its perfection. The Psalms let us sing, and therefore know and feel, the inner workings of that heart. These songs draw us so close to Jesus that, as we sing, we lose the distinction in the lyrics between us and him.

God wants us to know Jesus so personally that he lets us sing his son's life as if it were our own. And that's because in so many life-giving ways, it is (Colossians 3:4).

Many of the Psalms are written in the first person. The "I" in the Psalms is, first and foremost, the awaited Messiah—especially in the Psalms of David. As we'll see more fully later, David knew this. He knew that the Spirit of God spoke through him (2 Samuel 23:2).

As he tells his life experience in the Psalms, David writes his way into truth that transcends him. Reaching a millennium ahead of time into the life and work of the Messiah, the words that describe David's pain poetically sometimes describe Jesus's pain literally, as we saw with Psalm 22. In singing David's words as they worshiped God, God's people were identified and identifying with their truest King, singing his life experience as their own. What better way to express our full, personal identification with Christ than to sing his life in the first person? It's solidarity with the Savior, loving Withness in song.[15]

Paul describes his own desire to have a heart like the Lord's by saying he wants to know Jesus both in the power of Jesus's resurrection and in the pain of Christ's suffering (Philippians 3:8–11). The Psalms provide this personal knowledge. Martin Luther said that the Psalms spoke more clearly of Christ's death and resurrection than any other book in Scripture—keep in mind, that includes the gospels![16]

The Psalms let us share Christ's joy in defeating death and in the salvation his victory would spread throughout creation. But they also let us know how it felt and what it cost to do the lonely, often sorrowful work of saving the world (Psalms 22, 40). The Psalms prepare us for faithful, Christlike life in a fallen world.

Paint It Black

Jesus was "a man of sorrows, acquainted with grief" (Isaiah 53:1 and following). So it's no coincidence that about two-thirds of God's songs are laments. It's good and necessary to sing for joy as we experience life's loveliness, its bright and lofty moments. As we'll see, the Psalms take us to those shining heights. But David could say with Dylan, "Behind every beautiful thing I sense a kind of pain."[17]

In Scripture's longest cry of the heart, David longs for personal and global transformation according to God's law. And he just plain cries as he sees godding all around him. "My eyes shed streams of tears, because people do not keep your law" (Psalm 119:136).

Have you ever pleaded, angry and sobbing, with loved ones as they sped toward self-destruction, and wept bitterly as they got there? Jesus wailed as he beheld Jerusalem, his beloved, belligerent city: "O Jerusalem, Jerusalem, the city that kills the prophets and stones those who are sent to it! How often would I have gathered your children together as a hen gathers her brood under her wings, and you would not!" (Matthew 23:37). Echoes of Psalm 81:8 and 11: "O Israel, if you would but listen to me!...but my people did not listen to my voice."

Do you ever lie awake in the dark, angry and afraid, feeling desperately alone? As the shadow of the cross loomed ahead, Jesus knew that his disciples would not stay with him: "The hour is coming...when you will be scattered...and will leave me alone" (John 16:32). Psalm 102 expresses this haunted isolation: "I lie awake; I am like a lonely sparrow on the housetop....My days are like an evening shadow."

It's so hard to know how to process life's lows in a way that neither trivializes nor traps us within them. What do we do with all the dark, potentially poisonous stuff inside?

Sing it out. Just like Jesus did.

Music Therapy

The Psalms help us to get it all out without losing it altogether. They let out the sighs and screams, and they even have built-in pauses to let us be silent, when words just won't do.[18]

Music in itself is a glimpse of the peace and order missing from our chaotic lives and hearts. Composing music forces us to think in categories of connectedness: symmetry, continuity, consistency, and sometimes rhyme. Even if we claim to be moral anarchists, we're frustrated when our work doesn't come out "right"—when the sound just doesn't match the storm we're trying to expel through it. Same if we're just listening to music.

We know when the song just doesn't get it or come out right in the way we need to hear it. At the concert, we get upset at the band for not performing as well as they do in the studio. (This is part of why U2 is the best ever; they're even better live than recorded.) That there's a "right" we just feel when music gets us, and that it's usually a lot of hard work for the artist to get there, is an often unseen ray of warming light in the cold, lonely process of trying to express the dark.

Rage vented in hard, screaming rock music is not necessarily anarchistic, even when it tries to be. There's a huge and noticeable difference between a musically trained and tailored scream and a wild, warbling freak-out. The former can leave you awed; the latter is just odd. And even in the well-produced stuff that's meant to preach anarchy, it's artistic anarchistic.[19] There's carefulness in the composition, care which, ironically, requires self-control. To sing artfully about burning the whole place down requires the fire-extinguishing restraint the song calls us to abandon. Art points us toward truth, even when it despairs of ever finding it, or when we don't know if we can live with it once we do.

"With or Without You" by U2 is my all-time favorite rock song. And it just came on in the coffee shop where I'm working! (Or, "working," as my good "friend" puts it.) I love the whole atmosphere of the song: the vocals, the instrumentals, and the lyrics. Other bands and solo artists have tried to cover this song. It always goes bad.[20] The original artists, in every way, own this song (and that's one of the reasons I'm not quoting it—too many quotes costs too much money).

What I love most about the song is its integrity—how it remains true to its core throughout. Like a lake swelling in a relentless downpour, Bono's pain rises within him as the song goes on. Eventually the dam bursts in a wail that releases the song's essential tension. But following that cry, there's no neat and tidy wrap-up, no resolution to try harder and do better and to look on the bright side—there's no resolution at all. It's just a repeat of the title several times and some final, speechless, ghostly lament in falsetto. The music pounds on with the propulsive beat that carried it all along and adds some new guidance from the Edge's guitar, but then it all fades, suggesting a distraught soul who's done with words but not done with what's shredding his soul. And time carries him, no less burdened, into the increasingly silent periphery of other people's notice and care. *This song makes me so happy!*[21]

If we can avoid slipping into the dishonesty and willing blindness of relentless darkness,[22] of nihilism angsting about nihilism, it can be a big, sad, refreshing breath of fresh air to hear and sing a song that does not go softly into the light. Kind of like the deep, cleansing, shuddering breath after some serious sobbing—we can let sadness have its course without getting addicted to it.[23] After we're done with the song and the song's done with us for now, we can look at life again, more clearly for having cried those cleansing tears. If you're a Christian, imagine having honestly dark and darkly honest songs, directed toward God and written by God, to do all this for your soul. You've got them!

Psalm 88 could make a cat poster hiss and spit. It opens "God of my salvation, I cry out day and night before you," canters on to sunny lines like "You have put me in the depths of the pit, in the regions dark and deep," ambles blithely to a very Abraham/Job/Jeremiah/Hosea/Paul/Jesus-like "Your dreadful assaults destroy me," and ties a precious ribbon around the whole pretty package with lyrics written long before Dylan or Disturbed ever let us hear the sound of silence: "Darkness has become my only friend." Very true to life, very true to Jesus's life. But not the exclusive truth.

Psalm 88 is self-contained, sealed-off sadness, but it opens when it joins 149 other songs that run the range of human emotion and experience and give it all aesthetically attuned, authentically and artistically conceived catharsis. As God's word, it understands and meets us in the dark. But Scripture doesn't encourage the self-harm and isolation that tempts tortured souls through music that is honest, but not true.

Concussion Protocol

The sadness in the Psalms rises from life's separations, the dis-integration that defines the fallen world and is amplified beneath the ceiling of self. The Psalms feel the fundamental disconnectedness within the human heart and what we experience with special intensity beneath the ceiling of self: that gnawing, often depressing, and at times infuriating sense of unbelonging, incompletion and incompatibility in life, and within the self. Scripture tells us to expect it. The Psalms let us express it.

After the cosmic collision between our will and God's, we fell hard—the impact shocking and shaking everything that we are. We still have the headaches and dizziness, the nauseating feeling that everything is either too bright or too dark, the uncertainty and hesitancy on our feet as we step forward. Life's voices sound too loud or seem muffled even as they scream. Part of the stabilizing process is to realize that Scripture, especially in the Psalms, tells us it's okay to feel all shaken up and out of place. It would be crazy not to. Disorientation and dysphoria of all kinds make total sense in a fallen world.

We're naturally desperate to fit in somewhere, with someone. But we were made for more than just fitting in. The question has to be not so much "How can I fit in?" as "How can I be made whole?" At my size, I can fit comfortably into a car that would crunch and suffocate a taller man, but that doesn't mean that the me-sized car is actually good for me. It might be a Pinto.

We need to ask: how can my disjointed thoughts and feelings come to peaceful agreement, and how can this dis-integrated culture and world do the same? The Psalms are all about that cry for *shalom*—the state of being in which the condition of our body and soul meets the condition of the world, and it's all peace. Before *shalom* comes with the return of Christ, the Psalms teach us how to handle the hell of being torn apart by life's disconnections.

The Psalms sing the pain of life's dis-integrations: separation from our loved ones who die (Psalm 116: "precious in the sight of the Lord is the death of his loved ones"—think Jesus weeping at Lazarus's funeral); from the community of loving Witness (Psalm 42: "These things I remember, as I pour out my soul, how I would go with the multitude, leading the procession to the house of God"); from our former strength in life (Psalm 102: "He has broken my strength in midcourse; he has shortened my days"); from our bodies in death (Psalm 30: "What profit is there in my death… will the dust praise you?"); from God himself (Psalm 13: "Will you forget me forever?"); from justice (Psalm 73: "Behold, these are the wicked; always at ease, they increase in riches"); from freedom because of enslaving persecution (Psalm 129: "Many times they have ridden over my back with their plows"); from peace with God because of sin (Psalm 32: "Your hand was heavy upon me day and night; my strength was dried up as by the heat of summer");

from home while in exile (Psalm 137: "Our torturers demanded joyful songs from us....how can we sing the Lord's song in a foreign land?"); from friendship and trust (Psalm 41: "Even my close friend, whom I trusted...has lifted his heel against me"). Separations, fragmentation, disintegration of all kinds and in every place.

The Psalms give us wisdom and strength to understand, express, and endure life's lack of integrity, and they help us to participate in God's plan "for the fullness of time, to unite all things in Christ, things in heaven and things on earth" (from Ephesians 1:9–10).[24] Glimpsing the glory of all creation at peace, of all things made right and righteous, the Psalms cry out for God's kingdom to come in full, within us and throughout the world (Psalms 96, 98). They preview the world we want, and teach us to live faithfully in the one we've got.

As the one who'd reconcile creation to its Creator, Jesus felt life's separations as we do, and yet to a degree we can't comprehend. He felt dysphoria on a cosmic scale. The world was made through him, but when he came home for a visit, it was made quite clear to him that he was not welcome there anymore.

In some of Scripture's saddest words, John tells us that when the Lord arrived in the world, the world did not know him (John 1:10–11). This ignorance was not innocent. The more people realized who he was, the less they wanted him there. This still happens today. The more clearly we see Jesus for who he really is and not as the idol we make of him, the more our godding is provoked. Jesus images God perfectly; his presence ignites the hellish grudge we've had against God since the garden.

Ever since Satan spoke with our first parents, separation from God is not enough for us. God's silence is not enough. Hatred for our first love runs so deep, the only thing for it is to kill him. It's what Adam and Eve would have done in the garden if they were able, if God had possessed a physicality they could have touched and harmed. We know this because of what happened to Jesus, God in the flesh. When fallen humanity finally had the chance to kill its Creator, we seized it with a vengeance.

Remember, God's first step in saving the world was his separating the woman and her offspring from their new affinity for their true enemy. When creation hates its Creator enough to crucify him, it reveals a puncture wound in humanity's heart, put there by the serpent's fangs but also self-inflicted as we let the snake slither all around in our souls. One lesson from Satan was enough to school Adam and Eve in a whole history's worth of hatred for God.

It's All the Rage

Since the garden, we've never been fundamentally at peace with anyone or anything, because we're not fundamentally at peace with the one who created everything. This unsettledness, rooted in unholy hate, leads to a deep and pervasive anger, a felt hostility we can't explain but whose presence and power among and within us we cannot deny.

The Bible sees all the rage as continual aftershocks of the quake in Eden, the perennial antagonism between the woman and the serpent and their respective offspring. It's human godding's opposition to the authority of the God-man.

Psalm 2 tells us that the nations rage against God's appointed, anointed king—the Messiah. In Acts 4, Peter cites Psalm 2 as the significance of the multinational, political, personal, and religious hatred that culminated in Christ's crucifixion. Representatives of Rome, which ruled much of the world, along with many of Jesus's own people, were a malicious microcosm gathered to put God's anointed King to death. As John puts it, the world did not know the Word, and his own people did not receive him (John 1:10–11). By rejecting the Word, the world confirmed its rejection of the wholeness and peace only he could bring. Since the garden, we'd rather have hell on earth than be ruled by the King who reigns from heaven.

Of course, explicit opposition to Jesus isn't what every hater is thinking. And lest this overview of history sound self-important coming from a Christian, Christians are admittedly (and very obviously) not the only ones getting hated on in the world. Satan's venom spews in all directions, burning whomever it can. But the true face of humanity's deep-seated rage, turned toward the true God, does tend to show itself clearly at significant points in world history.

Christians in the wealthy West are prone to worship and with missionary zeal to export the Christ of the American suburbs to the broader world. We forget or are entirely ignorant of the fact that Christianity has very non-European roots, and that it has significantly shaped world history. In our day, in this culture, it's easy to be cheesy in our faith. By and large, our suffering is not a direct result of our faith in Christ. It's not so easy elsewhere, and it certainly hasn't been throughout history.

Eventually, autonomous empires get tired of people who insist that Jesus is King and that all people and nations are accountable to him. Christians in ancient Rome were savaged because they could no longer say in good conscience that "Caesar is Lord." Their insistence, however humbly, that "Jesus is Lord" was taken as a profound slight of Caesar and therefore a threat to the empire he ruled as a god. Plus, Christian preaching was bad for the economy. In various parts of the empire, conversions to Christ were forcing idol factories into bankruptcy (Acts 19:23 and following). For businesses built on lies, it's always bad when customers learn the truth. So Rome categorized Christians as criminals and subjected them, along with other enemies of the state, to the gladiator arenas or the cross, some of history's most sadistic forms of capital punishment.[25]

Nobody (except the man himself) naturally minds the Jesus who's cool with whatever we do. It's his claim to be our King that ignites a dormant, as yet unidentified rage within us. If Christ's enemies in more recent eras could put him back on that cross, they would. Not having that option, they do the next best thing: they persecute his disciples. This isn't a martyr complex. There were more Christian martyrs in the twentieth century than in all centuries after Christ combined.[26]

Jesus told the disciples in his day to expect such treatment, and how to handle it.

Death and Taxes

Despite the horrific persecution they'd endure, Jesus told his marked-for-death disciples to give proper respect to societal authorities. He even told them to pay the taxes levied by the empire that would slaughter many of them (Matthew 22:16–21). Does that strike you as weak, and even cruel of Christ? What kind of shepherd tells his sheep to grin and bear it as the wolves bear down upon them? Not Jesus. He's "the good shepherd" (John 10).

Contrary to the "gentle Jesus meek and mild" slanderous stereotype—the cartoonish Jesus at which Nietzsche (rightly) foamed at the mouth—God's suffering servant never disregards his disciples' emotional trauma as evil assails them. He did, however, tell his followers to respect and even to love their enemies, and to bless those who persecute them (Matthew 5:1–12). The really maddening thing is that Jesus actually practiced what he preached. He did this, from his heart, and expected the same of his disciples. Why?

Because by doing what seems impossible and even undignified, they'd be living out the heart of their heavenly Father, who looks with forgiving love upon a world that murdered his son.

To keep clear-headed on these confounding ideas, we have to remember that God's grace never comes at the expense of his justice. His love is not lawless, nor is his judgment without mercy. They all meet in Christ, in what he's done in the world and what he will do upon his return. Serving this God, persecuted Christians have been able to look upon their torturers with a deep and true desire that they, too, would find grace in the eyes of their Lord.

The respect Christians have shown to tyrants[27] is a quiet statement that the despots were not the gods they believed themselves to be. Christians were courteous to their killers because the King of kings told them to be, and because they actually loved them, just like their Savior did. They heard the word of their Lord, and they did what he said. James would be proud. So is Jesus.[28]

It's not that Jesus tells us to do nothing when we or others are abused. Remember that all of the Lord's "don'ts" come with a "do." When the Lord forbids murder on every level, he's also commanding every lawful effort to protect and prosper human life. Even though we are to love our enemies, we are to actively resist and oppose their satanic work. Part of the pushback Jesus allows his church comes through the Psalms, which are prayers, which in Christ are a powerful part of how God overthrows evil and evildoers in the world.[29]

Sinners praying for God to overthrow fellow sinners might seem hypocritical, like complaining over the mess we made and asking God to judge all the *other* mess-makers. But it's not hypocritical for God's people to cry out against evil unless they continue unrepentant in it. Full hypocrisy comes when we forsake the righteous Savior for the sake of godding and then curse God for how bad life is.

Our hearts heavy from confessed complicity in every evil and wanting to do something about it, we need a means of speaking and working against evil in a way proportionate to its severity. We need to be able to, as Eugene Petersen puts it, "curse without cursing."[30]

%)^*!%^$&(!

There isn't profanity strong enough to cuss it all out when we experience life's most cursed realities. God knows this. So, "there are psalms that lead us in our speech to God in times of violent desecration."[31]

Some of God's songs are "imprecatory"—they call God's judgment down upon those who relentlessly and unrepentantly pursue evil. Ecclesiastes 3 tells us that there's a time for everything under the sun. The Psalms provide the healthy, holy expression of every thing when its time comes, even holy hatred and retributive justice.

But doesn't Jesus say to turn the other cheek? Yes, indeed (Matthew 5:39). When someone slaps us in the face, we can overlook the offense (Proverbs 19:11). Jesus preaches against a retaliatory mind-set born of self-righteousness and wounded pride. He tells us to have an open door in our hearts for all people, but he never tells us to become doormats for anyone. In the face of injustice, the Psalms let our souls walk a biblical path between sinful activity and sinful passivity.

Paul tells believers to sing the Psalms (no exception granted for the rough ones) as evidence of the Holy Spirit's influence in their lives (Ephesians 5:18–19 and Colossians 3:16), and to "bless those who persecute you; bless and do not curse them....never avenge yourselves, but leave it to the wrath of God" (Romans 12:14, 19). The imprecatory psalms do exactly that. We get to sing it out, but we trust God to carry it out.

In Revelation 6, Christian martyrs are pictured as souls gathered under an altar. In verse 10, they cry out to the risen Christ for justice. "O Sovereign Lord, holy and true, how long before you will avenge our blood?" Jesus does not respond, "Well, *that's* not very Christian of you. What are you, *Old* Testament believers?"

Instead, they're told to wait a little longer, while God's saving work in the world continues, until the full family of God is gathered. That's when Jesus will return and apply justice fully. When the last sheep is brought into the fold, the Good Shepherd will deal with the wolves.[32]

The Psalms encourage, engender, and express this "patience of the saints" (Revelation 13:10) while letting us voice how hard it is to have and maintain. Just like the souls under the altar, many Psalms cry out, "How long, O Lord?" (Psalm 13) and many promise the coming of the Christ and with him full and final justice (Psalm 96). The totality of the peace promised lets us know that the psalmists were looking, perhaps without realizing it, beyond Christ's advent and to his return. Sunrise and sunset can look the same in a photo; we need to know what time the picture was taken or which direction the camera was facing to know the difference. The justice for which the Psalms cry dawned in Jesus's first coming and will be brought in full when the Son of God comes down from heaven once again. In the meantime, we need these patience-inspiring, peace-seeking Psalms, rather urgently.

At this moment in American history, some people are ready to go French Revolution on the whole place. Some see violence as a legitimate means to the end of their socially just cause, feeling that the powerful will only care when suffering touches their own kind. So consciences become increasingly comfortable with ideas they once opposed. "I never thought I'd do this, but there's no other way. And they deserve it."

Beneath the ceiling of self, there's no standard for justice but the self, or a community of selves. So legitimate grievances can go lawless and get lethal, and feel just fine about it. The Psalms warn us not to put our confidence in politicians (Psalm 146:3), but they are not vigilante anthems.[33] Imprecatory psalms express frustration and fury, but always from a fundamental posture of love, which requires patience and self-control and is the sum total principle of God's law.

For example, Michael LeFebvre writes that Psalm 109 "is often cited as the most cruel of the imprecations of Scripture." Exhibit A, verse 9. It cries out against an evil man, "May his children be fatherless and his wife a widow" (!!). We might think, even if David's anger against this guy is legit, why does he have to bring his wife and kids into it? But this is actually a grim call for mercy.

Given God's emphasis on the importance of family and the way he's structured it, this man David decries must be wretchedly evil. As we thought about in chapter 5, if Dad's that bad, then despite the deep pain it will cause, it's better for his family to be without him. Further, David maintains not only his personal innocence in the conflict (God would know if he's lying), but his personal, loving efforts to make peace with those the cursed man represents. "They encircle me with words of hate, and attack me without cause. In return for my love they accuse me, but I give myself to prayer. So they reward me evil for good, and hatred for my love" (verses 3–5). Loving your enemies while calling for their destruction seems contradictory, "but it was not contradictory to Christ who combined his curses with his tears."[34]

God Save the King

The Savior takes the suffering of his people very personally.[35] The resurrected Christ got in the face of Saul, whom we know as Paul, in a literally blinding display of messianic might. Jesus asked him, in light of his vicious persecution of Christians, "Why are you persecuting me?" (Acts 9:4). Through the imprecatory psalms, Christ stands for and with his persecuted people, allowing them to take their pain personally and to gain courage as they recognize its big-picture significance. Living as if Jesus is King earns the murderous ire of powerful Jesus-haters; it was this way when the imprecatory psalms were first written.

In the Old Testament era, God funneled his royal rule of the world through the kingdom of Israel. David and the people knew that he was God's chosen, anointed king, a prototype messiah whose dynasty the King of kings would claim and fulfill (Matthew 22:41 and following). So, the local skirmishes of the Old Testament era had cosmic significance. To oppose David was to oppose the expressed will of God, and the rule of God himself.[36] To sing against David's enemies was to sing ultimately against all systemic evil and injustice, whatever form they took in different eras, because evil is defined as such by its violation of God's righteous law.

Though the imprecations sometimes seem out of control and vitriolic,[37] it's significant that, like rage rock, they're contained in a song with a clear beginning and end. Paul tells us in Ephesians 4 (quoting Psalm 4) to be angry but not sinfully so, and to not let the sun go down on that anger. In that culture, sundown was the conclusion of the business day, so Paul is saying, "If you have legit business with anger, don't do anything unlawful with it and don't let it linger." The imprecatory psalms give to righteous anger its necessary vent and needed closure.

Three thousand years after theocratic Israel, we can sing imprecations against the obvious, systemic and vicious injustice we see in life, letting God and anyone else listening know how much we hate it. We cry out against evil, but only on God's terms. "Curses are not ours to invent and ascribe."[38] Having sung our hearts out, knowing that God hears and responds to prayer coming to him through Christ (John 14 and 15),[39] we can keep our hearts, mouths, and hands from doing evil in response to evil. This is how we "curse without cursing."

Some imprecatory language, as in Psalm 109, goes darker than we think God should allow. Some of it may be what D. A. Carson helpfully calls "the rhetoric of outrage," meant "not to inform but to ignite; it has…a great deal in common with a sudden scream….it vents confusion and terror."[40] He cites our friend Jeremiah's bitter complaint against God ("Why did I come out from the womb?") and notes that we're surely not to take the weeping prophet's words literally, as if he wished perpetual pregnancy upon his mother.

Some of the heated language in the Psalms is certainly, and purposefully, the rhetoric of outrage. But if the indignation that the psalmists are venting in such violent words is truly righteous, and especially considering that the Psalms were meant for public worship and not just private angsting, there's got to be a deeper, Spirit-inspired purpose and significance to these sacred curses. It's time once again to plop.

"Son of…"

When we take the Bible on its own terms, we see every passage in the sweep of the Covenant of Grace. All of the Psalms, and therefore the imprecatory Psalms, advance themes already begun and cannot be understood separate from those truths and the language in which they were expressed in prior Scripture.

Remember, Scripture uses labels like "children of" or even "son of" to indicate deep association with a way of life.[41] James and John, Jesus's disciples, were called "sons of thunder" not because Thor has kids, but because of their stormy temperaments. So, in the Psalms, cries such as Psalm 109's "let his children be fatherless" can and should be understood not only as the rhetoric of outrage, but ultimately as an expression of the perennial hope that the Messiah will once and for all rid the world of the serpent and his spiritual offspring. How do we know that this is God's intent in Psalm 109 (and by implication, other imprecations)?

Peter says the enemy in view of Psalm 109 is Judas,[42] the betrayer of Jesus, whom Jesus referred to as *"the son* of destruction" (John 17:12). David's imprecation broadens beyond one man to cover other children of the devil. "Sin has, in Biblical terms, both an individual and a corporate identity....Consequently, it is frequent and fitting language used in Scripture to speak of the total annihilation of a sinful nation."[43] I know what you're thinking, and you should be thinking it. But the basis for God's corporate judgments is never ethnic. God says on page 1 of his book and affirms throughout that all people bear his image (Genesis 1:26–28, 9:6, James 3). Judgment comes upon communities whose fundamental solidarity is satanic.[44]

The prayers for judgment against Satan's spiritual descendants are never uttered without deep mournfulness over the way children of God have acted like sons of hell.

Scripture records prayers of personal repentance (Psalm 51) and epic prayers of national repentance (Ezra 9 and Daniel 9). Biblical confessions of national sin begin with confession of personal sin. The prophets who led the people in prayer felt their own personal sinfulness deeply, but because they were part of the people, they considered themselves culpable for national sin as well. As Father Zossima put it, "Everyone is responsible for everyone and everything."[45]

Several of the psalms keep Israel's past sins ever before the people, to humble them in the present (Psalms 78 and 80). Wouldn't this pained sense of personal sin and corporate solidarity in sinfulness be a giant step toward peace for a fractured, divisive, and ever-dividing, blame-everyone-else culture like ours?

How about we Americans corporately repent for our brutality in the banishment of Native Americans from their homelands, and for the enslavement of Africans on American soil? How about we repent for the scores of millions of people of every ethnicity we've abused or just flat-out murdered between our shores, the unborn and the born, all the hurting people we've ignored because, well, we have stuff to do and social progress to make?[46]

Having confessed our own sin and taken steps to promote justice and mercy in our lives and culture, we can rightly and with a clean conscience cry out against the evil "out there." And as the imprecatory psalms essentially direct us, we can take the faithful fight directly to our truest enemy.

This Means War

The conflict between the woman, the dragon, and their respective offspring comes coursing down through history like a river of blood. In Old Testament times, when church and state could hardly be distinguished, God's people were sometimes called to take up arms in conflicts that were always fundamentally spiritual. The New Testament clearly articulates distinctions between church and state and between physical and spiritual warfare,[47] but it continues to remind us of the unseen realities at play in what we do see. The physical and metaphysical are ever intertwined.[48]

The devil gets much of his work done through those who do not acknowledge his existence. Thankfully, that's true of God as well. History tells of tyrants, satanic in their bloodlust, who'd think that belief in such a being is silly. There are benevolent rulers who reject Christ but do wonderful image-bearing work for the world. And, sadly, there are rulers who live like hell but draw fawning attention from Christians because they refer to Jesus as Lord. "They're baby Christians!" supporters say. No. Babies recognize their parents and act like them. The Psalms call attention to the true King, who works through (or despite) all lesser rulers to accomplish his righteous reign in the world.

As we've seen, David was no prince, but the shepherd-poet-prophet-warrior-Scripture-writing king of Israel understood the unique Christ-centeredness of his life, and therefore of his songs. He knew that his music was from the Holy Spirit, meant to teach his people about their true King.

For example, Jesus said that David wrote Psalm 110 while "in the Spirit" (Matthew 22:43 and following), meaning that he was consciously being led by the Spirit as he wrote (see Revelation 1:10 as an example of the same usage of that phrase). David's opening lyrics are cryptic: "The Lord said to my Lord, 'sit at my right hand.'" Wait. Who was David's Lord? David is Israel's king and no way is he bowing to a foreign ruler. And why does God call David's Lord his right-hand man? It's mysterious language that comes to clarity in Jesus Christ.

Jesus is both David's descendant and David's Lord, the God-appointed King who would ultimately sit at God's right hand[49] and who would fulfill all of David's Spirit-given words. Even the harshest.

Unlike Jesus, David fought in physical, brutal wars. Yet these fights, too, find their fulfillment and ultimate significance in the war Jesus did wage in this world, his shock-and-awe defeat of the one whose work stands behind all war. The Psalms fueled Christ's fight, and Christ's fight fulfilled the warful psalms.

The pain-filled psalms of judgment, which ought to be painful to sing, were composed to combat the devil's work, which deserves nothing but holy hate. It's right to call down God's judgment upon those who delight in continually carrying out that work.

Satan bit hard in the garden but got his head stomped at the cross. Ever since then, he's been doing whatever he can through whomever he can to rip and tear the world and its inhabitants before Jesus returns and renders him true dead. We need sobering, soldiering language to remind us that biblical faith in Christ is a fight, a very costly one with very personal casualties. Paul says that we do not wage war against flesh and blood (Ephesians 6:12). But, oh my, is it war.[50]

Rules of Engagement

In Ephesians 6, Paul tells Christians to suit up with "the whole armor of God," the spiritual weapons that God's people use to take the fight to their true enemy. Paul gets his military metaphor from Isaiah, who seems to be his favorite Old Testament prophet. In Isaiah 59, it's the Messiah who wears the armor and does the fighting. The Savior Isaiah foretells would fight on behalf of God's people, using spiritual weapons that demolish soul-enslaving philosophical strongholds set up against him (2 Corinthians 10:4–5). And so Paul tells believers to "put on Christ," to strap up in the strength of the Messiah.

In Romans 16:20, Paul braces his Christian brothers and sisters for the fight of their lives: "The God of peace will soon crush

Satan under your feet." It's Genesis 3:15 again! Except here, believers are crushing the serpent. Jesus beats the Enemy, but believers are so closely identified with him that his victory is described as theirs. Jesus has already won the war. What remains is for the risen Christ, through his word through his people, to keep on the attack until the Savior returns and slays the dragon true dead. The imprecatory psalms are on the cutting edge of that holy offensive.

Among the armaments Paul lists is the "sword of the Spirit," the word of God. We can sing the imprecatory psalms against modern slavery (Psalm 129 comes to mind) while spreading the gospel to both victims and perpetrators alike. We've seen how a once great enemy of the church was conscripted to the true King's service. Paul became a soldier for Christ who placed the gospel like a timed explosive into the relationship between a converted slaveholder and a fugitive slave. It was the charge that would explode whole systems of slavery in ages to come.

Singing the imprecatory psalms lets us acknowledge that the bite of a mortally wounded serpent still stings like hell, that there is still so much satanic oppression to oppose in this world. Yet these psalms remind us that we serve Satan's conqueror. As Christ with his spiritual sword cuts the enslaver's chains from people and communities (Revelation 19:15), we begin to learn redemption and reconciliation, love and peace—*shalom*—as a way of life.

Life Together

The Psalms call all people to reconciliation with the one true God and therefore to reconciliation with one another. These songs celebrate the peace that Jesus came to bring to the world, and to all peoples. "Praise the Lord, all you nations!…For great is his steadfast love toward us" (Psalm 117). John loves to highlight particular conversations as microcosms of the global peace the Psalms fight for and herald in song.

In John 4, Jesus instigates a conversation with a woman of Samaria. This woman had (at least) three social strikes against her. Strike 1: She was a woman. In that day, 'nuff said.[51] Strike 2: She was a Samaritan. As such, she was the victim and perhaps even a perpetrator of a longstanding, vicious, reciprocal racism with the Jews.[52] It was so bad, Jews would walk miles out of their way just to avoid Samaria, and the Samaritans were happy for them to take that hike. But on this day, Jesus took his disciples straight into the region of their racial nemeses. After sending them into town to get some food (awkward!), the Son of God sat down by a well to have one of history's most socially significant conversations.

As Jesus rests, the woman comes out to collect water at the well—what a coincidence!—and Jesus asks her for a drink. That Jesus even spoke to her shocked the woman. Her response in verse 9 reveals the perpetually raw wound of the racism that existed between their peoples: "How is it that you, a Jew, ask a drink of me, a woman of Samaria?"—*Why are you talking to me? Don't you know you're supposed to hate me?*

Typical of Jesus, his response seems off topic but is actually right to the point. He tells her that, if she knew the gift of God, and who it was that spoke to her, *she* would have asked *him* for living water—an Old Testament picture of everlasting life, which God alone can provide (verse 10, Jeremiah 17:13–14).[53]

Notice that Jesus was just fine with a woman from a despised people group approaching him as the middle man to receive something vital from God himself. Right away, Jesus removes any barrier based on sex or race between them, and therefore between her and God. The Old Testament had always taught, as Jewish leaders were notoriously guilty of ignoring, that those two barriers were never really there.[54]

It was the third social strike against the Samaritan woman that had her on the outs with God. When she asks for the living water Jesus spoke of, Jesus does not reply, "Sure! Here you go!" He tells her instead to go and get her husband. She replies honestly, "I have no husband." Jesus lets her know that he understands what she means by her careful reply. She was living with a man who was not her husband, and by implication claiming the benefits of marriage outside that covenanted relationship. She realizes that she's in the presence of a prophet. Amazingly, despite being called out for her sin, she feels comfortable enough with Jesus to open her heart to him. Her soul's deep pains and hopes come rushing to the surface in the Savior's gentle, kindhearted presence. She's captivated.

The woman then mentions the age-old disagreement between the Jews and Samaritans about the true and rightful place of worship: was it in Jerusalem on Mt. Zion or where the Samaritans insisted, right there in that very place they were talking? Jesus takes the conversational detour, knowing that they were arriving at its divinely intended destination. He tells her that the time is coming, and now is, when the true worshipers will worship neither in Jerusalem nor on the mountain where they talked, but "in spirit and in truth." But that doesn't address her question about the place of worship at all! Exactly.

The temple on Mt. Zion in Jerusalem was historically important in getting God's people grounded in their relationship to him, but the worship of God was always about the people, not the place. God's heart was with the worshipers wherever they assembled. The covenant of grace said, "I will dwell among *you*." The "yous" included people from everywhere on the planet. Wherever they assembled to worship, *they* were the sanctuary, the dwelling place of God. The New Testament confirms this by using temple language to describe God's worshipers.

Peter refers to Christians scattered way beyond Jerusalem as living stones, joined together to form a dwelling place for God (1 Peter 2:4 and following). No more need for the temple or its rituals, like animal sacrifices. And that's because Jesus, the Lamb of God, had given his life as the true offering foreshadowed by now obsolete temple ceremonies.[55] His redeeming work would bring home to God the true sons and daughters of Abraham from all over the map.[56] Jesus was talking to one such daughter at the well.

Wonderstruck and full of hope, the Samaritan woman leaves her conversation with Jesus so she can tell her people about the prophet who'd just broken society's rules of gender and race relations, had peered invasively into her life and spoken God's law softly and uncompromisingly, and had offered her the everlasting life only God could give—which all sounds to them rather messianic. Their own faithful hopes stirred, they come to see for themselves whether this Hebrew man Jesus is the Christ of God's word, the light of the nations (Isaiah 42:6, John 8:12).[57]

But she already knows he is. Before she leaves to find her friends, Jesus says to her, "I who speak to you am he."

Family Time

Only Christ's cross can crucify racism and kill xenophobia, because these are some of the sins he took upon himself and for which he suffered the hell they merit and the hell they inflict upon

God's image-bearers.[58] Only God's grace can rid a racist soul of the godding that stands behind that and every other self-righteous posture of heart, and only God's law can tell us what true love and acceptance look like among image-bearers. Reconciled to God through the redeeming work of Christ, we have every reason, right, and resource to be reconciled to one another. But still, it can be terrifying to take steps into new relationships, let alone into an entirely new identity, especially among former enemies.

As strangers and former enemies come together, good intentions abound, but so can suspicions and personal preferences in life that preclude (sometimes on purpose) different kinds of people from comfortable participation. So how, in practical terms, do you unite people so radically and racially different in the praise of one God?[59]

Well, how do we in our culture get profoundly different people from across the country to unite with the same heart and to love doing it? We see it all the time in sports. Focus on what unites them essentially (Sox nation!), get them to rally around a franchise hero (Miss you, Big Pappi!), and give them songs to sing together (Sweet Caroline!), however scattered they may be throughout the world (not all the faithful can make it to Fenway) and throughout time (some fans never saw 2004, sadly). The same goes, with much greater significance, for the worldwide church in all its varieties of people and social contexts. Show them their place in the one who fulfilled God's great promise going all the way back to humanity's beginning. And give them songs to sing together.[60]

The Bible functions as a family album for God's children, complete with ancestries. The Bible's songs serve as family anthems. Singing them today keeps God's family tied together through time and space. They remind us who we really are, who God's children have always been, and they help us welcome new family from all across the world.

The Psalms are perhaps the clearest example, and certainly the clearest expression, of the loving Withness that the gospel brings in Christ. These songs are never more powerful, never more themselves, than when a diverse group of people united by love for Christ sing them together. The Psalms can unite the world's people because they are the songs of the world's Savior.

Paul writes, "I am crucified with Christ" (Galatians 2:20) and that believers have been "raised together with Christ" (Colossians 3) and "seated with him in the heavenly places" (Ephesians 2, Psalm 22:1, 16, 2 and 110). Across time and space and all kinds of separations, all believers can sing out their union with the life, death, resurrection, and reign of their Savior. Whatever he's done, whatever he's doing, whatever he will do—we are with him, and therefore with one another as the historic people of God. The Psalms are the perfect songs for the diverse people who together are the temple of the living God.

Imagine a Sunday, stretched into its various stages across the globe, in which every Christian gathered in the public praise of God, and Christians imprisoned or hiding in the shadows, were all singing from one songbook. No matter what selections they sang in particular places, they'd be singing together, on the day Christ rose from the dead, the God-breathed words of their resurrected Savior. In a very real way, our voices, united in singing his songs, are his voice in the world. What an expression of unity that would be, and what a statement to the rest of the world about the resurrection and reign of its true King!

We might think, Cool. But what about the impossibility of our all singing in the same style? Same response. Cool!

Isn't it interesting that, while we have the texts of the psalms, we do not have inscripturated tunes to go with?[61] Nor does the Spirit command a particular style of singing. This suggests a liberty God wants us to have in composing culturally specific musical vehicles to carry God's universally applicable lyrics into the various gathering places of God's temple.

For you musical artists—what a gift you'd give the world, to compose culturally specific arrangements of the psalms where the tune really fits the text.[62] Your artistic arrangement would help the diverse people of God feel more and more at home in God's worldwide family.[63] The triune God delights in this kind of community (Psalm 133, Ephesians 4:1–6), because God *is* true community. Engaging his songs together is a beautiful and vital way of imaging him.

Oldies but Goodies

But aren't these songs, or at least a lot of them, too dated to be sung in our day? Awkward as it may feel at first, singing Old Testament texts makes perfect sense in the New Testament era. Singing the Psalms not only expresses our historic solidarity as God's family; it demonstrates how all of God's inscripturated words work together in harmony and do their unifying work in the world today.

Remember how the New Testament uses temple language for God's worshipers. The Psalms are full of temple imagery. The collection contains songs written before, during, and after the building and eventual destruction of the temple built by David's son, Solomon. We sing our love for Mt. Zion in Jerusalem, the location of the temple, where the very stones are precious to us (Psalm 102:14). We sing those words today with the understanding the New Testament gives us, living in the reality toward which centuries of psalm writing were building among the people of God, experiencing the truth that Jesus told the woman at the well: the people of God are the true temple. To sing about the place (the temple or its location) is to sing about the people. Peter calls believers living stones who are to "love one another earnestly from a pure heart" (1 Peter 1:22).

Paul uses covenant of grace language as he calls the Corinthians away from the godding that dominated their pre-Christian existence and that was putting up a nasty, scrappy fight as it was cornered by God's word. "What agreement has the temple of God with idols? For we are the temple of the living God; as God has said, 'I will make my dwelling among them'" (2 Corinthians 6:16).

In Ephesians 5 and Colossians 3, Paul tells Gentile converts from all over the ancient Near East to sing the Psalms as the regular experience and expression of their union with Christ and therefore unity with one another. As successive generations sing the Psalms across the world, the same lyrics take us more deeply into their always intended truth and build us more fully toward completion as God's temple. "The psalms themselves, even while continuing to celebrate the Zion promises and the coming Davidic kingship that goes with them, already sing about, and by singing help to bring about, an implicit personal version of Temple theology. Devout worshipers, individually or corporately, can themselves become, as it were, an extension of sacred space."[64]

This mature understanding and use of ancient material is part of what Jesus means when he tells the Samaritan woman that God is seeking those who will worship him in spirit and in truth.

True!

John loves to use the word "truth" to mean not so much the opposite of false, but reality, fulfillment, the real thing and not just the symbolic picture or preview.

As John opens his gospel, he tells us of John the Baptist, who came to bear witness about the light of the world (Jesus) but who was not the "true" light. The apostle isn't saying that John was a false light, a lying prophet.[65] He means that John was not the source of the light that his ministry shone into the world. The moon does not shine with its own light, but hopefully we don't look up with disdain on a clear night at the glowing silver orb and scream, "Liar! Poser!" The moon is not the true light; it shines with the light of the sun. So, too, the ministry of John the Baptist shone with the light of Jesus, the light of the world. Jesus was and is the "true" light.[66]

"Trueness" is a bit more complicated in humanity than it is among the stars. We begin this life as a mix of truth and lies, of bearing God's image but in a form badly banged up by our godding. So when God redeems people through Christ, the Holy Spirit gets to work on them, growing them into the affections and priorities that marked the life of the Savior, in whom God's image finds its "true" form, its perfect expression.

Supernaturally sown back into our souls are the roots that our godding has ripped out, stolen, from our essential humanity. A flower can live rootless, but not well, and not for long. The Holy Spirit takes people who humbly realize their rootlessness and grafts them back into their source of life. Taking into our souls God's breathed-out words, we grow full and fresh and tall, blooming like spring as we face the light of the world. In his truth, we become our true selves (Psalm 1).

So that we can bear the fruit God means us to in life, Jesus sets our sights upon his Kingly reign of the world. We learn to see his reign already at work in the world, especially in lives redeemed and evil opposed, and we make it the work of our lives to see God's kingdom come in full. Jesus promises to supply us with all that we need every day in that effort. "Seek first the kingdom of heaven and his righteousness, and all these things will be added to you" (Matthew 6:33).

The Psalms put our hearts in that kingdom-seeking posture; they call us and people of all nations to join together in praise of

God: "Clap your hands, all peoples! Shout to God with loud songs of joy!" (Psalm 47). The Psalms even call nature to get in on the act. "Let the sea roar and all that fills it....let the rivers clap their hands...before the Lord, for he comes to judge the earth. He will judge the world with righteousness" (Psalm 98:7–9).

The Psalms hail Christ for who he says he is, the one with all authority in heaven and on earth (Psalms 2, 24, 45, 110, 145; Matthew 28:18–20). The King's goal is global. He sends his church on a history- and civilization-spanning march for human wholeness and world peace, *shalom* that embraces the planet itself. And he's given us songs big enough to fit, and powerful enough to help bring forth, his good plans for his world.

Real, true peace means a diversified oneness, a loving Withness shared by all of created reality. The Psalms cry out prophetically for this *shalom*, in visceral praise of the one who'll bring it and in imprecatory defiance of those who oppose it. Taken all together, the Psalms are the truest and boldest peace and protest anthems ever written.

Going Green (with Envy)

Total loving Withness is the picture painted by God's moral law, the Ten Commandments, which the Psalms celebrate. As we've done throughout the book, let's call the mocking bluff of those who view God's law as repressive and invasive or so ridiculous it's laughable. The truth at the heart of these awkward antiquities leads to the love and peace we all claim to want so desperately in our day.

To get the full effect of how tyrannical and/or silly God's word can sound to enlightened ears, let's go old-school and look at two of the Ten Commandments in the Elizabethan English of the King James Version: commandments 10—thought policing!—and 4—no fun allowed on church day!

Exodus 20.17 readeth: "Thou shalt not covet thy neighbour's house; thou shalt not covet thy neighbour's wife, nor his manservant, nor his maidservant, nor his ox, nor his ass, nor any thing that is thy neighbour's."[67]

This is God's word? "Don't be jealous that your neighbor's got a better ass?!" That might apply on many levels, but the bottom line is: Don't be greedy about what belongs to someone else. To do so is unloving, self-serving, and it's the reason why the world is always at war.

James writes, "What causes war among you?[68] Is it not this, that your passions are at war within you? You desire and do not have, so you murder. You covet and cannot obtain, so you fight" (4:1 and following). Take any war in history, and doesn't it come down to this? Even war waged for right reasons presupposes that the enemies have done something selfish, something terribly and murderously wrong. So doesn't true and full world peace demand the complete renovation of the human heart down to this level?

The fourth commandment is a good crossover command between the two divisions of the ten, commands 1–4 focusing on our love for God and 6–10 on love for our neighbor. Command 4 shows us how honoring God is good for other people and all creation.

Exodus 20:8–11: "Remember the sabbath day, to keep it holy. Six days shalt thou labour, and do all thy work: But the seventh day is the sabbath of the Lord thy God: in it thou shalt not do any work, thou, nor thy son, nor thy daughter, thy manservant, nor thy maidservant, nor thy cattle [livestock in general] nor thy stranger that is within thy gates: For in six days the Lord made heaven and earth, the sea, and all that in them is, and rested the seventh day: wherefore the Lord blessed the sabbath day, and hallowed it."

How much better could we function in life if we were routinely well-rested? God says that on the Sabbath, which means cessation, rest is mandatory. Notice that God's love here extends through his people to the stranger who is among them. The stranger gets to enjoy the spiritual and physical rest God mandates for his people. And so do the animals! In every sense, we get to rest our asses.

In a sarcastic light, we might view these and all of God's detailed commands as the backward thoughts of ancient bumpkins.[69] But read rightly, they beautifully demonstrate God's concern expressed throughout Scripture that humans honor one another from their hearts and that they relate, in a position of primacy but not tyranny, to the natural world they inhabit.

People passionate about protecting and preserving the environment will find Scripture to be a friend. Psalms 8 and 104, among so many others, stand out in their celebration of the natural world. God's interrogation of Job in chapter 38 and following is a rhetorical tour of nature, from the animal kingdom to the constellations named after some of those fantastic beasts.[70] God asks Job, "Where were you when I laid the foundation of the earth?… Have you commanded the morning since your days began?…Can you…loose the cords of Orion?…Can you guide the Bear with its children?" There's even language that almost conjures the image of "mother nature." "From whose womb did the ice come forth…?" In Scripture, God presents himself as the master, parent, and caretaker of the natural world, the world he loves, delighted to make, and sent his son to save.

C. S. Lewis writes that true lovers of nature "want to receive as fully as possible whatever nature…is saying."[71] Scripture tells us that nature speaks as a beautiful world in pain. "The heavens declare the glory of God" (Psalm 19).[72] God's is the name that nature whispers and shouts; his is the power behind nature's sights and sounds, its stillness and its storms. Creation aches to be free from the bondage inflicted upon it due to human godding (Romans 8). Though creation's lapsed caretakers crucified Christ, nature seemed to recognize and welcome its Creator; even the un-living stones nearly came alive when God came near. Jesus once said to people who were irritated by the loud praise the crowds were giving him, "If these were silent, the very stones would cry out" (Luke 19:39–40).[73]

The Spirit of God walks with the image-bearer who loves the planet this way, all the way until the conservation champion might make the environment the focal point of her worship, or treat the land, the beasts, the creeping things and the birds as inherently equal to or even superior to God's image-bearers.[74] At that point, in a terrible irony, the environmentalist rejects the true nature of the world she loves and participates in the godding that wrought its terrors and miseries (Romans 1:22–23).[75]

The Bible points us to a better way: human cultivation and conservation of the earth in anticipation of God's kingdom come in full, which Scripture describes as the new heavens and the new earth, creation and humanity free from the godding that put the planet in such pain to begin with.

There's always been a symbiotic relationship between the condition of our personhood, body and soul, and the condition of the world. When Adam and Eve sinned, the earth brought forth hurtful thorns. Nature felt the new need to defend itself. Hosea, who understood the pain of betrayal, writes, "The Lord has a charge to bring against you who live in the land. There is no faithfulness or steadfast love, and no knowledge of God in the land. There is only cursing, lying and murder, stealing and adultery; they break all bounds....Therefore the land mourns...and all who live in it waste away; the beasts of the field and the birds of the air and the fish of the sea are dying" (Hosea 4:1 and following).

As the perfect bearer of God's image, Jesus is the perfect care-taker of creation. He reminds us of his Father's care for the sparrow in the wilderness, and at his word the storms fall silent. Creation aches for the day of Christ's return, when its redeemed caretakers feel the fullness of the freedom for which Christ has redeemed them (Romans 8:19 and following). "Then shall all the trees of the forest sing for joy" (Psalm 96:12). In the meantime, it's the Holy Spirit's joy to grow us in the grace that makes creation sing.

What a Wonderful World

Because we broke the world, Jesus begins to make it new by making us new. Paul says that anyone who is in Christ is a "new" creation. This newness is not the abolishment of the old, but its fulfillment, renewal, and reinvigoration. Jesus aligns our affections down the line of his law and blesses them with boundless capacity for expansion—no ceiling! Loving Withness among the world's caretakers blesses the world itself.

Paul's understanding of "new" matches John's understanding of "true." They both knew their Old Testaments! Newness is a consistent refrain in Isaiah. His prophecy reads like a symphony, with twists and turns, light and dark, screams and solace, planetary and personal unease joined together and yielding after agony to a peace large enough to envelop the world and all who dwell within it, the peace that can only come when the Maker of all descends, as promised in his covenant, to dwell with his creation. Isaiah, espe-cially in the final chapters, takes us deep into the life, mission, and especially the pain of the Messiah, and he proclaims ahead of time the glories to come when the suffering servant succeeds in his work, when the whole world feels the fullness of his victory.

Isaiah 65:17: "For behold, I create new heavens and a new earth, and the former things shall not be remembered or come into mind."

Peter picks up on Isaiah's language and hails the coming of the new heavens and earth (2 Peter 3). God isn't going to delete the current edition;[76] he's going to perfect it, to bring it to its designated end, and then some! He tells us that the defining characteristic of the new heavens and earth is righteousness. Same goes, therefore, for the image-bearers who through Christ are new creations.

Jesus is not just righteous; he is the personification of righteousness. For Jesus's disciples, then, justice isn't just something we're to strive for; it's something we're meant to do and even to embody. The Bible never separates social justice from personal righteousness.

Do you want to *know* true justice, not just as something you desire to see in the world (at all levels of power and in the criminal justice system itself), but as that through which you see the world? Do you want justice to be something you feel in your bones and exude from your pores? Sounds weird, but it's something of what Paul means when he says that believers are the aroma of Christ (2 Corinthians 2:15).

Christians are meant to radiate righteousness—not self-important moral rectitude, but real, deep, true, Christ-centered justice. This justice speaks the truth in love and feels its strength in the care of widows and orphans.[77] The Old Testament prophet Micah says, "He has told you, O man, what is good; and what does the Lord require of you but to do justice, and to love kindness, and to walk humbly with your God?" (Micah 6:8).

These qualities are what most people say they want to be all about, but like the earthy, enchanting smell of percolating coffee as we step inside from a frozen winter's morning, the aroma leads us to a particular place. Some people love the smell of coffee, but hate the taste. Same with justice. We love it if we define the terms, but if it means worshiping Jesus, *bleck*!

But if you want this world to be truly just no matter what you have to give up to see it happen, if you want righteousness bad, you can sniff it out in God's law and find its truth, its reality, in the One who kept it fully and from his heart.

This righteousness, God's righteousness, is something that hearts made "true and new" in Christ crave from the core of their being. Jesus says, "Blessed are those who hunger and thirst after righteousness" (Matthew 5:1–12). When his disciples return with food after his conversation with the Samaritan woman, Jesus says to them, "My food is to do the will of him who sent me" (John 4:34). In Psalm 42, the psalmist thirsts for God like a deer pants for water, and in Psalm 119, David writes, "I open my mouth and pant, because I long for your commandments." All-pervasive righteousness is the answer to the prayer Jesus teaches us: "Your kingdom come; your will be done on earth as it is in heaven."

You New and True, and the Whole World, Too!

The Psalms sing out ahead of time this full, holistic, and holy planetary state of being. They celebrate world peace like it's already here. That's faith.

Faith dips its brush in the colors of what will be and paints the present world accordingly. This is why some psalms hail the world with reckless glee as a place of bounty, joy, and placidity; it's enough to make Pollyanna tell David to calm down and get real.

In Psalm 37:25, David seems to have forsaken sanity—again. "I have not seen the righteous forsaken or his children begging for bread." What?! Either David is blind or he thinks only the wealthy and well-fed are righteous in God's sight. You can feel James getting quick to anger at the thought. David surely took care of the poor in his kingdom, but just as surely could not provide for every single true worshiper in desperate straits. So why does he say such things?

Such tracks are part of an album that most often grounds us and sometimes buries us in the grit and grime of everyday life. Even within Psalm 37, David lets us know his words are forward thinking (verse 27 and following). No single psalm, much less a single verse within it, is a standalone in God's songbook. Like all of God's written words, they inform and interpret one another. The better-than-real-life Psalms point us ahead of time to the "new" heavens and the "new" earth. And some of them even have a label to match—they're called "new" songs.

These songs, and those that make similar statements, are songs of salvation, the holistic salvation the Scriptures speak of from Genesis to Revelation, accomplished by Jesus and applied progressively to the world until its full application at his return. So Psalm 96, "Sing to the Lord a new song; sing to the Lord, all the earth!"

Isaiah calls for the "new song" as he contrasts past and present injustices with the future currently forming in his day, the coming age then underway but inaugurated with Messiah's arrival and completed upon his return. "Behold, the former things have come to pass, and new things I now declare, before they spring forth I tell you of them. Sing to the Lord a new song, his praise from the end of the earth" (Isaiah 42:9 and following).[78]

John writes of the "new" as well. In Revelation, the full number of God's family sing a "new song" in praise of the risen Christ and the redeeming, world-saving work he's done (Revelation 5). And John brings "new" and "true" together in his first New Testament letter, calling "true" worshipers to live out, along the lines of God's law, the newness they have in the Lord and in which they'll be fully formed when he returns.

First John 2:7–8: "Beloved, I am writing you no new commandment, but an old commandment that you had from the beginning. The old commandment is the word that you have heard. At the same time, it is a new commandment that I am writing to you, which is true in him and in you, because the darkness is passing away and the true light is already shining."

Typical of John and his nuancey use of language, he uses "new" in the way we typically think of it: the opposite of old, that which hasn't been before. But then he infuses "new" with the sense of "true" we see in his gospel. In teaching believers how to distinguish real believers from fake ones—true from false—John affirms that the commandment he's giving to believers has been there all along in God's word. But that commandment is new in that it finds its fulfillment, its lived-out reality, its truth in Jesus and in the people Jesus has redeemed. It's happening as the darkness is passing away (1 John 2:8), yielding against its will to the "true," invincible light (John 1:5, 9). God's word is truth—and the Bible is a true literary work of art!

The Psalms are the pitch-perfect songs for the era in which we live, between the advent and the return of Jesus, the time that "is and is coming" as Jesus described it in his history-making, history-defining conversation with the woman at the well. Jesus is the hinge upon which the times turn; the Word is the one in whom time and eternity touch.

Christ's finished work renders the future as certain and fixed as the past.[79] This gives us hope for the present, as we live in the agony of estrangement, journeying through the valley of tears in the shadow of death (Psalms 84, 23), on our way to the new heavens and the new earth (Psalm 98), which teem with love and peace, God's word ruling all around us and within us, like the air we breathe.

The Psalms are all about integration, wholeness, *shalom*: eternity and time, body and soul, heaven and earth, and every kind of image-bearer—united in loving Withness, together forever in God's all-encompassing presence, blessed perpetually with God's all-pervasive peace (Psalm 133). By coming to Christ and trusting his word, we start that walk toward perfection, toward a totality of *shalom*, now.

Peace in Our Time

The Psalms condition us for this walk toward perfection, steadying our steps as we travel the path the Savior trod before us. This path, as it did for Christ, leads to and through our death. But we need not ultimately fear any evil, not even the Evil One. Satan reminds us that death awaits—do all your godding now!!—and tries to convince us that everlasting life is a fanatic's fiction that prevents us from living life now as the gods we are. But his is a losing argument, especially in the days since Jesus proved it false.

For those trusting Christ, Jesus's atoning death and his resurrected life mean "the death of death."[80] Paul tells us that death, while still active in a fallen world, is on its way out of creation. "The last enemy to be destroyed is death." Death's shadow remains, but its sting is gone (1 Corinthians 15:55).

Unless the Lord returns in our respective lifetimes, you and I will one day die. "It is appointed unto man once to die, and after that, the judgment" (Hebrews 9:27). We know what will happen for all who are in Christ because of what happened to Christ himself. Paul calls the resurrected Christ the "firstfruits" of those who've died in him—the first and best of the crop that lets you know what the rest will be like when harvest time comes (1 Corinthians 15:20).

Jesus's resurrection means that the world itself will feel and come to fullness in his resurrected life. The seismic separations of the created order are stitched up in the scars of the Savior. Full healing will happen. The world will be free.

As Revelation closes, John sees the garden of Eden once again. But now, where access to the tree of life had been forbidden because of our first parents' sin, the way to life is once again wide open. People from all nations and tribes are coming and going freely. They're together, in perfect, loving Withness. And the serpent is nowhere to be found. Until then, while we sing of that freedom, we're still at war, and we still hurt, so we still need the psalms of imprecation and lament. But we won't need them forever.[81]

John tells us in Revelation 21 that God will wipe every tear from our eyes. No more unrighteous anger and sadness, and, apparently, no more righteous anger and sadness, either. We might be tempted to miss them, but there's nothing to mourn here!

As well as these dark emotions serve us now when given and guided by God's word, being upset that we'll eventually have to lay them aside is like being upset that we have to leave our winter clothes in the closet as we pack for the beach. That gear was good to wear for a time, to keep us from the world's cold, but now it's time to bask in the sun.

Or for those in the ancient Near East, it was blazing, dehydrating desert blight that symbolized death and pain. In Psalm 121, "the sun will not strike you by day, nor the moon by night," and in Revelation 7, "never again shall they hunger; never again will they thirst. Neither shall the sun beat down on them, nor any scorching heat." You might prefer Aspen to Maui as a picture of heaven.[82] Either way, no worries. The new heavens and the new earth will suit you well. And treat you well.

At peace with God, you'll be at peace with creation. Body and soul, you'll personify in your unique way the righteousness that pervades the whole world. You'll experience a oneness with God's creation not felt since the garden of Eden, and one that's even fuller. Childlike, you'll look under the rocks and stare unblinded into the bright and open sky. You can ask why all you want, hearing answers from the Lord himself, answers as big, if not bigger, than your questions. Hearing the Word of God speak to you, firsthand and face to face, you'll never stop saying, "Wow."

The eternal day when all of this begins is on its way. "At present we are on the outside of the world, the wrong side of the door. We discern the freshness and purity of morning, but they do not make us fresh and pure. We cannot mingle with the splendours we see. But all the leaves of the New Testament are rustling with the rumour that it will not always be so. Some day, God willing, we shall get in."[83]

The Bible tells us that God is more than willing. And Jesus Christ is the way.

The Lord of the Dance

"The one god that Nietzsche could tolerate was one that laughed and danced."[84] Brilliant as he was, Nietzsche missed so much about the Messiah in his raging invectives against the faith.

Jesus, the man of sorrows, endured what he did in this world for the joy that was set before him (Hebrews 12:2). His work was to gather into his trinitarian family "true," Spirit-filled worshipers, who would be God's people, his temple, who would find in him their eternal home. That work continues and grows stronger in the world, and there's no human being happier about it than the Lord Jesus himself. If you are not part of this family, the children of God around the world and the angels in heaven would rejoice in your homecoming. And your Savior would even sing about it.

> The Lord your God is in your midst,
> a mighty one who will save;
> he will rejoice over you with gladness;
> he will quiet you by his love;
> he will exult over you with loud singing.
> (Zephaniah 3:17)

Part of why God became human is so he could sing with a human voice, with us, as one of us. He took up God's breathed-out songs and lifted them in praise to his heavenly Father, singing and fulfilling every syllable—the ecstatic rejoicing, the deep-souled anger and mourning—leading us, the true us, the new us, in love and joy to live together in a world of endless *shalom*. There and then, we will forsake all that God's law forbids, and all that God's law requires is all that we will ever want, and all that we will ever do.

Because the new heavens and earth are defined by the righteousness that dwells there, and because God's moral law is the standard for righteousness, there's a sense in which we can read the Ten Commandments not only as precepts, but as promises—promises made to God's new creations, to you if you know or come to know the one who fulfills all of God's word.

You will have no other gods before the true and living God—finally free from our godding! You will not fashion God according to your image—you'll see the God-man face to face! You will not take God's name in vain—you'll speak of God, and to God, as he truly is. You'll keep the Sabbath—for all eternity, your body and soul will be at peace. You'll honor all those in authority—you'll meet, respect, and be respected by royal figures like King David and Queen Esther, as well as your Father Abraham and Mary, the Mother of God. You will not be unjustly angry, nor will there be any need for righteous indignation. You will not commit adultery, and not just because there's no more marriage. Your faithfulness to others, and others' to you, will define all your relationships. You will not steal—in God's presence, there's no begrudging others their blessings. You will not lie to or about others—you'll speak nothing but the truth and that in love. You'll not covet—in the presence of Christ, you'll have all you could ever want (Psalm 23:1).

Humanity is a song best sung by the original artist. In our godding, and especially beneath the ceiling of self, that song has been stolen from us. *We* have been stolen from us. We've been robbed. We are both victim and culprit as we try to reinterpret, if not rewrite, God's song. But our covers serve only to cover up the glory with which God intended his favorite creations to shine, the glory that shines in brilliant perfection in Jesus the Christ. The Lord Jesus is God and man; Son of God and Son of Man; the eternal Word, in whom all things cohere and have their meaning, made flesh; God forever blessed and the most blessed human being to ever live. And he lives forever!

In love, God spoke, God breathed, to tell us all of this. God gave us his written word to tell us of the Word incarnate, in whom you and I can be true and new, whole and free, forever. Jesus told us that all of this is true, and he gave his life and rose again to make it reality.

Jesus is no liar, and he is no thief. He came so that we can live, and live abundantly. He offers you that life, his life, your life. He offers you to you, recovered, redeemed, renewed—a living picture of what's to come for all creation.

The last line of the little Bible, God's breathed-out songbook, is the cry of the entire creation seeking and feeling its wholeness in the word. May it be our heart's cry, together, forever:

"Let everything that has breath praise the Lord. Praise the Lord!"

Digging Deeper, Ascribing Credit, and Some Fun along the Way

Chapter 1

1   Bob Dylan, "Not Dark Yet," *Time Out of Mind* (Columbia Records), 1997.

2   Twenty One Pilots, "Hometown," Blurryface (Fueled by Ramen), 2015.

3   It's a really bad statement that loses an idea's meaning entirely. But it's a really bad idea whose statement can't help but express the exact opposite of the idea's intent. Some understandings of truth would blame this problem of internal incoherence on the limits of language. It's common in "postmodern" times to assert that words cannot convey truth and that they have no knowable meaning except what the reader/hearer ascribes to them. Thus, no real communication is possible. But these views fall prey to the same suicidal inconsistencies of the incoherent ideas they're seeking to exonerate. Notice, it takes words to express the idea that words can't communicate, and it's easy to understand what's meant by those words. For example, "It's impossible for you to understand this sentence." You understood it, didn't you? Words convey meaning, and meaning can be known. More fun like this in chapter 5!

4   See especially the work of D. A. Carson, *The Gagging of God: Christianity Confronts Pluralism* (Grand Rapids: Zondervan, 1996) and *The Intolerance of Tolerance* (Grand Rapids: Eerdmans, 2012).

5   Possibly taking a second place finish to the church's condemning Galileo in relation to his teaching that the earth is not the center of the cosmos. This condemnation is considered exhibit A of Christianity's refusal to accept truth if it contradicts church dogma and therefore a blunder of cosmic proportions in the historical case for the intellectual credibility of the faith. See Owen Barfield, *Saving the Appearances: A Study in Idolatry* (Hanover: University Press of New England, 1988), especially chapter 7, p. 50 and following for the contention that the Galileo saga was really more about epistemology than astronomy, that the church's concern was not so much a heliocentric view of the cosmos as the danger of elevating scientific hypotheses from providers of analysis and explanation of empirical reality to arbiters of truth, even, potentially, moral truth. Even if current scientific theory explains physical phenomena satisfactorily (for now) should we really call it "truth"? And that raises the further, and deeper question: could popular scientific reasoning really provide humankind with everything in life worth knowing? Rationalism answered yes and has taken Western history and humanity to many unfortunate, dehumanizing places as a result. See chapters 3 and 4 of this book.

6   Referencing Romans chapter 1, Descartes writes: "…we seem to be told that everything that may be known of God can be demonstrated by reasoning which has no other source than our mind." From his *"Meditations on the First Philosophy—Dedicatory letter to the Sorbonne"* in Forest E. Baird, Walter Kaufmann, *Philosophical Classics: Volume III, Modern Philosophy, Second Edition* (Upper Saddle River: Prentice Hall, Simon & Schuster, 1997), p. 21.

7   Ibid., p. 19.

8   Kant never wanted it to go this far. He thought that every person could know, by the right use of reason, what is good and right behavior and that each person was compelled within his very being to follow this moral law. See chapter 3 for a bit more on what he called the "categorical imperative." See chapter 4 on whether reason by itself requires and can foster morality.

9   There is more to this one, as we'll see in chapters 3 and 5 especially. "Perception is reality" can mean that reality is composed of perception. For a fascinating article on this, see the April 25, 2016, piece by Amanda Gefter and Quanta, "The Case against Reality," https://www.theatlantic.com/science/archive/2016/04/the-illusion-of-reality/479559/. If we assume that this is true, though, it still raises questions about whose perception is ultimately most constitutive of reality. And as we'll focus upon in chapter 4, this understanding of reality cannot possibly lead to good ethics. It would seem to trend the other way. There's quite enough devaluing of one another's lives as it is—how much worse would it get were we to believe, to "know," that other lives and even our own lives are not actually real, but only (someone's) perception?

10   For a thought-provoking message on this topic and its connection to the central message of Christianity, have a listen to Dr. Carl Trueman's "The Foolishness of God" at http://www.geneva.edu/chapel/17-18-chapel-messages.

11   Even if we appreciate Jesus, beneath the ceiling of self we can never say that he is any greater than our opinion of him. So it's common in our culture to hear something like, "Oh, it's really nice that you believe in Jesus, but that's

just your opinion, after all. It's got nothing to do with me." Well, of course, when we express our personal faith it's an expression of our personal opinion, but only beneath the ceiling of self does it follow that opinions can never express truth.

12 The philosophical principle of the ceiling of self is nothing new. The biblical book of Judges repeatedly summarizes the way of life that the ceiling protects: "Everyone did what was right in his own eyes." And it shows us the consequences of that life. If you can make it through Judges without wanting to cry or vomit, you haven't read it right.

13 See C. S. Lewis, *The Abolition of Man* (New York: Simon and Schuster, Touchstone, 1996)—an absolute must-read if you are or are studying to be a teacher, or are just interested in philosophy of education, methodology and pedagogy in general. Lewis demonstrates with what now seems to be prophetic vision that the principles taught to elementary-aged school children in his native UK back in his day would be the undoing of Western society, because these principles attack and erode the essential constitutive principles of humanity. See chapters 5 and 6 of this book.

14 "This is why we can do a fine job curdling the imagination by stressing 'creativity,' for the creative child is encouraged to think of himself as a little god, with all his bright ideas coming from within. The older tradition has the poet as hearer before he is a crafter of verses. The Muse comes to him." Anthony Esolen, *Ten Ways to Destroy the Imagination of Your Child* (Wilmington: ISI Books, 2010), p. 200.

15 The new theme song to an old kids' cartoon called *Liberty's Kids* sums up this philosophy perfectly. Check out the lyrics to "Through My Own Eyes" by Kayla Hinkle and Aaron Carter.

16 For example, see the episode of *Sid the Science Kid* entitled "Sid's Holiday Adventure." For an intriguing view on holidays and their relationship to Christian worship (including the encouragement of Christians to celebrate Christmas as a secular holiday), see Dr. Michael LeFebvre's two-part blog, "Holidays and Holidays," at https://gentlereformation.com//2012/12/03/holidays-and-holy-days/ and https://gentlereformation.com//2017/11/30/holidays-and-holy-days-part-2/.

17 Lacey Sturm, *The Reason—How I Discovered a Life Worth Living—Revelations of a Rock Princess* (Grand Rapids: Baker, 2014), p. 84.

18 Sia, "Chandelier," *1,000 Forms of Fear* (EMI April Music Inc., Sony/ATV Music Publishing) 2014.

19 See Jean M. Twenge, *Generation Me: Why Today's Young Americans Are More Confident, Assertive, Entitled—and More Miserable Than Ever Before* (New York: Free Press, 2006), p. 107. Twenge's work helpfully chronicles and poignantly laments the deep struggles of today's youth (I cite her more recent work chapter 5). She places some, but not enough blame for it on parents and previous generations. How can young people be expected to get over themselves when they're taught so early in life that they can never reach beyond themselves? With all due respect to the author, though she shares some helpful hints at behavior modification, her solutions in many cases amount to rearranging the furniture in a burning room. She deals (effectively) in surface statistics and addresses some underlying causes, but never goes deeper. Nothing fundamental in the human condition is addressed, so no lasting help is discovered.

20 Fun. "We Are Young," *Some Nights* (WB Music Corp./Warner Chappel Music Inc.), 2012.

21 This line appears on a brilliant poster with "Meetings" instead of "Community" as the lead word. See Despair.com. I love this site and its products.

22 As Christian philosopher Francis Schaeffer put it so memorably: "If there is no absolute by which to judge society, society is absolute."

23 American College Health Association. American College Health Association–National College Health Assessment II: Reference Group Data Report Fall 2012. Baltimore: American College Health Association, 2013. Solman further notes, "In a sample of 14,000 students from universities and colleges in the U.S., Asian students were the least likely to receive counseling, take psychotropic medication or to seek support from family, friends or religious communities. Black students were the most likely to seek support from religious communities. Multiracial students were the most likely to participate in counseling and to seek support from friends and family members. White students were the most likely to seek medication for mental health concerns. About half the students who received help did so on their college campus." Amy Solman, LPC, CADC, MA, Mental Health First Aid for Higher Education. Chapters 2 and 3 provide a bit of backstory to the report's findings on patterns in the relationship between race and religion.

24 Twenge, p. 105.

25 It's common now to lament the decline of the Christian West, but what's often overlooked is that the rise of Christianity around the world is reflected in minority communities within the West, and more specifically the kind of robust, Bible-believing Christianity that European-based cultures have largely rejected. See Soong-Chan Rah, *The Next Evangelicalism: Freeing the Church from Western Cultural Captivity* (Downers Grove: IVP Books, 2009). His analysis is often angry and cathartic, but insightful and helpfully provocative nonetheless. I do wish he'd examined more fully the theological convictions at the core of the specific kind of Christianity that is on the rise among minorities in the wealthy West. As we'll think about in chapters 2 and 3, this ascending Christianity has everything to do with a high view of Scripture as truly and essentially the word of God.

Chapter 2

1 Lacey Sturm, "Heart Work," *Reflect Love Back Soundtrack Vol. 1* (RLB Records/FOLLOWSPOT Records), 2019.

2 One of many insults Christians have for one another. This one in its truest sense refers to the practice, condemned throughout Scripture, of requiring more or different than God does in obedience to his commands. It's saying "Thus says the Lord" when the Lord hasn't said so. Jesus often rebuked the teachers of his day for putting upon people burdens that God never had.

The term is often used today to criticize someone who is overly, and perhaps arrogantly, concerned with exacting, formalistic obedience to relatively unimportant rules.

3   See John 1:1–14, Isaiah 7 and Matthew 1, and 1 Corinthians 15 for key passages, respectively, on these biblical claims that are made and refined progressively throughout the Bible as Genesis moves toward Revelation. These beliefs at the core of historic Christianity are summed up in an ancient church creed called "The Apostle's Creed." We'll focus much in this book on Jesus's deity and his full-fledged humanity. For an emphasis on his being born of a virgin, please see J. Gresham Machen, *The Virgin Birth of Christ* (London: James Clarke and Company, 1958). See also Machen's *Christianity and Liberalism* (Grand Rapids: Wm. B. Eerdmans, 1923) for an examination of whether historic, biblically faithful, and historically honest Christianity is compatible with the denial of Scripture's emphasis on the supernatural, most notably Jesus's virgin birth and his bodily resurrection. Machen was a brilliant scholar, a believer in the historic Christian faith, and very well respected by scholarly atheists of his day.

4   See "A Gift of a Bible" on any number of easily accessible websites. Here's one: https://vimeo.com/10754567. This is quite a moving few minutes, as Jillette recounts what he considers to be "a very good man" who gave him a Bible and talked with him briefly after one of his shows.

5   The particular James who identifies himself here is James the brother of Jesus. This James became a leader in the early New Testament church. The New Testament book of Acts tells us about his leadership in general and his approach to God's word and Christian believers. That he was a well-respected leader in the church is clear in how Acts 15 highlights his role at the pivotal Jerusalem council, which dealt with how the law of Moses was to be understood and applied, particularly by the Gentile Christians flooding into the predominantly Hebrew Christian population of the early church.

6   The Bible has a built-in epistemology (understanding of knowledge). Epistemology deals with questions of how, why, and what we can know in life. For an introduction to the topic, see Esther Meek, *A Little Manual for Knowing* (Eugene: Wipf and Stock Publishers, 2014). Scripture's epistemology is Semitic, Hebrew. In the Hebrew mind-set, knowledge and reason are intimately connected to affection and emotion. We must not try to dice up the categories of our lives such that head and heart, belief and practice are separate from one another, let alone opposed to one another. See this chapter's section entitled "We Don't Need No Education." For you philosophy fans, see the three-volume set by Alvin Plantinga (*Warrant: The Current Debate, Warrant and Proper Function*, and *Warranted Christian Belief*), which focuses on the nature, causes, and categories of belief and religious belief in particular.

7   "Apostle" comes from a Greek word meaning "one who is sent." The twelve apostles were leaders of the highest authority in the early New Testament-era church. All of them knew Jesus personally and interacted with him following his resurrection. The apostle Paul's interaction with the resurrected Christ was a traumatic one, coming in the context of a violent,

confrontational, prophetic vision. See Acts 9. We'll engage Paul's teachings starting next chapter.

8   This title means "the second giving of the law." It chronicles the journey of the Israelites out of slavery in Egypt to the land God promised to provide them as their own. Because the all-talk faith that James decries was rampant among so many of them, this journey included forty years of a sort of pre-habitation exile from the Promised Land.

9   James would tell us to give the good seat that we secured to someone else, especially a socially marginalized person who may come to worship (see James 2). But we could still camp out for that purpose!

10   As we'll explore in chapter 5, the Bible teaches that humans share certain character qualities with God, which allow us to safely absorb some of that heat and to give it productive vent. But for reasons we'll get to in a bit, we try to harness that god-like fire as if we started it, as if it exists to serve us. Thus we set ourselves up for the flameouts we started to think about last chapter.

11   For a humorous example of this principle played out in a deadly serious situation, see the Old Testament book of Numbers, chapters 22 and 23. The saga detailed here is rich with irony and even includes good fodder for people particularly concerned about animal rights. See chapter 10 also on the latter. God loves all of creation, the "creatures" included (Psalms 104, 145, John 3:16, Romans 8).

12   Pastor and theologian John Murray puts it perfectly: "As will be our conception of Scripture, so will be our conception of the Christian faith." John Murray, *Collected Writings*, Volume 3 (Carlisle: Banner of Truth, 1982), p. 256.

13   Kevin Vanhoozer deals helpfully with the issue of theological prioritization in *First Theology: God, Scripture and Hermeneutics* (Downers Grove: InterVarsity, 2002).

14   See Jonathan P. Hill, *Emerging Adulthood and Faith* (Grand Rapids: The Calvin College Press, 2015).

15   We'll explore these commands as we go, but for a quick survey, see the New Testament book of Galatians, chapter 5, and then read Jesus's handling of such commands in Matthew, chapters 5–7, an address commonly called "The Sermon on the Mount."

16   Pharrell Williams, "Happy," *Girl* (Back Lot Music; i Am Other; Columbia), 2013.

17   Everclear, "Wonderful," *Songs from an American Movie Volume One: Learning How to Smile* (Capitol; EMI), 2000. Listen also to the band's "Father of Mine" for the same pained theme.

18   Title to a song by Depeche Mode.

19   For a thought-provoking rethinking of the commonplace practice among Christians of having and making pictures of Jesus, see any edition of theologian J. I. Packer's contemporary classic, *Knowing God*, chapter 4.

20   In chapter 10, we'll focus a lot on Jesus's conversation with a Samaritan woman, who, despite never having met him, immediately recognized him as a Hebrew man (John 4). To be the Savior of the world, Jesus needed to be a

Hebrew man. For particularly helpful passages on this point, see Isaiah 49:5–6 and John 8:12; Romans 1:16–17; and Matthew 1 and 5:17–18.

21 It's easy in the wealthy West to live out the faith as if it's a Western, white phenomenon and to do missionary work as such, taking in the name of Jesus the material styles and comforts of the North American suburbs to the far reaches of the world (and then taking it all back when we leave). How often do we come home from those trips envying the deep and vital faith of those to whom we came to minister? Rather than bringing to them a heavily Westernized faith (a quiet, colonialistic micro-agression?), what if we sought to find common ground with them, and to learn from them, by focusing—in our preaching, teaching, prayers, and songs upon the Bible—the very non-Western words that unite us? More to say about the uniting power of Scripture, and God's songs within it, in chapter 10.

22 This idea deserves exploration. Studies that document the exodus from established churches focus, understandably and necessarily, on polling data and survey questions about people's surface-level perceptions of church life. It's hard to quantify the tectonic theological shifts taking place in church and popular culture, especially given fluctuation and equivocation of basic terms such as God, Jesus, and faith. Unexamined or unannounced equivocation of terms inevitably skews statistics, but we may never know how they've done so in the reports we read. Given our day's pathological biblical illiteracy, depending on how one defines "God," a self-identified Bible-believing Christian who isn't actually familiar with Scripture may answer survey questions very similarly to a self-identified atheist who isn't familiar with the Bible. Some people reared in the multifaceted religious and political insanity of our popular culture would be shocked to learn that Jesus is not an American patriot, much less a liberal Democrat or a conservative Republican. He's not even a libertarian!

23 See also the Old Testament's concluding book, Malachi. As the last word from God for nearly four centuries, a prolonged, painful silence broken by the arrival of Jesus, Malachi serves as a summarizing indictment of a long history of beliefs and behaviors that God detests, and that Jesus would address in his saving work. See Malachi chapters 3 and 4 especially.

24 See the New Testament letter of Ephesians, especially chapter 2, which is the practical application of the truths its author writes in chapter 1.

25 See Ephesians 6. I owe the observation about children to commentator William Hendriksen. See the New Testament commentary series bearing his name (but contributed to by other scholars), specifically *New Testament Commentary: Exposition of Galatians, Ephesians, Philippians, Colossians and Philemon* (Grand Rapids: Baker, 2002).

26 See the introduction to Peter T. O'Brien, *The Letter to the Ephesians* (The Pillar New Testament Commentary) (Grand Rapids: Eerdmans, 1999).

27 See Ephesians 4.

28 See my blog post, "Paul's Agony," at https://gentlereformation. com//2013/05/17/pauls-agony/.

29 Theologian Gordon Fee.

30 The theology of tens of thousands of professing believers who attend football stadium–packing churches refuses to acknowledge life's shadows. Life's dark times and emotions, and in some cases any negativities whatsoever, are considered unrealities that we must banish by the blazing, positive, holy force of our faith. A simple study of Jesus's life, the "man of sorrows," refutes this false, trauma-inflicting understanding and expression of Christian faith. See Psalm 22, Isaiah 53, and the New Testament's four gospels. Unhealed diseases and difficulties in life in general, these people tell us, come to us, or won't leave us, due to our lack of faith. Such faith is fine for those doing materially well enough in life, especially the "pastors" who benefit from the tithes and offerings of their mega congregations, but is devastating to souls in life's dire straits and feeling doubly desperate as they're told they must generate (or pay for) a personal faith strong enough to banish all their problems. See chapters 4, 5, and 10 for an exploration of Scripture's teaching regarding life's maladies and when, how, and why they'll resolve.

31 Carl Trueman, "What Can Miserable Christians Sing?" in *The Wages of Spin: Critical Writings on Historical and Contemporary Evangelicalism* (Fearn, UK: Christian Focus, 2005), pp. 157-63.

32 See Bono and Eugene Petersen on the Psalms, https://www.youtube.com/watch?v=-l40S5e90KY.

33 I attended a pastors' conference during which the preacher lamented the accusation of inaccessibility often levied against ministers in his theological circles. Paraphrasing him, "You can tell them, yes, my sermons are inaccessible, but Jesus isn't." But Jesus has chosen the preaching of his word as a vital means by which he comes close to people! "Faith comes through hearing, and hearing through the word of Christ" (Romans 10:17). Even if all the hearers are academicians, and a highly technical sermon could truly stir all souls present, without an appeal toward the tangible transformation of the hearers' wills and an encouragement toward the tangible actions apart from which James says faith is not only fake, but dead (James 2), these messages do little if anything to bring God near. Under the guise of stimulating the mind, these sermons numb the soul and leave an autonomous will pleasantly unbothered, and perhaps even flattered for having followed the pastor so ably on his journey into theological obscurity.

34 Attendance numbers do not necessarily indicate that a church is faithfully doing the work that God calls her to do. We can read the numbers in lots of illegitimate ways. Church leaders who pride themselves on cultural relevance might think, "We must be doing something right. Look at how many people pack this place every week!" while church leaders who pride themselves on cultural irrelevance might think, "We must be doing something right. No one wants to worship here!" We must be careful that mere attendance data inspire neither false confidence nor unnecessary discouragement. For a wonderful study of what, according to Scripture, marks a true and faithful church, see Pastor Barry York's *Hitting the Marks: Restoring the Essential Identity of the Church* (Pittsburgh: Crown & Covenant Publications, 2018).

35 Such a term actually exists: supralapsarianism. Some of these words represent profound topics of vital practical import. Others represent an ultimately unholy trespassing into truth comprehensible only to God. Such trespassing ends up trampling the hearts of God's people. Theologians and pastors who think they can handle the heavy stuff are inflated with pride, and in the hearts of the people who suffer under their preaching, Scripture's portrayal of God is twisted into an abstract, distant terror. The challenge in theological exploration is for us to remain at all points humble, to take the walk into deeper truth only so far as Scripture will take us and not one step further, and to seek in every truth explored the practical and personal application to our lives, toward the goal of loving God, people, and the world with all that we are. See 1 Timothy 1:5 and the development of this theme in chapter 9 of this book.

36 I owe this phrase to a good friend, Shane Anderson.

37 Jesus experienced this in his preaching ministry. There were times where huge crowds were desperate to be around him, hanging on every word he said, especially if he was healing the ill and miraculously feeding the hungry. These were good and beautiful blessings straight from the Savior's heart. But when he called people to love the giver first and the gifts second, when he pressed upon them in his preaching what it meant to be his disciples, the crowds would often walk away, disappointed and disillusioned. See John 6.

38 A socially conscious Christianity that helpfully points out and decries the "colonializing" influence of American business and politics around the world should also be aware of the way our missionary efforts can do the same thing theologically among those who call for our help. See *World* magazine, April 14, 2018—"Mary Li Ma, Great Awakenings: Understanding Christianity's Appeal to Chinese Hearts" by Angela Lu Fulton.

39 For a sobering, and saddening, look at particular instances of Christian worship from the perspective of those who do not worship Jesus—and are sometimes hired to play in the praise band!—see "Some DFW Musicians Spend Their Sunday Mornings at Church—Hung Over From Secular Gigs" by Taylor Frantum, Alaena Hostetter, Jacob Vaughn, March 20, 2018 at http://www.dallasobserver.com/music/6-dfw-musicians-tell-us-whats-it-like-to-gig-at-church-10477625. It would be hard to believe that these are isolated incidents in just one part of the country. For a more expansive and perhaps more heartbreaking analysis of popular Christianity in the midst of and as co-opted by popular politics, see David French, "The True Sin of American Evangelicals in the Age of Trump," from *National Review* at htpps://www.nationalreview.com/2018/03/evangelicals-support-donald-trump political-realities-2016-election/.

40 And so small group Bible studies are often spent exploring first, and perhaps exclusively, what a particular passage of Scripture means to *us*, rather than seeking what God's always said through it, and then seeing how that truth applies to each of us personally. This approach basically puts us in control of what a Bible passage means, which means we can live it out however we like and claim God's approval for doing so.

41 On the high school level and below, Bible class in Christian schools is sometimes given to whatever Christian faculty members have the extra time to teach it, regardless of their academic background in the subject. Would we treat any other school subject this way? We've so imbibed the idea that detailed truth about God exists in the realm of the unknowable (unlike the facts and principles of science, history, and literary studies) that we consider any Christian with a kind heart and a willingness to teach sufficiently prepared to do so. Having standards this loose in the chemistry lab could have explosive results, literally! We affirm that "all truth is God's truth" but we consider God's word the truth that requires the least preparation to teach. The Bible is arguably the most influential book ever written. It is theology, philosophy, history, and ethics. Within its pages we find poetry, prophecy, and some of the most profound and penetrating analyses and critiques of humanity and particular civilizations ever penned. This world of a book touches with unparalleled profundity every aspect of life, and its teachings have deep, definitional implications for every academic discipline and societal vocation. And it is especially the children and young adults among us who, at their vital stages of life development, ought to benefit from the personally devoted and deeply studied preparedness of their Bible teachers.

42 "In brief: the connection between humility, conviction and rationality is to be found in the critical test of endurance." Kevin J. Vanhoozer, *First Theology: God, Scripture and Hermeneutics* (Downers Grove: InterVarsity, 2002), p. 367.

43 For a sobering, instructive study of the fading interest in social justice causes among those who once championed them as young adults, see Steve L. Porter, Felicia Heykoop, Barbara Miller, and Todd Pickett, "Spiritual Formation and the Social Justice Turn," *Christian Scholars Review*, Volume 44:3, Spring 2015.

44 See C. S. Lewis, *The Problem of Pain* (New York: The Macmillan Company), 1944.

45 E. J. Young, *An Introduction to the Old Testament* (Grand Rapids: Eerdmans, 1952), p. 10.

46 See Hebrews 11.

47 See James K. Hoffmeier, Dennis R. Magary, *Do Historical Matters Matter to Faith? A Critical Appraisal of Modern and Postmodern Approaches to Scripture* (Wheaton: Crossway, 2012), p. 134. Hoffmeier is quoting Philip Jenkins, *The Next Christendom: The Coming of Global Christianity* (New York: Oxford University Press, 2006) p. 14. By "liberal" Jenkins is referring to organized churches that, within their practical faith and life, deny the actual, physical resurrection of Jesus Christ. Not coincidentally, these churches are not comfortable with understanding Paul's description of Scripture as "inspired," i.e., God-breathed (2 Timothy 3:16) to mean that Scripture is truly, completely, and directly the actual word and words of God. For related discussion on the term "inerrancy"—that the biblical books are without error in their original manuscripts—see James R. A. Merrick, Stephen M. Garrett, R. Albert Mohler, Jr., Kevin J. Vanhoozer, Michael F. Bird, Peter E. Enns, and

John R. Franke, *Five Views on Biblical Inerrancy* (Grand Rapids: Zondervan, 2013).

Chapter 3

1　Friedrich Nietzsche, *The Gay Science*, trans. by Walter Kaufmann (New York: Random House, 1974), p. 181.

2　Lacey Sturm, "Life Screams," Lacey Sturm, "I'm Not Laughing," *Life Screams* (FOLLOWSPOT Records), 2016.

3　By 1648, Europe had spent three decades in the throes of a war largely driven by religion, politics, and a really nasty mix of the two. The war started in 1618 and was called—wait for it—"The Thirty Years War." The bland title illustrates well how drained of life people felt after long, dragged-out conflicts in which all sides claimed God and the Bible as the moral force behind their blood-spilling. See Justo Gonzalez, *The Story of Christianity, Volume 2: The Reformation to the Present Day* (San Francisco: Harper, 1985).

4　For a superb study on how the Bible was put together as the Bible, see the work of Michael J. Kruger, *The Question of Canon* (Downers Grove: IVP Academic, 2013) and also *Canon Revisited: Establishing the Origins and Authority of the New Testament Books* (Wheaton: Crossway, 2012).

5　"If religion was the principal villain of the Enlightenment, then science was its hero." Isaac Kramnick, ed. *The Portable Enlightenment Reader* (New York: Penguin, 1995), p. xii.

6　Kevin J. Vanhoozer, *First Theology: God, Scripture and Hermeneutics* (Downers Grove: InterVarsity, 2002), p. 237.

7　Kant "concluded that questions reaching beyond the bounds of possible experience are not only unanswerable, but unaskable, and thereby launched a radically empirical movement that has gathered strength to our own time."—Monroe Beardsley, *The European Philosophers from Descartes to Nietzsche: Modern Library Classics* (New York: Random House, 1960), p. 368.

8　In the name of reverent praise, such words enslave the object of faith and make him subject to the whims of the worshiper. When God is silent, politicians become divine, or at least the prophets (and benefactors) of whatever allegedly objective, transcendent repository of truth society currently worships. This is the essence of the thievery we thought about last chapter: belief in divine silence allows lesser voices to speak and rule with god-like authority.

9　See Michael Horton, *Beyond Culture Wars: Is America a Mission Field or a Battlefield?* (Chicago: Moody, 1994). Horton demonstrates that America's founding fathers were neither the secular humanists that politically correct revisionist historians wanted them to be nor the unified batch of Bible-believing Christians that some Christians wanted them to be. They represented various strains of theological thought and together comprised, as Horton argues, a mixed bag.

10　See Justo Gonzalez, *The Story of Christianity, Volume 2: The Reformation to the Present Day* (San Francisco: Harper, 1985), p. 194

11　"The principle is valid: 'It is not essential, and hence not necessary, for every one to know what God does or has done for his salvation;' but it is essential to know *what man himself must do* in order to become worthy of this assistance." Immanuel Kant, *Religion Within the Limits of Reason Alone*, Theodore M. Greene and Hoyt H. Hudson, trans. (New York: Harper & Row, 1960), p. 47.

12 Immanuel Kant, *Lectures on Philosophical Theology* (Ithaca: Cornell University Press, 1978), p. 160.

13 Ibid., pp. 165-6.

14 D. A. Carson, *The Gagging of God: Christianity Confronts Pluralism* (Grand Rapids: Zondervan, 1996), p. 68. One benefit of postmodernism is its rebuke of this blindspot in Enlightenment thought. Postmodernism issues the humbling reminder that none of us sees and understands life without built-in biases and sometimes unrecognized agendas. Not every bias is bad, but whether we busy ourselves with metaphysical questions for which we claim there are no knowable answers, or are practitioners in the "hard sciences," none of us, and therefore none of our work, is free from prejudice(s).

15 One of my favorite teachers used this term in a class on an unrelated topic. It's one of the many reasons he's one of my favorites. To protect the guilty, I'll not reveal his name.

16 Jefferson didn't mention the seventh commandment on his list of the commandments he found worthy of observing. This may well be because of his personal affinity for adultery. See Marvin Olasky, *The American Leadership Tradition: The Inevitable Impact of a Leader's Faith on a Nation's Destiny* (Wheaton: Crossway, 2000), p. 26. Jefferson "scorned any Scripture he could not control" (Olasky, p. 43).

17 "In denying the power of men to reject the law deliberately, Kant repeated the methodological mistake that Plato made when he denied that men can knowingly do evil. Kant...used his theory to dismiss the contravening evidence as illusory." John R. Silber, in Immanuel Kant, *Religion Within the Limits of Reason Alone*, Theodore M. Greene and Hoyt H. Hudson, trans. (New York: Harper & Row, 1960) p. cxxix.

18 Kant's lamenting of the capacity and actuality of human cruelty is impressive in its sincerity and circumspectness, yet his longing for a league of nations sheds light on the naïveté at the root of his otherwise relatively sober analysis of the human condition. He just can't bring himself to see how truly and radically corrupted humanity is, driven to evil right down to the first instances and motives of willing. Were Kant to admit this, he'd have to revise or abandon his cherished insistence on man's essential and necessary autonomy. But were he to step away from this philosophical fantasy and embrace a more reasonable, realistic view of humanity, he'd be in a position to understand the need for and to thank God for providing what the Bible proclaims in Jesus, the supernatural transformation of the corrupted human will by an unconditional saving grace. This grace replaces a pretended autonomy with true love and loyalty for God and people and the world itself. See chapters 8–10 of this book.

19 Theodore M. Greene comments on the humanitarian sentiments present in typical Enlightenment thinking: "This humanitarianism rested on the

newly acquired conviction of the essential goodness and infinite perfectibility of human nature. As God must have created man good, the vitiating causes which had perverted him must have been man-made, that is, contingent and removable." So it was reason that would undertake a "labor of purification." Greene, in Immanuel Kant, *Religion Within the Limits of Reason Alone*, Theodore M. Greene and Hoyt H. Hudson, trans. (New York: Harper & Row, 1960), p. x

20 Isaac Kramnick, ed. *The Portable Enlightenment Reader* (New York: Penguin, 1995), p. xiii.

21 A term meaning "before the flood." In the Bible's account of human life before the great flood described in Genesis 6, people lived for centuries.

22 Isaac Kramnick, ed. *The Portable Enlightenment Reader* (New York: Penguin, 1995), p. xiii.

23 Ibid., p. xxi. Kramnick is summarizing the view of J. L. Talmon, who believed that the Enlightenment's blind optimism about human potential set the stage for governments to declare godlike power over their citizens.

24 Ibid., p. xviii.

25 Major Enlightenment thinkers and artists were actually rather racist in their view of humanity. It's an embarrassment to people who are otherwise fans of the Enlightenment's worship of human reason. You can see why their thoughts segued so easily into Darwinism. Debates abound as to the science involved, but the ethical and racial implications of Darwinism are as uncomfortable as they are unavoidable: some kinds of people are just better, more evolved, than others. Only the strong survive! Might makes right, and in the Enlightenment, most of the might was white.

26 From a presentation by Calvin College sociologist Dr. Jonathan Hill, during the Eli Lilly Youth Theology Network Annual Consultation, held in Indianapolis, Indiana, on February 3–5, 2016.

27 Isaac Kramnick, ed. *The Portable Enlightenment Reader* (New York: Penguin, 1995), p. xx.

28 Ibid., p. xxii.

29 For a horrifying fictional accounting of cruel actions undeniably realistic and carried out by the allegedly civilized, see Fyodor Dostoyevsky's *The Brothers Karamazov*, the section entitled "Rebellion." We'll interact with this work next chapter.

30 See Chapter 8 on this.

31 Kant writes, "However the origin of moral evil in man is constituted, surely of all the explanations of the spread and propagation of this evil through all members and generations of our race, the most inept is that which describes it as descending to us as an *inheritance* from our first parents." Immanuel Kant, *Religion Within the Limits of Reason Alone*, Theodore M. Greene and Hoyt H. Hudson, trans. (New York: Harper & Row, 1960), p. 35. As we'll see in chapter 8 especially, Scripture teaches that our sinfulness was introduced to us, but that once our first parents willingly embraced it, sinfulness became the default mode of humanity. (Genesis 3, Psalm 14, Romans 3, Romans 5). Kant liked that Genesis recognized an outside contributor to our being corrupted,

but he despised the idea that corruption is also an inherited reality. Why, then, do humans have such a propensity toward and proficiency with evil? Kant said we can't know. "But the rational origin of this perversion of our will…that is, of the propensity to evil, remains inscrutable to us…There is then for us no conceivable ground from which the moral evil in us could originally have come…" *Religion*, pp. 38–9. The Bible gives us this "conceivable ground," but Kant rules its teaching out of bounds because, even if true, such truth lies beyond the reach of our reason. How convenient!

32 "Kierkegaard consolidated the opposition to Kant's moral optimism in asserting the power of men to fulfill their personalities in the despair of defiance. Nietzsche joined Kierkegaard in affirming that man's freedom can be diabolically, no less than heteronomously, expressed….No weak personality leads a civilized nation to moral disaster and a continent to ruin." John R. Silber, "The Ethical Significance of Kant's Religion," within Immanuel Kant, *Religion within the Limits of Reason Alone*, Theodore M. Greene and Hoyt H. Hudson, trans. (New York: Harper & Row, 1960), p. cxxix. We'll meet Kierkegaard in chapter 7 and Nietzsche in a few pages.

33 Joan Osborne, "One of Us," *Relish* (WB Music Corp; Warner Chappel Music Inc.), 1995.

34 See the work of philosopher Michael Polanyi on tacit knowledge. Dr. Esther Meek expounds and expands on his work in *Contact with Reality: Michael Polanyi's Realism and Why It Matters* (Eugene: Wipf and Stock Publishers, 2017).

35 I'm not trying to blame Kant for everything wrong in history. Just the history that's happened since he lived. Kidding. Kant is a convenient scapegoat because of the immensity of his influence and the multitudinous ways in which the ceiling has influenced our lives. He and Descartes, my other scapegoat, brought about monumental shifts in their time not only with regard to the content of popular thought, but down deep to the level of *how* people thought. But history subsequent to Kant, and obviously all that happened before him, has of course brought to us many more thinkers and philosophies that have shaped the lives we have and the people we are. For a more detailed study, see John Frame's *A History of Modern Philosophy and Theology*. Frame writes this about Kant in his relationship to prior thinkers heading in the direction he codified and advanced as definitively modern thinking: "Descartes, Locke, and their followers had tried to reason autonomously, without the constraints of divine revelation. But it was Kant who developed a comprehensive *rationale* for autonomous reasoning. It was Kant who argued that we must reason autonomously and *must* never reason in any other way. These arguments so persuaded mainstream philosophers and theologians as to transform those disciplines in radical ways. Those arguments are still with us; we deal with them all the time. And many philosophies and theologies after Kant mirror elements of his philosophical system." John M. Frame, *A History of Modern Philosophy and Theology* (Phillipsburg, NJ: P&R Publishing), pp. 251–2.

36 Yes, I'm thinking here of the Miley Cyrus song. It's epic.

37 This is a sincere compliment as well as a critique born of sad irony. Nietzsche wrote, "A very popular error: having the courage of one's convictions; rather it is a matter of having the courage for an attack on one's convictions." This courage is rare, indeed. Given the prevalence of Nietzsche's dogmatic, destructive invectives and the fact that it's always easier to destroy than to build something true and lasting, it seems debatable whether Nietzsche, despite his obvious and demonstrable brilliance, had the courage to be humbled and corrected by any views that stood contrary to his.

38 Friedrich Nietzsche, *Thus Spoke Zarathustra: A Book for None and All*, trans. Walter Kaufmann, (New York: Penguin, 1966), p. 3.

39 Nietzsche, *The Gay Science*, p. 181.

40 Nietzsche accused Christians of doing the same thing with their talk of heaven and earth. But the Bible's distinction has to do with the eternal vs. the temporal, not reality vs. perception, which is the stuff of Kant's ceiling, and which grants humans ultimate authority in practical life. The Bible is not okay with that; it presents Jesus as Lord of all of life, time, space, and eternity (Psalm 24, John 1, Colossians 1). See chapters 5 and 8 of this book.

41 Friedrich Nietzsche, *Twilight of the Idols*, trans. Duncan Large (New York: Oxford University Press, 1998), p. 45.

42 The following are notes from a fall of 1885 draft for Nietzsche's *The Will to Power*. "The Germans of today are no thinkers any longer: something else delights and impresses them....The will to power as a principle might be intelligible to them....But who knows? In two generations one will no longer require the sacrifice involved in any nationalistic squandering of power and in becoming stupid." —Friedrich Nietzsche, *The Will to Power*, trans. by Walter Kaufmann and R. J. Hollingdale, (New York: Random House, 1968), pp. xxii–xxiii. This volume by Nietzsche reflects in its heated and frenetic writing the ravages of his physical illness and decaying intellectual coherence. It's uncharitable to use it as fodder for criticism of his essential thoughts and contributions to philosophy, especially because of the just straight evil actions of his sister, a Nazi sympathizer, who arbitrarily composed the volume from his remaining writings so as to support the Nazi movement. Nietzsche's comments from his draft notes serve as an ironic rebuke of his sister's efforts and the weak-minded, despicable thinking— Nietzsche would call it "decadent"—that would in coming generations slanderously hail him as an inspiration. For a helpful read, see Sean Illing, "The alt-right is drunk on bad readings of Nietzsche. The Nazis were too." https://www.vox.com/2017/8/17/16110846/alt-right-nietzsche-richard-spencer-nazism. Illing writes, "Nietzsche was a lot of things...but he wasn't a racist or a fascist. That he's been hijacked by racists and fascists is partly his fault, though. His writings are riddled with contradictions and puzzles." As we're arguing in this chapter, Nietzsche is a great wrecking ball, but a terrible builder. Christian philosopher Merril Westphal recommends "Nietzsche for Lent."

43 One who gives a defense for a particular belief system, not someone who is sorry he or she holds it.

44   C. S. Lewis, *The Four Loves* (New York: Harcourt, Brace and World, Inc. 1960), p. 109.

45   Beyond the question of whether Nietzsche's Messiah would be good for the world, we have to ask: would he even be good according to Nietzsche? Nietzsche seems to recognize in his writing that he's bound by his own philosophy to hate his Messiah. The authentic man would inevitably personify everything Nietzsche stood against; he'd be an ultimate power who lords his glory over everyone else by the sheer force of his existence and the ethical example of his well-lived life (as he alone defines it). As soon as Nietzsche could say in rapturous praise of his Messiah, "Now *that's* how you live a noble, independent, free-thinking life!" he would by this very praise have proclaimed a template for the well-lived, truly human life and therefore have discouraged deviations from it. If held consistently, Nietzsche's most cherished values would first worship and then crucify their messianic personification and fulfillment.

46   Kevin J. Vanhoozer, *First Theology: God, Scripture and Hermeneutics* (Downers Grove: InterVarsity, 2002), p. 344.

47   Have a listen to Sheryl Crow's desperate demands as they turn to a tender, tortured plea in "Strong Enough."

48   Walter Kaufmann writes, "And the most important single clue to Zarathustra is that it is the work of an utterly lonely man" in Friedrich Nietzsche, *Thus Spoke Zarathustra: A Book for None and All*, trans. Walter Kaufmann, (New York: Penguin, 1966), p. xiii.

49   See also Chap Clark, *Hurt 2.0: Inside the World of Today's Teenagers—* (Grand Rapids: Baker, 2011). Clark argues that the age-old adage "Kids today are just like kids have always been" does not apply so much in our day.

50   Friedrich Nietzsche, *Thus Spoke Zarathustra: A Book for None and All*, trans. Walter Kaufmann, (New York: Penguin, 1966), p. 18.

51   Lacey Sturm, *The Reason—How I Discovered a Life Worth Living—Revelations of a Rock Princess* (Grand Rapids: Baker, 2014), p. 56.

52   Ibid., p. 55.

53   Ibid., p. 56.

54   This was very much the view of Jesus as well. This book, chapter 8 especially, is really just an exploration and explanation of his understanding of the written word of God. And if we're Christians, shouldn't we embrace Christ's view of Scripture? But that view has largely vanished from the landscape of American Christianity.

55   Francis A. Schaeffer, *He Is There and He Is Not Silent* (Wheaton: Tyndale, 1972).

Chapter 4

1   Second to Safety, "Esther," from the unpublished album *Esther*, 2019.

2   For a sad and sobering read, have a look at the FBI's own 2016–17 survey report of active shooter incidents in the United States, https://www.fbi.gov/file-repository/active-shooter-incidents-us-2016-2017.pdf/view. The report's purposely (and appropriately) dispassionate tone should icepick our nerves, re-sensitizing us to the horrors of our era.

3   Some people believe that this expression is found in the Bible. It was perhaps most famously used by Ben Franklin in his *Poor Richard's Almanac* and is usually regarded as a sort of Deistic inspiration for people to work hard, because God rewards such independent efforts.

4   For a haunting tale on this topic, told by a Japanese Christian through the story of embattled Catholic efforts to Christianize Japan, read Shusaku Endo, *Silence* (New York: Picador, 2016). This edition contains a foreword written by Martin Scorsese, the director and driving force behind the feature film based upon the novel.

5   Prolific and popular atheist Christopher Hitchens, upon hearing that Christians were praying for him in light of his terminal cancer, and of the establishment of September 20, 2010, as "Everybody Pray for Hitchens Day," wrote: "I don't mean to be churlish about any kind intentions, but when September 20, 2010, comes, please do not trouble deaf heaven with your bootless cries. Unless, of course, it makes you feel better." See Larry Alex Taunton, *The Faith of Christopher Hitchens: The Restless Soul of the World's Most Notorious Atheist*, (Nashville: Nelson, 2016), p. 172.

6   The effort of this book is to take the Bible on its own terms, for what it says about the written word of God and therefore about itself, rather than to reinterpret those claims in light of the currently acceptable (but always subject to change) dictates of contemporary, popular postmodern philosophies. Postmodernism has helpfully reminded us that Jesus was no modernist. Yes and amen. But are we really to believe he was a postmodernist?

7   U2's "City of Blinding Lights" from *How to Dismantle an Atomic Bomb* (Island; Interscope), 2004, is a beautiful meditation on this.

8   John 8:31–32. Note the irony of misusing Jesus's words as an ironic explanation of how leaving the faith feels. He says that his words are vital to knowing the truth that sets us free. See also Jesus's prayer in John 17.

9   See, for instance, Jon Stewart's *The Daily Show* interview with Ehrman at http://www.cc.com/video-clips/uj00dz/the-daily-show-with-jon-stewart-bart-ehrman.

10   With a notable exception being Bill Maher, who interviews true Christian scholars (though not, to my knowledge, those espousing a theologically "conservative" view of Scripture) on his show *Real Time*. Maher tends to treat them with respect, even as he disagrees vehemently and can't for the life of him understand why an intelligent person would be a Christian.

11   For substantial, direct refutations of Ehrman's claims, see Andreas Kostenberger, Darrell Bock, and Josh Chatraw, *Truth Matters: Confident Faith in a Confusing World* (Nashville: B&H Publishing Group, 2014). See also Michael F. Bird, Craig A. Evans, Simon J. Gathercole, Charles E. Hill, Chris Tilling, *How God Became Jesus: The Real Origins of Belief in Jesus' Divine Nature* (Grand Rapids: Zondervan, 2014).

12   Bart Ehrman, *God's Problem: How the Bible Fails to Answer Our Most Important Question—Why We Suffer* (New York: HarperCollins, 2008), p. 16.

13   Ehrman, p. 200.

14   Postmodern Scholar Peter Rollins calls the idea that the Bible is a

document at one with itself, "the ultimate fantasy of the Fundamentalist." See Peter Rollins, *The Fidelity of Betrayal: Towards a Church Beyond Belief* (Brewster: Paraclete, 2008), p. 17. Rollins uses "fundamentalist" to refer to close-minded Christians who just won't listen to good, solid reason and common sense about the many serious problems of authenticity and historical, scientific, and literary integrity of their precious book. For a popular language critical appraisal of some of Rollins's work, especially as it influenced the so-called "Emergent Church," see my 2009 series labeled "The Emerging Church" available through www.rpwitness.org.

15 Have a listen to the debate between Christian apologist James White and atheist Dan Barker, particularly "The Triune God of Scripture Lives," which takes a turn in the direction of this particular subject. With no charity, not even a condescending attempt at it, Barclay presses the point of the ignorance and incapacity of the ancients who wrote Scripture to address the matters of life that he finds to be the most important, true, and compelling, i.e., the matters of the material world. Also available is White's debate with Bart Ehrman, "Did the Bible Misquote Jesus?" on Ehrman's book *Misquoting Jesus: The Story Behind Who Quoted Jesus and Why* (New York: HarperCollins, 2005). These debates and so many others can be found at http://www.aomin. org/aoblog/2011/01/19/available-debates-by-dr-james-white/.

16 In fairness, Ehrman does try to interpret the biblical authors (when, as with Paul's letters, he thinks we can know who wrote particular parts of Scripture) on their own terms. For instance, he insists that Paul believed that Jesus actually rose, physically, from the grave and argues against Christian commentators who would try to allegorize the essential and pivotal event of Christian faith. Ehrman's criticism here is enough to make the Bible-believing Christian cry out "Amen!" This is by design. Ehrman stands such people up only to cut them off at the knees. Ehrman doesn't defend *what* Paul believed; he only defends the fact that Paul believed it. Following his strident defense, Ehrman utterly (and quickly and condescendingly) discredits Paul as a competent commentator on such things. It's not a point-by-point refutation of Paul's beliefs about the resurrection, which, as Ehrman rightly affirms, drive Paul's view of suffering. Instead, he just dismisses Paul altogether because of his unfortunate but inevitable ineptitude in seeing reality for what it is.

17 Ehrman, *God's Problem*, p. 244. Despite this comment, Ehrman claims elsewhere to personally love the Bible, calling some of its authors "religious geniuses" and saying that all of its authors should be listened to, notwithstanding the fact that they "contradict each other all over the map." I wonder if Paul made his list of geniuses. Ehrman claims that none of the biblical authors were inspired more than any other genius, like Mozart or Shakespeare. Ehrman is trying to disagree with a typical Christian belief, that the Bible is truly God's word. Interestingly, though, Paul does not claim to be "inspired" by God, nor does he claim that any of the biblical writers were. He says that the words, not the authors themselves nor simply the ideas that their words convey, but the very words themselves are "God-breathed," a word typically translated as "inspired" (2 Timothy 3:16). Peter says that the writers of Scripture were

"carried along" by the Spirit in their writing of Scripture (2 Peter 1:19-21). This is a crucial distinction to make, and it explains at least partly why Protestants during the Protestant Reformation refused to treat any of the Pope's teaching as inherently infallible. The Reformers insisted that Jesus was the only human being worthy of this kind of trust and possessing this kind of authority. They believed that the rest of us, no matter how high our rank in the church or how prominent our churches, can and do err. "Scripture alone" was the only infallible rule for faith and life.

18 It's ironically comforting for the Bible-believing Christian that Ehrman seldom goes after a genuine, well-informed, relatively contemporary opponent. In fact, when he finally invokes one—Fyodor Dostoyevsky, perhaps the greatest of all novelists and a Bible-believing Christian who wrote with stunning depth and lived-in experience about suffering—Ehrman never interacts with his view of the pertinent matters. Instead, he simply quotes his favorite among Dostoyevsky's literary creations, Ivan Karamazov, as we'll see later in this chapter. Inexplicably, Ehrman decides not to interact with the worldview of the author who expresses through Ivan and with painful perfection the blazing anger people feel as they see suffering in the world. Such brilliant explications of beliefs with which he disagrees were typical of the great Russian writer. He never cheapened those ideas by presenting less than a compelling case for them. (No disrespect, but Ehrman could really learn from this, and he's smart enough to know that.) In fact, as with Ivan, Dostoyevsky sometimes makes a more compelling case for his opponent's arguments than they do. It's as if he's saying, "I get it. I really do. But you're missing something here, something huge." Dostoyevsky teaches that what's missing from atheism, and therefore its quieter form, agnosticism, is any basis upon which to be morally outraged at the suffering and evil in the world. You even lose your ability to secure a lasting understanding of what's good in life. As he asks through one of his characters, "How can man be good without God?"

19 Ehrman expresses a condescending, but no doubt sincere appreciation for some of the notes he gets from people who disagree with him. "These e-mails are always well meaning and many of them are very thoughtful....It is a *little* surprising to me, though, that so many people have such a simple understanding of suffering and want to share it with me as if I hadn't heard or thought of that one before" (Ehrman, p. 263). A well-informed Christian reader might think similar things of Ehrman's book on suffering and its commentary on Scripture.

20 R. C. Sproul, *Lifeviews: Make a Christian Impact on Culture and Society*, (Grand Rapids: Fleming H. Revell, 1986), p. 43 and following.

21 "Nausea" by Jean-Paul Sartre is the story of one man's struggle to come to terms with life and the meaning of his own existence. See *Nausea, The Wall, and Other Stories: Two Volumes in One*—translated by Lloyd Alexander (New York: MJF, 1975).

22 Richard Wolin, *The Terms of Cultural Criticism: The Frankfurt School, Existentialism, Poststructuralism* (New York: Columbia University Press 1992), p. 128. Cited from *Sarte, L'Etre et le Neant* (Paris: Gallimard, 1950), p. 134.

23 Nietzsche said it would take time for Europe to really reckon with God's death. There would be an adjustment period as the news of God's death settled in. And as it typically happens when we deal with death, Christian Europe's reaction was mixed. Some reacted with mad, blood-lusty euphoria, eager to cut down any civil or church authority who dared invoke the dead deity. Denis Diderot's graphic declaration, "Men will never be free until the last king is strangled with the entrails of the last priest," pretty much said it all for the militant souls eager to be the Enlightenment's enforcers and executioners, the cutting edge of this great forward movement of freedom and tolerance, especially in France. Others reacted with the fixed, blinking stare Nietzsche describes through the eyes of his madman (see chapter 3). They just didn't get it. Bitterness and denial, an inability or unwillingness to reckon with a new reality: all classic reactions to death and all seen in the wake of God's death in Europe.

But once the initial shock and gut-level reactions gave way to calmed and carefully processed reactions—once we got over our rage for ever having been so unenlightened to believe in God to begin with and ever having done obeisance to all the power-hungry people claiming to serve him by ruling us, wouldn't there have been an overall sense of relief, a profound sense of freedom and new life and possibilities? We're still waiting...

24 John Lennon's beautiful atheistic anthem, "Imagine," expresses not just a dream but a hopelessly naïve fantasy.

25 Bill Maher responds to this by saying that in these cases, the state was being treated as God, so religion is still to blame. C'mon, Bill. Isn't that a bit of confirmation bias? It is if you don't put forward any solid, lasting philosophical basis upon which anything can be deemed good and valuable, and to which powerful people who believe that they must by the sword enact "good" are accountable. Atheism absolutely cannot give you this. To his point, though, governments are indeed sometimes treated as gods, especially the ones who claim to be religiously neutral. It's not "religion" that's to blame for mass murders, it's particular people living out their religious views, whether atheistically or theistically related. See Maher's discussion with Christian scholar Ross Douthat at https://www.youtube.com/watch?v=kJQjpG-lGY4.

26 Albert Camus, *Resistance, Rebellion, and Death*, trans. by Justin O'Brien (New York: Alfred A. Knopf, 1969), pp. 72–3.

27 See Sproul's helpful discussion in *Lifeviews*, pp. 61 and following.

28 From the preface by Paul Ramsey, Gabriel Vahanian, *The Death of God: The Culture of our Post-Christian Era* (New York: George Braziller, 1961), p. xv.

29 Penn Jillette, "Time for Atheists to Stand Up and Be Counted" at https://www.cnn.com/2016/06/02/opinions/atheists-reason-rally-jillette/index.html.

30 Maher, on the politically correct pathology of forbidding the criticism of favored religions, Islam in particular, "We have to stop saying...well, we should not insult a great religion. First of all there are no great religions. They're all stupid and dangerous. And we should insult them. And we should

be able to insult whatever we want. That is what free speech is like." He notes that murder of infidels is disturbingly and tellingly common in the Muslim world, not an aberration carried out by a crazy few. "This happens way too frequently. It's like *Groundhog Day* except if the groundhog kept getting its head cut off." Read more at http://www.inquisitr.com/1740217/bill-maher-on-charlie-hebdo-all-religions-are-stupid-and-dangerous-video/#O2k3UozUVC57mp4K.99.

31 Harris says, "I will grant you that the worst books ever written are in the Old Testament." https://www.youtube.com/watch?v=1JrYCHC0bkE. Here, Harris is in the process of answering a woman who claims that Mohammed himself was a peaceful person.

32 From Kai Nielsen, "Why Should I Be Moral?" *American Philosophical Quarterly* 21 (1984), p. 90. Cited in William Lane Craig, *Reasonable Faith: Christian Truth and Apologetics* (Wheaton: Crossway, revised ed., 1994), p. 6.

33 Play off of Jeremiah Burroughs (1599–1646), *The Evil of Evils: The Exceeding Sinfulness of Sin* (Ligonier, PA: Soli Deo Gloria, 1992).

34 A theodicy is an attempted explanation, in favor of God, of God's allowance of and manner of dealing with evil in the world.

35 First published in 1879–80. "Supposing one were asked to name a book calculated to give an unbeliever today a clear notion of what Christianity is about, could one hope to do much better than *The Brothers Karamazov*?" From the foreword by Malcolm Muggeridge, *The Gospel in Dostoyevsky*, the Bruderhof, ed. (New York: Orbis, 1988), p. 3.

36 Paul Ramsey, Gabriel Vahanian, *The Death of God: The Culture of our Post-Christian Era* (New York: George Braziller, 1961), xix.

37 *The Gospel in Dostoyevsky*, p. 51.

38 Ehrman, *God's Problem*, p. 276.

39 Time and again, rather than reporting suspected abuse to authorities, Planned Parenthood has repeatedly looked the other way, performed abortions on victims as young as 12 years old, and then returned those victims into the waiting arms of their abusers…This reputation has led to Planned Parenthood becoming a haven for sexual abusers and sex traffickers. Planned Parenthood is a favorite place to take their victims to cover up their crimes. See https://www.liveaction.org/what-we-do/investigations/aidingabusers/.

40 See Rod Dreher, "U2's Moral Stain," at https://www.theamericanconservative.com/dreher/u2-abortion-moral-stain-ireland/.

41 Here is the webpage for a wonderful organization called Deeper Still. Their tagline is "Freeing the abortion wounded heart." Having worked closely with a family ministered to by a local chapter of this great group of people (the wife is now a counselor in the organization), I can personally and highly recommend their beautiful, life-giving, encouraging work. http://www.godeeperstill.org/.

42 Ehrman, *God's Problem*, p. 278.

43 The full quotation comes from Sanger's essay, "Planning Your Children," June 1936. In context, she's making an argument for the widespread distribution of contraceptives, especially to poor communities bereft of them.

"When this is done," she writes, "every child will be a wanted child, born to its rightful heritage of love, care, and comfort." See the Margaret Sanger Project's posting at https://www.nyu.edu/projects/sanger/webedition/app/documents/show.php?sangerDoc=143717.xml.

To the point of my argument in chapter 4, note her assumptions and biases regarding proper family structure and planning; and especially consider the plight of children who result from what she calls "blind accident." Whatever your views on abortion, contraception, and Sanger herself, please read the full piece to understand this image-bearer in context. Doing this honestly and fully will require an examination of the results of her views regarding children born of what she calls in this article "blind accident"—a rather pejorative way of describing all unplanned pregnancies. Understanding Sanger in context also requires an examination of her views advocating eugenics. In 1920, Sanger said, "...birth control is nothing more or less than the facilitation of the process of weeding out the unfit [and] of preventing the birth of defectives." See "Eugenics and Birth Control" here, http://www.pbs.org/wgbh/americanexperience/features/pill-eugenics-and-birth-control/. The organization sponsoring this post is PBS, hardly a bastion of pro-life politics.

44 Larry Alex Taunton, *The Faith of Christopher Hitchens*, pp. 144–5.

45 Richard Wurmbrand, *Tortured for Christ* (London: Hodder and Stoughton, 1967), p. 34, cited in William Lane Craig, *Reasonable Faith: Christian Truth and Apologetics* (Wheaton: Crossway, revised ed. 1994), pp. 67–8.

46 Taunton, *The Faith of Christopher Hitchens*, p. 101.

47 How can children possibly be truly safe, their rights truly protected, in a society that respects no higher authority for truth and ethics than the individual self, or a collection of individual selves—a society that feels free to redefine or discard any concept, word, value, social more whatsoever? If we say that our worldview won't allow the kinds of terrible abuses that still largely lack public support, can we identify axiom(s) within that worldview that can with philosophical integrity and internal consistency remain unassailably and unalterably the same, thus safeguarding kids? What legal designations/terms are safe from redefinition these days? And therefore, what citizens, and in particular what children, are truly safe? See the next chapter for a more specific discussion on the deadly wordplay common to a self-as-truth culture.

48 And in the even more ancient world, the world of the Old Testament, biblical ethics stood in staggering, humane contrast to the morality of surrounding nations and cultures. For example, the much-hated dictum mentioned in Exodus 21:23, "an eye for an eye," was actually a principle of justice and restraint. It stipulates that the severity of the punishment must fit, but not exceed, the severity of the crime. By Jesus's day, this principle had been abused to justify a vengeful, vindictive way of life. Jesus preaches against that retaliatory posture of heart in Matthew 5:38–39. See chapter 7 and especially 10 for an exploration of Jesus's relationship to some of the most violent and seemingly vitriolic passages of the Old Testament.

49 Please have a listen to my sermon entitled "The Abolition of Inhumanity" at https://www.sermonaudio.com/sermoninfo.asp?SID=3120911211910,

which builds a biblical case against slavery as we saw it on American soil, and in particular against Christians who tried to use the Bible to defend it. See also Joseph S. Moore, *Founding Sins: How a Group of Antislavery Radicals Fought to Put Christ in the Constitution* (New York: Oxford University Press, 2016), and Bono's interview with *Rolling Stone* from December 2017 at https://www.rollingstone.com/music/music-features/bono-the-rolling-stone-interview-3-203774/. Bono (real name Paul Hewson) recognizes within Paul a stunning ability to see above and beyond his cultural milieu, but tends to toe the line of popular sociology and social mores. He doesn't seem to recognize, or at least agree, that the Apostle's culture-defying prophetic wisdom, like the New Testament itself, to which Paul was a primary contributor, rises not from Paul's correcting the Old Testament, but from his seeing Old Testament truth fulfilled in and applied anew by the risen Savior, Jesus Christ. See Matthew 5:17–18 and chapter 8 of this book for Jesus's own view of the Old Testament and his relationship to it.

50 For particularly remarkable displays of this respect, even in the midst of great injustice, note in both the Old and New Testament eras the respectful ways in which God's servants addressed pagan political rulers who had the power to kill them, horribly and unjustly, and in some cases were legitimately psychotic. See Daniel 3 and the Apostles' trials before various civil authorities throughout the book of Acts, chapter 4, for example.

51 Pastor Tim Keller was asked to address the question "What Can Christianity Offer Our Society in the 21st Century?" as the keynote speaker for the 2018 National Parliamentary Prayer Breakfast in Westminster Hall, London, on June 19, 2018. It's a 25-minute clip very worth your watching. https://www.youtube.com/watch?v=AkcouxJE6o4&feature=share: Keller argues from Scripture and the history of the Christian church that human rights have always been a central concern to Christ's true disciples. He quotes Gregory of Nyssa, who spoke against slavery and asked the rhetorical question, laughable given the ethics and economic structures of the day, "How much money for the image of God?" His point, of course, is that human beings are priceless and must not be treated as property.

52 See Tim Keller, *Generous Justice: How God's Grace Makes Us Just* (New York: Dutton, 2019).

53 For some, the discovery of similarity between Bible stories and ancient pagan myths is deeply unnerving. But what those who delight in introducing believers to these connections hardly ever mention is just how dramatically the biblical accounts differ from what seem at first to be their counterparts. The biblical narratives flat out contradict and correct these others stories. They mention the same things—a worldwide flood, the resurrection of a divine son—but the biblical narratives correct the others. It's as if God is saying to them through his own word, "Yep…you're definitely onto something. But you're way off when it comes to the most vital elements of your stories. This is how it really was, and this is who the true God really is…" For example, with regard to creation and flood narratives in particular, "The rest of the ancient Near East has nothing like Genesis 1–11," Bill T. Arnold and Bryan

E. Beyer, *Encountering the Old Testament: A Christian Survey* (Grand Rapids: Baker, 1999, 2008), p. 78.

Against the claim that Christianity is not unique because other religions (and Christian cults) include divine sons rising from the dead, historic Christianity maintains that Jesus was not simply the Son of God, but God himself, and very conscious of that fact. See *The Apostles' Creed* and the gospel of John, 1:1–18 and chapter 21 in particular. We'll visit these later. This, and the Christian faith's essential monotheism, set it apart from every other faith—and that's not even getting into the unique reason for and the consequences of God's becoming human in Jesus. Criticizing Christianity for inconsistent monotheism doesn't hold up, as we'll see in chapter 6, but criticizing it for being just like other religions is profoundly, and sometimes purposefully, ignorant and/or deceitful. On the resurrection of Jesus, see *The Reason for God*, chapter 13. Keller refers frequently in this chapter to the excellent work of N. T. Wright, world-renowned historian and New Testament scholar, on the historicity of Christ's resurrection.

54 In the wake of the terrorist attacks of September 11, 2001, some Christian leaders proclaimed the death of postmodernism—a complex system of thought that's typically and broadly understood as the defining philosophy of our day, and which assumes the ceiling of self as gospel truth. It was a game changer for some, like Christopher Hitchens. But for him, it just shifted things politically and opened his eyes to the blindness of his fellow atheists who could not bring themselves to feel the full weight and moral outrage that those terrorist acts should have elicited from them. Those events demonstrated the deadly moral hypocrisy of the strains of thought that cannot call evil what it is, but by no means did they kill that thinking. And it seems rather egotistical for Americans to assume they would, given so many other atrocities that have happened around the world in postmodern times. The idea was probably that postmodern thinkers in America would finally wake up to the moral bankruptcy of their worldviews, but people don't easily give up the godhood that self-centric truth promises them.

55 I'm using "Israel" in the big-picture sense to describe the Hebrew people. By Jeremiah's time, the kingdom of Israel had been divided into two kingdoms, "Israel" in the North and "Judah" in the South. Jeremiah's work focused on Judah.

56 Compare these words to the "Beatitudes," the opening section of Jesus's Sermon on the Mount, which lists character qualities that Jesus personifies and that he builds by his grace into his true disciples. John had the kind of heart Jesus describes as "blessed." We don't know for sure, but it would seem strange if John was not familiar with Jesus's teaching on this point. Those final words to him may have called these suppressed truths to his wounded heart before his life was taken violently for his Master's sake.

57 Even after Jesus's resurrection, which John never saw, things were a mess at times among Christians. Several New Testament epistles are written to God's growing family to correct their childish behavior; they were fighting with each other and giving their Father a bad name. How the times haven't changed! See 1 and 2 Corinthians especially, the latter written with Paul's heart bursting in joy over the way the Corinthian believers had heeded his loving correction from the first letter. And then there was the increasingly vicious persecution from Roman rulers who didn't take kindly to Christian insistence that Jesus, not Caesar, was Lord. From every angle, times were hard for believers. Christ did not exempt his disciples from suffering; he told them to expect it.

58 It could be that Jesus's doubting disciples just couldn't believe their eyes—it was too good to be true! As we thought about with Peter, God's written word proves a more lasting and reliable witness than the happy sights we're afraid to trust as true.

59 Dr. Byron Curtis writes, in informal correspondence, "Job's literary form is the closest thing we have to Greek drama or Shakespeare's *Lear* in all the Bible....The usual assertion that the speeches are dramatic art is no mark against the historicity of the book, or of Job, or of his friends." The Bible is composed of many literary genres, and genres within genres (i.e., the historical narratives of the gospel include Jesus's use of fictional stories—parables—to tell deep spiritual truths). Each of these literary forms and styles require distinct approaches to interpretation, and together they demonstrate the variety and artistic beauty with which God wrote his heart to us. For helpful introductions to the book of Job, see Francis I. Andersen, *Job: Tyndale Old Testament Commentaries* (Downers Grove: InterVarsity, 1976): Daniel Estes, *Handbook on the Wisdom Books and Psalms* (Grand Rapids: Baker Academic, 2005); and for help in recognizing the Bible's various genres and digging more deeply into biblical truth, see Leland Ryken, *How to Read the Bible as Literature...and get more out of it* (Grand Rapids: Zondervan, 1984) and *Words of Life: A Literary Introduction to the New Testament I* (Grand Rapids: Baker Book House, 1987); and Walter Kaiser, Moises Silva, *Introduction to Biblical Hermeneutics: The Search for Meaning* (Grand Rapids: Zondervan, 1994, 2007).

60 Psalm 14 opens with this lyric: "The fool has said in his heart, 'There is no God.'" In Scripture, the fool is someone who knows what is true but willingly acts otherwise.

61 C. S. Lewis, *Mere Christianity* (San Francisco: HarperCollins Publishers, 1952, 1980), pp. 38–9. Lewis makes his argument for God's existence based upon the moral code—what he calls the "tao"—deeply embedded in humanity and therefore deeply suggestive of a basic moral order built into the universe by a supreme, morally good being. This argument is valid and runs in keeping with what Paul writes in Romans 1:16–21. However, it seems that Lewis's argumentation isn't as immediately compelling to the "average person" as it may have been in his day. In an age that defines truth, especially moral truth, self-referentially and that therefore has little concern for the logical cogency and internal consistency of the personal moral beliefs based on this ever-shifting standard, people don't bite as easily onto an argument for moral truth whose hook is its cogent logical reasoning. The "moral argument" will have a hard time in a culture whose former moral–philosophical structures have not only crumbled, but been pulverized. His work still shines, though, in exposing the shallowness and self-contradictory nature of still typical strains of atheistic thought which pride themselves on their eminent reasonableness.

62 New International Version.

63 One of Ehrman's arguments is that New Testament folks like Paul really believed that Jesus would return very soon and that Jesus's not having done so helps to discredit their whole system of belief and hope. But expecting God's intervention to be imminent, only to have to wait a long time, is nothing new. As is typical, the opening chapters of the Bible are already on it. In their telling us of the very first people, they give us an example of the pained patience with which believers must embrace God's promises to intervene very directly and personally in human history. Right after humanity's first sin, God promised to provide a human savior. The first woman thought that perhaps this promise would be fulfilled with her first child. But no. Not by a very long shot. Was Eve wrong to hope to the point of expectation that salvation would come soon? Not at all. God's promises are detailed enough to incite persevering hope but vague enough to prohibit presumption (and very specific predictions about the Savior's arrival in the world).

64 William Lane Craig, *Reasonable Faith*, p. 67.

65 Ibid., pp. 111–2.

66 Sturm, *The Reason*, pp. 113–4.

67 *The Gospel in Dostoyevsky*, The Bruderhof, ed. (New York: Orbis, 1988), pp. 15–16.

68 "Time for Atheists to Stand Up and Be Counted" at https://www.cnn.com/2016/06/02/opinions/atheists-reason-rally-jillette/index.html.

69 See J. Ed Komoszewski, M. James Sawyer, and Daniel B. Wallace, *Reinventing Jesus: How Contemporary Skeptics Miss the Real Jesus and Mislead Popular Culture* (Grand Rapids: Kregel, 2006), p. 110 and following, among many other sections of this book dealing with Ehrman. It's not simply that Ehrman is challenging long-held Christian beliefs; nothing new there. It's the disingenuous, unscholarly way he's doing it while passing off his work to an uncritical popular audience as in-depth, scandalous-because-it's-true scholarship. Much of it has to do with Ehrman's ironclad insistence on the legitimacy of the "patchwork quilt" concept of Scripture (also countered in this and many other books). For instance, when questioning whether one text in the gospels is original and therefore raising questions as to the theological import of the passage, Ehrman "never once" consults a parallel passage in another gospel that states clearly, and indisputably, what the disputed text as we have it indicates. This is shoddy work on Ehrman's part, indicating that his personal narrative about the gospel narratives, the Bible as a whole, and Christianity in general does not allow for counterpoints from the very source whose veracity and trustworthiness he seeks to undermine. The authors of *Reinventing Jesus* are very charitable and respectful in their assessment of Ehrman's work (as of 2006): "Unfortunately, as careful a scholar as Ehrman is, his treatment of major theological changes in the text of the New Testament tends to fall under one of two criticisms: Either his textual decisions are suspect or his interpretations are suspect." The authors mention a previous work

of Ehrman's that received severe criticism, which Ehrman had, as yet, not answered. "For a book geared toward a lay audience, one would think that he would want to nuance his discussion a bit more, especially with all the theological weight that he says is on the line" (p. 113).

70 If it's objected that religious belief is circular in reasoning, the same could be said of atheism. And to prevent all these matters from devolving into a grand philosophical "I know you are but what am I?!"—we can compare the basic foundations of each belief: the god—or inviolable, presupposed, unproven ideas that function as such—in each system and do a compare-and-contrast as to how these principles, if consistently lived, look in the world, and see which thought systems are self-referentially coherent and consistent.

71 See chapter 10 on this especially.

72 "The Wedding at Cana" in *The Gospel in Dostoyevsky*, pp. 213-5.

73 A play off the title of a glorious song, *We Could Be Heroes*, by David Bowie. My favorite cover of the song is by the Wallflowers.

Chapter 5

1 C. S. Lewis, *That Hideous Strength* (London: The Macmillan Company, 1965), p. 351 footnote.

2 Lacey Sturm, "I'm Not Laughing," *Life Screams* (FOLLOWSPOT Records), 2016.

3 Neil Postman, *Amusing Ourselves to Death: Public Discourse in the Age of Show Business* (New York: Viking Press, 1985) cited in Jonathan Watt, *Languages of the Gods: A Faculty Integration Paper, Prepared for the Faculty and Trustees of Geneva College*, 2003. Some people are not able to exercise this gift as well as others; this, of course, does not diminish their humanity in the least. Stating such obvious truth is sadly necessary because there is no shortage of ways in which humans routinely dehumanize each other. As we'll examine next chapter, it's really only the Bible that provides a basis by which the human worth and value of every single human person is established regardless of their relative ability to participate in distinctively human activities.

4 One of my best friends, when we were in college, bought and restored an old Ford Pinto, painting it black except for a purple racing stripe right down the middle. It was a beautiful bomb. Thankfully, it never exploded on him or anyone else.

5 Proverbs 18:21—Proverbs is called one of the "wisdom books" of the Old Testament. It specializes in pithy but profound statements about how life works, tinged often with the kind of sarcasm and irony appropriate to a world full of people who all deep down believe themselves to be so wise. For instance, Proverbs 26:4–5: "Answer not a fool according to his folly, lest you be like him yourself. Answer a fool according to his folly, lest he be wise in his own eyes." Damned if you do and damned if you don't. Many people might be surprised that the Bible contains such blunt realism, such a deep understanding and therefore often dark analysis and commentary on how life really works in this world. With his brevity and rhetorical fire, James in many ways echoes Scripture's Wisdom Literature, which also includes the Psalms and the

book of Ecclesiastes. Like these books, James has a keen eye for bullgeschichte and calls it out when he sees it.

6   Words force choices—such as whether or not to keep listening or reading. Thanks for your choice! (My condolences regarding the self you let die in that sacrifice.) Whether or not we want to view it as a death—I admit that's really morbid—words always change us. In place of the us that existed before the other person spoke emerges a different version of us, hopefully wiser and better equipped to navigate life, but not necessarily so. The only thing we know for sure is that we're different and there's no going back.

7   "This reflects God's own nature on the one hand; it is a natural and normal thing for this God to speak, not some anthropomorphic projection onto a blank deistic screen! On the other hand, it reflects the fact that, within God's world, one of the most powerful things human beings, God's image-bearers, can do is to speak. Words change things....The notion of 'speech acts'...is fairly new in philosophy. It would not have surprised the ancient Israelite prophets." N. T. Wright, *Scripture and the Authority of God: How to Read the Bible Today* (New York: HarperCollins, 2011), pp. 36-7.

8   That doesn't mean that we're lying all the time, but that's only true because we can't know what a lie is without having an idea of what truth is. If the ceiling of self holds, it does mean that none of our words can ever really be called "true," and that means that none of our words can ever really be trusted. See how complicated this gets!

9   Beneath the ceiling of self, godding adults have preached their dogma to their mini-me progeny. We've taught little gods to raise hell whenever someone opposes them (except when we tell them what to do, of course; they need to respect *our* godhood). Rather than letting them fail, we change the rules of life's games and remove beneficial resistance that could build their personal strength. By telling them there is no truth higher than the self, we leave children vulnerable to predators who troll for unsteady souls and flatter them with lethal positivity. Proverbs 27:6 tells us, "Wounds from a friend can be trusted, but an enemy multiplies kisses." Life gets really dangerous when we can't tell our true friends from our real enemies.

10   If you're thinking, "tough loss!" then ouch!

11   See Esther Meek, *Contact with Reality: Michael Polanyi's Realism and Why It Matters* (Eugene: Wipf and Stock Publishers, 2017).

12   "If we contextualize our subjectivities with precision, we acknowledge that no two temporal subjects can be identical, and therefore every claim to the existence of a community or culture—is a hasty generalization. Subjectivity and community become one. Both are fictions. Just as the postmodern self disintegrates into an ultimately incoherent collection of subject positions, the postmodern community disintegrates to such a degree that our selves and our communities become difficult to distinguish: we can share neither with an 'other.' Temporality and the inevitable change that attends it renders the postmodern community as illusory as postmodern subjectivity. The community we depend upon to legitimate our interpretive activity appears to be there... until we look for it." Calvin L. Troup, *Temporality, Eternity, and Wisdom: The*

Rhetoric of Augustine's Confessions (Columbia: University of South Carolina Press, 1999).

13 "Use Your Illusion" is the title to a Guns N' Roses album from the '80s. Yes, I'm old.

14 Philip Rieff, *The Triumph of the Therapeutic: Uses of Faith after Freud* (New York: Harper & Row, 1966), p. 17.

15 See "Did NAACP president lie about her race? City investigates" by Jeff Humphrey and Melissa Luck, June 12, 2015, at https://www.kxly.com/news/local-news/spokane/did-naacp-president-lie-about-her-race-city-investigat es_20161121042949505/176695501 and a follow-up, "Rachel Dolezal, the white woman who posed as black, charged with welfare fraud" by Allyson Chiu, May 25, 2018, at https://www.washingtonpost.com/news/morning-mix/wp/2018/05/25/rachel-dolezal-the-white-woman-who-posed-as-black-charged-with-welfare-fraud/?noredirect=on&utm_term=.9b48cc20d76e.

16 I'm glad that the phrase "illegitimate child" is not used as frequently as it once was. It's an evil expression. There are no illegitimate children, no matter how illegitimate the actions of those who contributed to their existence.

17 Germaine Greer, prolific feminist author and noted public intellectual, openly criticized this action by John and Furnish. She considered it evidence of the emptying out, the deconstruction and therefore the destruction of the concept of motherhood. "It's gone," she laments. See the May 25, 2015, article by Jenn Selby in the online *Independent* at https://www.independent.co.uk/news/people/germaine-greer-criticises-elton-john-for-naming-husband-david-furnish-as-sons-mother-on-birth-10274618.html.

Such objections are powerful and important pauses on the path to meaninglessness. But if godding is the fundamental basis upon which such vital words are defined, the standard back to which objectors call us, then these pauses can only be commas, not full-stops, as we continue to write ourselves into nihilism.

18 See John Sikkema, "A Behind-the-Scenes Look at Recent Changes to Family Law in Ontario," April 21, 2017, at https://arpacanada.ca/news/2017/04/21/haunted-hetero-normative-family/ and "ARPA Presents to Committee Reviewing Bill 89 by the same author, April 11, 2017, at https://arpacanada.ca/news/2017/04/11/committee-cloth-ears-arpa-presents-committee-reviewing-bill-89/.

19 Christianity is, of course, accused of this. God gives his own son as a bloody sacrifice to satisfy his justice. As we'll see in chapter 7 especially, it's precisely at the points where Christianity seems most offensive that we discover how truly, drastically, beautifully, and freeingly it differs from every other belief system.

20 Cited by D. C. Schindler in *The Catholicity of Reason* (Grand Rapids: Eerdmans, 2013), p. 43, from Immanuel Kant, *Religion within the Limits of Reason Alone*, trans. Theodore M. Greene and Hoyt H. Hudson (New York: Harper & Row, 1960), p. 157.

21 "Kant's programme involved a shifting of transcendentality, so that its location was not the objective structure of reality but the objective structure of human rationality. Along with the shift there went a displacement of divinity and a change in the ontology of space and time, so that they became functions more of human rationality than of the real world. It was not that there was a secularization...so much as a displacement: the locus of the divine ordering of space and time was now the human mind rather than the eternal structures of being." Colin E. Gunton, *The One, the Three, and the Many: God, Creation, and the Culture of Modernity—the 1992 Bampton Lectures* (Cambridge: Cambridge University Press, 1993), p. 156.

22 See the April 14, 2018, edition of *World* for "Ze said, xe said" by Andree Seu Peterson. Terse and informative, the piece's unfortunately humorous tone belies its serious, sobering subject matter and belittles (surely unintentionally) those for whom gender identification and therefore language designation are matters of personal existential crisis.

23 Former student Zack Bowman, in a podcast entitled "Let God Die (So God Can Live)." His comment comes in episode 86, which has for its discussion topic: "Life Beyond Commiseration" at http://www.letgoddie.org.

24 Fourteen years of philosophical and sociological change show up in the sequel to *The Incredibles*, somewhat minimally given the time-gap and seismic social shifts occurring in that near decade and a half. Perhaps the most revelatory scene along these lines happens quickly and involves one brief line. Elastagirl tells her husband in the midst of a heated discussion about their children and their respective life-trajectories, "They're young! They haven't decided what they are yet." A notable contrast to what we might have expected her to say in the relatively ancient past when the first *The Incredibles* was released, perhaps something like, "They haven't decided what they want to be yet." We've gone from children deciding what they want to do as a life's vocation to children deciding what they are ontologically. At least she doesn't want to force such heavy conversations upon her kids before they're ready.

25 Sigmund Freud (1856–1939) and his theories on sex and sexuality have radically, deeply, and pervasively influenced Western culture, to the point that we now consider as self-evident truth the idea that one's sexual orientation and preferences are definitional of one's personhood, i.e., ontological. See C. S. Lewis's critiques of Sigmund Freud in Armand Nicholi, *The Question of God: C. S. Lewis and Sigmund Freud Debate God, Love, Sex, and the Meaning of Life* (New York: Free Press, 2002). See also Rosaria Butterfield, *Openness Unhindered: Further Thoughts of an Unlikely Convert on Sexual Identity and Union with Christ* (Pittsburgh: Crown & Covenant, 2015), which explores the history, philosophy, and rhetoric of pop culture's dogma regarding issues of sexuality and personhood.

26 See John Sikkema, "Five Bills in Five Years: Gender Ideology in Ontario," from March 21, 2017, at https://arpacanada.ca/news/2017/03/21/five-bills-five-years-gender-ideology-ontario/.

27 See also Walt Heyer, "Research Claiming Sex-Change Benefits is Based on Junk Science," from April 13, 2017, at http://thefederalist.com/2017/04/13/research-claiming-sex-change-benefits-based-junk-science/. This is an opinion piece but coming from an author who can not only sympathize but

empathize with gender change. Yes, anecdotal evidence can go both ways. But if you've studied the subject, which voices tend to be silenced and marginalized—those militantly in favor of all these operations to the exclusion of other options, or those seeking to propose alternatives? For a scholarly examination of the issues from a socially conservative viewpoint, see Ryan T. Anderson, *When Harry Became Sally: Responding to the Transgender Moment* (New York: Encounter Books, 2018), and for a direct counterargument, including criticism of some of the scholars and scholarship cited above, see Kelly R. Novak, *Let Harry Become Sally* (Andover: Hypothesis Press, 2018).

28 Canada is, as of this writing in 2018, considering whether to allow physician-assisted suicide (referred to as MAID—Medical Assistance in Dying) for minors and for the mentally incompetent with consent. To read the questions under current consideration, see the pertinent page published by the Council of Canadian Academies at http://www.scienceadvice.ca/en/assessments/in-progress/medical-assistance-dying/subquestions.aspx. I'm indebted for this information to Andre Schuten, legal counsel and Director of Law and Policy for the Association for Reformed Political Action. Mr. Schuten has argued related cases before the Canadian Supreme Court.

For an admittedly over the top, but not by much, satirical survey of cultural trends along these lines, see my blog post *A Lament for Sally* from July 2, 2015, at https://gentlereformation.com//2015/07/02/a-lament-for-sally-and-the-rest-of-us/.

29 Part two of Colin E. Gunton's lecture series, found in *The One, The Three, and The Many: God, Creation, and the Culture of Modernity, the 1992 Bampton Lectures* (London: Cambridge University Press, 1993), p. ix.

30 My dad! Rutledge Etheridge, *Brother John* (New York: Ace, 2001).

31 Listed at the very end, along with other seemingly disjointed bits of story, of a Kindle edition of *That Hideous Strength* by C. S. Lewis. See *The Space Trilogy, Omnib: Three Science Fiction Classics in One Volume: Out of the Silent Planet, Perelandra, That Hideous Strength.*

32 Philip Rieff, *The Triumph of the Therapeutic*, p. 19.

33 See Jean Twenge, "Has the Smartphone Destroyed a Generation?" from the September 2017 issue of *The Atlantic* at https://www.theatlantic.com/magazine/archive/2017/09/has-the-smartphone-destroyed-a-generation/534198/ For somewhat of a counterpoint, see Andrew Zirschky, *Beyond the Screen: Youth Ministry for the Connected But Alone Generation* (Nashville: Abingdon Press, 2015). Because there is little examination of the philosophical, theological, and sociological subcurrents upon which the iGeneration rode into culture, Twenge's analysis, while informative and helpfully sobering, seems to assign too much blame for disheartening trends to the technology by which the deep things of human life come to expression. Correlation is not causation. The tech certainly agitates those deep waters, and in many ways social media tech can be like a loaded weapon, but it's our ethics that decide which way our lives will go. The tech takes us on the admittedly blisteringly fast ride that our hearts were already asking for. Zirsky's thesis is that teenagers are simply doing

with contemporary technology what teens have always done with tech; they're making it social. He does approach the cultural phenomena from a theological angle, suggesting ways to encourage via the tech the kinds of deep personal fellowship that he claims the teens are seeking through it. Zirsky's analysis is a helpful call back from the proverbial ledge upon which many panicked parents feel perched in their efforts to love and protect their kids, but he tends to lionize the social media habits of youth. I wish his work had given more attention to the depersonalizing and dichotomizing elements of these habits, which border upon and often become obsessions. The typical tendencies to pull away from people in one's presence in favor of the phone and to project and invest our energies in an inevitably fabricated and sometimes self-consciously fake image of ourselves have undeniably dangerous and damaging effects.

34 Cecil Kuhne, ed. *Seeing Through the Eye: Malcom Muggeridge on Faith* (San Francisco: Ignatius Pres, 2005), p. 16.

35 Said by a student of mine, summarizing her struggles with anxiety.

36 "Paul Tillich reads cultural history as a series of anxiety attacks....he might have characterized postmodernity as the anxiety of truthlessness." Kevin J. Vanhoozer, *The Drama of Doctrine: A Canonical–Linguistic Approach to Christian Theology* (Louisville: Westminster John Knox, 2005), p. 2.

37 Each successive generation in this culture has felt the philosophical winds shift more intensely and the temperature dropping lower as a long-coming storm (which started across the Atlantic) approached more closely. That storm has arrived, has opened upon the young, and pours down with increasing ferocity. Those who snidely decry what they perceive as whining and weakness in this generation should remember and be moved to compassion by the fact that they, unlike so many young adults, weren't born drowning.

38 "Temporality and the inevitable change that attends it renders the postmodern community as illusory as postmodern subjectivity. The community we depend upon to legitimate our interpretive activity appears to be there... until we look for it." Troup, *Temporality*, p. 168.

39 James White, citing James Le Fanu in *Why Us: How Science Rediscovered the Mystery of Ourselves* (London, Harper, 2008), in "The Triune God of Scripture Lives." You can watch the debate at https://www.youtube.com/watch?annotation_id=annotation_3162430005&feature=iv&src_vid=UNZh-4pDio0&v=UNZh-4pDio0#t=19s.

40 See Numbers 6:22 and following. God told Aaron, Israel's "high priest," that the blessing that begins in verse 24 was to be given to the people of Israel, especially as gathered in worship. Significantly, the corporate blessing is composed in the singular. "The LORD bless you...." "You" is singular, indicating the solidarity of God's people beneath his love and blessing. As we're starting to see in this chapter and will see more fully next chapter, God, from his very being, loves oneness composed of beautiful diversity.

41 Italics added. "...hitherto it has thought to perform it analogically, by means of mechanical or organic models. Now we can pass beyond these, knowing that they are inadequate, and address ourselves to the task directly,

using whatever methods the nature of the material demands." John Macmurray, *Persons in Relation* (Amherst: Humanity Books, 1961, 1999) p. 12, second paragraph, pp. 12–3.

42 In the Sermon on the Mount Jesus begins his messianic ministry by correcting popular opinion about God's written word, saying frequently, "You have heard that it was said...but I say to you." However, Jesus never corrects Scripture itself, his citation of which he prefaced by saying, "It is written." See chapter 8.

43 Jesus healed people of dreadful diseases and tamed nature, but primarily as an authentication of his claim to fulfill the Scriptures. His miracles served his message. See Luke 5:17 and following.

44 See Acts 5, especially verse 39 on this point.

45 James White's debate with Dan Barker is illustrative here. Barker says that if White were to predict that a meteorite would crash the next day into the building where they were debating, were to tell him the mineral composition of said astral stone, that he would believe that his opponent is a prophet and that his God is the true god. Yet Jesus fulfilled hundreds—hundreds!—of ancient prophecies written centuries and even millennia before him, in exacting detail. Skeptics object, *But that was so then! And the documents claiming those fulfillments have been tampered with!* Well, when they have been altered, such alterations have been admitted and corrected. The "critical" editions of the Hebrew Old Testament and the Greek New Testament contain histories of textual transmission through the centuries, list aberrations, and even rank the relative reliability, based on age and number of manuscripts known, of translation decisions within canonically controversial texts. See Karl Elliger, Willhelm Rudulph, and Institute for New Testament Textual Research, eds. *Biblica Hebraica Stuttgartensia* (Peabody: Hendrickson Publishers, 2007) and Kurt Aland, *Greek–English New Testament* (Stuttgart: Deutsche Bibelgesellschaft, 2008).

Christianity has nothing to hide, and the Bible has nothing to be ashamed of in its contextually grounded claims of prophecy and fulfillment. The New Testament, which tells us of Jesus and his fulfillment of the Old Testament, "...is by far the best-attested writing of antiquity." Walter A. Elwell and Robert W. Yarbrough, *Encountering the New Testament: A Historical and Theological Survey* (Grand Rapids: Baker Academic, 2005), p. 28. There is no shortage of good, scholarly, credible works by Bible-believing Christians who counter the typical skepticism described above. And, of course, there are counterpoints. But the common dogma that faith is opposed to reason goes insufficiently challenged in pop culture. Scripture tells us that unbelief is not a problem of evidence, it's a problem of ethics (Psalm 14, Romans 1).

46 C. S. Lewis, "Miracles," *God in the Dock: Essays on Theology and Ethics* (Grand Rapids: Eerdmans, 1973), p. 25.

47 Dietrich Bonhoeffer, *Dietrich Bonhoeffer's Works, Volume 2: Act and Being* (Minneapolis: Fortress, 1996), p. 81.

48 Augustine, *Confessions*, 1.6.10, cited in Troup, *Temporality*, p. 154.

49 And yet, lest we degrade the importance and unique power of the spoken word, the Bible lets us know that its written words were meant to be preached. Paul commands and encourages Timothy, "Preach the word" (2 Timothy 4:2). In context, Paul tells Timothy to do this despite, and in some ways because of, the fact that people will not want to hear the faithful biblical preaching he's commending. The Holy Spirit makes the reading, and especially the preaching, of God's word effective in the freeing and renewing of God's image-bearers.

50 See Kevin DeYoung, *Taking God at His Word: Why the Bible Is Knowable, Necessary, and Enough, and What That Means for You and Me* (Wheaton: Crossway, 2014).

51 Sinclair B. Ferguson, *From the Mouth of God: Trusting, Reading, and Applying the Bible* (Carlisle: Banner of Truth, 2014), p. 3. This is an excellent resource from a scholar whose every writing is worth far more than the purchase price and who is considered to be one of the finest preachers in the English speaking world.

52 From Revelation 21:5, italics mine.

Chapter 6

1 Halsey, "Strangers," *Hopeless Fountain Kingdom* (Astralwerks), 2017.

2 Prior to delivering a lecture at Ohio State University, Christian apologist Ravi Zacharias was shown a building on campus hailed as "America's first postmodern building," designed by the architect to have no design, reflecting life's senselessness and meaninglessness. Zacharias asked his tour guide if the architect built the basement according to the same principles. Silence ensued. Recalling the incident, Zacharias says, "You and I can fool with the infrastructure as much as we would like, but we dare not fool with the foundation because it will call our bluff in a hurry." Meaninglessness cannot be understood absent meaning, as demonstrated by that very expensive architectural exercise in unintended irony. Read a portion of that recollection at https://www.thegospelcoalition.org/blogs/justin-taylor/ravi-zacharias-on-postmodern-architecture-at-ohio-state/.

3 Stories that are bizarre by design or that purposely promote ideas widely recognized as horrific and hurtful could be "great" in the artistry of their telling, but even then, they have to have a certain amount of coherence and internal integrity to make any sense to the audience. Even the most extreme artistic proclamations of randomness are inevitably received, processed, and evaluated by the minds of its observers, which function according to particular categories of cognition and feeling. The artist's attempt to convey meaninglessness, and the observer's effort to make sense of the senselessness, imply the art's failure to make its intended point.

4 If you've not had the pleasure, look up and listen to Brian Regan's "Stupid in School." The first time I heard it, I laughed so hard tears actually shot out of my eyes.

5 Some might prefer the term "humanity," as in, "The humanity of the film was its greatest virtue." I mean essentially the same thing by "humanness" but want to bring it in line with my "ness" words throughout the book. I also

want to distinguish the term from "humanity" as it refers to the collective mass of human beings.

6   Christopher Hitchens had a feisty interaction with his ardent admirer, Bill Maher, on the trend in the 2000s to mock then-President George Bush as a moron. Hitchens refers to such mockers as the unintelligent ones. Maher is clearly stung, and the audience boos. Hitchens cusses the crowd out. Hitchens meant a lot to Maher; it's rare if not completely unique to see on his face the evidence of hurt feelings. Maher's tribute to the late Hitchens includes this interaction. https://christopherhitchens.net/bill-maher.

7   A subtle example of the dehumanizing, deflating effect of denying moral truth occurs in the first *Night at the Museum* film. Ben Stiller plays the "meh" motif, up to and even through the climactic speech he gives to unite the culturally and chronologically diverse statues-come-to-life within the museum at which he works. Teddy Roosevelt, a person of genuine and great historical consequence, hails the bland everyman as a great man. Stories about "average" people doing something way above average can be great as the character reaches up and beyond typical, predictable experience. But Stiller's character does nothing of the sort. He gives a blah speech about how we should all pull together to get along. It's totally deflating. Nevertheless, Robin Williams's Roosevelt, the blood and guts warrior who spoke of the need to strive courageously in the arena, beams at him. Pure shenanigans. Maybe it's an intentional link to Stiller's other films, tethered all the way back to *Reality Bites* with its proto-emo sensibilities. Something like: life is meaningless; just enjoy the details. So out of that meaninglessness comes a spark toward selflessness that's relatively inspiring. Yawn. The only way this sequence has integrity is if its intent was irony: living statue Roosevelt delights in someone that would make real-life Roosevelt sick. But sadly, it seems the scene's intent was to play it straight. We're supposed to think insipid is inspiring. If it works, then we're seeing how radically reduced our sense of inspiration has become.

8   At least in her opening scene. At the end, she dithers about helplessly as Robin battles the Sheriff of Nottingham, brilliantly played by Alan Rickman (Snape from the Harry Potter films).

9   Watson speaks to this in an interview you can see at https://www.youtube.com/watch?v=u9zSPpDNQaw.

10   See the full review at https://www.rollingstone.com/movies/movie-reviews/star-wars-the-force-awakens-103677/.

11   In *Thor: Ragnarok*, the hero condescendingly praises a woman who fought on his home world of Asgard in an elite female-only band of warriors. Thor tells her that it's about time such a group existed and got their rightful respect, complementing his comments with a thumbs-up and a wink. The chauvinism fits Thor's character, but I wonder if the filmmakers weren't pushing back a bit through the god of thunder and having some fun mocking mandated salutes to feminism in a way that wouldn't get them in trouble on social media. The interviews in the film's bonus material more than make absolution for any such rebellion, though, as the actors fall all over themselves to make sure audiences know how thrilled they are to have strong

female leads in the film, especially as inspirational examples for the kids who will see it.

12 For the 2018 season of the WNBA, it was announced that tickets sales will fund a number of businesses, included Planned Parenthood. It's hard to imagine an organization that's done more to harm to girls and women.

13 See 1 Kings 10; Judges 4; Luke 2:36 and following; Acts 18:26.

14 The significance of this expression is the subject of sharp, perennial disagreement between Catholics and Protestants. But the Council of Ephesus in 431, an early church deliberative assembly important to the defining theological beliefs of both church groups, declared that because Jesus Christ is fully God, the virgin Mary should be called *Theotokos*—Greek for God-bearer. See Luke 2:34ff and John 19:26ff. See also Philip Schaff, *History of the Chrisitian Church, 8 Volumes* (Peabody: Hendrickson, 1994).

15 Feminism as a term covers a wide range of philosophically complex and sophisticated strains of thought. My focus in this chapter is on its most popular expressions in our culture, which seem so self-defeating. Despite movements like #MeToo, popular feminism seems practically servile to sexually greedy men who prowl about in entertainment and news media and in the hookup culture in general. For an introduction and overview of feminism as a philosophy and as a critic of traditional philosophy, see Eve Browning Cole, *Philosophy and Feminist Criticism: An Introduction* (New York: Paragon House, 1993). Cole writes that feminist philosophy does not try to see with a "God's-eye view," as does traditional philosophy, but rather avoids "the flight into abstraction whenever possible" and, latching itself to particular historical situations, seeks "the liberation of human beings from all forms of oppression," p. 2. As we've explored, though, it's precisely the forced separation between the metaphysical and the physical that renders laudable efforts for human liberation rootless and aimless, and leaves them susceptible to becoming their monstrous mirror opposites (Matthew 22:37-40).

16 "The work of art is the object seen in light of the eternal; and the good life is the world seen in light of the eternal. That is the connexion between art and ethics." Colin E. Gunton citing (and simplifying a bit) a Ludwig Wittgenstein observation. See Colin E. Gunton, *The One, the Three, and the Many: God, Creation, and the Culture of Modernity—the 1992 Bampton Lectures* (Cambridge: Cambridge University Press, 1993), p. 176.

17 Gunton notes that art, for most of its history, has incorporated some kind of redemptive vision. It presupposed that reality was meaningful. Art "…is therefore inextricably involved with the question of moral good, which does not mean that it must be didactically moral, but rather must in some way or other come to an understanding of its relation to human moral reality." Gunton, *The One, the Three, and the Many*, p. 175.

18 My deft use of expressions like this one demonstrates my ability to relate to young adults in my work as a college chaplain, and foreshadows similarly my abiding relevance for readers, no matter what your current age or when in history you read this. Dope verbage like this is consummately and constantly, epically and everlastingly, amazeballs.

19 Here, I'm not considering *Harry Potter and the Cursed Child*, written as a play, as truly a part of the Harry Potter book series.

20 It drives me crazy when people do that, depriving us of the joy of discovering and reacting, totally unprepared, to the stories and characters who may end up meaning so much to us. There's a reason it's called "spoiling" and not simply "revealing."

21 J. K. Rowling, *Harry Potter and the Sorcerer's Stone* (New York: Scholastic, 1997), p. 291.

22 Though there does seem to be a divide in Rowling's mind between big evil and little evil, between malicious deception and the situational ethics in which lying is considered no big deal. Ethics is a complex subject, and in a fallen world, the right thing to do can be hard to figure out. The great moral guide in Harry's world seems to be love, but it doesn't take too long before different people begin to define love in different ways, revealing their deepest and perhaps unspoken or even unrealized ethical commitments. See chapter 9 of this book.

23 In quoting as many musical artists as the publication could afford, and in mentioning portions of popular films, I am not saying, "See! They're trying to express what the Bible teaches!" I'm trying to treat them according to my best assessment of their authorial intent, and to see if and how what these artists say, sing, and put on film engages biblical truth.

24 Some Christians try to spot Jesus anywhere and everywhere they can in popular art, regardless of the artist's intentions. On the other hand, the film version of *A Wrinkle in Time* is criticized for ditching the Christian worldview that Madeleine L'Engle, the book's author, intended to convey. See Kim Renfro's critique at https://www.thisisinsider.com/wrinkle-in-time-movie-changes-book-religion-christianity-ending-2018-3. Contrast this with the Lord of the Rings trilogy. Its brilliant director, Peter Jackson, said candidly that he did not share the Christian worldview of J. R. R. Tolkien, the author of the beloved book series upon which the films are based. But Jackson and his crew committed early on to try to be true to that worldview in their telling the tale of Frodo and his epic jewelry. See the interviews of Jackson in the bonus features included with the extended versions of the films.

25 Harry is obviously meant to be a "Christ figure." But even there, we should be cautious. That concept has been reduced to apply to any literary character who is heroically self-sacrificial. Eagerness among Christians to see Jesus everywhere in their favorite stories may say more about the thinness of popular Christian theology than it does about the implicit presence of biblical truth in all aspects of life.

26 See chapter 4 on this.

27 The Bible is a metanarrative, an overarching story that unifies and makes sense of the various details of life. And audacious artist that he is, God claims that his work is definitive. It's *the* story of life, and therefore of humanity. As we dealt with in the endnotes of chapter 4, in every era of its composition and as a composite whole, the Bible sees itself as the corrective, not the counterpart, of other religions and their metanarratives, including atheism (Romans 1, Psalm 14).

28 See Sinclair B. Ferguson, *The Holy Spirit (Countours of Christian Theology)*, (Downers Grove: InterVarsity, 1999).

29 Hold your horses, Hebrew-scholar honchos. I'm not saying that Genesis 1:26 and following is a prooftext for the Trinity, only that the complexity of the being of the triune God is at least consistent with, if not slyly implied by, the pluralization "Let us…" The "plural of majesty" gains true majesty as we see within it the presence of a reality-defining truth whose expression grows and gains strength, definition, and precision throughout Scripture, culminating in the crystalline clarity of Matthew 28:18–20.

30 Especially in the poetic sections (see the opening of Psalm 24), the Hebrew Scriptures advance ideas by repeating them with slightly different wording. "Whom shall I send…" means the same thing as "…who will go for us," but the second clause advances the first, moving the question from God's inner thoughts to his outward invitation, to which Isaiah responds eagerly. Given the rest of Isaiah's writing—chapter 61 especially—and the development of Scripture's doctrine of God since Genesis 1, to understand the pluralization "us" as merely a plural of majesty is to sever this linguistic device from the theological context in which the author employs it.

31 Paul expresses the same theology by the same linguistic means as he gives a quintessential Christian blessing in 2 Corinthians 13:14: "The grace of the Lord Jesus Christ and the love of God and the fellowship of the Holy Spirit be with you all."

32 See Wayne Grudem, *Systematic Theology: An Introduction to Biblical Doctrine* (Leicester: InterVarsity and Grand Rapids: Zondervan, 1993). There are many—oh, so many—systematic theologies. This one stands out for its accessible language and the author's exemplary fairness and kindness to people and viewpoints with which he personally disagrees.

33 "For Kant, the mind is constitutionally lonely." D. C. Schindler, *The Catholicity of Reason* (Grand Rapids: Eerdmans, 2013), p. 42.

34 Colin E. Gunton, *The One, the Three, and the Many: God, Creation, and the Culture of Modernity—the 1992 Bampton Lectures* (Cambridge: Cambridge University Press, 1993), p. 118.

35 Gunton citing Samuel Taylor Coleridge. The fuller quotation is "Plato… perceived…that the knowledge of man by himself was not practicable without the knowledge of other things, or rather that man was that being in whom it pleased God that the consciousness of others' existence should abide, and that therefore without natural philosophy and without the sciences which led to the knowledge of objects without us, man himself would not be man." Gunton, p. 15, citing from *The Philosophical Lectures of Samuel Taylor Coleridge*, edited by Kathleen Coburn (London: Pilot Press, 1949), p. 176.

Natural philosophy and the sciences assume our ability to, with increasing but never exhaustive or infallible accuracy, understand and express reality. Even if we still insist that we are bound by our perceptions of that reality, we simply could not live life were it not possible to reach mutually agreeable perceptions, which suggests that we have far greater access to actual reality than we like to admit when our common access to truth reminds us uncomfortably of our moral accountability to it.

36 One of the arguments for maintaining abortion rights, and often the exception granted by those who oppose them, has to do with life created through rape or incest. I knew a woman who was the result of incestuous rape. Once again, I'm not coming close to pretending that I can understand what a victim goes through. My concern is the popular idea that carrying through with such a pregnancy, rather than killing the child conceived, is what will more seriously damage and further traumatize the mother. It is typical of the biblical God to take some of the worst, most dehumanizing wickedness humans can endure and to bring from it deeply humanizing good, and even actual human life. The crucified and now risen Christ can attest to this, and he does so in Scripture. See Philippians 2 for Paul's use of this truth and motif as a foundation for ethics.

37 Esther Lightcap Meek, *Loving to Know: Covenant Epistemology* (Eugene: Cascade, 2011), p. 216.

38 Skylar Grey, "Love the Way You Lie," *Don't Look Down* (Aftermath; Shady; Interscope), 2013. The song portrays an evil inside-out of loving Withness as the singer expresses an undying loyalty, an addiction, to a mutually abusive relationship.

39 Bram Stoker, *Dracula*, Kindle edition, a public domain book.

40 As we thought about in Psalm 139, God is everywhere. But we're too busy searching for God to consider what it might actually mean to find him. In *Miracles*, C. S. Lewis captures memorably the essential disingenuousness of some of our supposedly open-minded spiritual searching. "There comes a moment when people who have been dabbling in religion ('Man's search for God'!) suddenly draw back. Supposing we really found him? We never meant to come to that! Worse still supposing he has found us?" cited from Alister McGrath, *Doubting: Growing through the Uncertainties of Faith* (Downers Grove, 2006), p. 105.

41 "Remember your mortality"—also the title of a fantastic album by Flyleaf, when Lacey Sturm was their lead singer.

42 C. S. Lewis, *The Weight of Glory: And Other Addresses* (New York: Harper-Collins, 1980), p. 46.

43 See Rosaria Butterfield, *The Secret Thoughts of an Unlikely Convert* (Pittsburgh: Crown & Covenant Publications, 2012).

44 McGrath, p. 105, citing C. S. Lewis from *Miracles*.

45 G. K. Chesterton, "The Ethics of Elfland," *Orthodoxy* (SnowBall Classics Publishing), 2015.

46 "...I inquire whether the happy life is in the memory." —After mentioning Adam as the possible source of this memory. "Unless we knew it, we would not love it." Augustine, *The Confessions*, trans. John K. Ryan (New York: Doubleday, Image, 1960), p. 249.

47 Augustine, p. 251.

48 Sherlock Holmes in *A Study in Scarlet*. This is not to say that the character believed the Bible, much less its version of how humanity came to be. In context, Holmes is recounting Charles Darwin's belief that the power to appreciate and produce music existed long before our ability to speak. Holmes's musings on that point produce his eloquent foray into the subject that so captivated Augustine, the mysterious, deep-seated sense of connection humans have to our species' origins.

49 Chesterton, "A Defense of Heraldry," *The Defendant* (Dover Publications, 2012).

50 Rosaria Butterfield, *Openness Unhindered: Further Thoughts of an Unlikely Convert on Sexual Identity and Union with Christ* (Pittsburgh: Crown & Covenant Publications, 2015), p. 3.

51 Augustine, p. 278.

Chapter 7

1 Nietzsche, from *Beyond Good and Evil*, section 188.

2 Sia, "Jesus Wept," *This Is Acting* (Inertia; Monkey Puzzle; RCA), 2016.

3 See Harry Potter on this, especially *Harry Potter and the Half Blood Prince*. Rowling gently and poignantly guides us through young Harry's heart as he learns heartbreaking, idealism-shattering truths about his father's past.

4 D. A. Carson, *How Long, O Lord? Reflections on Suffering and Evil*, 2nd ed. (Grand Rapids: Baker, 2006), p. 205.

5 See especially the gospel of John on this. From sentence one, John draws our attention to Jesus Christ. Jesus says that to know him is to know God the Father (John 14). Throughout his gospel, perhaps nowhere more powerfully and poignantly than chapter 17, John focuses our hearts upon Jesus's relationship to his heavenly father and his understanding and acceptance of the redemptive work his father gave him to do.

6 Two of the best are D. A. Carson, *How Long, O Lord? Reflections on Suffering and Evil*, 2nd ed. (Grand Rapids: Baker, 2006); Christopher J. H. Wright, *The God I Don't Understand: Reflections on Tough Questions of Faith* (Grand Rapids: Zondervan, 2008). For a heavier read, due largely to its being written in 1663, see Thomas Watson, *All Things for Good: An Exposition of Romans 8:28*, available from various publishers.

7 There are still similar customs in various places in the world. In South Sudan, for example, when people want to welcome an elder from another clan, they cut a cow in half, letting its blood seep into the dirt road that leads into the village. The visiting elder jumps over the animal and proceeds in promised peace into what could otherwise have been enemy territory. Similar to what God was saying to Abram, those receiving the elder are saying, "If any harm befalls you, let what happened to this animal happen to us."

8 See Exodus 3 and "the burning bush" incident for an important example. Here, God speaks out of a holy fire the name by which he wants to be known among his people. Jesus applies this name to himself. His enemies understood the significance of his statement and tried to kill him because, in their minds, he'd committed the severest of blasphemies. See John 8:48 and following.

9 See Psalm 8; Matthew 5:44-45; and John 3:16.

10 Each of these truths unfolds into fuller detail as Scripture moves ahead, but the pivotal nature of the passage is shown in God's changing Abram's name and in the content of what God promises: to give Abraham a son when it was biologically impossible for Abram and his wife to have one.

11 Put this way by Dr. Rick Gamble, during lectures given at Reformed Presbyterian Theological Seminary.

12 There is actually an idiom in Hebrew that denotes God's "flaming nostrils." It was a Hebrew way of symbolizing God's anger, similar to what we mean by red-faced, or even the very similar description "nostrils flaring." In Psalm 18, David celebrates a God-given victory by picturing him as a fire-breathing dragon.

13 "Kierkegaard consolidated the opposition to Kant's moral optimism in asserting the power of men to fulfill their personalities in the despair of defiance. Nietzsche joined Kierkegaard in affirming that man's freedom can be diabolically, no less than heteronomously, expressed....No weak personality leads a civilized nation to moral disaster and a continent to ruin." John R. Silber, from "The Ethical Significance of Kant's *Religion*" within Immanuel Kant, *Religion within the Limits of Reason Alone*, Theodore M. Greene and Hoyt H. Hudson, trans. (New York: Harper & Row, 1960), p. cxxix.

14 The great problem Kierkegaard sought to tackle in his day was: "how to become a true Christian when one has the disadvantage of living in the midst of Christendom." Justo Gonzalez, *The Story of Christianity, Volume 2: The Reformation to the Present Day* (San Francisco: Harper, 1985), p. 291. Kierkegaard wanted a real faith in a living God, not an existentially inconsequential system of abstractions and theological theories that treat the content of Christian faith as mind candy and which, as a result, can't help but trivialize the pained life we live in a fallen world.

15 Kierkegaard has a brutal field day with a moralistic reading of Genesis 22. His commentary is a sharp, on-point rebuke to all who treat the Bible as just a book full of moral object lessons taught through its characters. Still today this text is preached as if God's reason for giving it is to teach us to sacrifice our best and most beloved belongings to him. So Kierkegaard imagines a preacher who handles the text that way, and then a faithful parishioner coming to him the next day: "I did it! I killed my boy, I gave God my best!" Awwwkwarrrrd...See Søren Kierkegaard, *Fear and Trembling and The Sickness Unto Death*, Walter Lowrie, trans. (Garden City: Doubleday, 1954).

16 Kierkegaard writes of the "knight of faith," a symbolic person who represents a perfection of faith Kierkegaard said he could not attain. Kierkegaard stares with horror and admiration at a faith that absorbs everything that staggers his soul, at a trust too wonderful and terrible for him to touch, at a loving loyalty too otherworldly to grasp. Kierkegaard finds this mystifying, majestic, monstrous faith displayed in the unthinkable actions of Abraham in Genesis 22. See *Fear and Trembling* under "Problem 2," p. 78 and following of the previously cited edition.

17 "It is supposed to be difficult to understand Hegel, but to understand Abraham is a trifle. To go beyond Hegel is a miracle, but to get beyond

Abraham is the easiest thing of all. I for my part have devoted a good deal of time to the understanding of the Hegelian philosophy…but when in spite of the trouble I have taken there are certain passages I cannot understand, I am foolhardy enough to think that he himself has not been quite clear. All this I do easily and naturally, my head does not suffer from it. *But on the other hand when I have to think of Abraham, I am as though annihilated.*" Søren Kierkegaard, *Fear and Trembling and The Sickness Unto Death*, Walter Lowrie, trans. and intro, (Garden City: Doubleday, 1954), p. 44, italics mine. Georg Wilhelm Friedrich Hegel (1770–1831) was a prominent German philosopher. His work was important enough to occupy the serious attention of the philosophical greats who succeeded him, such as Kierkegaard and Nietzsche. See John Frame, *A History of Modern Philosophy and Theology* (Phillipsburg, NJ: P&R Publishing, 2015).

18 Abraham was no saint. When he and his wife had to journey through Egypt, Abraham gave his wife to Pharaoh to do with her what he wanted. His reason? His wife was beautiful and he knew powerful Egyptians would want her and therefore might kill him. So he told her to lie and to tell people that he and his wife were siblings. Honest Abe? Not so much. Faithful, loving, protective husband? Not in that situation. But Abraham also had moral highlights of culture-defying self-deprecation and death-defying courage.

When he and his nephew Lot had to part ways because their respective employees were not getting along, Abraham deferred to Lot and let him choose which land he'd like to live in. It likely wasn't a true offer, but nor was it untruthful. It was in that culture an opportunity for the social inferior to show respect and deference and say, "So kind of you! But of course you must choose first." Lot ignored the social cue; his response was more akin to, "Cool. I'm taking the good land. Later, Uncle Abe!" Abraham let this insult to his honor pass, and even rescued Lot later when things went hellfire and brimstone in the city he'd chosen to live in, a profoundly evil place to which Lot had essentially sold his soul. See Genesis 13 and following. Abraham and Lot, just like the rest of us, needed a Redeemer, the Savior who'd come through Abraham's son.

19 Kierkegaard, *Fear and Trembling*, p. 35.

20 In the Greek, you can see the Greek word that gives rise to our English word "logic."

21 Kierkegaard, *Fear and Trembling*, p. 47.

22 Note in Genesis 21 how many times "his son" occurs, contrasted with verse 8, where we're told that Abraham made a great feast to celebrate a significant time in his young boy's life. Even when Isaac is not referred to as "his son Isaac," we're told how much Abraham loved and celebrated his boy.

23 By this point in Genesis, we've read of God's moral stand against evil, of his mercifully not destroying Adam and Eve following their rebellion, but also of his flooding the world in an unimaginable cataclysm of judgment. And yet even there, he'd sent a preacher named Noah to warn people for a century about the coming judgment and to offer them escape. God was not to be trifled with, but nor was he a tyrant.

24 Kierkegaard, *Fear and Trembling*, p. 64.

25 Peter Rollins writes against the idea that the Bible is a text at one with itself, calling that belief "the ultimate fantasy of the fundamentalist." Peter Rollins, *The Fidelity of Betrayal: Towards a Church Beyond Belief* (Brewster: Paraclete, 2008), p. 17. "Fundamentalist" is used somewhat derisively here to refer to close-minded Christians who can't or won't engage serious scholarly questions regarding the composition and content of the Bible. That Christians within particular streams of Christian thought have had this attitude is as sad as it is undeniable. Yet there are a growing number of relatively new, excellent scholarly works that join the tide of older, classic works (such as B. B. Warfield's *The Inspiration and Authority of Scripture*) in tearing holes in the old but newly dusted off patchwork quilt model. Please read both sides of the argument and see what you think. It's actually more historically accurate to say that the "canonization" of Scripture was much more a process of recognition than one of invention. The definitive assembly of God's written word was confirmed by the church, not created by the church. See especially the work of Michael J. Kruger, *Canon Revisited: Establishing the Origins and Authority of the New Testament Books* (Wheaton: Crossway, 2012) and *The Question of Canon: Challenging the Status Quo in the New Testament Debate* (Downers Grove: InterVarsity, 2013).

26 See chapter 3.

27 See the work of Geerhardus Vos, especially *Biblical Theology: Old and New Testaments* (Eugene: Wipf and Stock Publishers, republished 2003). The acorn analogy is from Dr. Rick Gamble and based upon Vos's analogy of a rose.

28 Notice, God has to "put" enmity—hostility—between the woman and the serpent, between Eve and Satan, it means they'd been getting along just fine. I owe this insight to my friend Dr. Michael LeFebvre. Part of God's grace in saving people is his helping us to realize the hellishness of our separation from him. We feel our godding's consequences and we hate them, but we won't put two and two together to admit their cause. By his word, God helps us to see and to confess that connection. His grace alerts us to the true nature of our godding, while the ancient Enemy keeps trying to gloss it up and call it freedom. We'll explore this more fully next chapter.

29 God's arrangement of life in the garden is referred to as the covenant of works. Adam broke this covenant and, as we'll see next chapter, Christ kept it (Romans 5). The covenant of grace, beginning in Genesis 3:15, runs through the rest of Scripture and, subsumed within it, as its historical heightening and advancement, are many other covenants such as the Noahic covenant (Genesis 9), the Mosaic covenant (which includes the Ten Commandments of Exodus 20) and the Davidic covenant (2 Samuel 7). For a wonderful guide to Scripture through the lens of God's covenants, see David McKay, *The Bond of Love: God's Covenantal Relationship with His Church* (Fearn, UK: Christian Focus, 2001).

30 The "major" prophets are Isaiah, Jeremiah, Ezekiel, and Daniel and are named such simply for the length of their prophecies and the expansive nature of their content. The "minor" prophets are Hosea, Joel, Amos, Obadiah,

Jonah, Micah, Nahum, Habakkuk, Zephaniah, Haggai, Zechariah, and the Old Testament's last book, Malachi. Reading the minor prophets in particular is like reading today's headlines. James in his style and thematic concerns is like a New Testament minor prophet.

31 Matthew begins his description of Christ's ancestry with Abraham. See Matthew 1:2 and following.

32 Kierkegaard talks about a "teleological suspension of the ethical," let's call it TSOE, in the "Problem 1" section of *Fear and Trembling*, p. 64 and following of the previously cited edition. Basically, Abraham put his ethics on pause, followed through with God's seemingly unethical command, trusting that he'd gain his heart's good desire, somehow, on the other side of it. He trusted that he'd get Isaac back, but he had to, in a sense, step out of his own moral constraints to get there. Thus, his trust in God is that much more credible. Abraham has consciously submitted himself to a truth that transcends his ability to understand and approve, but he could not do so if the command did not come from someone worthy of trust. Hmm… There's something to this, but not enough. This is where Kierkegaard perhaps fights a bit too much with the passage, or at least, expends too much energy on a good attack for a different battle.

Kierkegaard's TSOE depends upon the constant, unchangeable goodness of the one giving the bad command—otherwise, it could be used to argue for allegiance, however temporary, to terrible ideas, things, and people. If Abraham can sidestep God's character with a quick TSOE when he thinks God wants him to, how can he trust that he's really hearing from God and not listening to his own inner demons telling him to do terrible things? Kierkegaard's analysis is immensely helpful in getting us to understand, feel, and wrestle with a terrible text. But it's the covenant of grace that takes us beneath the dark, muddy and slippery surface to the gold buried beneath. Abraham's ordeal was an advancement in history and the most viscerally intense foreshadowing of this covenant in and through which the moral attributes of the relentlessly righteous, infinitely loving God, who desired to save a sinful world, meet and satisfy one another's requirements in Jesus Christ and his redemptive work. No aspect of God's character is suspended or put on hold as this covenant was proclaimed, as it advanced through history, and as it came to its culmination and fulfillment in Christ. See Peter's sermon in Acts 2 and Paul's argument in Romans 3–8 that in Christ, God's attributes are vindicated, not set aside or realigned. Looking to him, no believer has to nullify or temporarily suspend his or her ethics in living life in loving service to God.

33 That's the danger hidden within Nietzsche's wise observation quoted at the head of the chapter. C. S. Lewis picks up on it as well and rounds it out in a Christian ethical direction: take courage and perseverance, both good attributes in themselves, but give them to a person bent on evil, and the evil is as powerful and protracted as the person is brave and steadfast. Evil is parasitic upon good.

34 The story of Joseph, Genesis 30:22 and following.

35 Moses was one such suffering servant. After Israel commits a stunning act of idolatry, right at the base of the mountain where God was giving Moses the Ten Commandments, God tells Moses to back off so that he can destroy them all. Both Moses and Abraham take God very seriously. They don't think he's playing, and he isn't. God isn't playing; he's teaching. Granted, he's pushing his students to beyond the nth degree of their endurance in ways that would make a military drill sergeant blush. But in both cases, God remains true to his promise. Moses cites God's promise to Abraham as one reason why God must not destroy the people. Moses serves as the Christ figure in this exchange—one of the people, uniquely called by God to represent God to the people and the people to God, the prophet, priest, and king of Israel—who learns far more than Abraham knew, whose life was a living example of the kind of savior God would provide. Though God in his righteousness burns against sin, he will not consume those for whom his son intercedes. David dealt with the same issues.

The shepherd–king of Israel, the great defender of God's people and defeater of their enemies, David's writing and life-experience advanced beyond even Moses our understanding of the Christ to come. It's Jesus's pain ultimately but no less David's own pain when he screams out, "My God, my God, Why have you forsaken me?!" By no mere coincidence, Abraham, Moses, and David are three of the most significant people in history, three of the most heavily featured people in Scripture, and three people who, of all people that have ever lived, have come closest in their life's work and experience to the heart of God and the life of God's son who expresses it. This is why Jesus calls John the Baptist the greatest of all who'd ever come before him. Even greater than Abraham, Moses, and David—because John had the unique privilege of introducing people, in person, to the Savior whom those great figures before him could only see from afar.

36 It's especially unhelpful that in some English translations, the word "tempt" is used, as if the idea of sacrificing his son was enticing to Abraham. The King James Version does this, creating an apparent conflict with James as he tells us in chapter 1 that God tempts no one. Surely the KJV meant "test" by its word "tempt" and was simply using the common language of the time, but this translational dilemma demonstrates the need for the plop principle, to interpret Scripture by Scripture.

37 For an exploration of what many see as a contradiction between James and Paul on the basis of our being justified before God, please see/hear my sermon "Justification and Justification" at https://www.sermonaudio.com/sermoninfo.asp?SID=51611736111.

38 See J. I. Packer, *Rediscovering Holiness: Know the Fullness of Life with God* (Grand Rapids: Baker, 2009). Packer wrote the deeply moving afterword entitled "Holiness in the Dark: The Case of Mother Teresa."

39 C. S. Lewis wrote, "I believe in Christianity as I believe that the sun has risen, not only because I see it but because by it, I see everything else." This is from his essay "Is Theology Poetry?" in *The Weight of Glory*. As we've already seen in this book, Lewis is perhaps the most quotable and most often quoted—and therefore often misquoted—Christian thinker of at least the last century or so. To separate the accurate from the inaccurate citations, see William O'Flaherty, *The Misquotable C. S. Lewis: What He Didn't Say, What He Said, and Why It Matters* (Eugene: Wipf and Stock, 2018).

40 Though skeptics roll their eyes at it as gimmicky, it's worth a read: Lee Stroebel, *The Case for Christ: A Journalist's Personal Investigation of the Evidence for Jesus* (Grand Rapids: Zondervan, 1998). The book examines Scripture's claims regarding Jesus's resurrection as well as historically popular alternative explanations of Jesus's empty tomb.

41 Throughout the gospels, Jesus calls "blessed" those who really get it, who understand who he is and who trust him. See Psalm 1 and the opening section of the Sermon on the Mount, often called "The Beatitudes." Jesus is the blessed One, and those whom he makes into children of God increasingly take on the family likeness.

42 After Jesus rose from the dead, a disciple named Thomas would not believe it when others told him that they'd seen the Lord. Thomas wasn't having it. The talk of Christ-sightings probably seemed crazy to Thomas, if not also cruel. Thomas was spent. Like the other disciples, his heart had been ripped out by the brutal death of his beloved Master. Thomas said that unless he could see and feel the nail piercings in Jesus's hands and the spear-inflicted gash in Jesus's side, received when soldiers were checking to see if he was actually dead, he wouldn't believe in the resurrection. Because of this, he's often called "Doubting Thomas." In my opinion, that's mostly unfair, or at least uncharitable, not to mention that healthy skepticism can be a good thing. People forget that earlier on in Jesus's ministry, Thomas led the other disciples in a willingness to die with and for him (John 11:1–16). But after those events, when Jesus did in fact die, Thomas was understandably undone. He and the other disciples hadn't internalized what Jesus said would happen, and they didn't know their Old Testaments well enough to expect God's son to die and then to rise from the dead. They hadn't paid careful enough attention to Father Abraham (Luke 24:25–27).

But one day, in a closed-off room, Jesus appeared to the disciples. Thomas was among them. Jesus gave him the chance to touch his hands and his side, which still bore the scars of his suffering. We don't know whether Thomas took him up on the offer. What we do know is what Thomas said in response: "My Lord and my God!" (John 20:28). Jesus said to him, "Because you have seen me, you have believed; blessed are those who have not seen and yet have believed." Thomas doubted the testimony of his peers, and really, who could blame him? None of them were expecting the resurrection. But he and the other disciples should have understood and trusted the written words God had breathed out so long before and over so many centuries, the words that Jesus had preached and lived out among them. Given John's emphasis throughout his gospel on the word and words of God (1:1–5; 2:17; 6:31, 45, 68; 12:14–15; 17:17), it seems that he tells us about Thomas not to tattle on his doubt, but to trumpet the trustworthiness and Christ-centeredness of the Scriptures.

43 Emphasis mine.

44   Augustine called the Lord's Supper a "visible word."

45   The Bible is sometimes accused of an obvious inconsistency (and thus derided again as a backwards book fit only for the intellectually infirm) when it comes to the time Jesus's body was in the grave. Scripture says that the Savior would be in the grave for three days (Matthew 12:40 has Jesus making this prophecy) and yet clearly, if Jesus died on "Good Friday" and rose on "Easter Sunday," that's far fewer than 72 hours! But that's just the Hebrew way of calendar reckoning. Jesus died and rose again within three days; he rose on the third of three days. Once again, we Western critics of Scripture need to be reminded that the rest of the world doesn't think like we do (and is not the worse for it) and that when we seek to understand their lives, history, culture, and writings, we need first to try to see it as they see it.

46   Have a listen to Dr. Rich Ganz's wonderful message and personal story of conversion to Christ based on the very Scriptures that he thought he knew so well. The message is from April 13, 2016, and is called "The Best Bible Study Ever," http://www.geneva.edu/chapel/15-16-chapel-messages.

47   See the wonderfully helpful book by David Murray, *Jesus on Every Page: 10 Simple Ways to Seek and Find Christ in the Old Testament* (Grand Rapids: Reformation Heritage, 2013).

48   C. S. Lewis, *Perelandra* (New York: Scribner, 1996), p. 40.

49   From a lecture given at the November 2014 meeting of the Evangelical Theological Society in San Diego.

Chapter 8

1   Fiona Apple, "Criminal," *Tidal* (Epic Records), 1996.

2   Some of the Corinthian Christians were claiming that Christ was not risen from the dead because resurrections were impossible. Paul was stupefied. He couldn't believe that they didn't believe in the resurrection, given the vast amounts of evidence for Christ's resurrection and the eyewitness testimony (including his own) to which they had access. He mentions that there are well over 200 living eyewitnesses of Jesus's resurrection, which implicitly says, "Go ask them yourself!" Paul maintains that if Jesus is not risen, then Christianity is pointless and Christians are of all people most pathetic, still living in unforgiven sin and that he and the other apostles are liars for spreading the news of a resurrected Messiah. Most distressing to Paul was that the Corinthians were denying the authority and truthfulness of God's word as preached to them. He reminds the Corinthians that Scripture clearly taught that the Messiah must be crucified, buried, and resurrected. As a trustworthy source of truth, the apostles considered Scripture superior to even eyewitness accounts, of which there were plenty, including their own. Have a listen to "I Don't Know if I'm Agnostic and I Don't Care if I'm Apathetic," from April 15, 2015 at http://www.geneva.edu/chapel/14-15-chapel-messages.

3   We humans hate restraint so much that we'll invent our own realities to escape it—and not just in our minds. We've now got the tech to build another world and rule it as god. But even in that world, reality bites us in the microprocessor. The tech that allows us the most vivid experience of godhood is

subject to rules and regulations. If the tech breaks down, so does our deity. Virtual reality must answer to real reality. Even if we're fine with ignoring the difference between the two, in one way or another, real reality just won't let us forget.

4   See Luke 7:36 and following for a wonderful, and typical, example.

5   God's heart extends to all of creation, plants and animals included. Take a close look at the fourth commandment, and see also Proverbs 12:10. As we'll see in chapter 10, the Bible is the friend of the person passionately committed to the care, cultivation, and preservation of the earth. The Psalms celebrate and extol God's care for all his creation. See Psalms 8, 96, 98, and 104 as examples.

6   For you Harry Potter fans, maybe Adam and Eve were parseltongues!

7   We don't know whether God did add this stipulation to his command. It's significant that the author does not mention it, but we can't determine the significance of that silence with any certainty. There's a real vagueness, or at least a sometimes frustrating lack of detail in the opening chapters of Scripture, but this is natural given what Scripture is and how it works as the unfolding, increasingly detailed word of God whose essential purpose is to point people to life and wholeness in his son.

8   In book 2 of his space trilogy, *Perelandra*, C. S. Lewis writes a mesmerizing meditation on this interaction between Eve and Satan. He imagines the Eve-figure contemplating disobedience as a means of obedience and exposes the subtlety of the Satan-figure in encouraging that thought process. Perhaps it's more instructive than ironic that there are relatively recent books by professing Christians encouraging the same line of thought. See Peter Rollins, *The Fidelity of Betrayal: Towards a Church Beyond Belief* (Brewster: Paraclete, 2008).

9   Psalm 51:5 might be misunderstood to say that the act of conception is sinful. But as we'll see in chapter 9, God is quite in favor of human procreation. He told Adam and Eve to fill the earth with people! (Genesis 1:28).

10   A term referring to people from Asia, which would include the Middle East. Nietzsche viciously mocked what he considered to be the Jewish doom-and-gloom culture, which to him formed the only theological climate dark enough for belief in Jesus as God's son to rise.

11   Friedrich Nietzsche, *The Gay Science*, trans. by Walter Kaufmann (New York: Random House, 1974), p. 187, section 135.

12   Friedrich Nietzsche, *Thus Spoke Zarathustra: A Book for None and All*, trans. Walter Kaufmann (New York: Penguin, 1966), part 4, ch. 67.

13   For a thought-provoking, fascinating compare-and-contrast between two giants of social significance, see Andy Crouch's "Steve Jobs: The Secular Prophet." Written upon Jobs's death, this article recounts his contributions to society and the motives and vision behind them juxtaposed to those of Martin Luther King Jr. Don't worry. The Christian author of this article is respectful of Jobs. This is not one of those "now that he's gone, let's blast him" hit pieces that surface sadistically among the ideological opponents of highly influential, recently deceased people. http://andy-crouch.com/articles/steve_jobs_the_secular_prophet.

14 C. S. Lewis, *The Screwtape Letters* (New York: HarperOne, 1966), p. 44.

15 See Gabriel Vahanian, *The Death of God: The Culture of our Post-Christian Era* (New York: George Braziller), 1961.

16 From Andrew Solomon's June 8, 2018, article, "Anthony Bourdain, Kate Spade, and the Preventable Tragedies of Suicide" at https://www.newyorker. com/news/news-desk/preventable-tragedies. This is a well-meant but disturbingly shallow, if not hollow, attempt to help in the midst of a cultural crisis. Solomon writes, "For someone without a mental disorder or illness, would suicide seem like the permanent answer to temporary woes?" This question is profoundly naïve with regard to young adult culture; it begs the question with regard to suicide causality (and mental illness in general); and it's perilously and offensively close to stigmatizing many people who fall with legitimacy under the diagnosis of mental illness, a phrase that's sadly become a catch-all for harmful sociological behavior we can't understand. Complicating things further is the ever-expanding, sometimes arbitrarily and politically and financially driven definitions of mental illnesses. And the more we lump that which we can't understand into the category of mental illness, the more we stigmatize legitimate sufferers and disenfranchise those who know that what ails them runs deeper than mere biology. Once again, the deadly danger of the false dichotomy between the physical and metaphysical.

17 Lacey Sturm, *The Reason—How I Discovered a Life Worth Living—Revelations of a Rock Princess* (Grand Rapids: Baker, 2014), p. 62.

18 See the June 2015 article by Alex Schadenberg, "Doctor Will Kill Healthy 24-Year-Old in Euthanasia Who's Thought of Suicide Since She Was a Kid," http://www.lifenews.com/2015/06/22/doctor-will-kill-healthy-24-year-old-in-euthanasia-whos-thought-of-suicide-since-she-was-a-kid/. This article has been updated. The young woman described did actually take her life via physician-assisted suicide.

19 A heartbreaking counterexample is the fight to preserve the life of Alfie, a British toddler who suffered from a rare degenerative brain condition. Doctors declared him incurable, and despite his parents' heroic personal and legal fight to get him treatment, and even the offer of the Italian government to fly the boy to Italy to care for his needs there, "His parents lost or were turned away in the High Court, the Supreme Court and European Court of Human Rights. On Wednesday, the British Court of Appeal upheld a ruling that approved the withdrawal of care and sustenance. It also prohibited Alfie's parents from seeking treatment elsewhere." When it wants to, a godding government can say that neither we nor our loved ones have the right to life. As with Alfie, they can even prevent us from trying to live when others are very willing to cover the cost and provide all that's necessary for the fight. See "Alfie Evans, Terminally Ill British Toddler at Center of Court Fight, Dies" by Yonette Joseph, April 28, 2018, at https://www.nytimes. com/2018/04/28/world/europe/uk-alfie-evans-dead.html.

20 The analysis and opinion of Andre Schuten, legal counsel and Director of Law and Policy for the Association for Reformed Political Action.

21 So far, right-to-die fictional films still include token scenes of sadness and the "is this really right?" kind of moments, but ultimately the lesson is that suicide, or assisted suicide, is and can be a beautiful thing. And even if it's not, who are we to say that someone shouldn't off herself? But in real life, these deaths are unspeakably devastating to those left behind; they are victims of suicide as well. The Bible's emphasis on the personal nature of the world and the interdependent nature of all created life, especially human lives, opens potentially life-saving discussions about how we owe our lives to one another, and not just in the conventional way we might think of that notion. Scripture commands us to do everything in our power to promote the good of others, so that means we owe it to others to take good care of ourselves as best we can. It's not self-exaltation, but self-preservation as best we can manage, because whether they acknowledge it or not, our lives are inherently valuable to them. As we'll see next chapter, the content and sequence of God's commands to love teach us how to carry this out in life. Sadly, some hurting souls no longer believe that they are a good to anyone, or that they're good for anything. Thus, again, the importance of receiving and believing truth that is higher than we are.

22 To find a good and well-qualified counselor, see any of the following sites: National Board for Certified Counselors, http://www.nbcc.org/, CounselorFind or American Association of Christian Counselors, which gives referrals by location, http://www.aacc.net. Here's the national suicide prevention hotline, to talk with someone right away: 1-800-273-8255. Also, for organizations promoting mental health awareness and of help to students in particular, see Active Minds at http://www.activeminds.org and The Jed Foundation at http://safercampus.org. Many thanks to my friend and colleague, a pro in the field not least because of her deep compassion, Amy Solman.

23 Psalm 51 closes with mention of the animal sacrifices that, in the Old Testament era, accompanied confession of sin. All that religious butchering was a dreadful but necessary reminder of the awful cost and consequences of sin, and that, for redemption to be possible, an innocent life must take upon itself the guilt and consequences of godding for the guilty. The New Testament book of Hebrews tells us that the blood of animals can never take away sin (Hebrews 10). That was never the point. Those brutal tutorials continued only until Jesus came to offer himself as the true and essential sin offering. That's why John the Baptist called Jesus the Lamb of God (John 1:29).

24 In Genesis 1, God creates by issuing ten "Let…" commands. The tenth culminates in the creation of his image-bearers.

25 See endnote 18 in the previous chapter for a brief overview of Abraham's moral failures and successes.

26 N. T. Wright, *Surprised by Scripture: Engaging Contemporary Issues* (New York: Harper, 2014), p. 121.

27 From Job 13:15.

28 Or sometimes called "divine child abuse" or, as Spong likes to think of it, God the Father taking sinners to the "woodshed" only to have Jesus step in and take the impending abuse for us. This thought and these expressions are

relatively common among some of Christianity's most sarcastic and scathing public critics. It's an understandable inference for people ignorant of the true and deep significance of the cross, and especially for those unwilling to deal with the true and deep significance of sin, and their personal sin. But Spong is a scholar who simply, fundamentally, and categorically rejects the morality Jesus embraced and in service of which he willingly gave his life; Spong is a minister who dons liturgical robes even as he berates the Bible and belittles the historic Christian faith. See Bishop John Shelby Spong, *The Sins of Scripture* (New York: Harper One), 2005, and a public lecture describing the project, https://tvo.org/transcript/795848/video/archive/big-ideas/bishop-john-shelby-spong-on-the-sins-of-scripture. Spong wants to be theistic, but offers nothing in the place of the Christianity he tries to discredit except vacuous, baseless, and unsustainable sentiment. See chapter 3 of this book. Denominations and churches that embrace his approach to faith are dying. See chapter 2 of this book, and endnote 46 in particular. For a mature survey of the biblical material Spong loves to mock, see Joseph W. Smith III, *Sex and Violence in the Bible: A Survey of Explicit Content in the Holy Book* ((Phillipsburg, NJ: P&R, 2014).

29 "Hymn of Men Underground" in *The Gospel in Dostoyevsky*, The Bruderhof, ed. (New York: Orbis, 1988), p. 144.

30 Sturm, *The Reason*, p. 108.

31 Sturm, *The Reason*, p. 109.

Chapter 9

1 Death Cab for Cutie, "I Will Follow You into the Dark," *Plans* (Atlantic), 2006.

2 See my "Brooks, Baseball, and Battles Among Believers," at http://gentlereformation.com.

3 "Heterosexual" and "homosexual," especially when understood as categories of personhood, are byproducts of modernistic psychology, especially the work of Sigmund Freud with his emphasis on sexuality as the great subtext to human behavior. Dr. Christopher Yuan calls us to quit letting godless anthropologies, which in our culture are often uncritically taken as truth, to define all the terms for our understanding of human sexuality. Yuan vies instead for what all people, regardless of the labels we give ourselves, should pursue, what he calls "holy sexuality." See Christopher Yuan, *Holy Sexuality and the Gospel: Sex, Desire, and Relationships Shaped by God's Grand Story* (Colorado Springs: Multnomah, 2018).

4 This is my rendering of Philippians 4:6, italics added. The Greek word I've translated as "worry" is most often translated "anxious," but I want to avoid any implication that Paul is condemning as sinful the struggles we have with anxiety, and especially such struggles in the context of mental health. A related Greek word occurs in 2:28, and I've also rendered that "worry" in my mention of it. This is not to oversimplify a complex dynamic of personhood. It's just to bring related ideas together under the paragraph's thematic concern: that God's word calls us away from thoughts and activities that are

normal and natural to us. Paul is not condemning the besetting, sometimes crippling feeling of unsettledness increasingly common among us, much less those that are of clinical concern for so many. See chapter 5 on this.

5   Matthew 5–7.

6   See chapter 6's use of this passage in its discussion of the Trinity.

7   In the Bible, baptism is fundamentally about identification with someone and the truths that someone proclaims or even personifies. See Mark 1:4; Matthew 28:18–20; 1 Corinthians 10:1–2. When Jesus was baptized, he was officially recognized as God's son and set apart for his messianic work (Matthew 3:13 and following). Christians in "closed" countries—run by governments that declare Christianity illegal—understand the significance of baptism. Talking about Christianity can get you in trouble in those places, but if you get baptized, you've signed your death warrant. Baptism is seen as irrevocable identification with Jesus, a codified loyalty to someone and something higher than the state or the god whose worship the government mandates.

8   Sometimes our claiming to suffer for Christ is really more of a martyr complex. Truly persecuted Christians often demure and deny the severity of their suffering, while pseudo-persecuted Christians boast the scars of online cross-bearing: *The stupid reprobates couldn't handle the truth in my post; THAT'S why they cursed me out and unfriended me.* Sure. That's why.

9   Some may say that this hatred and rejection are deserved, or at least should be expected. Hate breeds hate. And where Christian words and actions have fallen short of God's standards for loving and respecting all human beings, then Christians should expect some return fire. But is it inherently hateful to humbly stand for and to speak out on behalf of Jesus and what he taught?

10 Paul is particularly good at this. See Romans 2 and Acts 17. He never compromises his message. He's conversant and confident enough in the Scriptures to identify the happy inconsistencies in other views of life, signs of truth that should point their practitioners to the true and living God, but that, because of their godding, fail to do so. To see in more detail what God requires of us in doing good to others, see the Westminster *Larger Catechism* on what God requires in the sixth commandment, at http://www.reformed. org. To sum up, it's a lot!

11 The term "non" is often used to designate someone who does not identify with any particular organized religion; we'll use the term "non-Christian" to designate anyone who does not believe the Bible to be what it claims, not because there are not true Christians who fit that category, nor to set up an oversimplified *us vs. them* divide, but just because trying to designate all of what someone might be and/or identify as takes too many words! Much of the New Testament addresses believers who were not acting as such, and the book of Hebrews in particular addresses those who've grown up surrounded by the word of God and have walked away from the faith.

12 In Romans 3, Paul cites Psalm 14 in claiming that no one does good. This is a statement ultimately about humankind's fundamental condition in this world as sinful. Sin has affected all that we are, think, and do. We are

naturally disposed toward self-worship, not the worship of the good God who made the world (Romans 1). The issue here is the way of life to which we belong, by which we are identified: either identified with Christ and covered by his righteousness, or outside of him and identified with our own unrighteousness. Psalm 14 articulates these categories, and Paul mentions them in Romans 5. Paul does not deny that "good" things can be done and are done by non-Christians. In Romans 2 he writes that those who do not know God's law in detail still do things detailed within it, not completely and constantly, not in such a way that they can exonerate themselves from sin or earn a right standing before God, but significantly and to the benefit of their fellow human beings. The good they do expresses the image of God we all bear.

13 Except perhaps Heath Ledger's stunningly portrayed Joker from *The Dark Knight*—the most philosophically consistent portrayal of evil I've ever seen on screen. In this film, the "Clown Prince of Crime" is all about anarchy, bringing down the moral posturing and social civilities behind which we hide our true, latent savagery. Very Voldemort-like but even darker and more self-assured, this Joker is truly, deeply, and unnervingly empty of care for any of his fellow human beings. His killing, maiming, and torturing doesn't serve other, preferred people or some allegedly transcendent moral cause as tyrants throughout history have claimed as justification for their atrocities. As Alfred, Bruce Wayne's butler, puts it, "Some men just want to watch the world burn."

14 Even if our answer is "I don't know," it demands we walk in certain ethical directions and away from others. One could use agnosticism to justify any action with regard to another human, because who's to say it's wrong to do that to humans, or whether a particular *Homo sapiens* should be considered fully human? Or, the same agnosticism could lead us to a cautious approach, reluctant to explore potentially harmful ideas and actions because of potentially devastating effects on organisms that might be considered human. One's particular version of agnosticism always has ethical standards and practical implications. Agnosticism is never the neutral morality/theology some want it to be. It's not the absence of certainty; it's the relocation of it. To be agnostic about something is to be sure you shouldn't come to a hard conclusion about that something, a belief that assumes other hard conclusions about what's knowable and the extent to which we are morally accountable creatures.

15 Even the most thorough historical and scientific analyses cannot ultimately answer questions of human origins, and they especially cannot answer questions of human value, and they're not terribly helpful with human ethics. They can do a lot of "what" but almost no "why."

16 Thus the classification of organizations that vie for "traditional" views of sexuality as "hate groups." While people and organizations can indeed act hatefully, that label is often brandished against any dissenting opinions that challenge the cultural dogma that our personal desires form the basis of unequivocal moral truth and personal ontology. See, as mentioned in the chapter 5 endnotes, Kelly R. Novak's *Let Harry Become Sally* (Andover: Hypothesis Press, 2018), a direct response to Ryan T. Anderson's *When Harry*

Became Sally: Responding to the Transgender Moment (New York: Encounter Books, 2018). Novak comes out swinging in the opening pages, begging the question of what defines truly hateful ideas and behaviors and smearing all dissenters to her thoughts with the label, and accepting uncritically similar labeling from organizations that thrive on the same rhetoric against dissenters. Once again, I encourage you to read both sides of the issue as expressed by their most competent, capable advocates. These two works on transgenderism and the deep struggles and traumas besetting people who personify the issue seem to qualify for such service.

17 Remember, beneath the ceiling, the self is the center of truth, beauty, meaning, and right. So, from that standpoint, to say that it is inherently hateful to promote scriptural standards of sexuality is to say nothing more than the obvious fact that we don't like what the Bible says about such things. In this case, hatred is basically meaningless; or at least, it loses the meaning that the accusers want it to have. Instead of crying, "Hate! We won't stand for that!" we might as well just say, "Opposition! We won't stand for that!" Reducing hate to mean mere opposition cheapens the concept. Hate really means something, but that's only because there is a higher standard to which each of us holds all people and by which we evaluate them as potential haters. The question is, whose standards do we consider to be the most accurate when it comes to accusations of hate?

18 Read through 1 John on this and note how many times the word "liar" is used.

19 See chapter 6.

20 The goal of education used to be learning to love what is truly lovely and to hate what is truly worth hating. But in our godding, love and hate and truth and right and beauty are all centered in the self, so "love" is intense affection for anything the self finds itself admiring or wanting or appreciating; and "hate" is what tries to discourage the same.

21 Psalm 61 expresses this beautifully. Verse 2: "…lead me to the rock that is higher than I."

22 We have to measure personal sincerity against objective truth. After all, isn't it the essence of abusive authority to tell us that no matter what we think and feel, we must comply, we must conform? But the opposite is true as well. To say that anything we think and feel is good and right is also a tyranny; it reduces the self to an unregulated mass of mere cravings and it means a whole lot of trouble for other people, depending on what we crave. Only tyrants think tyranny is loving.

23 As we thought about in chapter 6, self-preservation is not the priority it needs to be in our culture. Self-worship, including the darkness of self-loathing and self-harm, has taken its place. As sin always does, it's given us the opposite of what it promises us. We are indeed to love, to care for, and to seek the good of ourselves. How else should we treat one of God's favorite creations?

24 See Esther Lightcap Meek, *Loving to Know: Covenant Epistemology* (Eugene: Cascade, 2011).

25 Augustine taught that true education is a reciprocity of love. The teacher loves student and subject matter, and the student grows to love subject matter and teacher.

26 That's my translation. I'm not sure unhypocritical is an English word, but it really gets at the Greek. In the Greek word, we can see what becomes the English word for hypocrite, and it's prefixed by a "non" kind of word. Paul tells Timothy to keep to what he's taught, and to keep others from perverting it, so that believers can be anti-hypocrites.

27 C. S. Lewis, *The Four Loves* (New York: Harcourt, Brace and World, Inc., 1960). As in some of his other works, especially *The Great Divorce*, Lewis's work is flooded with beauty and wisdom, carrying us along into so many moments of "that's so deep, it makes so much sense and is so true to life!" But there are also some jagged rocks in the flowing river of those delights, statements that make you think, "You've got some bitterness against the fairer sex, don't you? Or at least against certain representatives and personality types within it?" He's clearly observed men practically emasculated by their waspy wives. Lewis wrote as feminism and the sexual revolution were increasingly strong and rising tides in the twentieth-century West. Times of cultural sea change draw out the depths of our beliefs. As we see in Lewis's work as it expresses his heart, it's profoundly difficult to distinguish in our souls between good and lasting convictions born of soul-steadying truths that keep us afloat in cultural storms, and brutish biases masking themselves as such, full of spiritual deadweight better tossed overboard for our own good and the good of others with whom we sail history's changing tides.

28 Eros can be taken to refer more deeply and fundamentally to desire itself, which results in but can be distinguished from matters of sexuality. For our purposes, we'll use the term to refer to desire in the context of sexuality.

29 If God's written words are his voice, these are some of his shouts. We might walk by a house and hear a dad screaming at one of his young kids. We whip out our phone to call CPS, not realizing that his beloved toddler was climbing a chair toward the open second-story window when no one else was looking. In the Old Testament book of Leviticus, for instance, God got loud in laws regarding sexual relationships. He wanted to teach his spiritually immature people to honor, respect, and protect one another; to actively watch out for and preserve one another's dignity in body and soul; to wean them off the opposite ways of life they'd seen as slaves in Egypt and to warn them away from such ways of life popular in the land he was giving them. In an excellent commentary on a difficult book, Allen P. Ross writes of Leviticus 18 in particular, "The chapter has a dual purpose: to warn Israel not to practice the abominations of the Egyptians and Canaanites; and to warn Israel that indulging in such wickedness would prompt God to expel them from the land as well." Allen P. Ross, *Holiness to the Lord: A Guide to the Exposition of the Book of Leviticus* (Grand Rapids: Baker, 2002), p. 339.

Leviticus is a sobering, sometimes stomach-turning read. Yet read against the cultures of the day, God's burning desire for his people's holiness and their freedom from the dignity-shredding customs that characterized pop cultures surrounding them is stunning, and beautiful. We need to remember that God used language and worked within and through cultural motifs that, though bizarre and extreme to us, would communicate clearly to his people the hellishness of that from which he was freeing them. As we observe sexual chaos and recklessness in our day and the lives left broken and trembling in its wreckage, this ancient, hard-nosed, and disturbing book seems more and more sophisticated and even gently sensitive to the deep needs of human beings. Notice chapter 18's tender emphasis on the dignity and sexual sanctity of each person's most intimate body parts, and its emphasis that sexual union—euphemistically, "uncovering nakedness"—involves deep belonging, not simply cohabitation, cf. Genesis 2:24 and Ephesians 5:31. Thus God's reserving sexual intimacy as a blessing to be enjoyed only within marriage. Admittedly, these deeper truths can be tough to spot on the surface of harsh-sounding strictures. But without God's warning us, sometimes in ways that can't help but grab our attention for their volume and content, we will wander, fully self-confident and self-justified, into the worst possible things for us, with heads held high and, in our minds, God and the world cheering us on the whole way. Naturally, the need for volume and blunt speech in the Old Testament era was greater, as God's church was born and just learning to walk. Compare Leviticus 18 to Ephesians 5. They communicate the same truth about the significance of sexual union, in language fitted for the respective audiences and their historical and cultural settings. See also Gordon J. Wenham, *The Book of Leviticus: New International Commentary on the Old Testament* (Grand Rapids: Eerdmans, 1979).

30 Referring to postmodernism as the "third culture," Rieff writes: "The third culture expects too much from sexuality. It expects a destruction of that identity which it now feels as a burden rather than as the protective and limiting commanding truths that permit each of us the freedom to be and do for ourselves, so continuously establishing ourselves." Philip Rieff, *My Life Among the Deathworks: Illustrations of the Aesthetics of Authority* (Charlottesville: University of Virginia Press, 2006), p. 131.

31 The Greek terms indicates a powerful desire and not necessarily a sinful desire. James even says that the Holy Sprit "lusts" in protective love for the purity of God's temple, God's people (James 4:5). For our purposes, and to simplify, we'll use "lust" to indicate sexual greed.

32 See "Oversexed ed" by Emily Belz, August 29, 2017, in the online edition of *World*. https://world.wng.org/2017/08/oversexed_ed.

33 As we've thought about, we encourage kids to consider very early on relationships they can't possibly comprehend and for which their minds and bodies are so obviously not ready. We teach them without necessarily naming it as such, that the pursuit of personal truth is what's most important, and that their feelings are the best guide toward it. This puts blinders on their souls so that they cannot perceive the true beauty and worthiness of another person, and prevents the full-fledged honoring of the other, which, in God's system, results in what's best for the development of the self. The capacity for

others-based love diminishes if it doesn't drown in the swelling, chaotic sea created by our godding.

34 Sitcoms such as *Two and a Half Men* routinely feature children as sexually savvy sages. I don't remember the show, but I remember my stomach turning at a commercial for a similar show in which a young child smiled at an adult with focused eyes and a crooked, suggestive smile. The adult's eyes bugged out, and the audience erupted in laughter. We just can't leave kids alone, can we? Maybe it's that seeing them have to deal with our hang-ups and take on our problems makes us feel better about it. We recognize that we're messed up, and we long for childlike innocence. But we also refuse to put down the godding that causes our hang-ups, so we can't have little examples of life free from polluted adulthood running around reminding us that we don't have to be the way we've chosen to be, reminding us perhaps of a time in our lives when our godding wasn't necessarily less severe, but was at least less complicated. When teenagers as young as thirteen perform on competitions such as *The Voice*, they often sing songs charged with sexuality, either deeply mature or overtly crass. The judges, the audience, and most disturbingly, their parents or other family members, think nothing of it.

35 In that culture, manhood and womanhood came earlier than what we're used to in the West. Being thirteen or so was enough. And yet, people we'd consider adolescents and not adults were, ideally, steeped in a way of life that looked toward and honored marriage, and that in general engaged children with the deep thoughts and self-forming, soul-stabilizing truths needed for them to navigate life; their culture didn't allow and expose them to sexual frivolity and frenzy. They learned self-control and a work ethic and sense of personal and communal responsibility utterly contrary to the godding, entitlement, and sexual chaos that forms the philosophical mold for kids reared in our time. The Scriptures treat children like the full-souled, burgeoning adults that they are, while pop culture in the wealthy West shackles them in a permanent, addled adolescence.

36 See Titus 2 and also many of the Proverbs, as a father addresses his sons in the same way. Proverbs 1, 5, and 7 are especially vivid examples. One sets the stage for the entire book, and 5 and 7 apply the book's principles to matters of sexuality.

37 NIV.

38 Or it might not be there at all, ever. That's okay! For some people, erotic feelings and physiological responses just aren't forthcoming, no matter how much they desire all levels of intimacy with their beloved. In a relationship based on trust and mutual understanding of personhood and identity that run far deeper than sexual preference or prowess, intimacy need not fit typical patterns to be truly intimate, intense, and mutually satisfying.

39 Lewis, *The Four Loves*, p. 134.

40 Lewis, *The Four Loves*, p. 160.

41 "Sex Is Not the Enemy" is the title of a song by the band Garbage.

42 The analogy breaks down, of course. In martial arts, you attempt to prove your mastery and control over the opponent, but as we love people, we're seeking to serve them, dedicating ourselves to their truest good and freedom.

43 Lewis, *The Four Loves*, p. 137.

44 See Ephesians 4 on this, as Paul cites and applies some of the Ten Commandments to his audience of new Christians. Every "knock it off!" has a "do this instead."

45 Yes, Paul writes earlier (verse 26) that wives are to "submit" to their husbands, and he means it. Which means that God means it. I leave that word out of the main body because we've learned to see that term not with biblically trained eyes, which would see, starting from Genesis 1, that any submission called for is defined in the context of respect, dignity, and ontological equality. This book is attempting to get at those biblical basics and to encourage that fully biblical view of fire-starting terms, and to help us unlearn the godding assumptions that keep us from seeing such truth as God spoke it. This book is not a church service, during which passages can be read in their entirety and carefully explained to those who hear biblical terms and are immediately incited to false interpretations. My goal is a selectivity that's scripturally faithful, and sensitive to how such terms are immediately heard and felt in a culture reared and formed beneath the ceiling of self.

46 In any given moment, we always act according to our greatest desire at that moment. Not necessarily our most deeply *felt* desire, but we ultimately in every moment submit to some undergirding something that moves us to action. Our affections are revealed in and they lead to our actions.

47 See Psalm 37:4.

48 God's not "keeping a record of wrongs" means that he does not actively revisit our confessed and forgiven sin as if it's still unaddressed. See Psalm 130 and a brutal, beautiful conversation Jesus has with Peter on this point in John 21. The latter is the focus of a chapel sermon I preached and called "Prison Break." Have a listen to "Prison Break," preached on March 28, 2018. http://www.geneva.edu/chapel/17-18-chapel-messages.

49 Scripture emphasizes God's proven track record of redemption when it comes to sexual sin. Jesus handles such hurting people with special compassion throughout the gospels, as we'll see next chapter in his conversation with a Samaritan woman (John 4). See also Luke 7:37ff.

50 This is one of the reasons that man-rompers are so deeply evil. They're physically and philosophically horrifying. Hopefully by the time this book is published, those pushing this pernicious idea will have repented of their desire to unleash such horror upon civilization. Although, if they were made from the same crazy comfortable material that makes up my baby daughter's onesie jammies, I might consider...NO! We've got to grow up; we've got to move on to maturity! Our past can't be changed, but we don't have to be chained to it.

51 Sometimes we think we need things the Bible calls sinful to make a bland life spicy. We equate moral rebellion with spirited personality. But let's take the focus off of us and put it on the world: Would we really be bored with world peace? Would we really sit around with nothing to do because we're done hating and hurting each other and say, "You know what this boring planet could use? A good murder!" Wouldn't we rather be in one another's presence without fear, wanting one another there and genuinely wanting nothing but what's best for one another? Impossible? For us, completely. For Jesus, not at all.

52 The Bible itself is a good case in point. It's the breath of God, superintended by the Holy Spirit who led people to write exactly what he wanted them to, and yet the humanness and particular personalities of each author really stand out.

53 See chapter 6 for a discussion of the opposite tendency we have in our godding. We don't deal with history as it is; we rewrite it in order to remake it in the image of our contemporary life dogmas.

54 God understands and kindly compensates for our weakness. Every time we're conscious of and tempted toward godding, he provides an alternate avenue of action, an exit toward godliness. See 1 Corinthians 10:12–14.

55 "Loyal opposition" is a term in classic rhetoric. A leader/thinker needed someone who for friendly purposes would act the antagonist toward his ideas, to sharpen and deepen the leader's thinking and to prepare the leader to engage true opposition.

56 Notice again, "Have you not *read* what was *said* to you by God…?" The Scriptures are the voice of God. The speech of God is active long after his spoken words were penned.

57 I love the song "I Can Only Imagine" by Mercy Me.

58 Take a look through the ten, either in Exodus 20 or Deuteronomy 5, and for now, just at number 10. Perfect love looks like no jealousy; no coveting. No illegitimate sense of ownership over another person. Where perfect love rules life, there is no need for the very legitimate jealousy that rises when promise-based relationships are threatened. Those threats don't exist. When the Lord returns, believers will be with one another, loving one another, in an even more sublime form of the loves we merely sampled in this painful, beautiful, often lovelorn life.

59 "To the Ancients, Friendship seemed the happiest and most fully human of all loves; the crown of life and the school of virtue. The modern world, in comparison, ignores it." Lewis, *The Four Loves*, p. 87. One of the blessings of the postmodern world is its emphasis on community. Withness, not individualism, is a virtue. Sadly, as we've seen, Venus loves to corrupt this virtue. Into the twenty-first century in the West, well beyond the sexual mores of Lewis's days, Venus corrupts yet another of friendship's blessings that Lewis extols. While Eros needs exclusivity, friendship can be a relatively promiscuous love. That's not to say we won't have our very close friends, but Lewis emphasizes the joy of having a community of friends, united around common interests and pursuits.

60 He calls himself "the disciple whom Jesus loved." This is not narcissism, nor is it a snide comment about the other disciples. It's a simple, humble statement of awestruck, blissed self-identification. Paul does the same thing

in Galatians 2:20. Throughout the letter called 1 John, the beloved disciple happily and frequently applies this description to all believers.

61 See chapter 6.

62 Lewis, *The Four Loves*, p. 91.

63 It seems impossible to avoid the conclusion that our obsession with sex and sexuality has contributed to the dysphoria felt by so many in our culture and fomented among children at younger and younger ages. Recognizing sexual attractiveness does not in itself imply sexual attraction, much less orientation, and still much less personal ontology. And even when sexual desire is clear, it's a tyranny to be taught that you must explore and maybe even follow through on every sexual impulse or proclivity you have lest you deny your true self. When natural curiosity gets dragged by cultural riptide into the towering, chaotic swells of a populace reckless and relentless in its sexual explorations, it's only natural to feel radically disoriented, to feel like you're drowning. It's natural to hold onto any feeling that seems solid just so you can survive. And when something helps us survive, it's natural to feel like we can't live without it. Even if we arrive at conclusions about our sexuality through what we consider to be measured, objective, and patient means, we still face the deeper questions of what really defines us, and who gets to decide.

64 NIV.

65 Philippians 1:6.

66 She was the great-great-grandmother of King David.

67 NIV.

Chapter 10

1 See Michael LeFebvre, *Exploring Ecclesiastes: Joy that Perseveres* (Carlisle: Day One Publications, 2016).

2 "Music and the metaphysical, in the root sense of that term, music and religious feeling, have been virtually inseparable." George Steiner *Real Presences* (Chicago: University of Chicago Press, 1989), p. 216. Cited by Colin E. Gunton, *The One, the Three, and the Many: God, Creation, and the Culture of Modernity—the 1992 Bampton Lectures* (Cambridge: Cambridge University Press, 1993), p. 176.

3 For example, the Song of Moses, Exodus 15:1 and following, Deuteronomy 31:30 and following, and the song of Mary, the mother of Jesus, Luke 1:46 and following.

4 An observation my friend and former teacher Pastor Tom Reid made, recalling his hearing it as a child.

5 2 Timothy 3:16; see chapter 3 of this book.

6 By Martin Luther in his preface to the 1531 revised edition of *The German Psalter*.

7 To the point of this chapter, it's a devastating irony that some of these churches feature the Psalms in their musical worship, sometimes exclusively. Sometimes those entrusted with a treasure lose sight of its true and deep value and therefore of how best to enrich others with it.

8   For me personally, and for lots of other Christians I know, such discoveries came in the course of studying philosophy, and the great writings of great Christian theologians of the past who recognized and brilliantly popularized the inherently personal nature of God's word. Reading Augustine's *Confessions* did this for me. I was reading and learning my own soul; I was discovering Scripture's capability to not only engage my deepest thoughts, doubts, joys, and anxieties, but to explain and even instruct them. God equips his church throughout history with preachers and teachers of his word who are especially gifted in helping hearers/readers draw close to his own heart. He calls them "shepherds after his own heart." See Jeremiah 3:15 and its beautiful, instructive anticipation of Jesus's self-identification in John 10. Then see Ephesians 4:10 and following.

9   By theologian John Calvin (1509–1564). For a wonderful, in-depth and challenging study of what it means in practical terms to love and follow Jesus, see Ronald S. Wallace, *Calvin's Doctrine of the Christian Life* (Eugene: Wipf and Stock, 1997).

10   Taken from "Songs from the Soul," a sermon preached in 1902 by theologian Geerhardus Vos. See Geerhardus Vos, *Grace and Glory: Sermons Preached in the Chapel of Princeton Theological Seminary* (Carlisle, PA: The Banner of Truth Trust, 1994).

11   Psalm 107 describes such a journey at sea. It matches, by no mere coincidence, that fateful sailing expedition we thought about briefly in chapter 5. See Psalm 107 and the end of Mark 4.

12   Debates ensue about what Paul means by "spiritual songs" and "hymns," especially because Paul likely did not mean exactly what we think of in our day by such terms. In the Greek, the word "spiritual" can modify songs and hymns and psalms, rendering Paul's command: "Speak to one another in psalms, hymns, and songs that are spiritual." Paul often uses the term "spiritual" to indicate the work of the Holy Spirit. See Galatians 5:22-6:1. If this is Paul's meaning, then we have a wonderful Trinitarian emphasis in this passage. We speak to one another with the word of Christ, by singing the songs the Holy Spirit gave us, to the praise of God. This Trinitarian emphasis is also typical of Paul. See 2 Corinthians 13:14 and the entirety of Romans 8.

13   Over and over, when New Testament writers call our attention to Jesus, they cite the Psalms. See Acts 2 and Hebrews 1, for example.

14   Vos, "Songs from the Soul."

15   Jesus would have sung and known all of the Psalms. He would have been reared on these songs, and they would have taught him to understand and navigate life as he "increased in wisdom and in stature and in favor with God and man" (Luke 2:52). After the Passover feast, the Hebrew people would sing a section of Psalms called "The Great Hallel," consisting of Psalms 113–118. Can you imagine what this would have meant to Jesus to sing this with his disciples as he left "the Last Supper" to give his life as the true and essential Passover sacrifice (1 Corinthians 5:7)? See Matthew 26:21 and following.

16 This is from Martin Luther's introduction to the Psalms in *The Luther Bible*, published in 1534. See https://wolfmueller.co/martin-luthers-introduction-psalms/.

17 Cited at the head of chapter 1. Bob Dylan, "Not Dark Yet."

18 These pauses come with the Hebrew word *Selah*, which seems to have been a musical or liturgical term calling for purposeful, quiet pause in the midst of song or at the very end, like those few moments before the applause when the lead singer bows her head and the band members stop playing. Psalm 3 contains both uses of *Selah*.

19 Like my use of an adjective rather than an adverb before "anarchistic." I'm no slave to the system!

20 True U2 fans will get this pun.

21 Despair doesn't dominate U2's lyrics, though. There is clearly the reach for higher truth, and conducted with musical brilliance, it leads us—especially at their concerts—into a transcendent experience.

22 See chapter 1.

23 The sadness in the Psalms is neither self-centered nor self-serving. It's neither self-induced nor philosophically self-defeating. The psalmists are not searching for reasons to be sad, nor are they operating from a moral base that comes back to bite them when they cry out against life's atrocities.

24 Here I replaced the ESV's "him" with Christ to clarify Paul's meaning. See the NIV translation for confirmation of Paul's intent.

25 It would be really hard to sell these early Christians the view of "the end times" embraced by many Christians in the West, that Jesus will rescue the church through and take them home to heaven in an event called "the rapture" before things get really bad.

26 Add to this the persecution and slaughter of believers in the Old Testament era, going all the way back to the first martyr, Abel, and the numbers would be staggering. As always, I do not intend these thoughts to be in any way dismissive of other groups of people who've been persecuted or slaughtered for their beliefs, or simply because, as in Soviet Russia, they were useless to the state. But the Bible does provide a coherent, consistent, and verifiable thesis as to the reason why such murderous affections and actions have so characterized humans and human history.

27 See the book of Daniel and the book of Acts, Matthew chapters 5–7, and Romans 13.

28 See Acts 7 as the New Testament's first recorded martyr, at the time of his death, sees Jesus in heaven, standing as his advocate and ready to receive him home.

29 James tells us in 5:16 that "the prayer of a righteous person has great power as it is working." Those who trust in Jesus are referred to as righteous (Psalm 1), not because of their own goodness but because of Christ's righteousness covering them. See Romans 3.

30 See Peterson's conversation with Bono, who publicly thanked Peterson for his translation of Scripture entitled *The Message*. https://www.youtube.com/watch?v=-l40S5e90KY from Fuller Studio.

31 From Dr. Michael LeFebvre's unpublished March 2003 paper, "Psalm 137," p. 13.

32 Peter hears that same cry from people in his day, and while he doesn't tell us exactly when Jesus will return to bring full justice, he does tell us why he hasn't yet. He writes to frustrated believers, increasingly mocked and attacked for their belief in a Savior they've never seen but who'd promised to return. Peter tells them it's just a matter of time; when all of those who will be saved are saved, Christ will return. In the meantime, and especially in the face of persecution, anger has its place among believers. James tells us not to rush to it, but neither he nor any other biblical author tells us that anger is out of bounds for the believer. Anger—rightly directed, slowly arrived at, and quickly put down when it's done (2 Peter 3, James 1, Ephesians 4)—has its place and it must have its nonviolent expression. Christ's persecuted people need catharsis.

33 Much less do they speak for our rage when the barista uses 2% rather than skim in our latte. These "first world problems" are not the pains that these Psalms scream. Perhaps that's one reason why the wealthy white West has such an "ick" reaction to them, and can hardly imagine singing them in praise of Thor, I mean, Jesus.

34 LeFebvre, p. 6.

35 As he's about to be martyred, Stephen sees Jesus in the heavens, standing as his advocate. See Acts 7 for the profound sermon that incited his murderers, a stunning overview of the Old Testament and its inherent Christ-centeredness. Verses 54–60 chronicle this courageous Christian's death.

36 In his war songs, David lists some of his enemies, and his name-dropping includes people and places who stood for and represented realities far greater than they. Edom and Moab are typical examples. See Psalm 83 and Isaiah 11.

37 Psalm 137 is perhaps the most vivid and violent. See Dr. Michael LeFebvre's excellent, faithful-to-Scripture and honest-to-our-emotions handling of this text in chapter 6 of his book, *Singing the Songs of Jesus: Revisiting the Psalms* (Fearn, UK: Christian Focus 2010).

38 LeFebvre, p. 15.

39 Jesus promises to give his followers everything they need to bring about the greatest desire of his own heart, the glory of his heavenly Father. Jesus teaches his disciples to pray along these lines in what's come to be called "the Lord's Prayer" starting in Matthew 6:9. In verse 33, Jesus promises that God will provide everything we need every day of our lives to make our seeking of the "kingdom come" successful.

40 D. A. Carson, *How Long, O Lord? Reflections on Suffering and Evil*, 2nd ed. (Grand Rapids: Baker, 2006), p. 87.

41 See chapter 7's discussion of the covenant of grace and the several examples of this particular language in light of it.

42 See Acts 1:16 and following.

43 "…we stand individually to account for our claim to union with Christ or not, so that even our individual faith is ultimately dependent upon our corporate identity." LeFebvre, 14.

44 Immediately the holy wars of the Old Testament come to mind. Though no amount of deeper, contextual understanding of these events can make those narratives easy to reckon with, there is a lot to be learned, and a lot of assumptions to be unlearned, as we approach them. A further exploration is beyond the scope of even this too-big book, but here are some excellent sources to consult: As recommended in an endnote in chapter 7, Christopher J. H. Wright, *The God I Don't Understand: Reflections on Tough Questions of Faith* (Grand Rapids: Zondervan, 2008); also, more specifically on the topic of holy war, *Show Them No Mercy: Four Views on God and Canaanite Genocide*, Stanley N. Gundry, series editor (Grand Rapids: Zondervan, 2003); and lastly and especially, a poignant, pained, and profoundly helpful sermon entitled "Is God a Moral Monster?" by Dr. Byron Curtis. He preached it April 8, 2015, during Geneva College's chapel service. You can find it at http://www.geneva.edu/chapel/14-15-chapel-messages. Upon learning that I'd asked Dr. Curtis to preach on this topic, one of his colleagues told him to "preach the hell out of it." Indeed.

45 See chapter 4.

46 At the time of this writing, controversy rages in America over whether to tear down from public property monuments honoring slave holders. Perhaps new monuments could be built—in somber, humbled, repentant memory of the human rights atrocities enacted on American soil. Greater exposure to the truth creates greater accountability before God. With as much access to the Bible as our culture has had, it's a wonder this nation still exists. Scripture calls us all to account. Can you imagine how beautiful, truly meaningful, and socially consequential it would be if Americans would join together first as image-bearers of God, and if God's children among them would remember that, though citizens of America, they are first and foremost citizens of Christ's kingdom and as such would together cry out for God's forgiveness upon the nation, upon us, for the godding we've done since before we officially existed as a nation? What a statement to the world that would be, that we would own our sin as a nation, and come humbly before the world's King to seek his grace and mercy! A lot of godding will need to go down for that to happen, and that's the kind of violence for which God's word equips us, and to which the imprecatory psalms give voice in our day.

47 In 1 Peter 2:17, the apostle tells believers to pay homage to the state. "Honor everyone. Love the brotherhood. Fear God. Honor the Emperor"—almost as if he had to add that last part so believers would know that, yes, "everyone" included the tyrannical fake god whose government sanctioned the crucifixion of God's son. But the New Testament also makes clear that the relationship between physical and metaphysical, body and soul, and in a similar way state and church, is one of distinction, not dichotomy. Like some twins, they're not identical, but they are closely related. All belong to God. No governing power exists except that which God has set up for his purposes. While I don't believe that Scripture calls Christians to establish a theocracy, I do believe that all governments owe their allegiance to the King of kings and ought to acknowledge it.

48 The idea that the spiritual and physical are opposite or opposing aspects of reality is an ancient form of ceiling-of-self thinking called gnosticism. It sees spirit as living in an antagonistic relationship with matter (which is seen as inherently evil), the idea that we're trapped in our physicality and in some cases that this means we can do whatever we want with our bodies, because it is our mind/spirit that is pure. John in particular seems to be combatting its rising influence. He opens 1 John by emphasizing the flesh-and-blood physicality of Jesus. Gnosticism is ceiling-of-self thinking in that it divides what God has joined together, body and soul, spirit and matter.

49 See 2 Samuel 7; Psalm 2; Mark 16; Acts 2, 7; Romans 8; Colossians 3; Hebrews 10; and 1 Peter 3.

50 These songs of war within God's songbook are just that—songs of war. See James E. Adams, *War Psalms of the Prince of Peace: Lessons from the Imprecatory Psalms* (Phillipsburg, NJ: P&R, 2017). This is the 25th anniversary edition. We understand why combat veterans use lots of profanity to describe the battles they've fought—that is, if they're able to speak about them at all. God gave us the Psalms as a means of healthy grieving and catharsis, which is often intensely emotional and requires strong language. The imprecatory psalms speak credibly to and for people who've seen life's most violent atrocities up close, keeping their catharsis within a moral framework that condemns the evil they've seen and promises resolution in the risen Christ.

51 See chapters 5 and 6 on biblical anthropology set against the dehumanizing patriarchalism of the days in which Scripture was composed.

52 See 2 Kings 17 and Ezra 9–10. The empire of Assyria conquered the northern section of Israel's split kingdom in 722 BC. The Gentiles brought into the land mixed martially and religiously with the Hebrew people remaining, leading them into the worship of other gods. Such people became known as Samaritans and were regarded by Jews as religiously impure half-breeds who'd corrupted the practical, political, and religious life of God's people.

53 Jesus laces his sermons as well as his everyday conversations with Scripture. That he used this reference with the woman would suggest her familiarity with Scripture, and Jesus's knowledge of it. He obviously knew the personal details of her life! His statements deliberately use biblical language to let her know that what her Scripture-informed heart was seeking was right in front of her, speaking to her!

54 The Psalms especially express God's heart for people of all nations, and exult in all kinds of people coming to worship the true and living God. See Psalm 87 and 117.

55 Now that he's resurrected and returned to heaven, all the ceremonies and accoutrements of temple worship and Old Testament era worship in general have no place among the people who are the place. And oh, how many and how diverse these people be! (Psalm 87, Ephesians 2). This is part of why Jesus advocates such a radically simple form of worship. Worshiping God in "spirit and in *truth*" (John 4:21–24) involves worshiping him in a manner appropriate to and reflective of the times, and this means in a way easily accessible to anyone anywhere in the world. No temple, no building-bound and culture-bound fixings required. Just people, any believing people in any place in the world, even prison! (Acts 16:25).

56 God tells Isaiah that the one to whom he in his universe-filling and transcending majesty will look is "the one who is humble and contrite in spirit, and who trembles at my word" (Isaiah 66:1–2). Hosea tells us that God would roar like a lion and that his displaced, disenfranchised children would "come trembling" from the nations that had been their historic antagonists (11:10). And it's not just that they'd come from among those peoples; it's that an untold number of them would *be* those people.

57 Though we're not told much about this woman, she clearly knew enough of the Old Testament to be expecting the Messiah and to be aware of the debates between her people and the Jews as to the proper place of worship. More than likely, then, she was familiar with the Psalms, songs vital to knowing and awaiting the true and coming King, the Savior, the Messiah.

58 Paul, ever on alert for threats to the gospel of Christ and the peace it brings among people, once spotted something hellish in the heart of Peter, something that could set fire to the bridges being built by Christ between Jews and Gentiles. In what must have been a supremely awkward moment among the apostles, Paul got in the face of his beloved brother in Christ. The apostle Peter had welcomed Gentiles into the faith of Abraham, but he was afraid of certain Hebrew countrymen who insisted that allegiance to Jewish religious custom was necessary to be in a right relationship with God. They were offended that Peter had been hanging out and eating with the uncircumcised Gentiles. So when Peter saw them approaching, he ditched the company of his Gentile Christian brethren. Other Hebrew Christians imitated his hypocrisy. Paul wasn't having it. He rebuked Peter "to his face." And the Holy Spirit thought this confrontation was an important enough teachable moment to include in his book—sorry, Peter! See Galatians 2:11 and following.

The Spirit's telling us about the imperfections and downright moral disasters of prominent believers is a refreshing reminder of the Bible's essential honesty, its objectivity and commitment to justice and truth. No one, not even Peter, an apostle who was in Jesus's inner, inner circle (along with James and John) was above confrontation and correction by Scripture. Christ's kingly law allowed no special treatment, no individualism, and no self-righteousness. Christ's church is on all levels all about loving Withness among all peoples and must live like it, or hear about it from her king. When we fail, he calls us to repentance.

59 In Romans 1, Paul defines the gospel as the power of God unto salvation for everyone who believes, "first for the Jew, then for the Gentile." The gospel's spread throughout the world is not a matter of ontological preference; it's a matter of historical sequence. Paul tells us that the gospel was announced to Abraham, and he makes lots of references to Abraham in the stunning exploration and exposition of the gospel that is his letter to the Romans.

60 The New Testament takes great pains to help Gentile Christians understand their family history, to know and feel and sing the "us" of the people of God across the world and throughout time. According to Paul, Gentile Christians share with Hebrew Christians not only a common faith in Jesus, but a common history as God's people. For these Gentile converts, the events of the Old Testament are family history. Paul writes in 1 Corinthians 10, referring back to Israel's exodus, led by Moses, from four centuries of slavery in Egypt and their journey through the Red Sea, "For I want you to know, brothers, that *our fathers* were all under the cloud, and all passed through the sea…" (italics mine). "Our fathers." In Christ, these Gentiles were new family; they belonged.

61 Particular tunes are mentioned in the Psalms, but there is nowhere near scholarly consensus on the idea that we have access to them.

62 It's really awkward when arrangements of the Psalms set tempestuous words to placid, limp tunes. Sometimes imprecatory psalms are set to light, if not jaunty, soundtracks. The jarring discordance legitimately raises the question of how seriously the arrangement takes the words; same for those who, in the worship service, can sing dark words of judgment and death blithely and transition seamlessly to announcements about the next church potluck.

63 Starting in chapter 1 of his excellent, best-selling book *The Reason for God*, Pastor Tim Keller poses and unpacks the question of why Christianity, as opposed to other faiths and worldviews, has worked so well among such radically diverse cultures and people groups across the world in uniting them all around the same truth, while allowing each of them to flourish as Christians within and to the benefit of their native cultural context.

64 N.T. Wright, *The Case for the Psalms: Why They Are Essential* (New York: HarperOne, 2013), p. 107.

65 See chapter 4's emphasis on John and Matthew 11.

66 John does this in chapter 1 of his gospel several times before arriving at verse 17, one of the most important passages in Scripture about the relationship between the Old Testament and the New. John writes: "The law came through Moses. Grace and *truth* came through Jesus Christ" (italics mine). Moses was not a false prophet, nor was God's law a lie. By his grace, God establishes loving Witness with those who trust him through Jesus. It's within this loving Witness that their lives begin to take on the fullness for which they were created, a fullness that takes shape along the lines of God's law, which is summed up in love. Within this loving Witness, we become who we really are; we grow into our fulfilled, real, mature, "true" selves.

67 The tenth commandment serves as the mirror image of the first. A heart focused exclusively in love upon the one true and living God will not covet, will not fixate jealously upon what God has kept from us and perhaps given to others.

68 Some translations say "fights" and "quarrels" but "war" really is the best rendering. As I preached through James, it became my favorite of the New Testament letters. Here's a sermon on this particular passage, entitled "To End All Wars": https://www.sermonaudio.com/sermoninfo.asp?SID=718118897.

69 The Holy Spirit loves to package truth in words the arrogant will mock and reject instantly, usually without any charitable, honest study of their deep meaning. The words would not have been awkward at all to the original audience; their strangeness to us is a function of time and culture. The Spirit knew that this would happen, and as an author, he loves to reward the careful reader. To those willing to learn from ancient wisdom, eternal wisdom, these passages are like a holy wink within God's word as it gazes upon us. These weird passages are a gauntlet for those who mock them, but they're a warm invitation into something wonderful for those who will trust God and see the weird texts through to their intended meaning and personal impact. If this all sounds like an attempted aggrandizement of the awkward, God himself tells us that he likes to do this: "God has chosen the foolish things in the world to shame the wise" (1 Corinthians 1:27). The Scriptures enjoy and employ irony, and the Holy Spirit loves the humble heart who wants to learn from God, rather than the one who wants to teach him a few things.

70 Yes, I am a Harry Potter fanboy.

71 Lewis, *The Four Loves*, pp. 34–5.

72 C. S. Lewis, a true scholar of ancient literature, considered Psalm 19 a top candidate for the finest poem ever written.

73 There's a nice thematic connection to Peter's calling Christians "living stones," assembled together in a temple, a dwelling place for God, to speak his praises (1 Peter 2:5).

74 In Romans 1, Paul describes these upside-down ascriptions of value as one expression of humanity's suppression of the knowledge of God, of God's revealing himself in the natural world around us and the moral world within us.

75 At that point, environmentalism tilts downhill toward the devaluing of humans, further into the willingness to destroy humans, and in some extreme cases it pines for the day when the trees will never again be cut down or even climbed upon, the day when humanity is gone and Mother Earth will be rid of her ungrateful children, her human parasites. As it always does, turning away from the Creator leads to the destruction, not the salvation, of the world.

76 But doesn't Peter say in this very chapter that the world will burn? Yes, and Peter also said that the moon was blood while preaching during bright daylight. See Acts 2 as Peter cites Joel 2. The issue is the totality and the revelatory, searing moral intensity of the purging that will take place. And what will be purged out of the planet? That which killed the world: our godding. In its place, Peter tells us, will come the world's rightful inhabitant: righteousness.

77 James 1:27. James is so many biblical things as a letter. It's New Testament Wisdom Literature; it's the Sermon on the Mount taken further; it's the voice of the Old Testament minor prophets (Hosea through Malachi) ringing true, louder and clearer in the New Testament era.

78 For a deep and soul-stirring exposition of this theme in Scripture, especially as it's expressed in the Psalms, see Geerhardus Vos, "The Eschatology of the Psalter," in *The Pauline Eschatology* (Phillipsburg, NJ: P&R, 1979) in the edition with the foreword by Richard B. Gaffin, Jr. See also Vos's *Biblical*

Theology: Old and New Testaments (Eugene: Wipf and Stock, 2003). His work is way more than worth the hard work it is to get through it. Vos was not only a true and profound theologian, he was the same as a preacher. He put aside the heavy academics (but not the essential substance explored and explicated in those academic works) when he preached. See the aforementioned *Grace and Glory*, a collection of his sermons preached at Princeton Theological Seminary, and especially his sermon "Rabboni," which is one of the most thoughtful and beautiful meditations I've ever read on Jesus's conversation with Mary just after he rose from the dead. Vos's work, in the academy and in the pulpit, shines with deep biblical learning come to its proper end in his heart as a Christian: profound love for the Savior, his word, people, and the world.

79 Paul writes with this in mind and consistently puts it before his hearers and readers, perhaps nowhere more clearly and powerfully than in Romans 8:28 and following. There, Paul describes believers in their timeless, essential standing before God, hailing what was true of them before they ever existed, what's happened to them in time and space, and what will be when Christ returns: "For whom God foreknew, he predestined to be conformed to the image of his son, in order that he might be the firstborn among many brethren. And those whom he predestined he also called, and those whom he called he also justified, and those whom he justified he also glorified."

80 Adapted from John Owen's *The Death of Death in the Death of Christ*. Available through Banner of Truth publishing.

81 Can't help but think of the U2 song "40," which is mostly Psalm 40. But I can't quote it because there's not enough money left to buy permission. Have a listen; you'll love it.

82 You should prefer Maui. It's actually called "paradise."

83 C. S. Lewis, *The Weight of Glory*, as quoted in a beautifully executed one-man play, *An Evening with C. S. Lewis*. British actor David Payne came with his crew in November 2017 to Geneva College to put on several performances. It was simple and profound. Highly recommended!

84 John Caputo, *Radical Hermeneutics* (Bloomington: Indiana University Press, 1987), p. 211.

Bibliography

Books and Online Articles

Adams, James E. *War Psalms of the Prince of Peace: Lessons from the Imprecatory Psalms*. Phillipsburg, NJ: P&R Publishing, 2017.

Andersen, Francis I. *Job: Tyndale Old Testament Commentaries*. Downers Grove: InterVarsity Press, 1976.

Anderson, Ryan T. *When Harry Became Sally: Responding to the Transgender Moment*. New York: Encounter Books, 2018.

Arnold, Bill T., and Bryan E. Bayer. *Encountering the Old Testament: A Christian Survey*. Grand Rapids: Baker Academic, 1999, 2008.

Baird, Forest E., and Walter Kaufmann. *Philosophic Classics, Volume III: Modern Philosophy*, 2nd ed. New York: Simon & Schuster, 1997.

Beardsley, Monroe C., ed. *The European Philosophers from Descartes to Nietzsche* (Modern Library Classics). New York: Modern Library, 1960.

Belz, Emily. "Oversexed ed." *World Magazine* (August 29, 2017): https://world.wng.org/2017/08/oversexed_ed.

Bird, Michael F., Craig A. Evans, Simon J. Gathercole, Charles E. Hill, and Chris Tilling. *How God Became Jesus: The Real Origins of Belief in Jesus' Divine Nature.* Grand Rapids: Zondervan, 2014.

Bonhoeffer, Dietrich. *Dietrich Bonhoeffer's Works, Volume 2: Act and Being.* Bernard Noble, trans.. Minneapolis: Fortress Press, 1996.

Browning Cole, Eve. *Philosophy and Feminist Criticism: An Introduction.* New York: Paragon House Publishers, 1993.

Burroughs, Jeremiah. *The Evil of Evils: The Exceeding Sinfulness of Sin* (Puritan Writings). Ligonier, PA: Soli Deo Gloria Publications, 1992.

Butterfield, Rosaria Champagne. *Openness Unhindered: Further Thoughts of an Unlikely Convert on Sexual Identity and Union with Christ.* Pittsburgh: Crown & Covenant Publications, 2015.

Camus, Albert. *Resistance, Rebellion, and Death.* Justin O'Brien, trans. New York: Alfred A. Knopf, Inc., 1969.

Caputo, John. *Radical Hermeneutics: Repetition, Deconstruction, and the Hermeneutic Project.* Bloomington: Indiana University Press, 1987.

Carson, D. A. *How Long, O Lord? Reflections on Suffering and Evil,* 2nd ed. Grand Rapids: Baker Academic, 2006.

Carson, D. A. *The Gagging of God: Christianity Confronts Pluralism.* Grand Rapids: Zondervan, 1996.

Chesterton, G. K. "The Ethics of Elfland," In *Orthodoxy.* New York: John Lane Company, 1908.

Chesterton, G. K. "A Defense of Heraldry," In *The Defendant.* Mineola: Dover Publications, 2012.

Chiu, Allyson. "Rachel Dolezal, the White Woman Who Posed as Black, Charged with Welfare Fraud." *The Washington Post,* May 25, 2018. https://www.washingtonpost.com/news/morning-mix/wp/2018/05/25/rachel-dolezal-the-white-woman-who-posed-as-black-charged-with-welfare-fraud/?noredirect=on&utm_term=.9b48cc20d76e.

Clark, Chap. *Hurt 2.0: Inside the World of Today's Teenagers* (Youth, Family, and Culture). Grand Rapids: Baker, 2011.

Coburn, Kathleen, ed. *The Philosophical Lectures of Samuel Taylor Coleridge*. London: Pilot Press, 1949.

Council of Canadian Academies. "Medical Assistance in Dying: The Expert Panel on Medical Assistance in Dying." Last Modified December 12, 2018. http://www.scienceadvice. ca/en/assessments/in-progress/medical-assistance-dying/ subquestions.aspx.

Craig, William Lane. *Reasonable Faith: Christian Truth and Apologetic*, revised ed. Wheaton: Crossway, 1994.

Crouch, Andy. "Steve Jobs: The Secular Prophet," October 8, 2011. http://andy-crouch.com/articles/steve_jobs_the_ secular_prophet.

DeYoung, Kevin. *Taking God at His Word: Why the Bible Is Knowable, Necessary, and Enough, and What That Means for You and Me*. Wheaton: Crossway, 2014.

Dostoyevsky, Fyodor. *The Gospel in Dostoyevsky: Selections from His Works*. Andrew R. MacAndrew and Constance Garnett, trans. Walden: Plough Publishing House, 1988.

Dreher, Rod. "U2's Moral Stain." *The American Conservative*. May 25, 2018. https://www.theamericanconservative.com/ dreher/u2-abortion-moral-stain-ireland/.

Elwell, Walter A., and Robert W. Yarbrough. *Encountering the New Testament: A Historical and Theological Survey*. Grand Rapids: Baker Academic, 2005.

Endo, Shusaku. *Silence*. William Johnston, trans. New York: Picador, 2016.

Enns, Peter. *The Bible Tells Me So…Why Defending Scripture Has Made Us Unable to Read It*. New York: HarperCollins, 2014.

Estes, Daniel. *Handbook on the Wisdom Books and Psalms*. Grand Rapids: Baker Academic, 2005.

Esolen, Anthony. *Ten Ways to Destroy the Imagination of Your Child*. Wilmington: ISI Books, 2010.

Falk, William. "The peacock on the plane." *The Week Magazine*. February 9, 2018. http://theweek.com/articles/754100/ peacock-plane.

Fanu, James Le. *Why Us: How Science Rediscovered the Mystery of Ourselves*. London, HarperCollins Publishers, 2008.

FBI. "Active Shooter Incidents in the United States in 2016 and 2017." US Department of Justice. https://www.fbi.gov/

file-repository/active-shooter-incidents-us-2016-2017.pdf/
view.

Ferguson, Sinclair B. *From the Mouth of God: Trusting, Reading, and Applying the Bible*. Carlisle, PA: Banner of Truth, 2014.

Ferguson, Sinclair B. *The Holy Spirit* (Contours of Christian Theology). Downers Grove: InterVarsity Press, 1999.

Frame, John M. *A History of Western Philosophy and Theology*. Phillipsburg, NJ: P&R Publishing, 2015.

Frantum, Taylor, Alaena Hostetter, and Jacob Vaughn. "Some DFW Musicians Spend Their Sunday Mornings at Church—Hung Over From Secular Gigs." *Dallas Observer*, March 20, 2018. http://www.dallasobserver.com/music/6-dfw-musicians-tell-us-whats-it-like-to-gig-at-church-10477625.

French, David. "The True Sin of American Evangelicals in the Age of Trump." *National Review*, March 13, 2018. https://www.nationalreview.com/2018/03/evangelicals-support-donald-trump-political-realities-2016-election/.

Gefter, Amanda, and Quanta. "The Case Against Reality: A professor of cognitive science argues that this world is nothing like the one we experience through our senses." *The Atlantic*, April 25, 2016. https://www.theatlantic.com/science/archive/2016/04/the-illusion-of-reality/479559/.

Gonzalez, Justo. *The Story of Christianity, Volume 2: The Reformation to the Present Day*. San Francisco: HarperCollins Publishers, 1985.

Grudem, Wayne. *Systematic Theology: An Introduction to Biblical Doctrine*. Grand Rapids: Zondervan, 1993.

Cowles, C. S., and Eugene H. Merrill, and Daniel L. Gard, and Tremper Longman III. *Show Them No Mercy: Four Views on God and Canaanite Genocide*. Stanley N. Gundry, ed. Grand Rapids: Zondervan, 2003.

Gunton, Colin E. *The One, the Three, and the Many: God, Creation, and the Culture of Modernity—the 1992 Bampton Lectures*. Cambridge: Cambridge University Press, 1993.

Hendriksen, William. *New Testament Commentary: Exposition of Galatians, Ephesians, Philippians, Colossians and Philemon*. Grand Rapids: Baker Publishing Group, 2002.

Heyer, Walt. "Research Claiming Sex-Change Benefits Is Based on Junk Science." *The Federalist*, April 13, 2017. http://

thefederalist.com/2017/04/13/research-claiming-sex-change-benefits-based-junk-science/.

Hill, Jonathan P. *Emerging Adulthood and Faith*. Grand Rapids: The Calvin College Press, 2015.

Hitchens, Christopher, and Douglas Wilson. *Is Christianity Good for the World? A Debate*. Moscow, ID: Canon Press, 2009.

Hoffmeier, James K., and Dennis R. Magary. *Do Historical Matters Matter to Faith? A Critical Appraisal of Modern and Postmodern Approaches to Scripture*. Wheaton: Crossway, 2012.

Horton, Michael. *Beyond Culture Wars: Is America a Mission Field or a Battlefield?* Chicago: Moody Publishers, 1994.

Humphrey, Jeff, and Melissa Luck. "Did NAACP president lie about her race? City investigates." *KXLY*, June 12, 2015. https://www.kxly.com/news/local-news/spokane/did-naacp-president-lie-about-her-race-city-investigates_2016112104294905/176695501.

Illing, Sean. "The alt-right is drunk on bad readings of Nietzsche. The Nazis were too." *Vox*, September 5, 2018. https://www.vox.com/2017/8/17/16140846/alt-right-nietzsche-richard-spencer-nazism.

Jillette, Penn. "Time for Atheists to Stand Up and Be Counted," *CNN online*. June 2, 2016. https://www.cnn.com/2016/06/02/opinions/atheists-reason-rally-jillette/index.html.

Joseph, Yonette. "Alfie Evans, Terminally Ill British Toddler at Center of Court Fight, Dies." New York Times, April 28, 2018. https://www.nytimes.com/2018/04/28/world/europe/uk-alfie-evans-dead.html

Kaiser, Walter, and Moises Silva. *Introduction to Biblical Hermeneutics: The Search for Meaning*. Grand Rapids: Zondervan, 1994, 2007.

Kant, Immanuel. *Grounding for the Metaphysics of Morals*. James W. Ellington, trans. Indianapolis: Hackett, 1993.

Kant, Immanuel. *Immanuel Kant Reader*. Raymond B. Blakney, ed, trans. New York: Harper & Brothers, 1960.

Kant, Immanuel. *Lectures on Philosophical Theology*. Allen W. Wood and Gertrude M. Clark, trans. Ithaca: Cornell University Press, 1978.

Kant, Immanuel. *Religion Within the Limits of Reason Alone*. Theodore M. Greene and Hoyt H. Hudson, trans. New York: Harper & Row, 1960.

Keller, Timothy. *The Reason for God: Belief in an Age of Skepticism.* New York: Riverhead, 2008.

Kierkegaard, Søren. *Fear and Trembling and The Sickness Unto Death.* Walter Lowrie, trans. Garden City: Doubleday, 1954.

Komoszewski, J. Ed, M. James Sawyer, and Daniel B. Wallace. *Reinventing Jesus: How Contemporary Skeptics Miss the Real Jesus and Mislead Popular Culture.* Grand Rapids: Kregel Publications, 2006.

Kostenberger, Andreas, Darrell Bock, and Josh Chatraw. *Truth Matters: Confident Faith in a Confusing World.* Nashville: B&H Publishing Group, 2014.

Kruger, Michael J. *Canon Revisited: Establishing the Origins and Authority of the New Testament Books.* Wheaton: Crossway, 2012.

Kruger, Michael J. *The Question of Canon: Challenging the Status Quo in the New Testament Debate.* Downers Grove: InterVarsity Press, 2013.

LeFebvre, Michael. *Exploring Ecclesiastes: Joy that Perseveres.* Carlisle: Day One Publications, 2016.

LeFebvre, Michael. *Singing the Songs of Jesus: Revisiting the Psalms.* Fearn, UK: Christian Focus Publications, 2010.

LeFebvre, Michael. "Psalm 137," March 2003. Unpublished, in possession of the author.

Lewis, C. S. *God in the Dock: Essays on Theology and Ethics.* Grand Rapids: Eerdmans, 1973.

Lewis, C. S. *Mere Christianity.* San Francisco: HarperCollins, 1952, 1980.

Lewis, C. S. "Miracles," *God in the Dock: Essays on Theology and Ethics.* Grand Rapids: Eerdmans, 1973.

Lewis, C. S. *That Hideous Strength.* London: The Macmillan Company, 1965.

Lewis, C. S. *The Abolition of Man.* New York: Simon & Schuster, Touchstone, 1996.

Lewis, C. S. *The Four Loves.* New York: Harcourt, Brace & World, 1960.

Lewis, C. S. *The Screwtape Letters.* New York: HarperOne, 1966.

Lewis, C. S. *The Weight of Glory: And Other Addresses.* New York: HarperCollins, 1980.

Lewis, C. S. *The Weight of Glory.* New York, 2001.

Lewis, C. S. *Perelandra.* New York: Charles Scribner's Sons, 1996.

Leonhardt, David. "It's Time to End the Scam of Flying Pets." *The New York Times*, February 4, 2018. https://www.nytimes.com/2018/02/04/opinion/flying-pets-scam-peacock.html.

Machen, J. Gresham. *Christianity and Liberalism*. Grand Rapids: Eerdmans, 1923.

Machen, J. Gresham. *The Virgin Birth of Christ*. London: James Clarke & Company, 1958.

Macmurray, John. *Persons in Relation*. Amherst: Humanity Books, 1961, 1999.

McGrath, Alister. *Doubting: Growing Through the Uncertainties of Faith*. Downers Grove: InterVarsity, 2006.

McKay, David. *The Bond of Love: God's Covenantal Relationship with His Church*. Fearn, UK: Christian Focus Publications, 2001.

Meek, Esther Lightcap. *Contact with Reality: Michael Polanyi's Realism and Why It Matters*. Eugene: Wipf and Stock Publishers, 2017.

Meek, Esther Lightcap. *Loving to Know: Covenant Epistemology*. Eugene: Cascade Books, 2011.

Merrick, James R. A., Stephen M. Garrett, Stanley N. Gundry, R. Albert Mohler Jr., Kevin J. Vanhoozer, Michael F. Bird, Peter E. Enns, and John R. Franke. *Five Views on Biblical Inerrancy*. Grand Rapids: Zondervan, 2013.

Muggeridge, Malcolm. *Seeing Through the Eye: Malcolm Muggeridge on Faith*. Cecil Kuhne, ed. San Francisco: Ignatius Press, 2005.

Murray, David. *Jesus on Every Page: 10 Simple Ways to Seek and Find Christ in the Old Testament*. Grand Rapids: Reformation Heritage, 2013.

Murray, John. *Collected Writings*, vol. 3. Carlisle: Banner of Truth, 1982.

Neuhaus, Richard John. *Freedom for Ministry*. Grand Rapids: Eerdmans, 1979.

Nicholi, Armand. *The Question of God: C. S. Lewis and Sigmund Freud Debate God, Love, Sex, and the Meaning of Life*. New York: Free Press, 2002.

Nietzsche, Friedrich. *The AntiChrist*. Anthony M. Ludovici, trans. Amherst: Prometheus, 2000.

Nietzsche, Friedrich. *The Gay Science*. Walter Kaufmann, trans. New York: Random House, 1974.

Nietzsche, Friedrich. *The Will to Power*. Walter Kaufmann and R. J. Hollingdale, trans. New York: Random House, 1968.

Nietzsche, Friedrich. *Thus Spoke Zarathustra: A Book for None and All*. Walter Kaufmann, trans. New York: Penguin, 1966.

Nietzsche, Friedrich. *Twilight of the Idols*. Duncan Large, trans. New York: Oxford University Press, 1998.

Novak, Kelly R. *Let Harry Become Sally*. Andover: Hypothesis Press, 2018.

O'Brien, Peter T. *The Letter to the Ephesians*. Grand Rapids: Eerdmans, 1999.

O'Flaherty, William. *The Misquotable C. S. Lewis: What He Didn't Say, What He Said, and Why It Matters*. Eugene: Wipf and Stock Publishers, 2018.

Olasky, Marvin. *The American Leadership Tradition: The Inevitable Impact of a Leader's Faith on a Nation's Destiny*. Wheaton: Crossway, 2000.

Olson, Roger E. *The Journey of Modern Theology: From Reconstruction to Deconstruction*. Downers Grove: IVP Academic, 2013.

Packer, J. I. *Rediscovering Holiness: Know the Fullness of Life with God*. Grand Rapids: Baker, 2009.

Peterson, Andrée Seu. "Ze said, xe said," *World*, April 14, 2018.

Porter, Steve L., Felica Heykoop, Barbara Miller, and Todd Pickett. "Spiritual Formation and the Social Justice Turn." *Christian Scholars Review* (vol. 44:3, Spring 2015).

Postman, Neil. *Amusing Ourselves to Death: Public Discourse in the Age of Show Business*. New York: Viking Press, 1985.

Price, Diana. "Bill Maher on Charlie Hebdo: All Religions Are 'Stupid And Dangerous.'" *Inquisitor*, November 19, 2018. http://www.inquisitr.com/1740217/bill-maher-on-charlie-hebdo-all-religions-are-stupid-and-dangerous-video/#O2k3UozUVC57mp4K.99.

Rah, Soong-Chan. *The Next Evangelicalism: Freeing the Church from Western Cultural Captivity*. Downers Grove: IVP Books, 2009.

Ramsey, Paul, and Gabriel Vahanian. *The Death of God: The Culture of Our Post-Christian Era*. New York: George Braziller, 1961.

Renfro, Kim. "'A Wrinkle in Time' ditches the book's explicit Christian references—and the movie really suffers because of it." *Insider*, March, 9, 2018. https://www.thisisinsider.com/

wrinkle-in-time-movie-changes-book-religion-christianity-ending-2018-3.

Rieff, Philip. *My Life Among the Deathworks: Illustrations of the Aesthetics of Authority.* Charlottesville: University of Virginia Press, 2006.

Rieff, Philip. *The Triumph of the Theraputic: Uses of Faith after Freud.* New York: Harper & Row, 1966.

Rollins, Peter. *The Fidelity of Betrayal: Towards a Church Beyond Belief.* Brewster: Paraclete Press, 2008.

Rollins, Peter. *The Idolatry of God: Breaking Our Addiction to Certainty and Satisfaction.* New York: Howard Books, 2012.

Ross, Allen P. *Holiness to the Lord: A Guide to the Exposition of the Book of Leviticus.* Grand Rapids: Baker, 2002.

Rowling, J. K. *Harry Potter and the Sorcerer's Stone.* New York: Scholastic Corporation, 1997.

Ryken, Leland. *How to Read the Bible as Literature…and Get More Out of It.* Grand Rapids: Zondervan, 1984.

Ryken, Leland. *Words of Life: A Literary Introduction to the New Testament I.* Grand Rapids: Baker Book House, 1987.

Schadenberg, Alex. "Doctor Killed Healthy 24-Year-Old in Euthanasia Who Thought of Suicide Since She Was a Kid." *LifeNews,* June 22, 2015. http://www.lifenews.com/2015/06/22/doctor-will-kill-healthy-24-year-old-in-euthanasia-whos-thought-of-suicide-since-she-was-a-kid/.

Schaff, Philip. *History of the Christian Church,* 8 vols. Peabody: Hendrickson, 1994.

Schindler, D. C. *The Catholicity of Reason.* Grand Rapids: Eerdmans, 2013.

Selby, Jenn. "Germaine Greer criticizes Elton John for naming husband David Furnish as son's 'mother' on birth certificate." *Independent,* May 25, 2015. https://www.independent.co.uk/news/people/germaine-greer-criticises-elton-john-for-naming-husband-david-furnish-as-sons-mother-on-birth-10274618.html.

Sikkema, John. "Five Bills in Five Years: Gender Ideology in Ontario." *Association for Reformed Political Action Canada,* March 21, 2017. https://arpacanada.ca/news/2017/03/21/five-bills-five-years-gender-ideology-ontario/.

Sikkema, John. "ARPA Presents to Committee Reviewing Bill

89," *ARPA CANADA*, April 11, 2017. https://arpacanada. ca/news/2017/04/11/committee-cloth-ears-arpa-presents-committee-reviewing-bill-89/.

Sikkema, John. "Haunted by the 'Hetero-Normative' Family," *ARPA Canada*, April 21, 2017. https://arpacanada.ca/news/2017/04/21/haunted-hetero-normative-family/.

Smith III, Joseph W. *Sex and Violence in the Bible: A Survey of the Explicit Content in the Holy Book*. Phillipsburg, NJ: P&R, 2014.

Solomon, Andrew. "Anthony Bourdain, Kate Spade, and the Preventable Tragedies of Suicide." *The New Yorker*, June 8, 2018. https://www.newyorker.com/news/news-desk/preventable-tragedies.

Spong, Bishop John Shelby. *The Sins of Scripture: Exposing the Bible's Texts of Hate to Reveal the God of Love*. New York: HarperOne, 2005.

Spong, Bishop John Shelby. "Bishop John Shelby Spong on the Sins of Scripture." June 20, 2005. https://tvo.org/transcript/795848/video/archive/big-ideas/bishop-john-shelby-spong-on-the-sins-of-scripture.

Sproul, R. C. *Lifeviews: Make a Christian Impact on Culture and Society*. Grand Rapids: Fleming H. Revell, 1986.

Steiner, George. *Real Presences*. Chicago: University of Chicago Press, 1989.

Strobel, Lee. *The Case for Christ: A Journalist's Personal Investigation of the Evidence for Jesus*. Grand Rapids: Zondervan, 1998.

Sturm, Lacey. *The Reason: How I Discovered a Life Worth Living—Revelations of a Rock Princess*. Grand Rapids: Baker, 2014.

Taunton, Larry Alex. *The Faith of Christopher Hitchens: The Restless Soul of the World's Most Notorious Atheist*. Nashville: Nelson, 2016.

Taylor, Justin. "Ravi Zacharias on Postmodern Architecture at Ohio State." *The Gospel Coalition*, January 13, 2014. https://www.thegospelcoalition.org/blogs/justin-taylor/ravi-zacharias-on-postmodern-architecture-at-ohio-state/.

The Economist. "The Right to Die." The Economist Group Ltd., June 27, 2015. http://www.economist.com/news/leaders/21656182-doctors-should-be-allowed-help-suffering-and-terminally-ill-die-when-they-choose.

Travers, Peter. "Star Wars: The Force Awakens." *RollingStone*, December 16, 2015. https://www.rollingstone.com/movies/movie-reviews/star-wars-the-force-awakens-103677/.

Troup, Calvin L. *Temporality, Eternity, and Wisdom: The Rhetoric of Augustine's Confessions*. Columbia: University of South Carolina Press, 1999.

Trueman, Carl. "What Can Miserable Christians Sing?" *The Wages of Spin: Critical Writings on Historical and Contemporary Evangelicalism* (Fearn, UK: Christian Focus, 2005), 157-63.

Twenge, Jean M. "Have Smartphones Destroyed a Generation?" *The Atlantic*, September 2017. https://www.theatlantic.com/magazine/archive/2017/09/has-the-smartphone-destroyed-a-generation/534198/.

Twenge, Jean M. and Keith W. Campbell. *The Narcissism Epidemic: Living in the Age of Entitlement*. New York: Free Press, 2009.

UNFPA. "Statement by UNFPA on U.S. Decision to Withhold Funding." *United Nations Population Fund*, April 4, 2017. https://www.unfpa.org/press/statement-unfpa-us-decision-withhold-funding#.

Vahanian, Gabriel. *The Death of God: The Culture of Our Post-Christian Era*. New York: George Braziller, 1961.

Vanhoozer, Kevin J. *First Theology: God, Scripture and Hermeneutics*. Downers Grove: InterVarsity, 2002.

Vanhoozer, Kevin J. *The Drama of Doctrine: A Canonical–Linguistic Approach to Christian Theology*. Louisville: Westminster John Knox, 2005.

Von Harnack, Adolf. *History of Dogma*. Boston: Beacon Press, 1959.

Vos, Geerhardus. *Biblical Theology: Old and New Testaments*. Eugene: Wipf and Stock, republished 2003.

Vos, Geerhardus. *Grace and Glory: Sermons Preached in the Chapel of Princeton Theological Seminary*. Carlisle: The Banner of Truth Trust, 1994.

Vos, Geerhardus. "The Eschatology of the Psalter" in *The Pauline Eschatology* (Phillipsburg: P&R, 1979).

Wallace, Ronald S. *Calvin's Doctrine of the Christian Life*. Eugene: Wipf and Stock, 1997.

Watt, Jonathan. *Languages of the Gods: A Faculty Integration Paper, Prepared for the Faculty and Trustees of Geneva College*. Faculty Integration Paper, Geneva College, 2003.

Wenham, Gordon J. *The Book of Leviticus: New International Commentary on the Old Testament*. Grand Rapids: Eerdmans, 1979.

Wenner, Jann S. "Bono: The Rolling Stone Interview: U2's frontman on the state of his band, the state of the world and what he learned from almost dying." Interview by Jann S. Wenner. *RollingStone*, December 27, 2017. https://www.rollingstone.com/music/music-features/bono-the-rolling-stone-interview-3-203774/.

Wolin, Richard. *The Terms of Cultural Criticism: The Frankfurt School, Existentialism, Poststructuralism*. New York: Columbia University Press 1992.

Wolfmueller, Bryan. "Martin Luther's Introduction to the Psalms." *World Wide Wolfmueller*, October 19, 2017. https://wolfmueller.co/martin-luthers-introduction-psalms/.

Wright, Christopher J. H. *The God I Don't Understand: Reflections on Tough Questions of Faith*. Grand Rapids: Zondervan, 2008.

Wright, N. T. *Evil and the Justice of God*. Downers Grove: InterVarsity, 2006.

Wright, N. T. *Scripture and the Authority of God: How to Read the Bible Today*. New York: HarperCollins, 2011.

Wright, N. T. *Surprised by Scripture: Engaging Contemporary Issues*. New York: Harper, 2014.

Wright, N. T. *The Case for the Psalms: Why They are Essential*. New York: HarperOne, 2013.

Zirschky, Andrew. *Beyond the Screen: Youth Ministry for the Connected But Alone Generation*. Nashville: Abingdon Press, 2015.

Videos

"Bono & Eugene Peterson—THE PSALMS." YouTube video, 21:42. FULLER studio, April 26, 2016. https://www.youtube.com/watch?v=-l40S5e90KY.

Ehrman, Bart. "The Daily Show with Jon Stewart." *The Daily Show with Jon Stewart*, 6:07. Video clip, March 14, 2006. http://www.cc.com/video-clips/uj00dz/the-daily-show-with-jon-stewart-bart-ehrman.

"Emma Watson and Dan Stevens Talk About the Feminism in *Beauty and the Beast*." YouTube video, 1:29. POPSUGAR Entertainment, March 9, 2017. https://www.youtube.com/watch?v=u9zSPpDNQaw.

Harris, Sam. "Sam Harris vs. 'Feminist' Islam Apologist 'Muhammad was peaceful'—'no he wasn't'." YouTube video, 5:15. "AustralianNeoCon1," December 9, 2012. https://www.youtube.com/watch?v=1JrYCHC0bkE.

"NPPB 2018—Revd Dr Tim Keller—What can Christianity offer our society in the 21st century?" YouTube video, 25:18. "Christians in Parliament," June 22, 2018. https://www.youtube.com/watch?v=AkcouxJE6o4&feature=share.

Maher, Bill. "Bill Maher's Tribute to Christopher Hitchens." Christopherhitchens.net, 1:39. 2012. https://christopherhitchens.net/bill-maher.

Discography

American Authors. "Believer," recorded in 2013. Track 1 on *Believer*. Mercury Records. Compact disc and digital download.

Apple, Fiona. "Criminal," recorded in 1996. Track 4 on *Tidal*. Work Records and Columbia Records. Compact disc.

Crow, Sheryl. "Strong Enough," recorded in 1993. Track 3 on *Tuesday Night Music Club*. A&M Records. Compact disc.

Cyrus, Miley. "Wrecking Ball," recorded in 2013. Track 6 on *Bangerz*. RCA Records. Compact disc and digital download.

Death Cab for Cutie. "I Will Follow You into the Dark," recorded in 2006. Track 3 on *Plans*. Atlantic Records. Compact disc.

Dylan, Bob. "Not Dark Yet," recorded in 1997. Track 7 on *Time Out of Mind*. Columbia Records. Compact disc.

Everclear. "Wonderful," recorded in 2000. Track 11 on *Songs from an American Movie Volume One: Learning How to Smile*. Capitol Records. Compact disc.

Fun. "We Are Young," recorded in 2012. Track 3 on *Some Nights*. Fueled by Ramen. Compact disc and digital download.

Grey, Skylar. "Love the Way You Lie," recorded in 2013. Track 9 on *Don't Look Down*. Interscope Records. Compact disc.

Halsey. "Strangers," recorded in 2016. Track 11 on *Hopeless Fountain Kingdom*. Astralwerks. Compact disc and digital download.

Osborne, Joan. "One of Us," recorded in 1995. Track 6 on *Relish*. Blue Gorilla Records. Compact disc.

Sia. "Chandelier," recorded in 2014. Track 1 on *1000 Forms of Fear*. RCA Records. Compact disc and digital download.

Sia. "Jesus Wept," recorded in April 2015. Track 18 on *This is Acting*. RCA Records. Compact disc and digital download.

Sturm, Lacey. "Heart Work," recorded in 2019. Track 7 on *Reflect Love Back Soundtrack Vol. 1*. RLB Records/FOLLOWSPOT Records. Compact disc and digital download.

Sturm, Lacey. "I'm Not Laughing," recorded in 2016. Track 3 on *Life Screams*. FOLLOWSPOT Records. Compact disc and digital download.

The Killers. "Sweet Talk," recorded in 2007. Track 5 in *Sawdust*. Island Records. Compact disc and digital download.

Twenty One Pilots. "Hometown," recorded in 2015. Track 12 on *Blurryface*. Fueled by Ramen. Compact disc.

Williams, Pharrell. "Happy," recorded in 2013. Track 1 on *Happy*. Columbia Records. Compact disc and digital download.

Suggested Reading

ARPA Canada: https://arpacanada.ca/.

Alpha and Omega Ministries, Dr. James White: http://www.aomin.org.

Barfield, Owen. *Saving the Appearances: A Study in Idolatry*. Hanover: University Press of New England, 1988.

Gentle Reformation Blog: http://www.gentlereformation.com.

"Chris Murphy on Abortion." *On The Issues: Every Political Leader on Every Issue*. Last modified September 18, 2018. www.ontheissues.org/Social/Chris_Murphy_Abortion.htm.

Yuan, Christopher. *Holy Sexuality and the Gospel: Sex, Desire, and Relationships Shaped by God's Grand Story*. Colorado Springs: Multnomah, 2018.

Copyright Information

Other Titles from
Crown & Covenant Publications

Prayers of the Bible:
366 Devotionals to Encourage Your Prayer Life
Gordon J. Keddie

Openness Unhindered:
Further Thoughts of an Unlikely Convert on Sexual Identity
and Union with Christ
Rosaria Butterfield

Hitting the Marks:
Restoring the Essential Identity of the Church
Barry J. York

150 Questions about the Psalter
Bradley Johnston

The Book of Psalms for Worship

Ascent:
Selections from the Book of Psalms for Worship (CD)

Crown & Covenant
PUBLICATIONS

www.crownandcovenant.com